Keningale Cook

The Fathers of Jesus - A Study of the Lineage of the Christian Doctrine and Traditions

Vol. I

Keningale Cook

The Fathers of Jesus - A Study of the Lineage of the Christian Doctrine and Traditions
Vol. I

ISBN/EAN: 9783337025731

Printed in Europe, USA, Canada, Australia, Japan

Cover: Foto ©Lupo / pixelio.de

More available books at **www.hansebooks.com**

THE FATHERS OF JESUS

*A STUDY OF THE LINEAGE OF THE CHRISTIAN
DOCTRINE AND TRADITIONS*

BY

KENINGALE COOK, M.A., LL.D.

IN TWO VOLUMES

VOL. I.

LONDON
KEGAN PAUL, TRENCH & CO., 1, PATERNOSTER SQUARE
1886

(The rights of translation and of reproduction are reserved.)

PREFACE.

THOUGH it is said that one who regards the wind will never sow, yet there are times and seasons which it is well to observe. The date of the constitution of a new Court of Parliament, established, if not upon the best and surest foundations, at least upon the widest, seems to offer a favourable occasion for the appearance of such a work as the present.

One who gives an equal ear to the voices in the air, will learn that, among other topics which excite men's minds, the question of the disestablishment of the English Church is raised. Somewhat confusedly, he will gather—

That "it would be a gigantic operation" (Mr. Gladstone).

That "it would involve an enormous loss to the moral stability of the whole empire" (Bishop of Salisbury).

That "it would prelude the downfall of much that is greatest and best in England" (Lord Tennyson).

That "the clergy have, unhappily for themselves, chosen to identify themselves and their cause, in the bitterest temper, with the fortunes of a political party and a social caste which has been proved to represent the minority of the people, and from whom political power has departed" (Sir W. Vernon Harcourt).

That disestablishment would "pauperize the priesthood, and paganize the people" (Bishop of Lincoln, 1877).

That it would "extend education."

That it would "leave a fair field in which the sects may compete for the glory of converting England."

That it would "arouse the latent energies of the Church;" that it would "cripple the Church for the present, and make it doubly strong in the future."

That it would elevate neglected curates into the chosen ones of their congregations.

That "the agricultural labourer resents, and justly, his virtual degradation in the Church which is his own" (Bishop of Chichester).

That Church Reform would "make the English Church again an integral portion of the national life."

Before it is decided to cast adrift from the national order and governance an institution of great bulk and power,—to launch it upon a sectarian, and possibly a reactionary career,—there are probably many millions of words to be said.

The question is stated to be outside of the sphere of practical politics for the moment; but it is at least within the scope of political diversions, for both parties have been playing at battledoor and shuttlecock with it. Furthermore, mooted questions do not now wait a century for solution. A statesman, when he says, " We see our way for five years," appears to think that he is speaking of a long period of time, and is content to leave to others to find mops for the deluge that may come a year or two later.

In the brief breathing time before the grapple of

the champions of privilege and secularism, it would seem a wise step for clerics and laymen alike to study not only what ecclesiastical functions and powers the future will leave in the hands which at present hold them, but also what elements of their doctrine will stand, what are true and vital and worth the holding.

A fair investigation of the groundworks and meaning of the faith might tend, on the one hand, to allay the oppositions of privilege and sectarianism ; and on the other, to refound a truly nationalized Church upon the broader and more lasting basis of the religious impulse which is to be found in the heart of all conditions of men.

To abandon untenable claims to the possession of an exclusive doctrine of salvation, and relax the constraining shackles of a defunct orthodoxy, would stimulate the pursuit of truth, and open the reformed Church to worthy men who at present shrink from the make-believe of subscription to doctrines which cannot face the light.

The position as premier Bishop of the much-abused heretic of five and twenty years ago, and the career of the lamented " Bishop of all Denominations," are examples of hope, and an augury of what might follow from appointing men of liberal mind to the staff of the Church militant, and leaving the door of the temple always on the latch to admit earnest work and sincere endeavour.

When ordination is open to men of unbiased conviction, and place shall follow merit alone, the clergy will find that, in order to lead, it will be necessary to be abreast of the best and most advanced thought of the time. At present we see the anomaly of the leading journals and reviews telling one story, the ecclesiastical organs another. The division into freedom and formula cannot continue for ever: the pearled grain may for a time be kept in one corner, the husk in another; but where, then, will be found the true and germinal corn, fit for sowing?

Without disturbing the mechanical framework of the Church too much, it may be possible to disestablish the Thirty-nine, and other articles of bondage; to trace back ceremonies to their foundations and meaning; to disendow creeds of all but universal truth and ethical reasonableness.

Our armed hand at present wields control upon the oldest sites of human history: our minds would do well to struggle to expand beyond the insular lines, and to learn how to make their own, without fear, what have been the deep religious thoughts of the world. The present century, by patient and unassuming labour, has discovered how much, in language and doctrine alike, we owe to a chain of tradition drawn from the Egypt and India of the past, whose forgotten hieroglyphs and most ancient hymns are now before us to show how far they are the parents of our speech and the inspirers of our thought. We may learn at last to how large a heritage we are entitled, as units of the human family.

TABLE OF CONTENTS.

I.—THE BOOK OF THOTH.
II.—AN ARYAN ANCESTOR.
III.—PRIMITIVE BUDDHISM.
IV.—THEISM AND ETHICS IN ANCIENT GREECE.
V.—THE SCHOOL OF PYTHAGORAS.
VI.—A RAY FROM THE SPHERE OF PLATO.
VII.—THE BROTHERHOOD OF THE ESSENES.
VIII.—DID JESUS KNOW GREEK?
IX.—THE TRADITION OF THE ELDERS.
X.—A CONTEMPORARY OF JESUS.
XI.—THE SACRED AND THE PROFANE.
XII.—THE GENIUS OF PARABLE.

CONTENTS OF VOL. I.

	PAGE
THE BOOK OF THOTH	1
AN ARYAN ANCESTOR	53
PRIMITIVE BUDDHISM	108
THEISM AND ETHICS IN ANCIENT GREECE	163
THE SCHOOL OF PYTHAGORAS	281
A RAY FROM THE SPHERE OF PLATO	326

THE FATHERS OF JESUS.

THE BOOK OF THOTH.

A GREAT engineering work, more stupendous than a pyramid, has made Egypt a highway for the leading nations; and the unique agricultural position of the country gives it prominence still, as it did of old. Simultaneously there has been felt a vivid interest and curiosity with regard to the ancient realm that was the sojourning place of the forefathers of our religion. Now it is opening out to us its hieroglyphic stores of buried millenniums, and disclosing not only the features of the mummy and a puzzle of cryptic writing, but the thoughts of men not too remote from ourselves for sympathy. At last, now that the laborious riddles of scholars are solved, we are reaching the wealth of the intelligent speech of our new-found brethren in humanity, a treasure that shines little the less clearly for having been buried so long.

"Whatever may be the antiquity of the Aryan mythologies, the Greek, the Etruscan, or the Hindhu, it is evident they only appear centuries after the Assyrian and Egyptian, and had not been committed to writing till a period comparatively recent compared with their venerable predecessors. . . . Babylonia has left behind it documents at least fifteen centuries before Christ, and Egypt at least two thousand years." *

* S. Birch, "Records of the Past," vol. x., Introd.

To this long entombment it is due that the political interest in Egypt and the philosophic interest in Egypt, although both present to-day, are yet wholly apart and distinct. Ancient Egypt has entirely passed away, leaving only its wondrous sepulchre. Of its sacred language and of the religion of those dead men whose legended cerements are treasuries of lore, Modern Egypt (with the exception, perhaps, of a few scholars at the Boulaq Museum) knows less than may be found in books that bear the imprint of Paris or London.

As in this section it will be our business to investigate the relationship of Egypt to those religious traditions which our societies of to-day hold as their own, it is right first to endeavour to disabuse the mind of a long-standing and ignorant prejudice. In that false judgment it is regarded as something approaching to blasphemy to esteem any elder religion as conceivably one of the mothers or nursing-mothers of our own, and so entitled to our veneration and our love. All that is outside of our own religious tradition and its Jewish stock, we have been wont to stigmatize as pagan and heathen,—if at all regarded of God, regarded as quite secondary and unworthy. It has been argued that our orthodoxy, be it taken on its lowest ground, and outside and apart from the special privileges to which it lays claim, is even then at least transcendental, whilst the outcome of the Egyptian and other heathen priestcraft is but a gross mass of idol worship, manifested in the most puerile and degraded form, darkened by superstition rather than enlightened by true spiritual light; a religion unsanctified by the grace of God that is ours. To persons holding such views it avails little to reply that much of the orthodox system itself is but blind image-worship and paltry lifeless ceremonial. They care nothing for differences of degree; it is difference in kind they insist upon. There exist light and darkness, religion and superstition; theirs is the religion and holy, the other is the superstition and unholy. Upon unlistening ears, too, would fall the argument that as, in spite of the idolatrous and ceremonial external of the popular cult, there is and has been in the Christian religion a living fount that has wrought its manifestation in pure and firm and noble lives; so with Egypt, beneath the gross and external Polytheism of the multitude, may reasonably be expected to be found deep springs, pure and undefiled, the very mystery of godliness itself. Such springs, and such alone, it might fairly be argued, if indeed they could be found, would be so free from stain as to be able to have had any parental relationship towards our own religion; if such, then, can be discovered, the ear of the wise should be opened to listen to the sound of the flowing of the ancient stream.

The Egyptian may be thought to have been too religious; he spent little trouble upon his ordinary dwelling-house, the temporary resting-place, but made the temple and the tomb of lasting materials to endure for ages.

As the Hellenic race was supreme in generosity of art, so was the Hebrew in tenacity of faith. Confronting ever the wonted worldly ways, was the passionate, often sublime, vehemence of the Hebrew prophets, who with untiring earnestness staunchly insisted upon the reality and unity of God, and upon righteousness or conscience as his way, and deeply stamped upon a great poetic literature the truth that in the doing of this righteousness lay the only course that could make man of any worth or blessedness. This view of God degenerated into exclusiveness, and this righteousness into formalism. But whence was this religious tendency in its original might derived? what was its spring? Was it wholly a primeval revelation? or, like the institution of Jesus, a new birth that was in great part a regeneration of the old?

Let us search the scriptures; what do they say of themselves?—

> "He shineth, then the land exulteth."
> "Creator of all good things."

"He careth for the state of the poor."
"He maketh his might a buckler."
"He is not graven in marble."
"His abode is not known."
"There is no building that can contain him."
"Thy Law is established in the whole land."
"Unknown is his name in heaven,
  He manifesteth not his forms;
  Vain are all representations."

What scripture is this? It seems familiar, as if it might be a paraphrase of our Hebrew Bible.

"The Lord God is a sun and a shield."—Ps. lxxxiv. 11.
"The Lord reigneth; let the earth rejoice."—Ps. xcvii. 1.
"The Lord is high above all nations, and his glory above the heavens."
  —Ps. cxiii. 4.
"The earth is full of the lovingkindness of the Lord."—Ps. xxxiii. 5.
"Who daily loadeth us with benefits."—Ps. lxviii. 19.
"The eyes of all wait upon thee; and thou givest them their meat in due
  season. Thou openest thy hand, and satisfiest the desire of every
  living thing."—Ps. cxlv. 15, 16.
"He raiseth up the poor out of the dust."—Ps. cxiii. 7.
"Thou hast been a stronghold to the poor."—Is. xxv. 4.
"He is a buckler unto all them that trust in him."—Ps. xviii. 30.
"Gods wood and stone,—the work of men's hands."—Deut. iv. 28.
"He made darkness his hiding place."—Ps. xviii. 11.
"Thy footsteps were not known."—Ps. lxxvii. 19.
"Thou art a God that hidest thyself, O God of Israel, the Saviour."—
  Is. xlv. 15.
"Behold, the heaven and the heaven of heavens cannot contain thee;
  how much less this house which I have built!"—2 Chron. vi. 18.
"A law shall go forth from me."—Is. li. 4.
"He appointed a law in Israel."—Ps. lxxviii. 5.
"They [the earth and the heavens] shall be changed, but thou art the
  same."—Ps. cii. 26, 27.
"My thoughts are not your thoughts, neither are your ways my ways."—
  Is. lv. 8.
"There is no searching of his understanding."—Is. xl. 28.
"After the wind an earthquake; but the Lord was not in the earthquake:
  and after the earthquake a fire; but the Lord was not in the fire:
  and after the fire a sound of gentle stillness."—1 Kings xix. 11, 12.
"Canst thou by searching find out God?"—Job xi. 7.
"Lo, these are but the outskirts of his ways; and how small a whisper
  do we hear of him!"—Job xxvi. 14.

But our familiar sounding quotation, to which the above and many other passages of the Jewish Scriptures show so distinct a likeness, is not from Judæa; it is from Egypt, from the beautiful Nile-Hymn, composed long before any known prophet uttered his voice in Israel. It is of the period of a dynasty that, by the majority of scholars, is considered to be contemporary with Moses.

The eminent churchman who renders it into English (Canon F. C. Cook) deems it a relic of primeval Monotheism.[*] It will suffice for an illustration of the Egyptian views in relation to the central doctrine of the Hebrew teachers, that of the reality and unity of deity. To the more pantheistic conceptions of the Egyptian psalmists, both in their higher and lower forms, we shall have to advert hereafter.

The following may illustrate the other central doctrine of the Hebrew seer, that the main way of life and of God is in the doing of righteousness, which alone brings permanent blessedness:—

"All men are in ecstasy,
Hearts in sweetness, bosoms in joy;
Everybody is in adoration.
Every one glorifies his goodness;
Mild is his love for us,
His tenderness environs hearts;
Great is his love in all bosoms.

*   *   *   *

Sanctifying, beneficent, is his name;
Veneration finds its place,
Respect immutable for his laws:
The path is open, the footpaths are opened:

---

[*] It is a question whether there is any certain ground for such a phrase as "primeval monotheism," unless employed in a loose and general sense. "The time has not come yet, it probably never will come," says Max Müller, "when we shall be able to assert anything about the real beginning of religion in general. We know a little here, a little there; but whatever we know of early religion, we always see that it pre-supposes vast periods of an earlier development." We do not even know who devised, and named after sun, moon, and planets, the seven days of the week. The most ancient nations we know of all use the same order, but though the tradition should have continued for a thousand centuries, have we any right to call it primeval?

Both worlds are at rest :
Evil flies and earth becomes fecundant
Peaceably under its Lord.
Justice is confirmed
By its Lord, who pursues iniquity."

This passage from the "Hymn to Osiris" is of a date considered to be two or three centuries earlier than the Nile-Hymn, from which the previous quotation was made. A very slight paraphrase also would allow this early writing to take its place almost unnoticed among the words of the Hebrew prophets.

When in our day of scientific investigation, which unfolds the hidden scrolls of the earth's antiquity, and dares not attempt to number the ages that have inscribed their record upon them, we hear the words "primeval Monotheism," we may be pardoned for wondering what they mean. Monotheism we understand, but what Monotheism was primeval? It was not that of the Hebrews, for, according to its own narratives, Israel was but a small tribe, little more than a family, when it entered the gates of Egypt, whence it emerged, after a few centuries of eventful history, a considerable people. May Egypt herself claim that primeval Monotheism, or must it be accorded to Assyria, to India, to China, or to the unknown land of Eden? Twenty-five centuries ago the question arose which nation of the world was most ancient, and Psametik, of Egypt, in whose long reign literature flourished, is recorded by Herodotus to have made an experiment to discover which was the primeval language, by observing the native articulation of children brought up by persons forbidden to utter a word in their hearing. The experiment was unscientifically conducted, and ended in the children borrowing the cry of the goats, and so making a word that was claimed to be the Phrygian term for bread. So long ago, then, Psametik knew no more of the origin of his race than we do. With the revelations of geology before us, it is idle to speculate as to national beginnings where we have no historic data to guide us; the question of "primeval Monotheism" is an impossible one; we know not whether the Sahara or the sea may not cover the remains of a myriad forgotten races; whether Egypt be the oldest link with this buried past we know not; all that we do know is that it affords the oldest history yet established. There is no rude nomad or tribal history of Egypt; nearly seven thousand years ago, at which period commence the landmarks of research, centuries before Adam, there is a reigning dynasty and a capital, where is worshipped a demiurgic deity called "The Father of Beginnings." Plato tells us (Timæus, v.) that when Solon had descanted upon the ancient mythology of Greece to the priests of Sais, one of them exclaimed, "Solon, Solon, ye Greeks are always boys, and aged Greek there is none." This he explained to mean that they had no ancient doctrines drawn from archaic tradition, whilst they themselves claimed that there were preserved in their own sacred writings the annals of Sais for eighty centuries. It is twenty-five centuries now since this claim was made.

The still current pseudo-spiritual views of ethnology, based upon misunderstandings of ancient fragments of allegoric lore, we may dismiss from our minds as readily as now we scout the pseudo-scientific view of the historian Diodorus of Sicily, who affirms the spontaneous generation of mice from the rich alluvial soil about Thebes, and argues thence the probability of Egypt's river mud beds having similarly produced man.

The "father of history"—if modern research will still allow him the title—says candidly (Eut. xv.), "I think the Egyptians have always existed ever since the human race began."

If we turn from the speculative to the actual, we may find a papyrus deemed by Egyptologists to be the most ancient book in the world, or about fifty-five centuries old. Therein Ptah-hotep, magistrate and sage, preaches as follows:—

"Beware of producing crude thoughts; study till thy words are matured!" There is no sign of youthfulness of life here, there is neither suggestion of the divine simplicity of Eden, nor on the other hand of the rude savagery of a race in an early stage of development. The remark is trite, venerable, cultured, and commonplace; and the wise man who uttered it must have been the heir of a civilization that a single thousand years' growth would have been quite inadequate to produce.

The ghostly presence of ancient Egypt dwarfs the Judæa that we have made so prominent in our old synopsis of the world; the stately calm that dwells by the untiring beneficent Nile puts to shame the petty cries of a self-assertive specially favoured nation, or the so-called miraculous preservation of a hardy tribe.

When the starving sons of Israel journeyed southwards, and left their rude tents and famine-stricken fields, they came to a land where there were mighty cities, graced with temples and palaces, obelisks and statues; where mathematics accurately directed irrigation, and canals aided agriculture with uses taught by the perennially watering Nile; where architecture was not merely commissioned to provide shelter, but made to subserve the proving of astronomical laws, and to afford standards of reference for cardinal points and measures of longitude; where fabrics were made that for evenness of thread would be the despair of Manchester—linen with more than five hundred strands in an inch, or five times finer than our fine cambric; a land where copper was tempered in a manner beyond the knowledge of our northern foundries, for it would cut stone without being hardened by alloy; and bronze wrought into blades that had the elasticity, as well as the keenness and hardness of steel; a land where the physicians composed treatises upon "the science of the beating of the heart" (Ebers papyrus). The root of our modern chemistry was there in the ancient name of the country,

Chemi, Kham or Ham, a word supposed to designate the black and crumbly nature of the soil, which re-appears in our word alchemy, or the black art. Our very Europe is Ereb, Greek Erebus, or the West.

In that busy land were storehouses of ancient learning, matured systems of ethics, and a priesthood as earnest and full of religion as any hierarchy that has existed on earth. Like all establishments, it had its evil side as well as its good, its comparatively dark and degraded eras as well as its enlightened and beneficent periods. It was well worthy to be the nursing-mother of the Hebrew or any younger race, and was this as naturally in religion as in language, where may be found Egyptian roots planted in the Hebrew, which have spread along one channel or another into our own English tongue.

The rite of circumcision appears to have been borrowed by the Hebrew, and certain other Palestinian tribes, from the Egyptians. Herodotus (II. 36) speaks of the Egyptians as "the only people in the world—they at least, and such as have learned the practice from them—who use circumcision." Again (II. 104) he says, "The Phœnicians and the Syrians of Palestine themselves confess that they learnt the custom from the Egyptians." The rite is known to have existed in Egypt as early as the fourth dynasty, which was centred at Memphis, or some six thousand years ago. It was variously followed in Palestine, being practised by the Edomites, but not by the generality of the Phœnicians, the Sidonians, or the Philistines. We may call to mind the observation attributed to Jesus on this subject (John vii. 22):—"Moses gave you circumcision; not that it is of Moses, but of the *fathers*." Who, then, are these fathers? Abraham was before Moses, and perhaps one of these fathers; as indeed one of his descendants is named in the confession with the first-fruit offering (Deut. xxvi. 5), "An Aramean ready to perish was my father; and he went down into Egypt, and sojourned there, few in number; and he became there a nation." But the fathers of Mennefer, or Memphis, the relics of which capital city are now nothing but funereal remains, were before Abraham.

The law of the Hebrews originates with Moses, and Moses, saved from the sacred river by the princess of Egypt when she was bathing, or more probably performing the rites connected with the yearly rise of the inundation, was "instructed in all the wisdom of the Egyptians." He is also said (Josephus, II. Ant. 10) to have conducted an Ethiopian war. There may have been troubles in the "waste Soudan" in those days, and of the reasons for the flight of the great leader from Egypt, the account we have is probably a very imperfect one.

In spite of the stupendous exactions of certain sovereigns, it would seem that life in Egypt was comparatively easy. The land needed not to be "tickled with the plough to laugh with a bountiful harvest;" the labourer, under a kindly rule, might have leisure for a considerable portion of the year, for the river, washing up rich silt from the highlands of Africa, prevents exhaustion of the land, and the consequent need of artificial replenishment. The Nile enriches year by year enormous tracts, and so softens the land that in many parts the agriculturists could dispense with the plough, and after sowing the seed had but to drive in his flocks to tread it in, or drag the mud with bushes. There was nearly always "corn in Egypt." The climate was, and still is, a mild and dry one, and the bodily needs are in consequence exceedingly small. A handful of grain, a single shirt, a hut of mud and cane sufficed for existence.

A strand, seven hundred miles long, by seven wide, enriched without labour by the regular rise and subsidence of the Nile, offered an unfailing means of subsistence to a proportionate number of persons; and that proportion of mouths to acres could be raised higher than was possible in any other country; or, food being readily provided, there remained a mighty force of surplus energy unused and seeking an outlet. This mass of vital force was embodied in the pyramids and other great works of Egypt. Such a country must have offered great enticements to settle to our nomad forefathers, and it is quite probable that Egypt formed the earliest settled community that we shall ever be able to trace. Time after time there must have resulted an excess in number. What was done with the surplus population? Diodorus Siculus states that, according to the assertions of the Egyptian priests, colonies had not only gone forth to Babylon, Greece, Palestine, but to so many different parts of the world that he shrank from recording them. It has even been asserted that Egyptian emigrants colonized our island, ages before it was known as Britain.

Though the actual labourer might receive but small benefit himself, he was the means of great and easily acquired wealth; and in addition to the kings and the pashas, large numbers of the priestly and literary classes were able to be supported without the cruel drain upon a people's resources due always to an inordinate proportion of non-producing classes. To the ranks of the sacred scribes belonged not only the high posts of the priesthood, but the more worldly functions of secretary and custodian of treasuries, granaries, and muniments; the scribes royal directed the War Office and the Admiralty of the river fleet; and the general body acted usefully as notaries, conveyancers, letter-writers, accountants, market clerks, managers of linen manufactories and of stone quarries, surveyors, engravers, architects, goldsmiths, sculptors, physicians, school-masters. Functions were to a certain extent hereditary, but the sacerdotal tribe was not a caste, but a class. Men of ability from any other social class might be admitted to the priesthood.

Man in a simple state of life is an observer of nature's methods. Among prominent objects of attention must always have been the apparent sources of life, and the recurrences of large events. The sun is the apparent origin of physical life, manifesting also a grand objective example of periodicity, which makes days and years and seasons; and marking out, in conjunction with stars, vast circles of time, which possibly expanded the minds of primitive men to large orbits of thought, as the miracle of his daily life-giving fire disposed them to love and adoration. Besides the sun, God's lieutenant of physical life, sex, the reproducer, has received reverence as the producer; the male element usually dominating as the sun, while, from a similar attribute and similar association with a stronger power, the moon and the feminine have gone together.

Natural observations and spiritual intuitions have been joined in correspondences, real or fanciful. The pictorial imagination has often sought to take the place of the spiritual revelation, and has led the mind astray from the true apprehension of the type. That the glorious solar orb should be recognized as the immediate cause of the life of our system, and so as a divine type, is a pantheism by no means inconsistent with the highest worship. When the priest of the esoteric mysteries worshipped Ra, or the creative sun, it was as a wondrous manifestation of the Supreme, or, as it were, the Supreme in specific action. The aspects of divine beneficence being manifold in their natural expression, the signs by which the eternal God was represented were to a certain extent interchangeable. God could not be beheld in his infinity, but he might be seen through any attribute, which attribute was adorable as God. This lofty and subtle Pantheism can only be held in its purity by the mind enfranchized from the rudimentary state and cleansed of the fluff of ignorance and narrow prejudice.

The litany of the priest ran:—

> "Homage to thee, Ra! Supreme power,
> He who discloses the earth, and lights the unseen,
> He whose principle has become his manifestation,
> Who is born under the form of the deity of the great disk."
> (NAVILLE, *Litany of Ra.*)

This was too metaphysical for the generality, who could not take in so purely intellectual a conception as that of the Amen-ra, or hidden fashioner, pouring his creative force into the recipient unseen, and producing a semblance of himself in the radiant sun. So the warmth of the poet invents endearing epithets for the sun as a person, singing that his soul shone in his shape, and that he dwelt in the interior of his dazzling disk; or, if of a metaphysical inclination, he argues that the divine emblem was "born as his own son," that he was wont to "address his eye," and "speak to his head," or, in other words, commune with himself. And the popular imagination demanded further substantivity and an extension of the concrete, and sought out many a quaint minor symbolism, and the artist put it into form. The "beetle that folds his wings, that rests in the empyrean," in some fanciful way, from rolling its eggs before it in a ball of dirt, is made a type, and the bull, as the largest creature known, is elevated to a divine symbol, and both are carven images at the door of the temple. Minor representations of divine attributes may be extended without limit, according as the mind seizes upon one or another external correspondence, or outward and visible sign of an internal and spiritual fact. One part of Egypt feels pride in its temples, where a sacred animal receives veneration as representing such or such a conception of divine power; in an adjoining canton the object of adoration is different, or worshipped in a different form. Certain cities marked out special triads or trinities of deity as objects of their peculiar worship. Rivalry intensifies each worship, until the spiritual attribute of the sign is forgotten. Each party has its god, the pantheistic fervour departs, universal religion wanes, and sects are born which are both polytheistic and idolatrous. The priest of enfranchised spirit sees still beneath the symbol its secret truth; to a partisan crowd this inner sense seems thin and vain; if he speaks, it is to deaf ears, so the acolytes continue to serve at the shrines, and the real magus and priest takes his place, perhaps sadly enough, at the head of the pomp and show which he knows and feels to be empty. The ineffable Amen-ra is forgotten amid the hosts of gods and goddesses that claim to be emanations of his but are nothing in themselves.

At another time we find supreme power worshipped under the name of Atoum. This was the red sun of the setting, and the sacred aspect may have been derived from his daily baptism in the horizon of the Nile.

"I am Atoum, Maker of the Heavens, Creator of Beings coming forth from the world, making all the generations of existences, Lord of life, supplying the gods" (Birch, *Eg. Rit.* ch. 79).

A monument contains a dialogue between the deceased and the water-god. "O Water! father of the gods! turn thy face towards me. Thou art the water which makes eternally young again." . . . "I am Atoum; I am the preferred of the sun. I am the blessed Ibis. I am the Water."

It is by no means impossible that this deity, in name at least, is the prototype of the Hebrew Adam, the root of whose name signifies a reddish colour.

Egypt was pantheistic and polytheistic at once; Pantheism being Monotheism made real, and vital, and warm, and Polytheism being Theism frittered away and degraded into countless superstitions and inanities. In other words, the object of Egyptian worship was a plurality in unity, the ignorant catching sight only of the exterior plurality, the seer penetrating deeper to the interior unity.

The Nile with the Egyptians was as marked an instance of periodicity and beneficence as the sun, and was worshipped as representative of many mystic attributes. As in the belief of the sages there existed a substantial sun that was but the emblem or presentment of an unseen life-giving power, so too was there a spiritual as well as a visible Nile. The first conception of this was the water of a firmament that was supposed

to enwrap the world ; an abyss on which the bark of the sun
was believed to sail ; as in the early Greek tradition is the office
assigned to Okeanos, or Ocean, a sort of liquid space. We
moderns only conceive of the firmament as being aërial and
vaporous, and refer to the Greek Ouranos as meaning heaven
or sky, but Ouranos itself we must father upon the Egyptian
word Urnas, or the Celestial Water. And, indeed, we retain
the root yet in our English word "urn," or water-vessel, and
in other words. Ur, in Egyptian, signifies water ; Uri, the
inundation of the Nile ; Ar, Aur, Aru, a river.*

"The Nile-God traverses heaven ; his course there corresponds to that of the river on earth," says the hymn. On
the spiritual or unseen Nile floats, according to the Egyptian
metaphor, the bark of the unseen sun ; and the disembodied
spirit vanishes from earth by that way, after the manner of
the sun duskily departing at eve.

One of the most serious and permanent of religious types,
in which the spiritual fact and its natural metaphor seem to
bear to each other more than a casual relation and correspondence, is that of water as an intervenience and ordeal to be
traversed between the corporeal and the spiritual world. As
in baptism the old self is symbolized as being washed away,
and the new self cleansed and brightened, so in death there is
the course across the river, be it known as Nile or Jordan, to
be faced. In this transit the most easily detachable part of
the still clinging earth-life is cleared away, and the soul is
ushered as far as may be into that state wherein there is no
wrappage of heredity or material veil to hide the real man,—
the state of naked truth.

The notion of a spiritual fact will entwine itself so closely

---

* The alphabetic hieroglyphs for the word *urnas* run as if the roots were *ura*,
great, very much, and *nd*, water. These signs are followed by the indented line,
which is the ideogram for water. (Birch, 547. Egypt. Saloon, 10 h. Lepsius,
Denkm., iii. 134 d, and ii. 4. Renouf, Egypt. Grammar, p. 5.) The same
ideographic sign is appended to words based upon the root signifying river, as in
arun-ta, the Syrian river Orontes.

with material emblems that it is often impossible to discover whether a glimmering consciousness of the fact first suggested the suitable emblem, or whether some ordinary event of physical life led the way to the idea. It may be, indeed it often is, from the clear view of a physical fact that we are enabled to proceed a step further to a conception of some deeper truth.

In Egypt the burial places were mostly in the mountains of the west, or sunset side, of the Nile; and when a death occurred on the eastern side, the ferrying of the mummy across the river became an important symbolic ceremony. By this passage was the soul, like the sun entering the underworld of the west, typified as sped on its way to the unseen. When a death took place on the western side of the Nile, the same procession was conveyed by boat across a pool within the temple precincts.

This symbolism of the passage from life to death has a very general acceptation under various allied forms. A correspondence, it is of course understood, is not a minute picture, but a foreshadowing, a whisper audible on one plane and in its own language, of what takes place on another, where the language in not the same. There has been a readiness, not explicable by the influence of the Egyptian ceremonial, or wholly derivable from the Jewish imagery of Jordan, to adopt the passage of a river as a type of the passage of the soul into disembodied being. Even the Greeks, though they borrowed the notion from Egypt, held the doctrine of the encircling rivers of Hades, and took their silent boatman Charon from the Egyptian Kharu, one of the imagined attendant demons of the death-process. But they added the strange superstition that those whose corpses by any mischance remained unburied or uncovered by soil, were not permitted to enter the ferryman's barge without previously passing a hundred years in vain wanderings to and fro upon the shore. The Greeks were imaginative rather than inspired;

a more real reason for the spirit's wandering close to earth would have been, not that the body was not buried, but that the soul was ;—that certain earthly ties were not put aside which drew the spirit down and prevented it from passing through that river on the thither side of which is the entrance to life.

Perhaps the root of this symbolism of water, whether Nile, Jordan, or Styx, as a mystic dividing line between the terrestrial and the trans-terrestrial, is to be found in a very commonplace fact. The natural boundaries of primitive peoples were mountains, seas, and rivers, amongst which rivers hold a special place, for they are manifest dividers, while an ocean stretches too widely away to allow the relation of the opposite shores to be perceived, and a mountain range seems less a landmark than a barrier.

In Shakespeare's time we find one and the same term denoting both a boundary and a stream :—

> " The undiscovered country, from whose bourn
> No traveller returns " (*Hamlet*, iii. 1).

> " Come over the bourn, Bessy, to me ;
>   Her boat hath a leak,
>   And she must not speak
> Why she does not come over to thee."
>   (*King Lear*, iii. 6.)

It is quite possible that the origin of the ceremonial of baptism is to be traced, by a gradual process of evolution, from the ferrying of the mummy across the Nile. It seems a short step from this to the "baptism into death" of the author of the Epistle to the Romans.*

---

* Baptismal purification and after-death judgment are associated in the following Assyrian fragment :—

"HYMN UPON THE LOT OF THE JUST AFTER DEATH.
" Wash thy hands, purify thy hands.
Let the gods, thine elders, wash their hands, purify their hands.
Eat sacred foods from sacred plates.
Drink sacred water from sacred vessels.
Prepare thyself for the judgment of the King of the son of his god."
              (Transl., J. HALÉVY, *Records of the Past*, vol. xi.)

So far as can be seen, we ought not to regard the ancient Egyptians as a priest-ridden people. We have seen in how many necessary occupations of practical life the Egyptian priest was engaged ; and in his more especial function he was not only ceremonialist, but philosopher and poet. Such natural outlet may reasonably be supposed to have kept the priestly mind free from that morbidness into which it is apt to lapse when the work to be done is all of an internal character. The secret lust of dominance, uncoiling itself in the spiritual sphere, is a more harmful evil than the rude power of open tyranny.

There was a very wholesome feeling in Egypt with regard to productive labour, though the law that enforced it was armed with a sanction that seems to us severe. Herodotus tells us (II. 177) "Amasis* established the law that every Egyptian should appear once a year before the governor of his canton and show his means of living ; or failing to do so, and to prove that he got an honest livelihood, should be put to death. Solon, the Athenian, borrowed this law from the Egyptians, and imposed it on his countrymen, who have observed it ever since : it is indeed an excellent custom."

The condemnation of the idle to death might owe a sanction to the fact that in a simple community of labourers he that did not labour was self-condemned to die of starvation, unless, indeed, he were within reach of the charity of others.

This sorrowful result of idleness is referred to in the Hymn to the Nile, the type of beneficent action in its fecundating and enriching power :—

> "Idle hands he loathes . . . .
> If the gods in heaven are grieved,
>   [as by idleness]
> Then sorrow cometh upon men."

* Aahmes, a king who enjoyed a long and prosperous reign, the termination of which marks the decline of Egyptian monarchy. He is said to have especially favoured the Greeks, and to have contributed to the temple at Delphi. During his reign Cyrus took Babylon, and after his death Cambyses established a Persian Dynasty in Egypt.

One of the confessions of innocence in the Ritual runs, "O Stripper of Words, I have not made delays, or dawdled."

Where religious feeling is pure and pantheistic, orthodoxy is genial and comprehensive. To add a new emblem of divinity to the pantheon is not to disturb the old; it is but to reveal another attribute of the unseen, which, when assimilated with what men have felt before, enriches the conception of deity. There were in Egypt and in Greece terrible degradations of religion; by those degradations it is no more right to judge the purest current of their thought than it is to condemn the inner spirit of our own faith by any popular presentment in which it is turned all awry, and well-nigh upside down. There were sectarian disputes in Egypt, but they appear to have arisen from local feeling and prejudice rather than purely religious difference or vital divergence of doctrine. A main danger against which we have to guard in our estimate of the glowing pantheistic faiths, is that of supposing that they were doctrinal in the sense in which we have known of doctrine from the metaphysical discussions of wrangling and ignorant ecclesiastical fathers, the dogmatic bulls of most Christian Emperors and Popes, and the paltry shibboleths of zealous extirpators of heresy, and promoters of auto-da-fé.

In a general view of the characteristics of the Egyptian system there stands out most impressively the importance in which was held from the earliest ages the question of life in the hereafter. Clement of Alexandria goes so far as to state that "from Pythagoras Plato derived the immortality of the soul, and he from the Egyptians." This at least shows that the subject appeared then to hold, and to have held, as prominent a place in the ethics of Egypt as is proved now to us, who hold many centuries of her history within our reach. The sense of vast sweep of time evidenced in astronomic knowledge, and the acquaintance with the Sothic period,*

---

* The astronomic year is approximately of $365\frac{1}{4}$ days, the civil year is of 365 only. In four years there would be a day wrong, which we correct by the extra day in Leap Year, but in $365\frac{1}{4}$ times four years, the days would come right again. This period of 1,461 years is the Egyptian Great Year or Sothic period.

may have led, we might naturally expect, to a consciousness of the shortness of the span of earthly life, and hence to a readiness to take in the idea of continued existence after death. The enduring pyramids and mighty mausolea represent the endeavour to outlive time; and their paintings and sculptures mainly portray the faith in the outliving of earthly life, and the passage into the state beyond.

A prominent picture in a recent Exhibition of the Royal Academy exemplifies a custom that proceeds from this tendency. At the Egyptian banquet in the midst of the gaiety is dragged in an image of the sacred boat of the dead, upon which lies the figure of a mummy wrought over with all the painted symbolism of death and judgment. Herodotus tells us that as the servant who draws this strange burden shows it to each guest by turn, he says, "Gaze here, and drink, and be merry, for when you die, such will you be." There was probably, in the bright faith of the Egyptian, as much joy as solemnity in the address.

We may briefly sketch that mystic passage of man as portrayed in the Ritual. In it we shall find much that yet lives in our beliefs.

First we have the embalmment in the Moum—a bituminous drug or wax—which converted the steeped body into the almost imperishable mummy. Bandaged in hundreds of yards of fine linen, placed in the case or cartonnage, over which were inscribed extracts from the ritual of the dead, and finally in the coffin of fragrant wood or of finest stone, the corpse lies upon the lion-shaped couch.

The solemn festal dirge peals from those that stand around:—

> "No man comes from thence
> Who tells of their sayings,
> Who tells of their affairs,
> Who encourages our hearts,
> Ye go
> To the place whence they return not."
>
> (Transl., C. W. GOODWIN.)

The tomb is described elsewhere as "the eternal horizon." At the funeral of priests and priestesses, and at a later epoch, there is a more doctrinal service, known as the Book of Respirations (translated by P. J. de Horrack), the papyrus of which is found deposited with their remains :—

"Thou dost enter the horizon with the Sun.
Thy soul is received in the barque Neshem with Osiris.
Thy soul is divinized in the Hall of Seb.
Thou art justified for ever and ever.
      Hail to the Osiris—
Thine individuality is permanent.
Thy body is durable.
Thy mummy doth germinate.

　　*　　*　　*　　*　　*

Thy body is rejuvenated.

　　*　　*　　*　　*　　*

Thy flesh is on thy bones,
Like unto thy form on earth.

　　*　　*　　*　　*　　*

Thou art divinized with the souls of the gods,
Thy heart is the heart of Ra.
Thy members are the members of the great God (Osiris).

　　*　　*　　*　　*　　*

Thy soul is divinized in Heaven,
To make all the transformations it desireth.
Thou comest on earth each day.
Strengthened by thine ornaments [of the mummy]
Thou art prepared for life.
Thou remainest in a healthful state ;
Thou walkest, thou breathest everywhere.
      [The gods of the lower heaven speak.]
He is received in the Divine Nether World.

　　*　　*　　*　　*　　*

He liveth in the truth.
He doth nourish himself with truth.

　　*　　*　　*　　*　　*

He hath given food to the hungry,
Drink to the thirsty,
Clothes to the naked.
He is favoured among the faithful (or, living),
And divinized among the perfected.
His soul is received wherever it willeth.

> He hath received the Book of Respirations,
> That he may breathe with his soul,
> With that of the Lower Heaven,
> And that he may make any transformation at his will,
> Like the Westerners;
> That his soul may go wherever it desireth,
> Living on the earth for ever and ever."

The following is from the Book of Hades ("Records of the Past," vol. xii.): "O God, who dwelleth in hell, who art with us and the sovereign of Amenti, you who cheer yourselves in your places, and who recline in your beds, raise up your flesh, unite your bones, close together your limbs, collect together your flesh, that the agreeable breath be wafted to your nostrils, . . . that your divine eyes may glisten. See the light by them. Arouse yourselves from your swoon. . . . Their refreshment is of water."

References to reviving water and vivifying air, as awaiting those who have crossed the abyss of death, may also be found in Assyrian and in Parsi sacred books.

There are some physical tendencies in the thoughts here to which we shall afterwards refer; following at present the ceremony.

After the mummy has been conveyed in the symbolic barge across the mystic ferry, the next proceeding is the dramatic representation of the judgment to come.

We need not dwell on the representation of this by masked priests, who would be unable adequately to realize in their acted parts of judge, accuser, mediators, assessors, and recording angel, that wonderful drama of death which fills the sacred pages of the Ritual, and is best enacted in the quiet chambers of the mind. The vivid ceremony, however, with its emblematic signs of good and evil, its scales in which the heart of the deceased is weighed against truth, its impartial judgment, its kindly mediators, must to many have been in itself a more impressive sermon than words.

Thoth, known to the Greeks as Hermes, is the author or

inspirer of the Book of the Dead.* He it is who contends for the soul of the departed, and justifies him against his enemies; he introduces the shade into the unseen world. He is known as the "Good Saviour," and the "Lord of the Divine Words."

He cries out, "O companions of souls made in the House of Osiris, accompany ye the soul of Osiris with yourselves to the House of Osiris! Let him see as ye see, let him hear as ye hear, let him stand as ye stand, let him sit as ye sit."

Osiris is the supreme judge, and the soul that is sufficiently justified to be allowed to enter the path toward him is already accounted as one with him, and is designated the Osirian, or the Osiris.

The Egyptians held the myth of a dying god, both the Nile and the sun being emblems of death followed by resurrection. "They differ from the Greeks," says Herodotus (II. 50), "in paying no divine honours to heroes." The hero was a supernal man who was imagined to be at length deified, or rather elevated to be a demi-god amongst the stars. The allegorical idea of the Egyptians was here lost in the Greek poetic fancy. The tradition of Osiris having lived on earth probably arose from the belief in everything great being a manifestation of the divine. Before man was recognized as being a manifestation of God, the name Osiris, which was afterwards given to departed spirits entering upon their heavenly journey, was bestowed only upon deceased kings. In the sculptures the king is represented in the attitude of a votary, with offerings to a double of himself, his human character doing homage to the eternal not-himself that was realized as dwelling in him.

Like the sun at its setting, the departed spirit passes out

---

* "The sacred books of the priests were all supposed to have been written by Thoth" (S. Sharpe, Egypt. Myth. and Egypt. Christ.). The transliteration of the Egyptian name of this deity is Tahuti.

of sight through the gate of the west. He makes a way in the darkness to see his father, whose beloved he is. He enters as a hawk, the symbol of time; he comes out as a phœnix (bennu), the emblem of the great solar cycle, and so of the soul's endless journey. As he wends along, towed in the ark, or mystic boat, to the heaven, he worships the Lord of Sunbeams, who illuminates the unseen world, who smites the evil, places the Osiris out of sin, and lets him be with the great blessed. He prays the god not to dissipate one who is the type of himself. So far proceeds what is known as the "Manifestation to Light."

The consciousness of divinity grows upon the spirit; he is under order for the hill of the West; the West is the great future; it is what the souls of the gods have had made for them; he feels his eternal life; no element can keep him back. From his heart is rubbed away the stain of corruption and evil. He approaches the Pool of the Two Truths. "I am the soul in his two halves," he says to himself, the interior shrine-dwelling life being united with the other, or by a transformation of two into one he is a completed and united soul; or he is the soul of the sun and of Osiris at once. The expression appears to be an archaic one, on which later holders of the Ritual put a various interpretation.

There are spiritual dangers, however, awaiting him, givers of blows for sins, and terrible beings from whom he has to be protected. Of such we are told, "Those who are in the Pool of the Persea are those born wicked, justifying what they do. For the night of the battle their march is from the East of the heaven. The battle is made in heaven and on the whole earth,"—as indeed is always the battle of good and evil. The divine protector is appealed to in most poetic language: "O Sun, in his egg, gleaming in orb, shining from his horizon, floating in his clouds, who hates sins, forced along by the conducting of Light, without an equal among the Gods, who gives blasts of flame from his mouth, illuminating the world with his splendour! save thou the Osiris from that God whose forms are mystic." Then follows a more realistic appeal: " O Lord of the Great Abode, Chief of the Gods! save thou the Osiris from the God whose face is in the shape of a dog, with the eyebrows of men; he lives off the fallen at the angle of the Pool of Fire, eating the body and digesting the heart, spitting out the bodies. He is invisible. . . . Eater of Millions in his name. He is . . . in the Pool of Fire . . . at the place of the Rejection. Every one who treads in it deficient falls to his blows."

The departed being then passes through many stations of adoration to groups of deities, which is called " Performing the Days." He emerges with enemies thrust aside, pure, in pure clothes of safety. It might be thought that his wanderings were now over, but, indeed, his experiences are only beginning. He has to be reconstructed. His mouth has to be given to him, or reopened; hands are made for him, and legs; and he receives his heart, which is at peace with him. A charm is obtained from each place where he has sojourned in life, and his mind is somehow reformed as he " shoots through every place in which he has been:" a passage, perhaps, through the illuminated sphere of memory. The faculties re-awakened, they have to be preserved. His heart is saved by being the heart of the Great One: " Giving my heart to the Gods, for my heart remains to me," he cries; " I prevail by it for ever." His heart, he is conscious, was his mother, was his being upon earth, was placed within him, and is returned to him by the chief Gods. He adores the soul that still is his, that is not separated. The symbolic presentment of the breath or soul, the gast or ghost, is the form of a bird with human head. A statuette of the Nineteenth Dynasty bears a dove with human head and wings extended over the bosom, to typify the soul.

Again evil creatures approach, crocodiles and vipers. They are repelled by the spirit, who proclaims that he has crossed, and has been healed, and is one with Osiris, and with other deities. He is at once the babe, and, by virtue of his sonship, the Great God. "There is not a limb of him without a god. Thoth is vivifying his limbs; . . . men, gods, spirits, the dead, mortals, beatified spirits, illuminated, do not make any attack upon him. He it is who comes out sound, Immortal is his name." He avoids decapitation, escapes dying a second time, eschews defilement, comes forth with authority, the son of Truth, the substance of the great gods. He feeds on celestial food, receives delicious breath, and his eyes unclose. For the birthplace of the heaven he is bound, in a ferry-boat of plaited corn straw. The sacred boat or ark is generally represented as overshadowed by the wings or feathers of two presiding deities, figures of the Goddess of Truth, which remind us of the Cherubim of the Jews; more indeed than do the Kirubi, the winged human-headed bulls so well known from the Assyrian sculptures, where they guard the entrances to palaces or temples. The sacred boat, when used in the processions, usually contained emblems of life, and sometimes the scarab, symbol of the sun. In later times an imprisoned serpent was the occupant of the ark, which shows a changed symbolism.

To return to our celestial voyager: he finds the doors of the heaven open; he passes on, holding the sail of the boat; he is not drowned in the good water; he sees Osiris there; the repose of the mild one is under the pools. "Wonderful," he says, "is my growth and my substance; my spirits and the power of my hand. . . . I spiritualize myself, I live. . . . I stand upon my feet, youthful through rest." He prevails over the waters; he has prevailed [by accomplishment] over what he has been ordered to do on earth. He prays to the Lords of Truth without fault, who are for ever filling the cycles of eternity, that his sin may be rubbed out in the Purgatory, that he may be saved from annihilation in the Region of the Two Truths. The Gods of the Empyreal Gate, the guardians of heaven, struggle against him, but he is one of the illuminated spirits that belong to Light. A flow comes out of Osiris to him, his shape becomes that of his divine prototype. The redeeming son of God incorporates him with his soul. He makes transformations, he follows the noble road, having got rid of the sins which detained him on earth. He can visit his mummy; every path is opened to the soul that is from the beginning, from the reckoning of years. He seeks to be guarded as a quick soul, and shut out from the shut-up souls and dead shades; he is new embalmed by the Heaven.

Still continue the purificatory steps that lead to more expansive life. The deceased, according to the vignette upon the papyrus, holds up the symbols of writing to the god that inspires the book and prays to make a good use of what in modern phraseology would be the "means of grace." " O great Beholder of his Father, Guardian of the books of Thoth! Let me come, spiritualize myself, make myself a soul, prevail and prepare myself by the writings of Thoth. . . . The Sun, the Lord of the two worlds, has ordered me to do truth." He journeys on, and welcomes the chief spirits who belong to the servants of the Lord of Things. He is created in the heart of the Great Gods; he washes in the Pool of Peace, drawing waters from the divine Pool. His inner life is presumably represented by this sacred imagery.

At length the mystic bark reaches the shore; he unwinds the rope and weighs anchor, in peace. He cries out, "Come —come—near—near. I have come to see my father Osiris." Every part of the boat that has come out of the dim eventide of death, by analogy with the daily dying sun, out of the dusk "heaven when the disk is red," then challenges the spirit to tell its name or purport. The name of the hold is darkness; of the sail, the firmament; of the rope, attachment; of the river traversed, the Visible. There is much in the illustrations of this spectral progress, that is without life and meaning to us yet, no doubt in part from our want of familiarity with what, had we been the cultured sons of ancient Egypt, we were presupposed to know. The re-invigoration of the prepared spirit still continues; his limbs are sound; the Great Lady has sustained him as well as the Sun; he has grown strong to turn back the Dragon of Evil. He puts abomination away; he does not injure the true food of his existence. He gains knowledge of spiritual beings; he labours, and then, striding towards gates that are closed, is acquitted by those who belong to them, and approaches his house after his labours to the delight of his two souls.

Soul with the Egyptian was a compound entity. Besides the mummy, or shed form of earth, there was the spirit (*akh ;* Gr. *pneuma*), which is the secret essence or intelligence and influx of God; the life (*bâ ;* Gr. *psyche*), or sensuous vitality; the form (*ka ;* Gr. *morphe*), or characteristic individuality of existence; and the shade (*kha-ba ;* Gr. *skia ;* Lat. *imago*), or emanational form. What he hates, we are told, is that he should "die a second time;" and in opposition to this is the "making for ever the time." The scene is now a wide space surrounded by the celestial Nile: it is the place of Many Waters; the deceased is there in peace, navigating in his boat, or acting as one of the wise dead, whose lot it is to mow the giant corn, whose ear is of three cubits. He learns the roads in this sanctuary of the dead, knows the ways of going in and coming out.

The Osirian is now justified before the tutelary gods of the regions of Hades. The scene still enlarges itself, and the action becomes higher. We approach the Hall of the Two Truths, and the majestic drama of the Judgment.

The Great God, Osiris, the Lord of Truth, sits on a lofty throne, wearing a mitre of gold with long feathers attached to each side, and balancing either way; he holds a sceptre, the crozier of authority, and the Tau cross, or emblem of life; and the flabellum of justice rests upon his shoulder. Mystic serpents are in the canopy above him. He is mild-faced, but inexorably calm, as Rhot-amenti, or judge of the unseen life, of the hidden being; he is the great prototype of the deity known to the Greeks as Rhadamanthus.

Before the divine Judge are placed sin offerings, and near him are seated the four mediators, or daimonic genii of the dead. Beneath his footstool is the dark cavern of descent to the world of chastisement. The deceased man holds up his hands in prayer, and is supported by the sister goddesses, Isis and Nephthys, the spirits of the upper and lower heavens respectively; each wears on her head the emblem of truth. In front of the Judge is the dragon (the Cerberus of the Greeks), guarding the mouth of the regions of death, and taking the part of accuser or diabolos. Ranged around the Judgment Hall are forty-two assessors, whose prerogative it is to examine the prisoner and report, each having his special province and function.

The following is the claim of a good man for gentle judgment. It is identical in some points with similar appeals to be cited in their place: "Homage to thee, Great God, Lord of Truth and Justice! I am come to thee, O my master. I present myself to thee, and contemplate thy perfecting. I know you, lord of truth and justice. I have brought you the truth. I have committed no fraud against men. I have not tormented the widow. I have not lied in the tribunal. I know not lies. I have not done any prohibited thing. I have not commanded my workman to do more than he could do. I have not been idle. I have not made others weep. I have not made fraudulent gains. I have not altered the grain measure. I have not falsified the equilibrium of the balance. I have not taken away the milk from the foster-child. I have not driven sacred beasts from the pastures. I am pure—I am pure" (Rit., ch. 125).

Such a claim had but to be verified. A large balance is in the midst, presided over by attendant deities. In the one scale is placed the conduct or character of the deceased, typified by the heart (or the funeral vase that held it); in the other is the ostrich feather, or the figure of the Goddess of Truth—Thmei, the Greek Themi, the Thummim of the Hebrew priest's breastplate; as the Urim presents a like analogy to the emblem of Rê or Ra, the sun, or Light. A small weight is moved along the beam, to make a balance, and so determine how much the heart falls short of its standard. Horus, the redeemer and divine son, takes the suppliant shade by the hand, and pleads his merits before the calm Osiris. Thoth, the deity of letters, as recording angel, inscribes on his tablets the actions of the deceased, and presents them before the Judge. The door of entrance is guarded, retreat is impossible; the trembling creature is before the tribunal of infallibility, with his heart all open to view, and his every action weighed in the balance. Osiris was president over judgment rather than judge; the recorded actions spoke for themselves; there was no impugning facts in the pure spiritual light; the conscience of the awakened spirit saw itself in the true bill of the jury, and in the verdict of the balance.

The sentence of doom being favourable, the spirit is designated *makkru*, or justified, a word which is presumably the origin of the Greek *makar* or *makarios*, which comes down to us in the epithet of the Beatitudes, usually translated "blessed." The virtuous soul is now admitted to the heavenly regions, before the entrance to which sits Harpakrut—Horus the child, the Greek Harpocrates, the type of youth and renewal of life; his finger on his lip, in symbol, not of secrecy, but of infancy.

Of these heavenly regions there were extended and varied ideas: there was within those realms a field of rest extending itself at the word of "the Majesty of the God;" there plants grew, and the name of the field was Aahlu, which is familiar to us in the word Elysium.

On the sarcophagus of Oimenepthah there is a representation of this judgment of the dead. The soul of a wicked man is being sent to inhabit the body of a pig; the Egyptian view as to which animal is manifest from the phrase found in the Ritual, "the abomination of a great pig." On a papyrus a soul is similarly portrayed as being sent into the body of a ram. Here we see an appreciation of the law that underlies the theory of transmigration, that the human spirit assimilates its form to its own ideal. The spirit is impure, it takes a swinish shape. This belief was probably not unknown to the Jews; indeed, we have proof that they discussed the question of the effect upon the condition of a man's life of his pre-existent qualities. It would seem not unlikely, then, that the doctrine may have had to do with the growth of the strange legend of the Gospel of the flight of a flock of demons into the bodies of a herd of swine. If in Egypt a man accidentally touched a pig, we are told by Herodotus that he straightway rushed into the river to cleanse himself.

When the soul, unworthy of the mansions of the blessed, has been dismissed at the Judgment to an incarnation suitable to his propensities, the communication between him and the place he has left is shown to be cut off by the presentment of a figure hewing away the ground with an axe; which may remind us of another physical symbol, the "great gulf fixed," designating the same truth of severance.

The sins of which the spirit under trial has to justify himself, "when he has been made to see the Faces of the Gods," are on many and various moral planes. A few may be cited from the Ritual. "O ye Lords of Truth, I have brought you Truth. Rub ye away my faults. I have not privily done evil against mankind. I have not afflicted persons or men. I have not told falsehoods in the tribunal of Truth. . . . I have not made the labouring man do more than his task daily. . . . I have not been idle. . . . I have not made to weep. . . . I have not done fraud to men. I have not changed the measures of the country. I have not injured the images of the gods. I have not taken scraps of the bandages of the dead. I have not committed adultery. . . .

I have not withheld milk from mouths of sucklings. . . . I have not netted sacred birds. I have not caught the fish which typify them. . . . I have not stopped a God from his manifestation." To each assessor he proclaims a separate quality of innocence. The proclamation of the virtue of the justified soul is full of beauty, and may remind us of familiar scenes of judgment in our own sacred tradition. "Let the Osiris go; ye know he is without fault, without soil, without sin, without crimes. Do not torture, do not anything against him. He lives off truth, he is fed off truth, he has made his delight in doing what men say and the gods wish. The God has welcomed him as he has wished. *He has given food to my hungry, drink to my thirsty ones, clothes to my naked, he has made a boat for me to go by.* He has made the sacred food of the gods, the meal of the spirits. Take ye them to him, guard ye them for him."

The passage italicized, and indeed the whole action of the Judgment, we may consider in relation to the august circumstances of the Great Assize as portrayed in the Gospels (Matt. xxv. 31). The deputy King there says to the justified souls, "Come, ye blessed of my Father, inherit the kingdom prepared for you from the foundation of the world. For I was hungry and ye gave me to eat; I was thirsty and ye gave me drink; I was a stranger and ye received me; naked, and ye clothed me; I was sick, and ye visited me; I was in prison and ye came unto me. . . . Verily I say unto you, inasmuch as ye did it unto the least of these my brethren, ye did it unto me." With the latter part may be specially compared the converse thought of the Egyptian prophet: He that gives food to the hungry, clothes to the naked, "has made a boat for me to go by;" in other words, has made ready the way of the Lord, or been the channel whereby the goodness of God is borne in unto creation. In one we have the divine assurance; In feeding the hungry, ye fed me; in the other, In feeding the hungry, ye enabled me to feed them.

Before the acquitted spirit may leave the Hall of Judgment, his knowledge or virtue is repeatedly made proof of. Each part of the hall, its door, sill, and lintel, refuse to open to him, or to let him pass over, unless he tells their name and meaning. The pure floor will not let him tread upon it without the name or purport of his feet being given. Finally, says the doorkeeper, "You have not passed yet, unless you tell me my name." "Toucher of hearts, Searcher of the reins," is the reply; and the spirit, by the aid of Thoth, here called the Reckoner of the Earth, is introduced to the regions beyond; past the roads of darkness, and far from the abode whose ceiling is of flame, and its circuit of undying basilisks.

The Judgment, it would seem, is but the introduction to the spiritual regions, where the new comer has yet to learn to dwell. The purificatory process is represented as continuing; there is a Basin of Purgatorial Fire, guarded by apes, near the openings of the secret doors of the west. The spirit is empowered to come in and go forth at will, severed as he is from earth, with faults obliterated and sins dissipated that detained him. By reason of this purity, "His soul is as a smoke against the devourer of bodies of the dead, flying over the dead, hidden from the suffocaters." Onward "the deceased passes; open ye the gates of the gateway, prepare ye his hall when he comes. Justify ye his words against his accusers. There is given him the food of the Gods of the Gate. There has been made for him the head attire which belongs to him, as dwelling in the hidden place, as image of the great waters, true soul of a created spirit."

There follows "The Passage to the Sun," "the book of vivifying the soul for ever." "The Osiris serves the Sun; . . . there are no shades where he is. . . . He does not walk in the Valley of Darkness, he does not go in the Pool of the Damned. He is not in the fissure a moment. He knows no terror in the place in which he is." He daily overthrows the seductive serpent of evil, by the aid of the deity of redemption,

VOL. I.   D

and the goddess of the vault of heaven, who strengthens him with the water of life and celestial food.

He is made to approach to see his house in Hades; he is like the Sun, and is seen as the Sun's boatman. The beings of light protect him; when attack is made against him, and his heart fails, support is given to him. His enemies are gods, spirits of the dead; "he makes his way, he tows thy boat, his actions are thy actions (the Sun's)," so that there is nothing of earth for god or spirit to attack, nothing of death for the dead souls to draw down to themselves. The disk of the sun is often represented as his eye, and similarly the spirit of the individual is regarded as an eye. [Compare, "If thine eye be single, thy whole body shall be full of light."] "His eye [his spirit] is at peace in its place; . . . the person of the Eye is then before the Gods. The person shines as he did at first. . . . The eye having been veiled before the Lord of that Land (the land of Eternal Birth) it has been made full, and at peace."

There is held festival of the names of the gods, which the spirit has to learn; and he is prepared to know Osiris in every place, under his different names or signs. In the House of Osiris are seven halls, and the names of these must be known, as they only admit of entrance to certain qualities of spirit. The descriptions are pregnant with meaning. The first is typified as the overthrower of numerous forms; perhaps signifying that every shell and subterfuge has to be thrown away, and the inner spirit to be clearly manifested as it is. The name written on one hall is Babble; beyond which doubtless many for long fail to pass. On another is the legend "Great Stopper of the Vain."

The spirit enters "the beginning of the gates of the Aahlu [Elysium], or the abode of Osiris"—gates of the meek-hearted. An appropriate deity holds a double sword at each gate. The name of these guardians is "Terrible;" one of them the spirit addresses as follows: "The fire which burns inextinguishably, . . . the heat which prepares annihilation, running to kill; no salvation, no passing over from its binding is thy name." But the spirit anoints himself with the ambrosia of life of the divine limbs, wraps himself in a pure, white linen garment, holds a stem of a palm-tree, and, purified, proceeds. Spells which imply spiritual knowledge and baptismal purifications which by cleansing justify, are his way of power.

He learns to traverse even the secret places of the valleys of hell, and to prevail against the evils, though not without many a prayer drawn forth by numerous terrors. There is "the Place of Waters; none of the dead can stand in it. Its water is of fire, its flow is of fire, it glows with smoking fire; if wished, there is no drinking it. The thirst of those who are in it is inextinguishable. Through the greatness of its terror and the magnitude of its fear, the Gods, the damned, and the spirits look at its waters from a distance. Their thirst is inextinguishable, they have no peace; if they wish, they cannot escape it."

The action of the book does not appear to be continuous; we revert to the process of awakening the dormant soul. "Isis says: I have come as the winds to be thy protection, to give as breath to thy nostril the north wind. . . . Nephthys says: The Osiris has been awakened."

Then follows "the chapter of building a House on Earth," which cannot be such a house as we know, unless the mummy is the refuge on earth that is signified. "Come ye," says Osiris to the Gods who are in his service; "behold the building of this house of this prepared spirit. He has come like the sun, the same as ye have. May ye give him his speech that he may glorify you as ordered by me. Look ye to what I myself do."

A dogma connected with the mummy associates itself with the narrative, but is overborne by a higher conception. There is an air of pride in contemplation of the body which wastes not while all flesh grows corrupt. The sun sheds its rays on the mummy on its lion-couch, and the spirit prays, "Hail, father Osiris. . . . I have come; I prepare this my body. This my body does not pass away. . . . I do not what thou hatest, but what thy thought wishes. No harm was done to me when I passed through thy belly, receiving no impurity, which thou hast given to every god and goddess; every beast and reptile, when perished, its soul departs after death, it is empty corruption. Hail, my father Osiris, . . . thou dost not corrupt. The eye of Light has not decayed away. I am! I am! I live! I live! I grow! I grow! I wake in peace. I am not corrupted, I am not suffocated there. I grow tall."

There is an orientation of the dead in his chest, which seems to have more to do with a funeral ceremony than to be an episode of the future state. The four winds represent deities, and each goes to the nostril of the defunct. "Unknown," says the Ritual, "is the extent of its mystery. It is not known to rustics." There is a more beautiful reference to the winds of heaven in the scriptures of the Zoroastrians.

We may conclude our extracts from the Ritual of the Dead by certain words of adoration which the departed spirit addresses to the great father Osiris, taking upon himself the character of Horus, or the son. "I have supported thee. . . . I have put forth my arm against the shamers of thy face. . . . I have brought to thee all fruit. . . . I have given thee thy spirit. I have given thee thy soul. I have given thee thy power. I have given thee thy force. I have given thee thy triumph. . . . I have given thee thy victory." "The spirit is returned to God who gave it;" and the address implies that whenever man works, it is God that is working; what spirit is in him is part of God, nay, part of God's life, and may be returned to him with increase, to the enlargement of the divine life, and eternal triumph and victory.

Another instance of this realized oneness with deity we may find in the Inscriptions of Queen Hatasu [Eighteenth Dynasty] ("Records of the Past," vol. x.). "Amen says,

'Thou hast satisfied my heart always. I give thee all the divine life, and all the divine peace which dwells in me; every power I possess, every strength which I have, and every joy which makes me happy.'"

The following is a prayer cited by Mariette Bey: "I ask thy majesty, in my faith, that thou mayest shine on my body, that thou enlighten my sepulchre. Give perfection to my substance, near thy substance. Open to me the doors of the dwelling of thy inferior heaven, that I may go out, that I may approach, that my heart may be pleased, that I may stay in the place that pleases me."

Another prayer is for the souls of the departed: "Approach thou to him. May he enter thy bosom every day! Give him strength to pass the gates of the inferior heaven! Give him the life which was before thee; the breath of the resurrection which is after thee; the entrance and the departure which are in thy power. He sees in thee. He lives in thee. It is in thee that he will never be annihilated."

Herodotus says of the Egyptians (Eut. xxxvii.): "They are religious to excess, far beyond any other race of men." True religion is an ideal and the holding to it; superstition is a morbidness that hugs itself rather than puts out the hand to wholesome work. There are traces, slight but suggestive, of a gradual decadence, through growing ecclesiasticism, of the Egyptian priesthood. The earlier temples had an open portico through which the national solemnities were open to the eyes of the people; the later temples had a wall joining like a web the columns that formed their front, and so acting in a separative manner, as was probably the original intention of the rood screen seen in our cathedrals. "Each Egyptian, like the Greeks," says Herodotus (Eut. xcii.), "takes to himself one wife only." In early times the priests were married men, their wives often being priestesses; and a man was proud of descent through a line of priestesses, as through a line of priests. But at a late time the superstition of celibacy found its way into their doctrines; and, indeed, from Egypt sprang those monastic sects of which, in another place, we may have occasion to speak more particularly in their relation to the followers of Jesus.

There is a curious passage in some versions of the Ritual (ch. cxv.), showing the Egyptian notion as to the original bi-sexual nature of man, which may remind us of the tradition of Genesis: "I, Ra, appeared before the sun. When the circumference of darkness was opened, I was as one among you (the gods). I know how the woman was made from the man."

In another place, Ra, as the sun, is imagined as being born of the great mother Neith (Athene), the sky: "Neith, the Great Mother, who gave birth to the Sun-god Ra, the Firstborn, when as yet no birth had been." (Pastophorus of the Vatican [Twenty-sixth Dynasty], "Records of the Past," vol. x.).

There are evidences of great secrecy having been maintained by the Egyptian priests with regard to their esoteric doctrines. Herodotus, who caught up from them a few fragments of their lore, says of the priests of Heliopolis (Ei-n-ra, the abode of the sun; with the Hebrews, Beth-shemesh, by a play of words corrupted into Aven): "What they told me concerning their religion it is not my intention to repeat, except the names of their deities, which I believe all men know equally. If I relate anything else concerning these matters, it will be only when compelled to do so by the course of my narrative." There was a name, too, of Osiris that he would not utter, which reminds us of the superstition prevalent among the Jews in the time of the translation of the Septuagint—an epoch of special Egyptian influence—in respect of the "I AM," the ineffable name of Jehovah.

Under the later sovereigns the Egyptian faith appears to have lost its simple character, and to have intimately united with foreign thought, the government extending an impartial patronage to all, and accepting all as necessary elements of pomp and of maintenance of popular power. The ancient indigenous kings had a different mode of regarding religion ; they were of the priesthood themselves, and had a single heart to deity as known to their race, without the later patronage of the churches for expedience' sake. In days of such corruption of primates, the body of priests and people is likely to grow careless and callous and sensual, while the naturally religious souls react into some extreme of fanaticism.

Of the Egyptian magic we know but little, though there are evidences that it entered considerably into their religious system. The inner sanctuary of their temples was a dark room, protected by courtyard after courtyard, gateway after gateway, antechamber after antechamber, from any but the qualified celebrants of the rites. Who knows what mystic ceremonies were transacted there ?

During thousands of years millions of human bodies were converted into mummies, or resinous mineralized substances that yet preserved their original organic form, and consequently retained a certain electric life. The process was a tedious and costly one ; what was its object ? what the incentive to so universal a practice ?

It is evident that the Egyptian view as to the state of the disembodied soul after death was various.

Herodotus tells us (II. 123), " The Egyptians were the first to broach the opinion that the soul of man is immortal, and that, when the body dies, it enters into the form of an animal, which is born at the moment ; thence passing on from one animal into another, until it has circled through the forms of all the creatures which tenant the earth, the water, and the air, after which it enters again into a human frame, and is born anew."

Herodotus had probably a not very accurate notion of the

Egyptian faith on this point, but there is an evident aversion expressed in the sacred books from the "second death," or the being reborn in an earthly body; though, with an inconsistency parallel with that of the Christian burial service, in one passage of the Ritual (ch. cxlvi.) the deceased is represented as exclaiming as with joy, when his soul is re-united to his body, that "he has overcome his bandages [of the mummy], and that it is given him to extend his arm."

By very few persons indeed is any of the ancient magic-knowledge now held in possession, or passed on as tradition. An old gentleman, however, the owner, perhaps, of the largest existing library of books on magic, told the writer of certain real or fancied methods of power which need not be named here; suffice it that they somewhat resemble the legend recounted by Euripides of ghosts whom the drinking of a libation of blood enables to gather strength to speak, and recover their old physical memory that the spiritual waters of Lethe had washed away. Lycophron, too, one of the court poets of Ptolemy Philadelphus, King of Egypt in a later period, tells a similar story in his "Cassandra."

On the Stele of Iritisen ("Records of the Past," vol. x.) is a reference to food from which ghosts might gain nourishment—the "white cream of the sacred cow, on which the manes like to feed."

In the "Tale of Setnau," which is a genuine Egyptian relic, we have the story of mummies who not only converse in their catacombs, but have even the power of emerging amongst the living. The charm possessed was thus communicated: "If thou art in the unseen, thou wilt have power to resume the form which thou hadst on earth." In passages we have already quoted from the esoteric books, there are references to the germination of the mummy, and to the power of locomotion at will that under certain conditions, is granted to the departed soul. We therefore conclude that the mummy was made use of by the friends of the deceased for necromantic purposes. It would enable his memory to be still cherished by those in whom the presence of the mummy kept it alive ; and while the spirit enters upon its mystic journey, it has yet a habitation in the physical by means of the embalmed form. In the eternal endo-physical is its true home ; and there is its higher life :—

> " He hath received the Book of Respirations
> That he may breathe with his soul."

The body exists, but he has left it, and its irregular and discordant breath, to enter the divine harmony of respiration. The book is the symbol of harmony or perfectedness.

Then comes in, however, a more mundane idea :—

> " That he may make any transformation at his will,
> That his soul may go wherever it desireth,
> Living on the earth for ever and ever."

The mummy could have but slight hold upon the spirit, could give it no true power, yet that little enabled them to say that the spirit lived in the finite as well as in the infinite. If it hovered about earth, careless to advance deeper into inner life, it might be glad, through the thrills of the cord of still existing union with matter, to be recalled by the magician's rites, and to flash some kind of message along its private telegraph wire to the earth sphere. The ears of the ghastly electric remains, not yet wholly bereft of the organic quality of man, could not hear, and he could have no knowledge through these rites of the events of earth, but he might perchance feel such semblance of sensation as could affect those undissipated organs. It would seem at first thought, on following this hypothesis, as if to leave behind one's mummy in a semi-organic existence of centuries was to commit a terrible power to the hands of one's enemies. That soul only, however, that was low and earthbound could be constrained to stoop down far, and upon the spirit of aspiring and heavenly quality could be exerted only a modicum of conjury, a feeble chain indeed after there had once been known the charm and potency of other and more spiritual spheres.

Opinion on the mighty subject of the uprise of life after death no doubt varied among the Egyptians at different epochs. The most spiritual knowledge in its decadence is what will produce the most degrading and materialistic superstition. The belief commonly held about the object of the mummy is that when the years of transmigratory wanderings were over, it might await the return of its soul, and further its re-incarnation. This might help to explain the Pyramids, and may be in accord with the statement of Herodotus; but the painting on the mummy cases, which represents the soul as a bird with human head hovering above the mummy as it lies on its lion-shaped bier, is a doubtful support to this view, although considered to typify it. The bird-soul bears in its grasp the character or emblem of life, and a sail or flag, which is probably the emblem of breath, while Anubis stands by in his customary attitude, as embalmist. It has been supposed that the soul is putting back life and breath into the mummy, but it is just as reasonable to suppose that it is the spirit's departure with those qualities that is represented. In another picture we have a scene of death beneath the vault of heaven, and two presiding deities seated, solemnly upholding the feather of truth, or symbol of justification; the corporeal body, painted red, is falling to the ground in death, while the spiritual form, coloured of the azure of heaven, stands upright in an attitude of prayer and adoration. William Blake's design of "Death's Door," whereby descends the worn-out pilgrim, who above emerges in glad renewal of youth, is a close modern parallel to the Egyptian picture.

But if the Egyptians held concurrent contradictory views on this subject, they are no more singular than ourselves, who, in "The Order for the Burial of the Dead," repeat in one place a pæan of felicity for delivery "from the burden of the flesh," and in another mistranslate Job into saying, "*In* my flesh shall I see God."

The fashion of mummy-making once instituted, the process might be continued without any clear reason but the strong power of precedent; and on this hypothesis we may be prepared to accept the references that are found to the use of the mummy, as, for instance:—

"Saith Nout: O, the Osiris, divine father and first prophet of Ammon Osor-ur, truthful, thou receivest the libation from my own hands; I, thy beneficent mother. I bring thee the vase containing the abundant water for rejoicing thy heart by its effusion, that thou mayest breathe the breath (of life) resulting from it; for I give water to every mummy. I give breath to him whose throat is deprived of it, to those whose body is hidden, to those who have no chapel. I am with thee. I reunite thee to thy soul, which will separate itself no more from thee" (Libation Vase of Osor-ur, Saitic Epoch [Louvre, 908]; trans. P. Pierret, " Records of the Past," vol. xii.).

"The chapter of the visit of the soul to the body in Hades. [Vignette—a soul flying to the body.] . . . He sees his body, he is at peace in his mummy, he is not molested, his body is not strangled for ever.—If this chapter be known, his body has not decayed, his soul is not thrust into his body for ever" (*Rit.*, transl. Birch, lxxxix.). The concluding words here imply a doctrine that the preservation of the mummy obviated a second incarnation.

Again, in a much later papyrus we find: "This good woman whose heart is wise, may she be counted as one of the chosen that serve Osiris; may her soul be restored to youth with their souls, may her body endure in the depths" (Rhind Papyr.).

The following from the Stele of Beka, in the Museum of Turin (" Records of the Past," vol. x.), will soberly complete the subject:—

"I myself was just and true, without malice, *a man* having

put God in his heart, and having been quick to discern his will. I reach the city of those who are in eternity. I have done good upon earth; I have harboured no prejudice; I have not been wicked; I have not approved of any offence or iniquity. I have taken pleasure in speaking the truth; I have perceived the advantage it is to conform to this practice upon the earth, from the time when action began until the tomb. My sure defence shall be to speak it in the day when I reach the divine judges, the skilful interpreters [the assessors], discoverers of all actions, the chastisers of sins."

The Egyptians, it must be allowed, had a very clear conception of right and wrong: the foregoing is an almost ideal record for an official, the chief steward of the public granary. It is to be noted that, though in the first person, the writing is probably the tribute of family or friends of the deceased.

The tablet concludes: "May your soul enjoy the right to go freely in and out like the eternal Lords who are established before the gods." On which M. François Chabas comments— "The chief bliss of the elect, according to the Egyptian creed, consisted in their faculty of unlimited motion in the whole universe. The usual prayers demand for the deceased the power 'of going and coming from and to everywhere under any form they like.'"

Like those familiar to us from Hebrew sources are the Egyptian stories showing a belief in the obsessions of demoniac influences. In the narrative of "The Possessed Princess," a little sister of the royal wife of one of the kings, we find it said: "There is an evil movement in her limbs." A person "acquainted with things" is sent for. The king orders, "Bring me the scribe of the houses of life, and those acquainted with the mysteries of the inner palace." She was found by these sages, we are told in the most matter-of-fact way, "in the condition of being under spirits," which were hostile to contend with. A cure or exorcism is made, and "she was right forthwith."

On the Rosetta Stone, a record of comparatively late Egyptian times, or about two centuries before our era, we find Hermes, or Thoth, the impersonation of learning, referred to as the "twice-great," or literally, the "great and great." He was afterwards more commonly known, especially among Alexandrian Greeks, such as had so large a hand in forming some of our theologic dogmas, as the "thrice great;" we may compare with this title the "Holy, holy, holy" that is so familiar to us.

Shu is the deity of light, and an instance of the many modes of personification of the divine existence in the solar attributes. The Amen-Ra is the hidden source; all other deities, even the Ra himself, being a manifestation only of that inner power; while Ra, or the visible Sun, is still further personified in his rays, his disk, his position—rising, setting in the horizon, shining below the world, or viewed in his human influence. The expression of our ritual, "Light of Light, very God of very God," has a ring of Egyptian metaphysics; and probably originated among Alexandrian bishops.

In Egypt the Divine Being is not so much God the Father as a more remote deific essence, through the intervening of so many deified attributes.

Osiris is the chief of the Egyptian Pantheon, the sun in a semi-human form, and the author of natural life; that spirit of the visible sun being the emanation of the invisible Supreme. Of this Osiris, Horus is the son, represented as the sun in his mid-day power, and venerated as being of his personal substance. He has many attributes and characters, some of which are not sharply defined from those of Osiris. He is the symbol of eternal youth, as is the sun in its daily death and resurrection. "The old man who becomes young" is one of his titles, and he is represented as achieving impossibility by treading under foot a crocodile, which cannot turn its head, and so typified an impossibility. In the mystic imagery of the Book of the Dead, he was able to make the crocodiles of darkness to turn back their heads. In the hieroglyphic texts Horus is known under many names; he is "The sole begotten of his Father," "The Holy Child," "The beloved Son of his Father," "The Lord of Life," "The Eternal One," "The God creating Himself;" and in his relation to man, "Horus the Redeemer," "The justifier of the Righteous."

> "Horus, he is my brother:
> Horus is my cousin:
> Horus has come to me out of my Father,
> He has proceeded from the brains of his head;
> *　　*　　*　　*　　*
> The Universal Lord."

In the records of the simple Egyptian faith of the period succeeding the expulsion of the Syrian invaders, when the national life appears to have expanded into a special fruitfulness, we find thoughts that seem not rude and strange to us, but homely and familiar. This was an epoch before the influences of foreign civilizations, Greek or Persian, were so intermingled with the proper tradition of archaic Egypt as to make it lose to a great extent its distinctive character. This was, too, the epoch of the Exodus, when the fathers of our religious traditions were "learned in the wisdom of the Egyptians."

Such hymns as the following find their kindred among the works of the Hebrew prophets and psalmists, both as regards simplicity, earnestness, and tendency of thought.

"Oh! Amen, lend thine ear to him
  Who is alone before the tribunal,
  He is poor (he is not) rich.
  The court oppresses him;
  Silver and gold for the clerks of the book,
  Garments for the servants. There is no other Amen, acting as judge,
  To deliver (one) from his misery;
  When the poor man is before the tribunal,
  (Making) the poor to go forth rich."
              (*Hymn to Amen.* Transl., C. W. GOODWIN.)

By substituting for the word Amen its literal meaning,

the Unseen, the language will become yet more familiar to us.

The following is a portion of another hymn from the same papyrus as the above :—

" I cry, the beginning of wisdom is the way of Amen, the rudder of (truth).
Thou art he that giveth bread to him who has none,
That sustaineth the servant of his house.
Let no prince be my defender in all my troubles.
Let not my memorial be placed under the power
Of any man who is in the house . . . My Lord is (my) defender;
I know his power, to wit, (he is) a strong defender,
There is none mighty except him alone.
Strong is Amen, knowing how to answer,
Fulfilling the desire of him who cries to him."

What follows is more distinctively Egyptian, else this might well have been the cry of some Israelitish sojourner.

The following is from a metrical psalm of a time preceding, perhaps by a century or two, the date of those last quoted :—

" Mind thee of joy, till cometh the day of pilgrimage,
When we draw near the land which loveth silence.

* * * *

He finished his existence . . . (the common fate of men).
Their abodes pass away,
And their place is not ;
They are as if they had never been born
Since the time of Ra [the Sun].
(They in the shades) are sitting on the bank of the river,
Thy soul is among them, drinking its sacred water,
Following thy heart, at peace.

* * * *

Not the least moment could be added to his life,
(When he went to) the realm of eternity.
Those who have magazines full of bread to spend,
Even they shall encounter the hour of a last end.
The moment of that day will diminish the valour of the rich.
Mind thee of the day when thou too shalt start for the land
To which one goeth to return not thence.

Good for thee then will have been (an honest life),
Therefore be just, and hate transgressions,
For he who loveth justice (will be blessed)."
(*Song of the Harper.* Transl., LUDWIG STERN.)

It is noticeable how these hymns differ alike from naturalism, from what is called Paganism, and from the highest thoughts of Greek philosophy. The earnestness there takes another form; here we feel the peculiar seriousness which has constituted one of the main elements of power of the ancient Hebrew prophets.

It will have been remarked how prominent a place is held by the sun in the Egyptian view of deity; and yet it would be unfair to call the Egyptian faith sun-worship. What is manifest stands with the Egyptian seer only for the border or fringe of the infinite life that is invisible except through myriad revealments. The symbolism of the life and death and progress through heaven of the sun has been so intimately worked in with the belief in the continuance of the soul below the horizon of the visible, that a materialist might argue thence that the course and renewal of the sun had suggested to man a similar return to life of his soul when hidden in the clouds of his day's evening. The argument would have plausibility and nothing more: in every great race under heaven of which we have any knowledge, there has lived the faith in the soul's continuance after death, while the physical symbols which have become associated with this faith have been widely different among different peoples. The symbols therefore are the temporary and accidental appendage of a permanent instinct, which finds for itself in every grand analogy of the natural world the best correspondences it may to the glorious vision that is seen as yet through a glass darkly.

In referring to the faith of Egypt, it is necessary to distinguish the ancient religion, not only from the modern, but from that of the period of foreign domination. A great religious centre was to be found in what, historically speaking, might almost be termed with propriety "Modern Egypt," that is to say, Egypt of the period about the beginning of our era. Then was Alexandria the main haunt and home of philosophy; there was to be found the Greek dialoguer; the Egyptian priest, such as Plutarch saw him; the ascetic Therapeut; the fanciful Gnostic: there met orientalized Greek, Grecized Jew, and Judæo-Egyptian; and there the influences of all the ancient faiths of the world seethed into argument and something at times not unlike spiritual chaos. But bright life and vision were not wanting; Philo, in spite of his excess in hunting out symbolic senses, not only where they were to be found, but where they were not, showed that there was not wholly lost the glow of the Hebrew teachings nor the subtle influence of the mind of Egypt.

How describe the influence upon human thought of this hoary nation of the Nile? The life of Egypt is the romance of the world, and it is only as in a romance that even part of the story can be told.

Manetho, the Egyptian priest of the fourth century B.C., was taken for a fabulist because he gives a list of dynasties extending over four thousand years, but has won more respect as scholarship has advanced. It is partly upon his narrative that the following is founded.

In the scorching plains, buried and forgotten, lay the pillars of Hermes, engraved tables of immemorial date. They bore upon them sacred truths, but the hieroglyph had lost its clearness through time and decay, and the meaning of the symbols had been effaced from the minds of men. Some political trouble, or dispute between rival temples, or some new tyrant's bid for popularity and power, had occupied men's minds. Perhaps a natural calamity had occurred, or the sanctuary that guarded the stones was laid waste, and the elucidator of their apocrypha slain. So lapsed a time long enough to let the graven obelisks pass out of memory, while the truths they had conveyed were also pushed aside and made remote by other interests. The crystal tablets stood no longer upright; they shone upon men neither in the letter nor in the spirit, being trampled under foot in both. Long they lay unnoticed, unknown of, while Hermes, god of thought, was a god only in name.

The tradition of a buried column feebly lingered on, like an old crone that seemingly neither lives nor dies. Now and then a half-remembered whisper of the lost wisdom would spring up like a summer wind and touch a susceptible ear; but the world seemed too old and men too busy to make more of it. And so for centuries.

Anon there came a stir, and this like a fresh wind on the waters. The people began to open their eyes with a new alertness, as for something great and strange to come, and to discover that over the trite maxims of the priesthood there lay some blight; they seemed dry, conventional, and unsatisfactory. Minds long confined expanded, and wondered where they had been, and where they were. From a state in which a revelation would have seemed a matter of no account, and a man professing to be its bearer one to be scouted and mocked and put out of the way, they found themselves in a state in which the idea of learning had in it something acceptable, and such fear as might cause the repulsion of its messenger began to be held as narrow and cowardly.

Over the sandy plain blew the wind, making ripples like a crisping river: some things it covered, others it bared. There was living then a strange mortal known as the Son of the Good Spirit; some learning he had, and much thirst for it. As one day he wandered with curious eyes, now turned skyward, now seeming as if they would pierce and burn through earth, with the air's breath fresh and delicate upon his brow that an eager mind had somewhat fevered; as the light of the growing dawn swam serenely over the landscape, he felt himself as in the presence of some crisis of his life. But the horizon was void. As the sun mounted higher, there was but a scrubby knoll, betokening, perchance, some ancient ruin, that broke the pellucid smoothness of the eternal circle of the view. It attracted him, and he went towards it to sit down and meditate upon what was moving him. As he sat longing for clearer articulation of his fervent thoughts, his hand fell idly upon the mound; his fingers played with the light friable earth. Soon, as he dreamed, a thrill came up the hand as if some magnet drew it, and there met his finger-tips something defined like a sacred sign or figure. He turned, and the magnet was exposed; the sun's rays glinted off the surface of a crystal rock, and glowed in a carven symbol on its face. Ardently he explored further, and the buried treasure of centuries was exhumed, the fabled pillar of Hermes. It was almost illegible; neglect had allowed the inscription to become choked with earth; the emblem and its significance were alike faint and clouded.

The discoverer rested not; he pored over his prize, and, line by line, symbol by symbol, fought his way back to the word and its meaning. After years of study he brought his boon into the light: law and geometry, rhythmic lore, hymns of the gods, the stories of the stars, the orders of the angels, the arts of healing, celestial revelations and universal principles illustrated by new thought, were recommitted to the people, The ancient sanction was a dower of welcome; spiritual learning revived, and the priest was once more an inspired man. The happy messenger, the Son of the Good Spirit, was greeted by the name of the second Hermes, and long revered for his boon, the restoration of the ancient scriptures.

When he departed, it could be said of him, as was said of a good minister of nearly five thousand years ago: "He had protected the poor, and defended the weak. Peace was in his words, and the Book of Thoth on his tongue." *

Plato knew his name as Hermes, and Livy as Mercurius Teutates; in Egyptian the name of the deity from which

* Brugsch, Hist. d'Egypte, i. 92.

these titles are derived is Tahuti, Theut, or Thoth. Trismegistus, or Threefold-greatest, he is also called. Clement of Alexandria discourses of him; Homer, a thousand years before, regarded him as the messenger of the gods and conductor of departed souls. His symbolic images were in the public places of Pelasgia and Greece, and took various fantastic forms, as the idea of his attributes became varied or corrupted.

The labours of the second Hermes were fading out in the day of Manetho himself, and the meaning of the pillars was hidden again under earth and the foot of man.

A third student of philosophic mind and sympathetic emotion came forth and strove to renovate the Hermaic name; but the charm had departed. His books are extant,* but about the time of his sojourn in Egypt, in an adjacent country there appeared another Hermes with a different name.

A man came forth who knew the old story of the neglect and decay of the life of the spirit under the dust and inertness of matter, and warned his school, in order that nothing might be lost through the blight of ignorance: "Cast not your pearls before the swine, lest they trample them under their feet and turn to rend you." But the pearls rolled far and got beneath the feet, and the narrow heel of doctrine trampled them, and ignorance brought dust and hid their clear beauty, and mock pearls were thrown among them: and though they are not wholly lost, they are, like the crystal columns of Hermes, obscured and overlaid.

Whoever has the talisman to aid him in his quest, as it was borne by the second Hermes, may find some of these pearls, and though there be among them some that are defaced, they may yet shine as brightly as when first they issued from the lips of the Disciple of the Light.

But until a true hunger and thirst excite men's hearts again, the traveller in the wilderness does but scratch in the sand above the lost jewels in vain.

* Hermetis Trismegisti " Poemander," " Clavis," etc.

AN ARYAN ANCESTOR.

WE have reasons for taking a personal interest in the Aryans. If we look for the traditional cradle of our race, a star overhangs the Orient. Our language finds its principal roots in a spreading centre which is ascribed to the regions lying south of the great river Oxus, and between Euphrates on the west and Indus on the east.

As members of the Indo-Germanic family, we own sonship to the Friesic tribes, who filled the wild fringes of Northern Europe, and made our Anglo-Saxondom by westward invasion, as no doubt they had made their own domain of Friez and Teutonland by incursion from their ancestral east.

This outset of Aryan expansion it would be prudent to style the beginning of a cycle, the dawn of a semi-historical period, rather than the first colonization of a world.

When the noble nomads wandering further eastward reached India (*Arya* in Sanscrit signifies noble) they found rude darker races to subjugate.

Somewhat degenerated from their ancient superiority, these conquerors themselves, or at least such of them as remained and multiplied in India, are now ruled by another and a stronger shoot of the Aryan branch which extended itself westward. Notwithstanding many a fusion and a wide scattering of itself by colonization, this Aryan shoot has not perished, but subsisting in us makes up the strength of England with distinction and unexhausted vitality.

The view we have expressed of the primitive Aryans as

the dominant race of an early period, will allow of room for the questions whether Egypt is not older still than Aryana, and whether the differences between the so-called Semitic languages of the Phœnician and Hebrew peoples and those of the so-called Indo-Germanic group are not differences due to variation rather than to absence of fellowship in origin. The hieroglyph and the oldest cuneiform have not yet been fully explored and compared with other ancient alphabets.

A clue which fairly illustrates the ramifications of the Aryan stock may be found in our word "wit," or "wot." This same word is to be traced with slight variation through the Gothic, the Anglo-Saxon, the old Norman, the German. In the Greek it is εἴδω or οἶδα, preceded by the obsolete letter *vau*. In Latin it is *video*. In Sanscrit it appears as *vid* and in the well-known *Veda*, making by a variation also *bodhi* and *budha*, both signifying knowledge. Perhaps it is the Assyrian *idû*, to know, or to oversee. In Zend it is the *A-vista* (*vid*), the book of knowledge. The Egyptian *ut*, *uit*, magic, has a strong likeness to this root, and magic in the old days had not been branded as quackery, but was regarded as a key of knowledge. The Hebrew, *bda*, to form, *bdd*, to devise, may perhaps also be added to the chain.

To return to Anglo-Saxon, the same root forms the name of the deity *Voden*, *Woden*, or *Odin* (old German *wuotan*), the equivalent of the Hermes or god of wisdom. From *Woden* it comes to us as *Wednesday*, the day, if it were not too much to hope, of wit or wisdom.

Another root, which also signifies to know, appears in our language in the verbs *ken, can, con, acquaint*, and *know*, and in the adjectives *canny* and *cunning*. It is Gothic *kunnan;* Anglo-Saxon, *can, cennan*, and *cnawan;* Swedish, *kunnig* and *kæanna;* Dutch and German, *kennen;* Danish, *kan;* Sanscrit, *gnâ, gânâmi;* Zend, *hunara*, Pazand, *khunar* (science), also Zend *vaen*, and Pazand *vinastan* and *ginastan*, to perceive; Greek, γινώσκειν; Latin, *cognoscere;* old French, *connoistre*.

Egyptian, *kan*, ability, service, power, courage, *khen, khennu, khent*, sanctuary, interior, concealed, *khennui*, intelligence, valour, seem to be akin. From this root—knowledge conveying power—come the words signifying king, old English *cyning*, German *könig*, and possibly the Tartar *khan*, and the Egyptian *ken, kannt*, titles. The prenomen of the writer, which is an old East Anglian place name and surname, contains the same root.

It may be interesting to add a few instances in which the connection between the older languages is readily to be traced.

Among Egyptian hieroglyphs may be found *más*, anoint; *masu*, anoint, dip. In Zend *mashyá* is clarified butter. In Hebrew and Syriac *meshuh, meshihha;* in Arabic *masih*, signify anointed.

In Egyptian *khab*, Assyrian *caccabu*, Hebrew *kôhhabi*, alike signify a star.

We find in Egyptian *makheru*, justified, especially in reference to the dead after judgment; in Assyrian *magaru*, obedient, happy; in Greek μάκαρ, blessed, happy, especially an epithet of the dead. In the Venetian dialect the word lives at the present day as *maggari*, an exclamation of good fortune.

Egyptian *kam*, a reed, *khem*, the masculine emblem; Sanscrit, *kalm;* Hebrew, *gma, gome*, reedgrass, rush; Greek, καλαμος; Arabic, *qalam;* German, *halm*; French, *chaume*, stubble; English, *halm, haulm*, would appear to be practically the same word, and so to afford a trace of a primitive relationship between Egyptian, Shemite, and Aryan.

A more singular word-history still may be found. Among the deities of the Veda, which gives the most ancient trace of the Aryans in India, is *Varuna*, the sky, and the god who resides in the sky. It is easy to perceive the connection between *Varunas*, the nightly firmament, and the Greek οὐρανός, the heaven or the sky,—*ouranos*, which with the obsolete Greek letter *vau*, might have been written *vouranos*. It is not until we turn to Egypt, however, that we reach the origin of the word. There the great water of the Nile was worshipped as a personification of the beneficence of nature. As to the Egyptian this mighty stream seemed to make a highway through the world, so was there imagined to be a splendid spiritual highway through the firmament. Along this the disembodied spirit was supposed to pass on its journey to the Unseen. This highway was the *Urnas*, or celestial water, personified as a deity of the sky. From this word, in its Greek form, we have named the star Uranus, and we have English words in common use which may remind us of the Egyptian root *ur, uri*.

The link between the Egyptian "Urnas," the Greek "Ouranos" and the Vedic "Varunas," appears to manifest itself in the Sanscrit root *vâri*, water. As it would seem, it is through ignorance of an Egyptian root and its application, that Max Müller derives "Varunas," the firmament, from the Sanscrit *var*, to cover.

Etymologists may now attack the question : Which is the original root, the Egyptian *uri* or the Sanscrit *vâri?* An obvious reason for the greater antiquity of the Egyptian root lies in the fact that the Egyptian doctrine of the ceaseless flow through heaven of the celestial Nile accounts for the application to the firmament of a word primarily signifying water.

This chain of lingual roots established, a question suggests itself : Is it possible that the region in which, through the yearly bounty of the Nile, agriculture was free from the curse which besets it elsewhere, was the land that occasioned the legend of the garden of Eden ? Upon this hypothesis, the Adam and Eve who were turned out of Paradise represent emigrants from a country too small to maintain its overgrown family. The memory of a paradise which they had lost, was preserved in Aryana like the dream of a golden age.

Did this legend, to which reference is made hereafter, take its rise among a set of primeval colonists—Egyptian exiles pining for home, and handing down to the far-off generations of their descendants an idealized reminiscence of their state of life by the Nile, where man might eat of the fruit of the ground without toil?

The story of the Garden of Eden is what is learnedly termed a Mythic Philosopheme; that is, an allegory made up of tradition and fancy. The garden itself is topographically impracticable, unless we could imagine the Levant done away with, and the rivers moved.

The present work, however, is prepared for the press in a part of England which, though now consisting of dirty acres of the ordinary kind, was the channel of a prehistoric river, the bed of which discloses the remains of crocodiles, sharks, and turtles, of the palæotherium, the hyopotamus, and many another extinct beast, and tells palæontologists that it once flowed by tangled jungle through simmering morasses toward a sub-tropical sea. It is necessary, therefore, to allow some latitude to the topographical descriptions of the garden of delight, as it is impossible to guess the age of the traditions upon which they may have been founded.

We may call to mind, to show the drift of the thoughts of the ancient scribe, that, combined with the Phrat, or Euphrates, and the Dekel, Digla, or Tigris, one of the rivers mentioned is the Nile (Gihon*) which compasses Cush, or Ethiopia; while the word Pishon, the name of the fourth river of the legend, and the one which has not been identified, is understood to mean "overflowing." Perhaps it may be found to be the Indus.

The word Paradise is familiarly applied to a garden

* Geón (Gen. ii. 13) was a designation of the Nile. "He maketh knowledge to come forth like a stream, as Gihon in the days of vintage" (Sir. xxiv. 25). The word "light" in the published text, in place of "stream," is due to an error made by the grandson of Jesus in the translation from Hebrew into Greek, the Hebrew equivalents of "light" and "stream" differing only one jot.

watered from a contiguous river: "I came forth as a canal dug from a river, as a water-pipe into a paradise" (Sir. xxiv. 30). The Sohar speaks of an earthly and a heavenly Paradise, of which the latter excels the former "as much as darkness is excelled by light."

If the early Nomads from Egypt went westward and southward, they might reach the Niger and the Congo, or be lost to sight in equatorial Africa, where perhaps their children are still, as lingual affinities suggest. If they went eastward, they would have choice of two ways, land and water. If they chose land, they would cross the line of the Suez canal, and avoiding the Arabian desert, would enter what we now call the Holy Land; and the first natural bar to their continued progress would be the river Euphrates. If they chose water, they would have to coast to replenish their stores, as there is reason to believe that neither steamships existed, nor vessels of sufficient tonnage to carry provision for a long voyage. They would simply skirt the peninsula of Arabia and find themselves in the Persian Gulf at the mouth of the Euphrates. "The oldest traditions of the early Babylonians," says George Smith in the "Chaldean Account of the Deluge," seem to centre round the Persian Gulf. If the wanderers chose the first bank of the river, they might meet their brothers of the land route not far from the site of Babylon.[*]

If instead of sailing up the Persian Gulf, they held resolutely to the east; after an open sea journey of three hundred miles, they would arrive in India.

The most important early records of man, so far as we know them, are confined within the comparatively small area which includes the borders of the countries just mentioned. A bee line from the Nile to the Indus is about fifteen hundred miles in length, just the distance which the Mormon pilgrims

---

[*] "The early inhabitants of South Babylonia were of a cognate race with the primitive colonists both of Arabia and of the African Ethiopia" (Rawlinson, "Herodotus," i. 442).

to the American west achieved in bullock waggons and hand carts, across a country without roads or bridges.

If the track of our forefathers was as here suggested, some memorial of the fact is to be expected to be found about their squatting places.

In Egyptian hieroglyphics *ur, uri*, as we have seen, stand for "water," "inundation ;" *ar, aur, aru*, represent "river." A Greek term for water is οὖρον. A Hebraized Egyptian word, signifying "river," and describing chiefly, though not exclusively, the river of Egypt, is *yeôr, iavr, iar* (Gen. xli. 1 ; Isa. xxxiii. 21, and xix. 6 ; Amos vii. 8, etc.). In Accadian (pre-Assyrian cuneiform), *ra* is to "inundate."

From this archaic root comes the Egyptian name of the Nile, *Naru, Nairu, Naiari*, probably denoting the streams at the furcation of the Delta, *na* or *nai* in Egyptian grammar being the definite article in the plural number.

A Hebrew equivalent for "river" is *nahar*, as in *Nahar Mitzraim*, "the river of Egypt" (Gen. xv. 18). *Aram-naharaim*, or "Syria of the rivers" (Judg. iii. 8, 10 ; and version of LXX.), is the Mesopotamia formed by the Tigris and Euphrates or by the Abana and Pharphar rivers. An old Greek word signifying "flowing" is νάρος.

In the case of the Egyptian roots in the Hebrew language the difficulty has to be met of distinguishing between primitive roots and words learned during the centuries of Hebrew servitude in Egypt.

The recorded migration of Abraham was from "Ur of the Chaldees," a locality regarded as existing somewhere in the region of the rivers Euphrates and Tigris. But the word "Ur" has been a *crux* for etymologists, and proclaimed diversely to mean "fire," "a city," "a castle," and "a region."

Sir Henry Rawlinson discovered on the Chaldean cylinders in the ruined temple at Mugheir (the site of which is so near to the Euphrates as now and again to be flooded by it), a reference to a "king of Ur," and to a temple of the moon at

Húr. Other inscriptions make it appear that this Ur was originally a maritime city. What more natural than that it should have been an archaic Egyptian colony, called by an Egyptian water name? Or what more probable than that in the course of time, families like that of Abraham should have branched off from the parent stock, having lost the tradition of their Egyptian origin, though retaining marks of their descent in the roots of their language?

An element transferable from generation to generation, and from race to race, which would appear to be as indestructible as etymological roots, and like them subject to change, attrition, and even a kind of inversion, is proverbial wisdom, even in its higher ranges of mystic thought. The results of earnest speculations, wise deductions, rare inspirations, and pure revelations, with the addition of ceremonial specialties, doctrinal petrifactions, and prejudices and beliefs whose inner meaning has perhaps been forgotten, somehow crystallize together, and make up the religious tradition of a nation.

Our own system we draw from the Hebrews, whose oriental idealism we have hardened by our occidental practicality into a body of doctrine which its parents would fail to recognize.

Similarly the Hebrews, apart from what was mystically born among them (all great ideas, as we know them, are in part a renewal of old ones, and in part a new birth of earth and heaven acting upon ourselves), drew largely from Egypt in their early days, from Assyria in a later day, and from Babylonian and Medo-Persian influences later still.

The earliest head of the Hebrew tribe was the Chaldean nomad, to whose birthplace on the Euphrates reference has been made; and the people themselves were directed (Deut. xxvi. 5) to make acknowledgment of their origin thus: " An Aramean . . . was my father; and he went down into Egypt, and sojourned there, few in number, and became there a nation."

If we affiliate ourselves to the Hebrew traditions, we have a son's right to examine into their lineage.

The links with Assyria, manifesting themselves in parallel deluge legends, dovetailing records of events, and kindred elements of language, we will not here recount, but turn to the Babylonian influences of the second captivity, a time when the Assyrian empire fell and a Medo-Persian sovereignty was established. Then flourished in great power and repute the Magi or priestly caste, who at that time were followers of the Zoroastrian religion. The late Emanuel Deutsch, being a Jew, expresses himself with some caution respecting these foreign influences, but allows that they were of the highest importance: "The analogies between the Persian creed of the time and the Judaism of the captives is so striking that we may fairly doubt which have most influenced the other; we only see clearly the extraordinary and radical change which, within the space of a few generations, came over the exiles under the influence of the civilization and religion of Persia."

We English have several reasons, then, for our interest in the Aryan legacy: We have an Aryan strain in our blood, derived from the westward migrants; we rule a very considerable group of the eastern settlers; and our religious traditions are derived from a so-called Semitic tribe claiming to have its origin somewhere near that sweet ancient spot between the rivers where the myth of Eden was attempted to be localized. And before those traditions were delivered to us they had received a new and great religious impulse from the long sojourn of the people among purely Aryan surroundings, and under the influence of the religious and scientific caste of the Medes and Persians.

We may yet have other interests in old Aryana, at least in its western borders: it is strange, indeed, that English enterprise and Hebrew patriotism together should not ere now have leased a piece of Syria from its bankrupt sovereign, and by making a track along the river valley to the Persian Gulf, have reopened the fabled garden of the world. Now that the rich land has lain fallow so long, is it not time to cleanse out its ancient choked canals, and banish the desolation that broods over it?—a desolation that is not so fatalistic but that it would flee before the busy hands of energetic men.*

The language of the ancient Aryans, whose traditions are now represented by the scanty remnant of the Bombay Parsis, is the sister of the Sanscrit of the Vedas. The Mohammedan extension of the seventh century drove out the depositaries of the traditions from their ancient haunts, but the Masdayasnian or Zoroastrian doctrines are not yet quite extinct, even after their continuance for four thousand years. The Parsis themselves are working like western students at the gathering up of the fragments of their scriptures; and, as regards ourselves more particularly, we do not yet know how much we are contributing to the preservation of these thoughts, in the sacred literature we hold so dear, until we know how much we owe to the sojourn of the Jews in Babylon, at the time when that city fell under Medo-Persian rule.

At the time of Jesus, the priests of the Zoroastrian religion appear to have been known to the peoples of the west as Mages.

Lucian (Long., 4) refers to those called Mages as "a soothsaying order among the Persians, Parthians, and Bactrians, and especially the Medes." Cicero affirms (De Divin., i. 23) that "No one can be king of the Persians, unless he have

---

* From a harbour facing Cyprus, along the line of a trade route to the Euphrates, would require a railway of about a hundred and thirty English miles, to be continued further alongside the river to the limit where it becomes navigable by steam. Unless some active race colonizes the district, the river, which a few years ago was a noble stream, two hundred yards wide as it flowed by Babylon, will become obliterated in reedy morasses, and the towns upon its banks be entirely ruined. There are groves of palms, belts of date-trees, wheat, barley, rice, coffee, fish in abundance; colonization should be no more difficult than in an unexplored country; the Sultan would scarcely be likely to refuse a concession; a wilderness would become a garden once again; and a new road be afforded between Europe and India.

previously gained perception of the training and science of the Mages." Philo tells us (Quod omn. prob. lib., xi.) that "Among the Persians is the order of Mages, who, investigating the works of nature for the observation of truth, do quietly by the clearest setting forth initiate themselves and others into the divine virtues." Some old reactionist Jew, reviving the hatred of foreign influences to which his nation was ever so largely open, decided that "Whoever learns a single word from a Mage is liable to death" (Schabb., f. 75 i. Bava-Bathra).

The date when the prophet Zoroaster (Zarathustra) flourished, is considered by those who have the best right to form a judgment to be about 2300 B.C., and the field of his earliest influence to have been Bactria, the modern Bokhara, north of Afghanistan. Here was a great trade centre for merchants dealing with the woollen and the gold, and manifold other products, of Central Asia.

Balkh (Bakhdi, Berekhdha, in the Zend Avesta) was the capital city, and in the great fire temple there the seer is believed to have preached to a large audience whom he addresses as "those that have come from near and from far."

He declares that the wise (the seven immortal benefactors or arch-angelic beings, who personify divine qualities, and are represented as emanations from deity) have manifested this universe as a duality. There is a contrariety between the life-giving and the destructive powers in this world, between this life and the other life ; between the knowledge acquired by study and experience, and the inborn celestial wisdom of the pre-existent spirit. God is ruler through the good mind. Immortality and wholesomeness are the attainment of the soul of the pure. Punishment is not arbitrary for shameful deeds, but the wicked man's own hatred for good impels him away from good. Whatever we do, is stored in the dwelling place of the heavenly singers, and meets us, when come the increasers of the days, the holy ones who assist at the resurrection; and when the weightiest life begins, which is the destruction of the terrestrial creation.

Philosophy, astronomy, and law are ascribed to Zoroaster. And the race which owned him as its teacher became a great nation.

The mythical region from which this people is represented as deriving its origin, is a semi-fabulous Eden,—Airyana-vaêjô (Sanscrit, Erangvejadesha; Pazand, Era-vezh). This is Iran the pure, of the good creation. It is said of it that it was a creation of delight, but unapproachable, else the whole corporeal world would have gone after it. But a curious historical reminiscence appears to mingle with the legend of Paradise. After the contrariety of the earth life has manifested itself, the region of bliss is found to have ten months of winter and only two of summer. This would point to the north of the route from Turkestan to China, or to the territory now known as Siberia. The antithesis here is very singular, and reminds us of that other garden legend, where the primitive state is perfection, the after condition one of briars and thorns. In the undisturbed city, men live long; there is no weeping, no falsehood, no avarice. In every forty years, from one woman and one man, one child is born. Their law is goodness, and their religion the primeval religion, and when they die they are righteous. Their ruler is a messenger angel from God, Srôsh the obedient, and their chieftain a homotaurus, who lives on the seashore.*

From this very inconsistent region the Aryans emigrate in bands. Sogdiana, Mervè, Margiana, Bactra, Nisa, Herat, Cabul, Candahar, Arachosia, Etymander, Khorasan, India and Ragha in Media, the designations being according to modern or classic names, are more or less fully identified as the quarters of the Orient over which they squatted.

* *Vide*, Avesta, Vendidad, Fargard I. Mainyo-i-khard, XLIV. and LXII.—Another Avatar epoch, or rather, Zodiacal period, was marked by Oannes, or the fish deity, who, the Assyrian student George Smith observes, is supposed to have arisen from the Persian Gulf.

Herodotus tells us that the Medes were anciently called by all people Aryans. They were indeed Aryans, and probably the most important of the groups of emigrants, perhaps the mother-tribe. They must have extended themselves even to the south-west of what was Media proper, for in 2234 B.C. Babylon, which so often in after days changed hands, became the seat of a Median dynasty. It seems probable that Armenia, too, was in part absorbed by these dominant Aryans, for an inscription of Sargon at Khorsabad, describing Assyrian victories (eighth century B.C.) refers to far-distant Media, stretching onward to Albania. That is to say—past Ararat toward the north.

We have not at present any connected history of the Zoroastrian Medes from their earliest period. History says little more of them than does the Book of Genesis, which (x. 2) refers to the Madai as of the descendants of Japheth. But their literature makes us conscious of their presence. It was spoken of by tradition some two centuries before our era as having consisted of two millions of verses; a development which, it has been said by competent authorities, would require the effluxion of a thousand years.

In the ninth century B.C. the Medes were an independent and distinct people, whom the Assyrians (in a monument of 880 B.C.) claim to have defeated. Possibly in the earlier references to them they were not differentiated from the general Aryan stock.

In the eighth century B.C. Ecbatana, the Median capital, was built. In the Book of Tobit is a reference both to this city and also to the ancient city Ragha, the capital of the earliest Aryan settlement in Media, according to the Zend Avesta. In this century, too, a Median monarch conquered Persia, and his granddaughter married a Persian noble, and became the mother of Cyrus.

Afterwards we find the Medes and Persians regarded as a sort of twin race. They had descended from the same mother Arya, and each seems to have helped the other. Media was the cradle of the Persian power, producing a hardy race, breeding fine horses, and the men themselves not to be bought by gold. Under Cyrus the fortunes of Persia obscured the name of the Mede; but the latter was the more advanced in the arts, and the influence of the Magian tribe was prominent in the Persian system. The book of the chronicles kept by the learned caste was ever before the monarch for his instruction.

The Medo-Persian empire extended itself over all the Asiatic regions that lie between the Mediterranean and the Indus. Luxury followed upon the increase of wealth and centralization; and the stern Macedonian at length overran the whole empire, and brought in a new dynasty and a new *régime*. In the burning of the palace at Persepolis, through a foolish weakness of Alexander, the royal copy of the Zoroastrian scriptures was destroyed, and by far the greater part of them is not now extant. Perhaps, as the scriptures of other nations have been so unexpectedly recovered, there may yet be found among ruins at Pasargada, Ecbatana, Ragha, Susa, or Persepolis, some records of Aryan thought, as it was both before and at the date of the cuneiform inscriptions of Darius. The language in which what we have of the Aryan scriptures is written, is older than that variety of cuneiform. The more modern Parsi books, such as were gathered, translated, or composed in the early centuries of our era under the Sasanian dynasty of Persia, are still faithfully Zoroastrian, and serve to explain the allusions in the older books. There is, therefore, something substantial to turn to when we seek to examine the influences that so strongly affected our religious ancestors, the Hebrews, when they came under the Medo-Persian rule during the period of their stay in Babylonia, consequent upon the various deportations of Nebo-kudurri-ussur in the sixth century B.C. Some never returned from this and the earlier transportations, having become naturalized in the strange land which they had been carried off to populate, and having obtained, some of them, political employment, others a comfortable position with foreign servants under them, others again a profitable opening for traffic. Even the literary classes did not all return to Judea at the time of the patriotic revival, when Jerusalem was allowed to be re-established. Nahardea, in Babylonia, remained a centre of Jewish colleges from the time of the exile for several centuries, and was the seat of learning which produced Hillel the Great, who left Babylon to take the Presidency at Jerusalem.

That beautiful patriotism which took the exiles home, notwithstanding the cosmopolitan influences that had been acting upon them through their intercourse with other peoples, eventually gave rise to a very narrow and bigoted Judaism. That this Judaism was at no time more isolated or self-contained than the religious system of other peoples, save and except by reason of a proud churlishness which for a time marked a dominant faction at Jerusalem, may be seen from the foreign elements that are to be found in the Apocalyptic and Apocryphal books, the Talmud, and the New Testament.

The Talmud affirms that the very names of the angels the Jews learned in Babylon. They had, indeed, learned what became the Kabbalistic theory of existence; and, with a beautiful angelistic faith, had borrowed also a too large reliance upon the petty powers of demonology.

It has been said that, while the Hindus and the Greeks regarded as animated the whole of nature, the Persians imparadised the creation as being the abode of angels. How spiritual their conceptions were may be judged from relics still existing, which probably represent much older strata of thought than the date of the books implies:—

"To the Celestials the bounty of the Most High hath vouchsafed a body which admitteth not of separation which doth not wax old, and is susceptible neither of pain nor defilement."

"Mezdâm separated man from the other animals by the distinction of a soul, which is a free and independent substance, without a body or anything material, indivisible and without position, by which he attaineth to the glory of the angels.

"By his knowledge he united the Soul with the elemental body.

"If one doth good in the elemental body, and possesseth useful knowledge, and acts aright, and is a Hirtâsp [one who refrains from much eating and sleep for the love of God], and doth not give pain to harmless animals;

"When he putteth off the inferior body, I will introduce him into the abode of Angels, that he may see me with the nearest angels" (Desatir, or Sacred Writings of the Ancient Persian Prophets. Bombay, 1818).

Among the answers to the question, "How is it possible to seek the preservation and prosperity of the body without injury of the soul, and the deliverance of the soul without injury of the body?" are the following:—

"Suffer not anxiety; since he that is anxious is heedless of the enjoyment of the world and of the spirit, and decay happens to his body and soul."

"With a malicious man carry on no conflict."

"In always doing of good works, be diligent; that it may come to thy assistance in the heavens."

"Be not reliant on much treasure and wealth; since in the end, it is necessary for thee to leave all" (Mainyo-i-khard, ii. 20, 54, 96, 97).

There is little doubt which of the extracts that follow— Zoroastrian, Buddhist, Hebrew, Christian—is the latest version of a fine metaphoric conception:—

"One can escape from hell if one uses heavenly wisdom as a covering for the back, heavenly contentment as armour, heavenly truth for a shield, heavenly gratitude for a club, heavenly devotedness for a bow, heavenly [or the spirit of] liberality, for an arrow . . . in this manner it is possible to come to heaven and the sight of God" (Mainyo-i-khard, p. 315 ff. Paris MS. and ed. E. W. West, xliii. 5).

"And converting Sila (Virtue) into a cloak, and Jhânam (Thought) into a breast-plate, he [Sakyamuni] covered mankind with the armour of Dhammo (Law) and provided them with the most perfect panoply" (quoted by Turnour, in "Jour. of the As. Soc. of Bengal," 1838, p. 796).

"And he put on righteousness as a breast-plate [or, coat of mail], and salvation for a helmet upon his head; and he put on garments of vengeance for clothing, and was clad with zeal as a cloak" (Isaiah lix. 17).

"Wherefore take up the whole armour of God . . . having girded your loins with truth, and having put on the breast-plate of righteousness, and having shod your feet with the preparation of the gospel of peace; withal taking up the shield of faith, wherewith ye shall be able to quench all the fiery darts of the evil *one*. And take the helmet of salvation, and the sword of the spirit, which is the word of God" (Ephes. vi. 13).

The origin of man is always likely to be a matter of interest; we will accordingly gather together from the various corners where it lies in fragments the legend of the Aryan protoplast, and endeavour to rehabilitate our mythical ancestor in order to compare him with his Hebrew congener.

First must be exhumed an ancient theory which we will venture to designate that of double evolution. One process is confined to the physical world, regarded as the *nidus* of life. In the Aryan mythology, a bull is the first and sole inhabitant of the earth, to which succeeds man. In the Indian books the succession of animals is much more complete. The incarnations of Vishnu, some of which are not without their parallel in Assyrian legend, are successively as a fish (cf. Dagon,

Oannes, Jonah), a turtle, a boar, a lion, a pigmy, a rude man armed with an axe, a hunter or warrior with a bow, an agriculturist furnished with a plough, a priest or religious teacher. The final incarnation seems to imply a mysterious subversal of the whole order, a completion of the cycle, a saviour heralding destruction. Another similar scheme of succession consists of plants, worms, insects, fish, serpents, tortoises, cattle, wild animals, man. These successive embodiments may fairly be taken to represent the evolution of physical life.

The simultaneous process which eventually results in man, is that of a spiritual being gradually descending, by a sort of fall as it were, into a region of grosser life. The Parsi Bundaheshn, or Book of Genesis, which is a compilation of old fragmentary lore, refers to a statement in the Law, or ancient scripture, concerning beings who fed first on water, then on the fruit of trees, then on milk, finally on meat. Eating, it will be remembered, had something to do with the Adamite fall; but here it would really appear that a gradual materialization is adumbrated, the spiritual entity becoming more corporeal, stage by stage, until eventually he can make organic the chemical atoms of the terrestrial sphere, and is fitted to adopt the embryo animal body, which, by its own process of evolution, is being prepared for him. The reverse process with regard to food heralds the millennium, to which we will refer more fully in its place.

The cosmogony to which these developments belong is cyclic. A period passes in tranquillity without evil, then ensues a period of evils and wars; then, as good and evil mingle, appears the level of life as we know it.

In the works of Mirkond, the Persian historian, we find it stated that a being bearing the name of Kaiômart is asserted by the Magi to be identical with the Hebrew Adam. The following passages from the Avesta will serve as introduction to the myth of our Aryan ancestor, who, like as the Kabbalists regarded the first or archetypal Adam, is not so much the actual protoplast as the medium of production of the human race:—

"The Fravashi (angelic counterpart) of *the pure Gayo-marathan* praise we, who first heard the mind of Ahura-Mazda, and his commands, from which he created the race of the Aryan regions" (Khordah-Avesta, Farvardin Yasht, 24, 87).

"This word have I (Ahura-Mazda) spoken . . . before the creation of this heaven, before the water, before the earth, before the trees, before the creation of the four-footed bull, before the birth of *the pure man, the two-legged*, before the body of this sun was created according to the wish of the Amĕsha-çpĕntas [the seven personified divine attributes whose duty is the preservation of the universe]" (Avesta, Yaçna, xix. 16). The "pure man" here is Kaiômart or Gayo-marathan.

"All the good, mighty, holy Fravashis of the pure, praise we, from Gayô-marathan unto Çaoshyańç the victorious" (Yaçna, xxvi. 32). We will refer later to this Caoshyańç or Sosiosh.

"Praise to the Fravashi of the Bull, of Gayô(marathan), of the holy Zarathustra, the pure" (Yaçna, lxvii. 63).

"Praise be to Ahura-Mazda. Praise to the Amĕsha-çpĕntas, praise to Mithra who possesses wide pastures, praise to the Sun with swift steeds, praise to the Eyes of Ahura-Mazda, praise to the Bull, praise to Gaya(marathan), praise to the Fravashi of Zarathustra, the holy, pure. Praise to the whole world of the pure, which was, and is, and is to be" (Khordah-Avesta, Qarset Nyayis, i.).

"May all Fravashis of the pure . . . from Gayomart to Çosios, here be mentioned" (Prayer after the Afergâns [written in Parsi, more modern than Zend]).

"Blessed be the souls of the lords, Desturs, Mobeds, Herbeds, believers, propagators of the faith, the disciples who have died on this corporeal earth. Blessed be the soul of Gayomars, and Hoshang, and Tahmûr and Jamshéd, etc." (Âferin of the seven Amshaspands [Parsi]).

"May the heavenly yazatas [angels], the earthly yazatas, the heavenly Time, the Frohars [the same as Fravashis, pre-existent spiritual counterparts, or the medium or power which holds body and soul together] of the pure, from Gayomart to Çosios, the victorious, the very majestic, the being, having been, about to be, the born, unborn, belonging to the region, belonging to other regions, the pious men and women, not of age and of age, who have deceased upon this earth in the faith —all Frohars and souls of the same be here mentioned" (Âferîn Gahanbâr, 4 [Parsi]).

"The Heavenly Understanding, created by Mazda, praise we" (Khordah-Avesta, Sirozah, ii. 2).

"The first after the Understanding among the pure creatures praise we" (Avesta, Vispered, xxii. 5). This description, according to tradition, denotes Kaiômart.

"We begin praise and adoration of the bull, of Gaya-(meretan), of Manthra-çpěnta [the holy word personified], the pure, efficacious" (Vispered, xxiv. 3).

These very catholic prayers and praises, which are no doubt of very different dates, show the primeval man, regarded as a mythological being, and having, indeed, come to be treated with adoration.

It is to later works than the Avesta that we have to turn to find any elucidation of the myth; the earlier writings concur in showing the existence of the legend which the later ones explain.

In the *Desatir*—a collection of writings of the ancient Persian poets—we find Kaiômart addressed as "the prince of the higher sphere." The Persian commentator names him "Ferzinsar, the son of Yasanajanan" (which we take to mean head or beginning of the Farsi, or Persians, son of the Spirit of Life), "whom they call Gil-shah [lord of clay] and Giomert;" and describes him as "sent by the benevolent and merciful Ruler of the world on the work of prophecy." He also describes him as having reclaimed man, and as held to be the Father of Mankind. The address to Kaiômart to which the commentator is referring is most passionate and poetic. It runs as follows :—

"He who created thee, and is the Creator of all, is mighty!

"And gave thee refulgence, and enlightened All!

"And sent forth upon thee a portion of his awful light!

"And next, according to his will, assigned thee a course which is everlasting!

"And placed thee high in the lofty eminence of the seventh Heaven!

"I pray of thee, O Father, Lord! that thou ask, by the splendour of thy soul, from thy father and Lord, thy Prime Cause and Lover, the Intelligence that glorified thee with light, and all the free and blazing lights that possess intelligence, that they would ask of their Father and Lord, the Intelligence of all intelligences, the first created Intelligence, the most approved wish that can be asked of the Being, most worthy of all Beings to be adored, the one worthy of the worship of mankind, the Stablisher of All, to make me one of those who approach the band of his Lights and the secrets of his essence; and to pour light on the band of Light and Splendour; and to magnify them, and to purify them and us; while the world endureth, and to all eternity, so let it be!

"In the name of the Lofty, the Giver, the Just, the Lord! O Ferzinsár! thou art the Prophet whom three sons obey.

[Persian note.—The mineral, vegetable, and animal kingdoms.]

"And the four mothers are under thy sway." [Persian note.—The four elements.]

Some writers have attempted to make Kaiômart a historical personage, as the first sovereign of the earliest dynasty of Persia, the Peshdadian. The annals of that dynasty Sir W. Jones describes as dark and fabulous, that of the Kaiani kings who succeeded them heroic and poetical, that of the Sasanian sovereigns historical. The Peshdadian may well be dark and mythical, seeing that the word signifies "before created." According to the legend, however, the son of Kaiômart was a king who discovered fire from flint, while his grandson's nephew was Jemsheed, the founder of Persepolis, who is said to have lived for centuries, and to have divided his subjects into castes.

On the supposed historical ground Kaiômart has a rival. Malcolm, in his "History of Persia," says: "In almost all modern accounts of Persia which have been translated from Mahommedan authors, Kaiomurs is considered the first king of the country; but the Dabistan, a book professedly compiled from works of the ancient Guebers or worshippers of fire, presents us with a chapter on a succession of monarchs and prophets who preceded Kaiomurs. According to the author, the Persians, previous to the reign of Kaiomurs, and consequently long before the mission of Zoroaster, venerated a prophet called Mah-abad (or the great Abad), whom they considered as the father of men. We are told in the Dabistan that the ancient Persians deemed it impossible to ascertain who were the first parents of the human race. The knowledge of man, they alleged, was quite incompetent to such a discovery; but they believed, on the authority of their books, that Mah-abad was the person left at the end of the last great cycle, and consequently father of the present world." This cyclic theory is cognate with that of the "rounds," learned in India by the modern theosophical Buddhists.

The ancient Persians "believe time to be divided into a succession of cycles or periods, to each of which they allot its own people, believing that a male and female are left at the end of every cycle to be the parents of the population of the next.

"The only particulars they relate of Mah-abad are, that he and his wife, having survived the former cycle, were blessed with a numerous progeny, who inhabited caves and clefts of rocks, and were uninformed of both the comforts and luxuries of life; that they were at first strangers to order and government, but that Mah-abad, inspired and aided by Divine power, resolved to alter their condition, and to effect that object, planted gardens and invented ornaments and forged weapons, etc."

The Avesta, however, makes no reference to Mah-abad, who must be considered a strictly Persian creation, the Dabistan making Kaiômart only the first king of the fifth dynasty of the monarchs of Persia, and the sovereign to whom is transmitted a celestial volume in perfect accord with the Mahabadian code.

Later Persian writers follow the chronology of the Jews, and trace the descent of Kaiômart from Noah. He reclaimed, says Ferdosi, his subjects from a state of savage barbarity, but his civilizing efforts brought him many wars with the deevs or magicians. The just king's army, however, was joined by all the lions, tigers, and panthers in his dominions, who left their native forests to aid him, and routed the deevs. There is another and slightly discrepant account of this supernatural aid to which we need not advert more particularly. After the victory Kaiômart is represented as retiring to his capital of Balkh.

This is but imaginary history. We will return to the myth, which has at least a philosophic conception for its basis. We gather it mainly from the Bundehesch and the Majmil al Tawârikh.

According to one account, the present cycle, taken out of the Endless Time, is to be twelve thousand years; for one half of this, the primeval man and the bull (the animal creation, we may presume) lived "without evil in the superior regions of the world." During this time six signs of the Zodiac were traversed. As the world came under the sign of the Balance, dissensions manifested themselves.

According to another account, the first model of existence incarnated upon earth is the Homotaurus, who, however, eventually succumbs to the attacks of the Principle of Evil. As he dies Kaiômart proceeds from him. Kaiômart is androgynous, as also is Adam in one of the two versions we have of the creation myth, and in the traditions handed down by the Kabbalistic Rabbins. R. Samuel Bar Nahman, who presided over twelve hundred students at Pumbadita * in the early part of the fourth century of our era, describes Adam and Eve as created conjoined, and is as absurdly specific as Plato's friends in the *Symposium* in describing the manner of such conjunction.

As opposed to the bull, who is typified by emblems of death and deprivation of speech, Kaiômart is a living and speaking being. He was formed radiant, white, with eyes looking up to heaven. He is essentially an immortal being, and a particular genius watches over his safety to enable him to withstand the power of the Principle of Evil.

The accounts we have of the myth, being of late compilation, differ among themselves, and wander into trivialities; but there seems evidence that Kaiômart represented man in a higher state than ordinary mortality. The same belief was held by the Rabbins concerning the primeval Adam. "Garments of light, these were the garments of the first Adam," was the commentary made by Rabbi Meir on the coats of skin, or fleshly bodies, while Adam's deep sleep was said to represent the lapse from the state of essential life.

Notwithstanding his immortality, Kaiômart did not survive the combined attack of the Principle of Evil, the Father of Death, and of thousands of deevs who fell upon him. But the elementary principles of his being were purified by sunlight, and confided to the genii of fire and of earth. After a number of years there grew from this seed a tree of life, spreading into two branches.

A poet in the Veda seems to be considering some such evolution as this when he asks, " Who has seen the firstborn,

* Mouth of the Bedaitha, a canal once joining the Euphrates and Tigris.

when he who had no bones bore him that had bones?" This is the very *crux* of the spiritual evolution theory.

The next stage brings us to the creation of strictly terrestrial man. In the Avesta itself Kaiômart is at once supernal and the physical protoplast; but in the later writings are frequent references to first parents of a kind not very different from the fabled Adam and Eve; while to Kaiômart, on the other hand, the Kabbalistic conception of the first and spiritual Adam manifests a similar resemblance.

The tree of two branches develops into two human beings, a male and a female, Meschia and Meschiâna (*mashya* is Old Bactrian for *man*), who are pure, and obedient to Ahura-Mazda. Heaven is destined for them, provided they be humble of heart, perform the work of the law, be pure in thought, word, and deed, and do not invoke the deevs. By so continuing they will be a reciprocal blessing to each other.

First they speak thus: It is Ahura-Mazda who has given the water, the earth, trees, animals, the stars, the moon, and sun, and all the benefits that spring therefrom. Then the spirit of opposition enters their thoughts, and all becomes inverted. They turn to the evil principle, and confess him author of their benefits. They eat and clothe themselves. Their food is of more substantial kind, step by step, until they reach flesh. Then they make a fire, obtain metals, and practice handicrafts, all without thanking God. They quarrel and lose the wish to be re-united. Finally comes the serpent, not in the well-known guise of the Hebrew story, but in that of which Dr. Donaldson thought he saw traces in the Eden legend, that of the phallic symbol. Excess begins, with arrogance and selfishness on the part of each and injury to both.

In the Avesta itself there is no trace of Meschia and Meschiâna, and it is therefore probable that they do not belong to the original Zoroastrian conception of creation, but have been evolved by an amplification of the myth. But if the legend of them is borrowed from that of Adam and Eve, it is singular that an element which some scholars have regarded as almost eliminated from the Hebrew account should appear distinctly in the Parsi version. If the latter, which is frequent in the books of later date than the Avesta, be borrowed from the Hebrew story, it must surely be from an earlier version of it than that which we now possess.

The myth of Kaiômart has the best evidence of being a veritable original; and, moreover, is in harmony with the cyclic beliefs of the Zoroastrians. The attempt to set down Kaiômart as the earliest of the kings of Persia, must be due to an endeavour after history-making. The further account of the historians, that it was owing to the increasing depravity of the race, by which it was rendered nearly extinct, that the all-merciful Creator called Kaiômart to the throne in order to save mankind, may also be regarded as an amplification of the legend. This reading, however, may not be wholly inconsistent with the cyclic idea, for the wearing out of one cycle by reason of depravity and declension, must surely be the beginning of the regenerative era, unless we are to believe, with the author of the Second Book of Esdras, who is evidently under Babylonian influences, that the world reverts to an archaic state of silence and lifelessness between period and period of life.

Was one and the last of such periods beginning or ending, the present writer wonders, when the spot in which he is revising these pages was the bed of a huge estuary, from which may now be gathered the remains of crocodiles and sharks, and of many a shell-fish that dwelt in the brine long before the fabled Adam and Eve were even thought of.

To each of these æonic periods a divine messenger is ascribed, and each messenger seems in a sense to be regarded as identical with the others, just as John the Baptist was regarded as a re-appearance of Elijah. The key to this is that each supernal man is regarded as but the missionary manifestation of the One Supreme Being;

and the idea, if pantheistic in excess, is not altogether an unworthy one.

We have alluded to the Principle of Evil in the Zoroastrian creed. There it appears personified as Aharman (Anrô-mainyus), but his existence is only permitted for a limited period by Ahura-Mazda (Hôrmezd), the Creator of all good. The sway of the Evil One extends only over the mortal life. In one of the oldest Gathas, or original hymns of the Avesta, some of which are considered to date from the time of the Prophet, we find, "Let not the mischief-maker destroy the second life;" meaning, according to the Parsi commentators, that in the second period his power to destroy ceases. This faith is more fully developed in expression in the *Desatir*, where we find: "Amongst the most resplendent, powerful, and glorious of the servants who are free from inferior bodies and matter, there is none God's enemy or rival, or disobedient, or cast down, or annihilated."

It is necessary to understand something of this before turning to the completion of the myth of Kaiômart. And it may be well to convey more distinctly the basis of the Parsi doctrines. They are founded, not unlike those of the Egyptians, the Brahmans, the Pythagoreans, and the Kabbalists, on the ancient conception of *Parô-asti*, or pre-existence. "The parô-asti is not the life in the other world, as we understand it, but it signifies the primary state of the soul, to which it returns after its separation from the body; this state is then identified with that of everlasting life."[*]

In the *Dabistan* the same belief is found, without which, it may be named, it is impossible to understand the Kabbala, Buddhism, the doctrines of Pythagoras, and certain sayings of the Apocryphal writers and of the Pharisees of the time when our era begins. The noblest modern expression of the doctrine may be found in Wordsworth's "Intimations of Immortality from the Recollections of Early Childhood."

[*] Haug. "Hadokht Nask." Notes.

The Persian faith is that souls are eternal and limitless, that they proceed from above, and are spirits of the upper sphere. Those who are imperfectly developed migrate from one body to another, until by the efficacy of good thoughts, good words, and good actions, they are fully and finally emancipated from the corporeal condition, and gain their higher rank. They are also, according to the quality of their good works, more or less in affinity with a particular star, and belong to the sphere assigned to that star.

The regaining of this primitive state with all the added gains of mortal experience, may well be deemed at least as difficult a process as that of birth as we know it. The resurrection is regarded as the great deed; in a very old part of Avesta it is designated "the greatest business." As the crowing of the cock awakes us and convinces us that what we saw in sleep was but a dream, so in like manner after death we shall realize that the corporeal world itself was but a dream that is passed away. The cock is with the Parsis the resurrection symbol.

In this difficult business of revival, man is not without a helper. There is Sosiosh (Saoshyâs, Çaoshyañç) the kindler, the victorious, the uplifted amid the corporeal. "He is so helpful that he will save the whole corporeal world; he is so high amongst the corporeal, that he, endowed with body and vital powers, will withstand the destroyer of the corporeal." He has a double attribute, probably owing to modifications of doctrine by lapse of time. He is a prophet appearing before the close of a millennium to rearrange the world, and prepare for the resurrection. He is the victorious dead-restorer, who raises the dead or causes the resurrection by means of the power and assistance of wisdom.[*] In the former sense he is a successor to Kaiômart; in the later he would seem to be almost identical with him in function.

As the millennium draws near, the force of nature weakens.

[*] "Mainyo-i-khard."

Men will pass three days and nights in adoration of the Supreme. As they began to corporealize themselves by feeding first upon water, and in succession upon fruit, milk, and flesh, so now they will reverse the process. They will cease to take flesh, then milk, then fruit, and finally will drink water only. Then will appear the Helper, and man will feed no more, and yet he will not die.

Our Aryan progenitor would appear to be rather a spectral being, but if we follow the creed of our Zoroastrian cousins, that on awakening from the sleep of heedlessness, we shall recognize that the earth life has been but an instructive dream, we ourselves, being yet within that dream, must now appear to be but shadows before that reverend ancestor who so long ago rubbed away the heavy mist from his eyes, and set us an example of the high destiny of man.

At first sight it would seem that to dwell upon the final or resurrection condition of the Zoroastrian Adam would be to turn away from the consideration of his genesis, and to be regarding the creation legend of the Parsis through lenses that invert.

But if we follow the Aryan belief that earth life, when spiritually regarded, is related to eternal life as but an episode devoted to corporeal sleep or dream, then either side of that shadowy period must equally be the fringe of the true state from which all our temporary existence draws its essential vitality. Under such an aspect, birth and death alike are rifts in the veil which covers us; and the difference between them is only in the direction of the soul's passage—whether into or out from the umbrageous avenue of mortality.

Notwithstanding our very natural and wholesome prejudices in favour of the existence in which we are called to manifest ourselves, and which forms for us the all-important present, the now hidden life may be the sphere from which proceeds that magic quality which bids chemical atoms uprise in organic force and beauty. If, as contradistinguished from the seventy years' journey in the caravan whose protection we have found temporarily serviceable, the unrealized dream state be the abiding and virtual life; then the ideal or standard man of any complete philosophy of creation, whether entering upon his perigee or apogee, must represent the strength and character of that more truly substantial life, in archetypal mintage undefaced, or as near thereto as may be attained, and he must be pre-eminent in earthly uses as well.

Kaiômart, or the pure man, as manifested in the Aryan books, is represented as the summit of the animal creation, differentiated from the lower degrees by his upright carriage, his articulate speech, his response to the mind of the Heavenly Supreme. He retains his hold upon essential life, perhaps in the continued consciousness of relation to his angelic counterpart. His pre-eminence of type is declared by his being described as the white man *par excellence*. This attribute of the arch-natural man was, perhaps, a mark of high distinction in the days when the myth of creation was embodied. The tribes among whom the Aryans made their way were probably for the most part dark and degraded aborigines of a lower race than themselves.

As the name of the Hebrew Haadamah implies a reddish colour, the essential difference of the Aryan prototype is that he is white. We esteem this whiteness a privilege still; maybe, when that legend was young, the tradition survived of the day when the vanguard of humanity somehow emerged from negrohood, and changed curly wool into hair. What, it may be curiously asked, are we doing to advance our race, in equal measure with the fathers and mothers of those days? With our Christianity, our commerce, and our "koom-posh," do we yet even dream what our next step is to be—to take us individually as much above ourselves as we seem superior to Soudanese and Bushmen, and they to gorillas?

But Kaiômart, or the ideal man, was not only white and radiant; he is represented as by origin an immortal being, with eyes looking up to heaven. The liquid of life had been applied to him in creation which rendered him ever beautiful and radiant, as a spiritual being who could dominate this body of mortality. The prophet Zoroaster is represented in the paintings and sculptures as endowed with a nimbus, a glory or crown of radiance, which is meant to typify the shining forth of the atmosphere that fills the world of light.

We may assume that Kaiômart was understood never to have lost the consciousness of the unity of the two worlds. That oneness, Persian writers have said, even distinguished ascetics may comprehend. To understand the theory of resurrection, as it chimes in with such views as these, and to make an intelligent analysis of the word itself (anastasis) as we find it in the philosophical language of Greece, it will be necessary to bear in mind a matter that is considered in Persian books as belonging to ancient lore ; a doctrine, moreover, that is revived by new believers in every age. This is the belief, as summarized by the authors of the Synopsis of the Dabistan, "that a man may attain the faculty to quit and reassume his body, or to consider it as a loose garment, which he may put off at pleasure, for ascending to the world of light, and on his return be reunited with the material elements."

It is logically manifest that these mystic passages of the soul must in a partial way be in themselves a resurrection and a new birth. If birth and death are entrances and exits in due form and ceremony with all one's belongings through the great portals of our mortal career, in which we are come to stay ; these other movements are like unencumbered and hasty errands, to execute which one steps out unnoticed through a private door, which is either left open or the master carries the key.

There is no double evolution necessary for this, for the physical frame is quiescent, held only by life's cord of ductile gold ; but the processes by which the spirit adapts itself to the degrees of the spheres or transcends from denser to rarer atmospheres, are told of only in the mazy utterances of seers themselves.

This kind of occultism is very mischief of moonshine unto the modern mind, well swaddled as it is by that most useful mother, mechanical and commercial realism. But whatever may be the right and wholesome way of practical life, philosophically we have no right to ignore the bridges by men in every age held to exist between the present "solid unreality" and the regions where are—

> "Trodden upon by noiseless angels,
> Long mysterious reaches fed with moonlight."

Such questions must rest upon their merits. Though speaking philosophically, an earth life may be but episodical; yet it is, at least apparently, a considerable episode, and the real business during its progress. To fill out one's existence from a plane, however superior, to which one is not adjusted at the time, instead of expanding into the best capacities of the life that is present, would indeed be to turn what may be truest sunshine on its own plane into merest moonshine on another. The materialistic mind in its own purblind fashion is no doubt conscious of this truth, but forgets the fact that morbid cravings after the life withdrawn, while they may be an infringement of a true and wholesome balance, are no more so than is the equally morbid resort to a hoodwink of false science and a puerile arrogance of certainty, assumed in order that all beyond a defined horizon shall be ignored.

If, by reason of our having journeyed "further from the east" to learn the mighty mechanics of the physical plane, we fail to sympathize with the dreams of our Aryan cousins, we may test the breadth of our own philosophic standing according as we fling away those beliefs as worthless with the feeble ridicule of ignorance, or accept them as a contribution to the large history and knowledge of man.

With this apology to the modern mind, the recital may be

resumed of the Aryan theory of mortal life as contained in the sacred assurances of the ancient religion.

Kaiómart we may take to represent man in a state midway between the corporeal and the spiritual, with vision extending into both worlds. Meschia and Meschiâna are drawn down more fully into matter, and are thus subjected to what may be called the Fall. In a Phœnician myth which has passed through Grecian hands a somewhat similar gradation may be found. Aiōn and Protogonos are the first that enter mortal life. Aiōn discovers the art of nutriment from fruit trees; and the offspring of the pair, apparently representing ordinary mortals, are Genos and Genea. These names are but philosophic expressions, Aiōn is Æon, or Time; Protogonos, firstborn, or first parent; Genos and Genea equally denote race, family, offspring.

Kaiómart having departed this life before the production of beings of separate sex, it might naturally be supposed that he returned forthwith to his spiritual state. It is probable enough that the cycle of existence was originally understood to denote the regular course of individual life made typical; but in the development of the theory it must have become doctrinally necessary to account for the close of an epoch as well as for its beginning. Artistically speaking, the idea of a general and specific blossoming of creation, and a simultaneous resurrection into superior opportunity of life, is more pleasant and picturesque than that of the same results produced, so to speak, insensibly, by the unostentatious coming and going of individuals. And indeed that there are cycles of human development, history tells us; therefore it is not surprising that a doctrine should have established itself of a cyclic period bounded by a creation and a resurrection of man.

Geology would lead us to believe that our earth as a continuous abode of man is indefinitely older than is necessary far to outstretch even a number of cycles, regarded as periods between which Mother Nature might pause to refresh herself, as it were, between throe and throe, each the creative act which renewed a world. Nevertheless, we shall find it easy to respect the cyclical conception of the history of man, and that without adopting literally the notion that the world's inhabitants die out at zodiacal intervals and are succeeded by a brand new race. How great civilizations fade out and are replaced by young and vigorous developments is a matter beyond the scope of the present argument.

As, in accordance with the cyclic creed, the day of resurrection approaches, the evil-doer, presumably the personification of the evil principle, is challenged to effect it. He will strive in vain; it is not in his province. But, nevertheless, the process begins. The various members which are to form man's supernal body are not drawn from earth as in creation—they come one and all from the celestial land. It will be remembered that humanity has been regarded as moving towards the spiritual confines by the reverse process in respect of nutriment to that of creation. After abandoning, degree by degree, the diet of flesh, of milk, of fruit, and of water, man ceases to eat, and yet he does not die.

One part of the light which is with the sun will enlighten Kaiômart, the other will enlighten the rest of men. Perhaps we may read this as a poetic expression of the fact that the spiritual ray reaches first the spiritual man. The spiritual entities now recognize the substantial forms that are the fit expression of each individual, and all the immortal denizens of the world assemble together with man, who is about to assume the final body, and return to the weightiest life.

As Kaiômart was the spiritual agent of creation, so Saoshyos fulfils the corresponding function in resurrection; he is the rekindler. There are also a number of other-world beings who assist: "the Increasers of the Days, who step forward to the maintenance of the pure world" (Yaçna, xlv. 3).

The perishable world has been a protection to the evil and the good, and, however inferior in itself, has become in its maternal office the very creation of the Supreme. But when the dividing is at hand, the state of the wicked, as to their souls, becomes hard. They are not like the demons, without spiritual counterparts (Fravashis); but their affinity is about to appear to them in uncomely form, the very image of their souls. The true followers of Ahura-Mazda comfort themselves during the trying process—the separation of the vital powers and consciousness—by the prayers that are themselves "the creations of the first world;" that is to say, of the world they are on the way towards, designated in the same Gâthâs as "the next world." The picture given is of the whole creation, "bodies together with bones, vital power and form, strength and consciousness, soul and Fravashi," subjected to the dread process, through which into the after-death state the soul's progress is portrayed. In the account itself it is impossible to distinguish the doctrine of a postponed and general, or simultaneous, resurrection, which nevertheless is spoken of as taking place after "the long time" and forming "the perfect resurrection." The soul is finding its proper food and raiment in the truths of the religious hymns; and passages which we will shortly cite will instance how the journey is understood to begin immediately.

There is a cyclic account, however, according to which the dead are resuscitated by an elixir which proceeds from the Bull and from the White Man (Kaiômart). Saoshyos gives of this elixir to all mankind, and they enter upon their immortality in a world without stain. There is some contradiction in the different developments of the legend, for it is otherwise given (Bundaheshn): "First will the bodily form of Kaiômart uprise, then that of Mashia and Mashiâna, afterwards that of the rest of mankind."

The confusion between the Parsi doctrines of immediate entrance after death into the life of the spiritual world, and of a resuscitation postponed until the expiration of a cycle, which requires for its completion the decrepitude of the physical world, is particularly noteworthy for us, seeing that the same dilemma has come down into our Christian ritual. In the Order for the Burial of the Dead there is the old mistranslation of Job, "in my flesh" for "out from my flesh:" there confronts it the beautiful account of a sowing in corruption, an uprising in incorruption. There is a pæan on the delivery from the burden of the body, and on the decarnate condition which ensues, as a state in which spirits or souls "live," and not only live, but live "in joy and felicity." And yet, as if the actual possession of life, and that a life of joy and of consciousness of the indwelling of God, were not enough to satisfy reasonable expectation, there is a superadded affirmation of a general resurrection at the last day—a moment which, however intelligible in the primal meaning of the phrase, is traditionally regarded as marking a remote future period following upon the wreck of the globe.

But large doctrines like these which sway great portions of humanity for thousands of years ought to be treated with respect rather than with a too hasty and merely intellectual criticism. Our forefathers the Druids, as Julius Cæsar records, wished to convince men of this as a primary truth, that souls do not die, but from one set of conditions pass after death to others; and they were confident, he says, that in this was the greatest excitation to virtue, by the lapsing of the terror of death. For those, then, whose lack of development prevents their attaining "anastasy" in the true sense of the word; for persons who departing this life would fail of a better resurrection and, cowering back again (*ab aliis transeuntes ad alios*), pass into lower elements, it is perhaps well and hopeful that a belief should continue in a real spiritual consummation, postponed, but somewhile to be reached. Moreover, though humanity, being inharmonious, moves with the irregularities of individualism or at most in a partial national progress; spiritual spheres, having the unity of their harmony, must consummate periods of development by a movement into fuller light in wholeness and simultaneity. And who can tell how far the great doctrine of a specific earthly resurrection, with its general enhancement of life, may not be due to a confused spiritual memory stirring in humanity? Why there should be a favourite expectation of rejoining a body composed of a familiar material substance is easily made intelligible by the consideration how difficult it is for the terrestrial mind to appreciate the vigour of trans-corporeal substance, or to realize how, if the life further on appears dim and phantom-like to us, we ourselves may probably appear still more frail, and clad in a ghostlike mist, in the eyes of those who live and upstand in the terrible strength of angelhood.

The following will exemplify the religious belief of the Aryans on the immediate future of the departing soul, as it concludes its own last earthly day, and enters upon its own resurrection, and its own judgment.

"Where are those tribunals, where do they assemble, where do they come together, at which a man of the corporeal world gives account for his soul? Then answered Ahura-Mazda, After the man is dead, after the man is departed, after his going, the wicked evil-knowing Daevas do work. In the third night, after the coming and lightning of the dawn" (Avesta, Vendidad, xix. 89–91).

"Zarathustra asked Ahura-Mazda, O Ahura-Mazda, most munificent spirit, creator of the settlements supplied with creatures, holy one! when a pious man passes away, where remains his soul that night? Then said Ahura-Mazda, It sits down near the head, chanting the Gâtha Ustavaiti, imploring blessedness. . . . On this night the soul has as much joyfulness as his whole living existence comprised. Where dwells his soul the second night? [The second and third night are described as the first.] On the lapse of the third night, when the dawn appears, the soul of the pious man goes forward, recollecting itself at the perfume of plants.* To him there seems a wind blowing from the more southern side, from the more southern quarters, a sweet scent more sweet-scented than other winds. Then inhaling that wind with the nose, the soul of the pious man considers, Whence blows the wind, the most sweet-scented wind that I have ever inhaled with the nostrils? Advancing with this wind, there appears to him what is his own religion [or law, the rule of life to which he has conformed] in the figure of a beautiful maiden . . . with a dazzling face. . . . Then the soul of the pious man speaks to her, asking, What virgin art thou, whom I have seen here as the most beautiful of virgins in form? Then answers him his own law, I am, O youth, thy good thoughts, good words, good deeds, and good religion, on account of which good religion in thy own possession every one has loved thee for such greatness, and goodness, and beauty, and perfume, and victoriousness, which overcomes enemies, as thou appearest to me. . . . The soul of the pious man first advanced with a footstep placed upon good thought ; secondly, upon good word ; thirdly, upon good action ; fourthly, upon the eternal lights. To him spoke a pious one, previously deceased, asking, How, O pious one, didst thou die? how come away from the fleshly dwellings, . . . from the corporeal world, to the spiritual life, from the perishable to the imperishable? how long will have been thy blessing? Then said Ahura-Mazda, Ask not him whom thou askest, who is come along the fearful, terrible, tremendous path, the separation of body and soul" (Hadokht Nask, ii. ; cf. Arda Viraf, iv. 8-35 ; Mainyo-i-Khard, ii. 110-157).

* Water was an older symbol, or instrument, of revivification : " Beatification of the just after judgment. . . . They have put there the sacred water. The goddess Anat, the great spouse of Anu, will cover thee with her sacred hands. The god Iau will transport thee into a place of delights . . . He will place thee in the midst of honey and butter. He will pour into thy mouth reviving water; thy mouth will be opened for thanksgivings" (Assyrian Fragments, transl. J. Halévy. "Records of the Past," vol. xi.).

In the Pazand, *sadis* or *sedish* is the term for this period of three days or nights, that the soul remains near the body after death. The Sanskrit equivalent is *trirâtrin*. In the book of the *Mainyo-i-Khard* (Spirit of Wisdom) it is written:

"He who is a world-adorning and spirit-destroying man is so destroyed, in a single punishment of the three days, as a raging fire when water comes upon it" (xxi. 10).

"Which is the good work . . . ? To wish good for every one . . . and to be undoubting about the existence of God, and the religion, and the soul, and heaven, and the account that is in the three days, and the reality of the resurrection of the dead and the final body" (*Ib.*, lxiii. 1–7).

"Be not reliant on life; since death occurs at last, and dogs and birds destroy the corpse, and the bones fall to the ground; and during three days (and) nights, the soul sits on the top of the head of the body" (*Ib.*, ii. 110–114).

"For three days after dissolution, the soul is supposed to flit round its tenement of clay, in hopes of a re-union" (Vaux, *Nineveh*).

In the earlier part of this section, reference was made to the traces of relationship and similarity existing between the Aryan doctrines and those which belong to what Christendom has accepted as its own religious traditions.

The Aryan approaches the question of the birth-process of death in a detailed and picturesque, it might almost be said matter-of-fact, way. The following passage will exemplify the deeper intensity of religious feeling in the Hebrew:—

"Come, and let us return unto the Lord; for he hath torn, and he will heal us; he hath smitten, and he will bind us up. After two days will he revive us: on the third day he will raise us up, and we shall live in his sight. Then shall we know, we shall follow on to know the Lord; his going forth is sure as the daybreak, and he will come unto us as the rain, as the latter rain that watereth the earth."

This singular fragment appears in the book of Hosea (vi.

i, 3) quite detached from any context. If we analyze the passage it will be difficult to see what it means if it does not belong to the same kind of prophetic or visionary depiction of after-death experience as those cited from the Zoroastrian books.

By the loose manner of Hebrew speech the phrase "after two days" is apparently reckoned as equivalent to "after three days" and also to "on the third day," as may be seen from what is quoted above when compared with Esther iv. 16, and v. 1, and also with the following: "Come again unto me after three days. . . . They came on the third day, as the king bade, saying, 'Come again on the third day'" (2 Chron. x. 5 and 12).

The confusion is caused by fractions of days being counted as wholes. From a few moments before a particular day begins to a moment after it is passed, the period is one of three days, for it breaks into three separate days.

We will refer presently to the Hebrew word used in Hosea to denote resurrection, and dwell for a moment here on its Greek equivalent in the Septuagint. The Greek verb is ἐξανίστημι, literally, "forth-up-stand," using the English verb both transitively and intransitively; and the construction differs slightly from that of the Hebrew original, being in place of "on the third day he will make us upstand," "in the third day we shall forth-upstand," or, to paraphrase the compound, "emerge on a higher plane erect." By a comparison of words the English reader may find the pith of the meaning of this one. We have well-known words compounded of the Greek verb signifying to stand, "apostasy" and "ecstasy," and may transliterate others from the verb above cited, viz. *anastasy* and *exanastasy*. A common measure is still manifest in these words. *Apostasy* is "offstanding" in the sense of defection; *hypostasy* is subsistence; *ecstasy* is "outstanding" in the sense in which (in the Persian passage already quoted) the spirit is described as finding its body a loose garment, which, under certain conditions, it is possible to stand out of. *Anastasy* is "upstanding" used in many senses, and is the well-known word which is usually and inaccurately translated resurrection. The invariable German rendering of the word is *auferstehung*, to which our Anglo-Saxon "upstanding" is the exact equivalent. The word *ex-ana-stasy* or "out-up-standing" combines the notion of ecstasy, or the spirit's freedom, with that of anastasy or its elevation. Whoever originally applied this Greek term to the subject in question, had evidently the clearest understanding of the metaphysics of the expression.

Our word resurrection is confusing, for it implies re-rising, or rising *again*, which is a thought quite compatible with the Parsi conception of a primal state of existence to which the spirit returns at death; but that is not what is intended by those who currently use the word. If it is designed to mean a re-establishment of the physical organism, that sense is not to be found in the original term.

The Aryan influences acting upon the Hebrews evidently tended to relax in some degree the reverential intensity with which the Hebrew mind had been wont to regard the mysteries of life. The following passage from the Talmud exemplifies a cheering view of the process of death:—

"Rabba, assisting at the agony of Rab Nachman, said to him, Master, I would that thou wouldst appear to me after thy death. Rab Nachman appeared unto him. Rabba asked of him, Hast thou suffered much?—As a hair that one should draw out of a cup of milk" (Moed Katan, 28 a).

It is naturally to be expected that Rabbinical literature will show traces of the Mazdayasnian lore relative to the threefold period of death's gestation of the soul. The following may serve as instances:—

"Tradition of Bar Caphra: There is supreme force of woe on the third day only; for, during a three-days' space, a soul wanders around the sepulchre, expecting to return into the body. But when it sees that the aspect of the countenance is altered, it recedes and relinquishes the body" (Bereschith R., c. 7).

"For the entire space of three days a soul flies above the body, expecting to return" (S. D., Job. xiv. 22, and Vajikra R., xviii.).

"For three days there is vehemence of mourning, because thus far the form of the face is recognized" (Koheleth R., xii. 5).

"Why, after a three-days' space, can a poor man lay aside mourning? ... After a three-days' space the flesh corrupts, and the looks are changed" (Tanchuma, f. xlvii. 1).

The authority referred to for this change is a passage in Job:—

> "Thou destroyest him irretrievably, and he passes;
> Thou changest his countenance, and sendest him away.
> Do his sons come to honour, he knoweth nought of it;
> Are they brought low, he perceives it not of them.
> His flesh only bears its own sufferings,
> And his soul groans only on its own account" (Job xiv. 20–22).

"They go forth to a sepulchre and look on the dead for three days" (Massecheth Semachoth, viii.).

"They make no attestation respecting a dead person except within three days after his death. After the three days' time they do not attest concerning him, for the aspect of his face is altered" (Jebamoth, f. 120, 1).

A similar tradition may be traced in the fifth century B.C. The ghost of Polydoros (Euripides, "Hecuba," 32) speaks: "Being raised up this third daylight, having deserted my body."

In the Johannine story of Lazarus (John xi. 17, 39) the fourth day is adduced as affording conclusive evidence of death.

The myth of Jonah, probably disfigured as it is from its original, may occur to us as having been cited in relation to this doctrine of the triple period occupied by the death process. The interior of the whale as a residence affords a powerful metaphor for the state of a transitional being during the three days of death, for there would indeed be there neither seafaring nor dry land, but a veritable suspension of realizable existence.

According to such studious Rabbis among the modern Jews as are conversant with Bible, Talmud, and Gospels alike, and hold out yearning and sadly unregarded hands towards their Christian fellows, the expression "son of man" denotes man in general, but as viewed in his immortal aspect; it so comes to signify a man who is regenerate, or born again, and so has become the glorified heir of the defunct "old Adam."

In this general sense, or rather in a particular sense typifying the general sense, would by them be understood such expressions as these: "As Jonah was three days and three nights in the whale's belly; so will the son of man be three days and three nights in the heart of the earth" (Matt. xii. 40).

"Destroy this temple, and in three days I will raise it up [literally, "awaken it"]. . . . He spoke of the temple of his body"* (John ii. 19, 21, cf. Matt. xxvi. 61).

"We heard him say, I will destroy this temple that is made with hands, and in three days I will build another made without hands" (Mark xiv. 58; cf. xv. 29).

"The son of man is about to be delivered up into the hands of men, and they will kill him, and the third day he will be raised [literally, "awakened"]" (Matt. xvii. 22).

"We remember that that deceiver said, while he was yet alive, After three days I am raised [literally, "am awakened"]" (Matt. xxvii. 63).

---

* The sense of this mystical allusion would seem quite obvious, were it not for the fact that the building of the *naos* was one of the labours set down for a Messiah: "When King Messias shall awake, given in the north, he will come and build the house of the sanctuary which has been given in the south" (Bemidbar, xiv., and Cant. iv. 16). Perhaps the saying was uttered in one allusive sense, and understood in another.

"He began to teach them, that the son of man must suffer many things ... and be killed, and after three days uprise. And he spake the saying openly. And Peter took him, and began to rebuke him. But he turning about, and seeing his disciples, rebuked Peter, and saith, Get thee behind me, satan: for thou mindest not the things of God, but the things of men" (Mark viii. 31-33).

"He used to teach his disciples and say to them, The son of man is delivered up into the hands of men, and they will kill him, and though killed, after three days he will raise himself [literally, "upstand himself." Here we find the word used for resurrection which was examined above in its form *anastasy*]. But they understood not the saying, and were afraid to ask him" (Mark ix. 31, 32).

"And from among the peoples and tribes and tongues and nations do they look upon their dead bodies three days and a half,* and suffer not their dead bodies to be laid in a tomb. ... and after the three days and a half the breath of life from God entered into them, and they stood upon their feet" (Apocalypse of John, xi. 9, 11).

These mystical passages we leave as we find them; if there be a triplicity in the process of death as the mature soul traverses and solidifies the essence of its experience of childhood, youth, and full age, it would be as true to the Aryan as

---

* The expression, "three days and a half," probably had a meaning with the writer. In Apocalyptic and Talmudical books, Vespasian is said to have besieged Jerusalem three years and a half, Antiochus also, Hadrian Bethlehem for a like time, and Nebusaradanus to have laid waste Jerusalem for three years and a half. The judgment of Nebuchadnezzar and Vespasian was said to occupy a like time. Perhaps the number is meant to imply the extreme of purgatory, for it is said that the judgment of the impious in Gehenna only lasts for twelve months. Clement of Alexandria describes this mysterious period as half a week, which brings it to the period specified in the Apocalypse. "The half of the week Nero held sway, and in the holy city Jerusalem placed the abomination; and in the half of the week he was taken away, and Otho, and Galba, and Vitellius. And Vespasian rose to the supreme power, and destroyed Jerusalem, and desolated the holy place. And that such are the facts of the case, is *clear to him that is able to understand*, as the prophet said" (Strom. I. xxi.). There was evidently something to be read between the lines here.

to the Jew; and any obscurity with regard to it would be only in our apprehension of so recondite a nativity.

The haze to which we have pointed as floating for so long a time over the subject of a concurrent and remote resurrection, as distinguished from the continuance of the soul's existence in immediate life, may be found in the story of Lazarus, which is no doubt an expansion of some incidents in the life of Jesus. Referring to the brother who is apparently departed, the Master says, "He will rise again [literally, "upstand himself"]." The sister replies, "I know that he will in the uprise [*anastasis, auferstehung*—upstanding] in the uttermost day." The final day to the sages meant probably the mortal life's final day—the uttermost hour of each individual on earth; but in the popular view this idea would seem to have brought a spiritual fact into too near and familiar relations for it to be welcomed. A lesson we may safely draw from the life of Jesus is that while standing on this plane he also stood, and stood *consciously* and with open eyes, on the grander interior plane of spirit. He responds in splendid and majestic utterance: "I am," embodied here before you, "the upstanding and the life [an idiomatic expression, possibly meaning by its conjunction of substantives, I am, or represent, the *anastasis*, or "upstanding life"]. He that confides in me [and realizes this fact of the higher life], though he die [which is a temporal fact only], yet will he live, and every one that lives and confides in me will never die." In other words, every one who attains to the realization of the spiritual fact as it is, will know that death is nothing and life is everything. The day he dies he will begin to awaken in the fitting paradise of his state.

We have brought forward this familiar account not only because it sheds light through the haze that lies upon the Aryan, and also upon the Jewish and Christian doctrines, but because of a somewhat fanciful relation which it bears to our Aryan ancestor.

Kaiômart, as we have found him in the Zoroastrian books, is regarded as "the firstfruits of them that slept"—"Kaiômart shall rise first [*auferstehen*, or "upstand," as the Germans render the original text], afterwards the rest of mankind."

The reported words of Jesus, "I am the resurrection" ("upstanding"), we have only in the Greek language. If we had the veritable Aramaic in which he is presumed to have spoken, the equivalent expression would have sounded something like *Aya ha Kaiáhmat*.

If one of the mages, then, who are related to have discovered by astromancy the cradle of his birth, had been among the auditors of Jesus, it would have sounded to his ears as if the mysterious Rabbi of Galilee were identifying himself with the Aryan representative of the life that upstands and vanquishes death. He might have thought that he heard a voice, I am Kaiômart.

This seems to be a curious fancy, and nothing more, for it is held that the Aryan word Kaiômart and the Semitic word Kaiáhmat have no root affinity.

There is another coincidence in respect of these words which is equally curious, and may be considered with interest by those who hold that in the sayings of Jesus there is a by-meaning which has not always been perceived. In the ancient symbolism, the male generally represents the more spiritual, the female the more physical life. If we could entertain the hypothesis that the word Kaiáhmat would remind a Zoroastrian of the glorified Adam of his legend, the second term would readily represent that other and more earthly half of nature which is wedded to the celestial part; and the words would run, "I am the Kaiáhmat and the Eve." The word Eve is merely the Hebrew *Havvah*, Life, in the Septuagint rendered by Zoë (Gen. iii. 20). The actual word in the Greek gospel text from which the quotation is made (John xi. 25) is also Zoë. The Hebrew word *Havvah*, as a kind of proper name, might possibly be familiar to the Hebrews to whom Aramaic was the vernacular.

An interesting piece of evidence may be adduced that the word which Jesus used to express resurrection was virtually *Kaiáhmat*. The word to rise, which forms its root, is used in many senses, as indeed is the Greek word *anastasis*, which signifies insurrection, and even the rising to one's feet from a chair, as well as upstanding in the sense of reaching the life after death. The Hebrew word employed in the same sense in the passage we have quoted from Hosea is *choomun*, containing the same root *Km* with *Kaiáhmat*. This root *Km*, *Kūm*, means also to establish, to set upright, to rise, to raise. In Mark v. 41, we find a record of the power of Jesus in restoring a poor girl who was nearly dead. He says, according to the English translation, "Maiden, arise," and by a very rare chance the Aramaic words of this encouraging address are given us, transliterated into Greek: *Taleitha koum* [or κούμι]. This is the identical root of *Kaiáhmat*.*

---

* The word shows but slight variation through a number of dialects. In Syriac it is *non-chachma* or *nu-choma*; Hebraic, *kouhma*; Peshito and old Chaldee, *chiamta*, *chaiman*; Chaldee and Arabic, *kaimna* and *kaem*, to raise; *kaihmat*, one who raises up the people. Arabic *kiyám*, standing upright, rising up, making an insurrection; *kimat*, plural *kiyam*, stature (*kayyám*, subsisting, eternal; *kayyimat*, straightness, orthodoxy); *kiyámat*, the resurrection, last day, last judgment. There is a modern Persian work entitled "Kiamat Nama," or "Resurrection-Compendium." The word in late Persian or Arabic will bear a trace of its popular Jewish signification, through Mohammedan influences.

The root *kum* may be seen in our own language in ac-cum-ulate, where it signifies rising, swelling, and so, mound or heap. It comes to us through Greek κύπτω, κύμβος, κῦμα; Latin, *cumulus*, *tumeo*, *tumulus* (tomb), *cyma*; French, *comble*, *cime*. A swelling with the idea of ripeness (found in the uses of *tumeo*) associates it with κυέω, κύημα. The Sanscrit is *evayámi*; Pazand, *káma*, lust; *keymi*, womb, old Bactrian *cagemā*; Pali *kámo*, wish, desire, lust; Tibetan, *kampa*, to long for; Egyptian, *khem*, the Lingaic emblem, also the bull symbol. In Aryana, as in Egypt, "these images only symbolize in a very expressive manner the creative force of nature, without obscene intention. It is another way to express *celestial generation*, which should cause the deceased to enter into a new life" (Mariette Bey). A section of humanity has exalted shame into a religion, and taboos all who will not bow down to its dark idol. And for these it will be difficult to realize that in perfect simplicity and good faith the phallic exaltation which repeats itself in response to the influx of the spirit of life, might appear to the Egyptian thinker to afford an analogical aid to the faith in the uprise of

Kaiômart is a word variously transliterated by foreign writers, and very variously derived. We find Kaiomorts, Kehomorts, Kajumert, Kayomers, Kaiomurs, Kajomorts, Kayūmart, Gayômard, Gayomars, Gaiomard, Gayomart, Gayô-mareta, Gayômaratan, Gaya-maretan, Gayomarathno, Gaiumardda, Gueiéhémereté, Giomert, etc. It has been said to mean mortal life, because *Khai* in Hebrew signifies living. (*Nephesh khayá*, a living animal-soul, is the term applied to Adam in Genesis.) It has also been derived from Sanskrit, *kaya*, body, form, and *mrita*, earth; and from Syriac words signifying the Living Word. On the other hand, it might as probably come from Zend *gâo*, bull, and *mard*, man. As expressing their earliest mythical hero, it is possible that the word Kaiômart may be archaic in the language of the Zoroastrians, and that its authentic roots may be difficult to find. In spite of the singular similarity between Kaiômart and Kaiáhmat, as well as between a hero who is the firstfruits of a terrestrial and then of a resurrection life, and resurrection itself regarded as personified; in spite, moreover, of the fact that a common root is found to join the Hebrew and Aryan words signifying to rise, we cannot convince ourselves that there is anything more in the resemblance than one of those singular appearances of identity such as are wont to lead too enthusiastic philologists astray.

In the clearness of their avowal that the truest image and ideal of man is to be found in his spiritual rather than in his corporeal principle, the Christian Scriptures transcend the

---

individual consciousness in resurrection after resurrection of the human form. In the native processes of the world we are in, must lie hidden the alphabets of the language of our future. But through the confusion due to warped social arrangements and unvitalized creeds, the letters of the divine handwriting in us may come to be even a perplexity and a scandal.

The Hebrew or Chaldee word is traceable through the Aryan tongues; the Pahlvi *kímunistan*, to wish, to desire, to ask (Sanscrit *káma*, a desire), has its substantive *kámeh*, for which the corresponding Pazand word is *khástan*, which also means to rise, get up; so that it is considered by philologists that the verb is in affinity with the Chaldee *kum, kim, koum, kaem*; Hebrew *qum*.

notion of Kaiômart as the typical man, represented though he be as essentially an immortal being. We may sum his attributes as follows: he is amphibious, by reason of being a heavenly creature and yet approaching earth, not sundered into sex, radiant, white, with eyes looking up to heaven. He is the firstborn of pure creatures, and the closest to the Heavenly Understanding, the first recipient of the commands of the Deity, the first who heard his mind, the Son of the Spirit of Life, and the first step from spirit in the direction of the production of the corporeal world, and, as the herald of men, the first to return by resurrection to "the pure world," "the wise realm," "the truthful kingdom," "the best place."

Reference has been made to the doctrine of the entrance of man into the terrestrial sphere by a gradual corporealization, and of his return to the primary existence by a reverse process, until such food as we know of is untasted and yet man dies not. Parallels have also been drawn from the apparently disarranged myth of the Hebrew Scripture, and from the interpretation of it by the Rabbins in a Kabbalistic sense not unlike the doctrine of the Zoroastrians.

The Pauline writings, which afford a concluding illustration of this parable of creation, still further develop the subject, and convey a double conception including at once both mortal and spiritual life, the latter as the triumphant element. The Adam is taken as representative of man in his materializing or falling state—that is, as an unspiritual, soulic (psychic), and pre-eminently terrestrial being; he is the living animal-soul. The Christ idea (the word having apparently a developed sense from the early conception of a Messiah or anointed king) is of man on his upward journey— man the spiritual, as represented by the standard uplifted by Jesus, which harmonized with a long-reverenced ideal.

The notion is of man weighed down by terrestrial sluggishness until awakened by the advent and the upleading of a messenger from the bright and glad heavenly state, and thus raised from a circle of depressed existence, from which without help he was slow to emerge. A string of familiar passages will best convey the sentiment—

"If there is no upstanding of the dead, even Christ has not been awakened. . . . If it were in this life only we had hope in Christ, we are more to be pitied than all men. But now Christ has been raised from the dead, the prime * of them who have fallen asleep. For since through man is death, so through man is upstanding of dead: for *as in the Adam all die, so also in the Christ will all be quickened* (made live creatures). . . . The last enemy that is to be brought to nought is death. . . . And when all things have been subjected to him, then also will the Son himself be made subject unto him that subjected all things unto him, that God may be the all in all. . . . An unspiritual (animal-soulic) body is sown, a spiritual body is upwakened. If there is an unspiritual body, there is also a spiritual. So also it is written, *The first man Adam became a living animal soul; the last Adam a life-giving spirit.* Howbeit the spiritual is not first, but the animal-soulic, afterwards the spiritual. *The first man is of earth, earthy; the second man is from heaven*" (1 Cor. xv.).

In the following, "ye died," seems to represent the Adam state, and the word Christ the quality of supernal life, as well as the person typifying it: "Ye died, and your life has been hidden with Christ in God: when Christ, your life, is manifested, then will ye also be manifested with him in glory." . . . Deaden earth-qualities and evil, "seeing that ye have stript off the *old man* with his doings, and have put on the *new man*, which is being renewed unto full knowledge after the image of him that created him; where there is no such thing as

---

* Απαρχη has a double sense as first both in time and quality; it is commonly used metaphorically, as in "the very prime of wisdom," "of philosophy." In Plato (Prot. 343, xxviii.) certain maxims are recorded as being inscribed on the temple at Delphi, and dedicated to Apollo as "the firstfruits of wisdom."

Greek and Jew, circumcision and uncircumcision, non-Greek, Scythian, bond, free; but Christ is all and in all" (Col. iii.).

"The son of his love . . . who is an image of the invisible God, firstborn of all creation . . . original, firstborn from among the dead" (Col. i.).

"The man Jesus Christ . . . manifested in flesh, justified in spirit, seen by angels, preached among Gentiles, believed on in the world, received up in glory," . . . "who brought death to nought, but brought life and incorruption to light through the good tidings." Some "saying that the upstanding has already befallen," turn aside. (1 and 2 Tim.)

"Being put to death in the flesh, but quickened in the spirit, in which also he went and preached unto the spirits in prison . . . good tidings preached to dead men also" (1 Peter).

"The power of his upstanding . . . if by any means I may reach to the upstanding from the dead. Not that I did attain or am already perfected. . . . I reckon not myself to have yet laid hold. . . . The state we belong to is in the heavens" (Phil. iii.).

"Ye have a chrism (Christ-unction) from the Holy One. . . . We have passed over out of death into life, because we love. . . . Let us love, because he first loved us" (1 John iv.).

These passages are mixed with much mystical matter of various kinds and value, generated at a time when there was an extraordinary spiritual stir, and consequently a consciousness apt to over-stimulate; but the quotations are clear enough to show a complete theory of an amphibious constitution of man, represented by "an old man," a typical or primal representative of bodily life, and a "new man," the type, herald, and kindler of the supernal life. They show, too, creation and resurrection as forming a cycle, and even evince a tendency to shift the simple cycle from each individual to whom it belongs to a composite cyclical event. The conception which they contain of a double Adam, or of man in polar opposite attitudes, may be illustrated from Talmudic lore. The orthodox Rabbinical views, as given in the Talmud, being fairly attributable in part to the new lights let in upon the Hebrews through their intercourse with the Median sages, will complete for us the not inharmonious chain of the myths of the ancestry of man, both Aryan and Semitic.

Mr. Taylor, the editor of the excellent edition of *Pirqe Aboth*, refers to the double idea of Adam or man, constituting "the doctrine that there is a correspondence in all respects between the upper world and the lower: 'Whatever exists above, exists also below.' Thus there is an archetypal and celestial Adam analogous to the lower Adam, and made literally in the *image of God*. There is also a *familia* above corresponding to the human *familia* below, with respect to which it is said, 'May it be Thy pleasure, O Lord our God, to make peace in the family above, and in the family below' (Berakoth, 16 b, 17 a). The condition or action of either of these communities must have its analogue in the other. 'He who occupies himself in Thorah for its own sake makes peace in the family above and in the family below. . . . Rab said, 'It is as if he built a palace above and below. . . . Moreover he protects the whole world, etc., and brings the redemption nigh' (Sanhedr., 99 b)."

Again, "a conception which pervades the Midrash literature is that there is an 'upper' and a 'lower' Adam: a celestial man, made strictly in the image of God, and a terrestrial man corresponding in detail to his archetype, of which he is the material adumbration. This twofold conception makes it difficult at times to estimate the precise value of the brief enigmatical sayings of the Rabbis on the Creation and the Fall. The matter is further complicated by their tendency to ignore the distinction between the potential and the actual: between the embryo and its development: between the 'idea' and its temporal manifestation.

"There are two aspects of the statement that man was

made in the *çelem*, or image, of God, according as we regard the resemblance to God as predicated of the actual man or of his archetype; and, as a consequence of this, there are also two ways of regarding the Fall, viz. (1) as a loss of the Divine image in which man was actually created, and (2) as a falling away of the terrestrial Adam from his archetype. In the 'Book of the Generations of Adam,' the Divine likeness is described as not wholly lost but perpetuated : 'God created man in the LIKENESS of God . . . Adam begat a son in his own LIKENESS, after his image (Gen. v. 1, 3); on which Ramban remarks, 'It is known that all that are born of living beings are in the likeness and image of their parents; but because Adam was exalted in his likeness and his image, for it is said of him that In the likeness of God made he him, it says expressly here that his offspring likewise were in that exalted likeness, but it does not say this of Cain and Abel, not wishing to dilate upon them, etc.' This agrees with the Targum of Jonathan, which introduces the remark that 'before this Eve bare Cain, who was not like him (Adam),' etc." This idea of an earthward development will remind us of the Zoroastrian beliefs, and especially of the conception of Kaiômart as being responsive to the mind of the Divinity, while Maschia and Maschiana typify human beings who are not on the prophetic heights of humanity, but are of its animal plane; and we may be reminded of the beautiful counterblast to unhealthy asceticism which we have quoted, that man the spiritual must, as things are, succeed rather than precede man the unspiritual. Man the spiritual, we may say, is built up or strengthened from man the corporeal; large and healthy root (postulating due openness to the Divine sunlight) makes large and wholesome flower.

The superficially opposing views which we have instanced can all be reconciled in the paradox that the Fall of man is his Rise; the earthward pilgrimage well pursued is the way of heavenly strength.

Creation, according to the Talmud, is not to be regarded as complete in Adam, or, as we should say, in the protoplastic state: "Everything that was created in the six days of Bereschith needs 'making' (*i.e.* preparation or concoction). The mustard, for example, needs sweetening; lupines need sweetening; wheat needs to be ground; even man needs amendment" (Bereschith Rabbah, XI.). "According to this view," says Mr. Taylor, "the 'image' and 'likeness' is that to which man *approximates*." So we logically come to this as the outcome of the old philosophic myths when brought together: Resurrection and creation are complemental; the spirit leaves its primary state, but by a fall which should inspire no hyperascetic horror; and it returns with a fresh armful, so to speak, of life and experience, to a state nigher than before to the Divine likeness of its origin. To infringe the laws of the lower Adam is to be a starveling in life, and miss the way that leads up to the true upstanding. "The first Adam reached from the earth to the firmament, for it is said that he was created *upon* or *above* the earth" (Chagiga, 12 a). "Twice didst thou form me" (writes the commentator, as cited by Mr. Taylor), "at first high, then low." But the regeneration is the old spiritual generation more fully realized.

"The sonship of Israel," says Mr. Taylor, "implies their possession of the Divine likeness in a higher degree than Adam, or man in general.... The primal man, the embryo of the race, is created an adumbration of Elohim; Israel is singled out for the distinction of sonship to IHVH." We who are of Aryan origin may not claim to any special distinction over Gentile humanity, but prefer to rank according as we are found. The less intensely Judaic of the Rabbis, moreover, would appear to have preferred the general to the special ground. "R. Obadiah of Sforno dilates upon man's faculty of acquiring a perfection with which he was not specifically created. He remarks ... that '*In imagine*' implies the twofold possibility, first, of rising to perfection by means of wisdom through which the love and fear of God are acquired, and, secondly, of lapsing into chaos and perishing, according to the words of the Psalmist (xlix. 21), ' If he will not understand, he will be like the beasts that perish ' [' Man that is in honour (his heavenly birthright and spiritual state) and understandeth not, is like the beasts that perish '] ; for if man had been wholly spiritual he might have been called actually *Elohim*, a word which is applied not only to God but to intellectual and incorporeal beings, as angels, and also to judges, in respect of the *mind* . . . which properly belongs to them ; but since he is in part material he is described, not as *Elohim*, but in lower terms, as ' *in the image of Elohim.*' "

These Hebrew subtleties may prove tedious, but we must not forget that the sages had to work out their thoughts in a narrow and constraining epoch. We who have the privilege of expanding our lungs in a freer air may treat Aryan and Semite as brothers, and make harmonious philosophy of our own from the most luminous we can find of their suggestions.

PRIMITIVE BUDDHISM.

IN the works of Marco Polo, the Venetian traveller of the thirteenth century, it is said of the founder of Buddhism, "Si fuisset Christianus, fuisset apud Deum maximus factus."

Had Sakya-muni risen from the dead to find himself the head of a Therapeutic, Ebionite, Nazirite, or Essene community, or of a Christian monastery of the period before the faith was absorbed into a political institution, and martyrdom exchanged for dominion, he would probably have taken it for granted that he was among an unknown family of his own disciples. "The monastic rules of the Buddhists, found in the Pratimoksha (a work dating from B.C.), are in their general tone, and even in some particulars, wonderfully like those adopted in the West." *

A student of that primitive faith which has become transformed into modern Christianity may now and again, in the difficulties of critical analysis, find himself indulging a wish for the discovery of a fifth Gospel. He would welcome the simple and unadulterated collection of inspired sayings which Matthew is recorded as having made in the original Hebraic tongue; he would even be glad to discover the Gospel of Marcion, the Evangel according to the Egyptians, or the Nazarenes, or the Hebrews, or any one of those numerous orderly narratives referred to by Luke, the polished and poetically-minded editor of later days. Or the English scholar

---

* *Vide*, S. Beal, "A Catena of Buddhist Scriptures from the Chinese;" Spence Hardy, "Eastern Monachism."

might be both inquisitive and proud if among ancient British relics there could but be disentombed a record giving the unconventional views of Simon the Zealot, who is said to have travelled westward as far as our island, and to have been crucified here. Or if any of the notes of unbelieving Thomas should be found, rendered into the languages of the countries he is traditionally reported to have visited, Parthia, Persia, India, there would indeed be a feast for the curious.

The difficulty with Buddhism is not that there are too few records, but too many. The Buddhist canon in China alone includes nearly fifteen hundred distinct works.

The peculiar interest in Chinese versions of books that have their origin in India, is that they afford a security that the originals have not been tampered with, or rather a means of discovering in what portions they are scarcely open to suspicion of modification of their primitive form. Wherever is found a parallelism, amounting almost to identity, between passages of a work in Pali (the native tongue of Buddhism), and a Chinese version of it made fifteen hundred years ago, the evidence is good that the passage so found has remained intact during that period at least, in spite of those changes of sectarian feeling, which almost insensibly leave their marks upon a text.

A translation from Chinese into English of an authentic Buddhist work,* when compared with a version already made from the Pali,† affords an excellent verification of Buddhist doctrines before they had become thinly drawn out into intellectuality, lost in the mazes of metaphysics, or extended into florid idolatry to suit the ignorant.

Between five or six centuries before the era by which we reckon, is the date of the young prince who grew up into the

---

* "Texts from the Buddhist Canon, commonly known as 'Dhammapada.'" Translated from the Chinese by S. Beal.
† "Buddhaghosha's Parables." Translated from Burmese by Capt. H. T. Rogers, R.E. With an Introduction, containing "Buddha's Dhammapadam," or "Path of Virtue;" translated from Pali, by F. Max Müller.

commanding prophet, the founder of Buddhism. When he died, leaving no written teachings behind him—as the story goes—his cousin and disciple, Ananda, took up the task of collecting the words of wisdom that his memory, and possibly the memory of others also, had stored. Probably a great portion, although put into form, was held in memory—not in manuscript—and only promulgated orally. Councils of disciples met to revise these growing collections—growing first, no doubt, out of accruing recollections, afterwards by the additions of ingenious commentators, editors, and improvers. It must not be forgotten that the prophet did not launch his gospel upon ears unaccustomed to the words of philosophy, but introduced it into the midst of the grand and long-established religious tenets of his country, from which beliefs moreover his own differed, as would appear, rather by being a heightening or revival than a contradiction.

The third of these Buddhist councils was held under King Asoka, about two centuries and a half before our era. Of this Asoka there are authentic inscriptions in existence of the date named. As a Hindu versifier of the present generation writes:—

> "There have I stood where Asok's pillar high
>   Through thousand years doth Asok's mandates bear;
> There still it stands unmoved athwart the sky;
>   One of the mightiest world did ever rear."

Whether perpetuated in writing, or orally, as was the manner of ancient priests, whose memories, by practice and through the worldly uneventfulness of their life, far transcended what we know of memory—while probably they had division of labour even in tradition, and no single priest knew more than a part of the whole,—the Buddhistic collections were soon gathered into a canon bearing the name of "The Three Baskets." But, in spite of the anxious care that had been bestowed, the pious collectors had been human, with their little tendencies to bias, their little incapacities of understanding, like ourselves, and there soon came to be disputes among the defenders of the faith.

The first redaction is said to have taken place immediately after the death of Sakya-muni, under the care of five hundred monks, three of the principal disciples of the master sharing the task of gathering together his words. The next redaction took place in about a century, for discord had already arisen, and the Buddhist leaders felt the necessity of assembling to decide upon difficult questions of authenticity.

Something over four centuries after the time of the master there were eighteen separate sects of Buddhists. Eighteen sects in four hundred years! At the same rate, this would only allow Christendom in its eighteen hundred years to have eighty bodies dissenting from one another.

In his preface to the "Dhammapada," Max Müller refers to "the problem, so often started, whether it is possible to distinguish between Buddhism and the personal teaching of Buddha." He argues as follows: "We possess the Buddhist canon, and whatever is found in that canon we have a right to consider as the orthodox Buddhist doctrine. But as there has been no lack of efforts in the Christian theology to distinguish between the doctrine of the founder of our religion and that of the writers of the Gospels; to go beyond the canon of the New Testament, and to make the λόγια of the Master the only solid rule of faith, so the same want was felt at a very early period among the followers of Buddha. King Asoka, the Indian Constantine, had to remind the assembled priests at the great council which had to settle the Buddhist canon that 'what had been said by Buddha, that alone was well said.'

"Works attributed to Buddha, but declared to be apocryphal, or even heterodox, existed already at that time (246 B.C.). Thus we are by no means without authority for distinguishing between Buddhism and the teaching of Buddha; the only question is, Whether in our time such a separation is still practicable.

"My belief is," continues Professor Müller, "that, in general, all honest inquirers must oppose a 'No' to this question, and confess that it is useless to try to cast a glance beyond the boundaries of the Buddhist canon. What we find in the canonical books in the so-called 'Three Baskets' is orthodox Buddhism and the doctrine of Buddha, similarly as we must accept in general whatever we find in the Four Gospels as orthodox Christianity and the doctrine of Christ."

This is a most lame and impotent conclusion, and in each case in which an accepted Christian text has been discovered to be the gloss of a commentator, and not found in the earliest manuscripts, and is at the same time manifestly at variance from the doctrine of the Founder, Professor Müller's argument can evidently be reduced to an absurdity. Had he said simply that the Three Baskets are the accepted scriptures of orthodox Buddhism, the Four Gospels of orthodox Christianity, he would have uttered that which, if a truism, is at least a fact.

It is disappointing to find a distinguished student of comparative religious lore so resigning himself to the abandonment of a difficulty. It must, however, be allowed that Western civilization is still very young in philosophic experience. Doctrinal fetters have long cramped the mind, and prevented its expansion in the ethical direction. Moreover, our country has not long emerged from insular barbarism, and four centuries ago was almost without culture in foreign languages and foreign thought. The time is not long past when, if a few bones of extinct animals had been placed before a naturalist, and he were asked to reconstruct the whole anatomy upon their basis, he would have smiled with the superior wisdom of ignorance upon his inquirer's absurd folly. Now he will not only build up the probable anatomical form, but certainly separate from the bones placed before him such as do not consist with the others but belong to creatures of a different type.

May we not hope, therefore, that as sympathetic study of ancient philosophy progresses, there may be found to grow a faculty of distinguishing between characteristic expressions of thought, as is done with different varieties of bones; and that to body forth the thoughts of a distinctive thinker with more or less fulness and certitude, we shall require but to have before us authentic relics known to have proceeded from him? For the criticism of thought, time must be allowed, as for other scientific studies.*

Professor Müller somewhat fritters away the force of his negative, and, while professing to maintain his stronghold, abandons his separate forts, when he continues as follows in respect to the Buddhist scriptures:—

"Still, with regard to certain doctrines and facts, the question, I think, ought to be asked again and again, whether it may not be possible to advance a step further, even with the conviction that we cannot arrive at results of apodictic certainty? If it happens that on certain points we find in different parts of the canon, not only doctrines differing from each other, but plainly contradictory to each other, it follows, surely, that only one of these can have belonged to Buddha personally. In such a case, therefore, I believe we have a right to choose, and I believe we shall be justified in accepting that view as the original one, the one peculiar to Buddha himself, which harmonizes least with the later system of orthodox Buddhism."

There is a large amount of force in Professor Müller's

---

* "Men of science ... have to deal with extremely abstract and ideal conceptions. By constant use and familiarity, these, and the relations between them, become just as real and external as the ordinary objects of experience ; and the perception of new relations among them is so rapid, that the correspondence of the mind to external circumstances so great, that a real scientific sense is developed, by which things are perceived as immediately and truly as I see you now.

"Poets and painters and musicians also are so accustomed to put outside of them the idea of beauty, that it becomes a real external existence, a thing which they see with spiritual eyes, and then describe to you, but by no means create" (W. K. Clifford, "Lectures and Essays").

concluding suggestion, and we may note as curious the fact that he has not carried on his parallelism of Buddhism with Christianity in regard to the applicability of the very searching test he puts forward.

Another Buddhistic student, Mr. D'Alwis, of Ceylon, takes a very different view from that of Professor Max Müller; he urges that "it is indeed possible, according to hints given by Buddha himself, to separate his genuine doctrines from the greater part, if not the whole, of what has been long accepted as the *logia*. For example, after a little investigation, we have found no difficulty in expunging the whole of the fable which goes by the name of Gotama's battle with Mára (Mára himself seems to partake of the nature of the Evil One, Death and Cupid). There is no more mystery in the very *logia* of Gotama than in works on other religions. We find no authority for the predictions regarding distinguished persons who lived in after times."

Mr. D'Alwis says further, "The Three Baskets do not contain entirely the words of Gotama. None of them are free from additions, and the discourses themselves show that they are not without omissions. . . . The formal conclusion of several of the Sútras, which is everywhere identically the same, is essentially the language of the disciples. The Kathá Vatthupakarana, the third book of the Abhidhamma, was added by Moggaliputta Tissou, with the avowed intention of refuting the doctrines in 'the apocryphal and heterodox works' to which Max Müller refers. . . . Then, again, we have grave doubts as to the genuineness of some of the books . . . the language of which, both as regards style and grammar, is different from the undoubted *logia* of Gotama. . . . Again, there is reason to believe that Ananda, the beloved pupil of Gotama, imported much of his own ideas into the Pari-nibbána Sutta."

The similarity between the account above given, and the questions arising out of the growth of the Christian scriptures, such as the dogmatic interpolations, the methods of the anti-heretical fathers, the Johannine influences, etc., may be noted by the way, and will be interesting to the historical student.

The order of the Three Baskets, or orthodox Buddhist scriptures, will throw some light upon the growth of a body of religious doctrine. The three great divisions are Sermons, Ethics, Metaphysics. Can we not, to speak broadly, follow the course of the great prophet, and hear the sermon? walk with the disciples, and be treated to ethics, instead of to the burning heart words of an inspired teacher? remove a little further and come upon the disputatious doctors with their metaphysics?

By what tests can we discover the prophet's own utterances amongst imitations? His mission is humanitarian; his utterances must manifest a human tenderness more markedly than an ethical systematization. He will at times be exceedingly simple from love of the little ones (intellectually speaking). At times, from the difficulty of drawing down heavenly truths into a lower and crasser sphere, he will resort to fable, and will scatter caskets for the wise, parables of enshrined significance, even paradoxes of startling form that live and are not forgotten, by reason of the very audacity of their conception.

It may be well to relate here in brief the story of Gautama's life. Legendary in part though it be, it no doubt contains a valuable proportion of fact.

Sakya, or Siddharta, was the son of Raja Suddhodana, of the clan of the Gautamas, who lived at Kapila, near Gorukpur, on the confines of Nepaul and Oude. The date of his birth is not known with absolute certainty, but 623 B.C. is most generally accepted. His mother, Suddhodana's queen, was named Maya. She died seven days after his birth, and the child was brought up by a maternal aunt. The story respecting his birth from the side of a virgin, which is said to have reached Jerome and to have been repeated by Ratramnus, would seem to be an afterthought of foolish followers; the legend is represented on very early temple sculptures.

A conjecture has been hazarded, from some peculiarities of burial rites and other indications, that the Sakyas, who are unknown in the records of India, were foreigners, and of a Scythian royal family. A short time before the reputed birth of the Muni, the Scythians had poured over Media, Judæa, and Asia Minor; and it is considered possible that one branch of these invaders had penetrated at an earlier date into Northern India. It has been conjectured that reference is made to them in the description: "It is a mighty nation, it is an ancient nation, a nation whose language thou knowest not, neither understandest thou what they say. Their quiver is as an open sepulchre, they are all warriors" (Jer. v. 15-17, Tr., S. Sharpe).

There is a legend cited from Wassiljew's "Buddhismus," by Schlagintweit in his "Buddhism in Tibet," to the effect that the Sakya tribe had been involved in a disastrous war during the life of the Buddha, and was nearly exterminated, its surviving members being compelled to wander. It is suggested that a son of the race may thus have been led to view existence as the source of pain and sorrow, rather than through the circumstances described in the story presently to be related. But it may be argued that the effect of a nomad life upon the members of a warlike clan is likely to be in the direction of increased hardihood and martial qualities, rather than in the direction of deep analysis of the problems of existence; while the idleness and luxury of a court might by reaction foster in a sensitive nature a tendency to a contemplative and earnest life.

It is said, according to one legend, that on the day of Sakya's birth were born also the daughter of a neighbouring king (Yasōdara, who, when the pair had reached their seventeenth year, became Sakya's wife), and Ananda, who after the prince became accepted as a Buddha, accompanied him as pupil and friend. If the story be true, the three friends, bound on a mission from the worlds of spirits to "assume a human form and to be born in the earth," must have started with a wonderful sympathy of impulse to time their simultaneous arrival here so exactly.

Sakya-muni, it is said, early distinguished himself by his qualities both intellectual and personal. This statement is probable enough, for an Englishman (the late R. C. Childers), writing nearly twenty-five centuries after the time of the immediate influence of the Buddha, says that "to those who are familiar with the Pali sacred books, nothing is more striking than the intense personality of Gautama."

The Scythians gave to their kings the title of "universal ruler," and were probably known as the lion among nations, if it is of them that the words were said, "The lion is come up from his thicket, and the destroyer of nations has moved his camp" (Jer. iv. 6). The legend of Gautama's birth is that there then appeared the flower (*Ficus glomerata*) which is fabled to manifest itself whenever one of the order of universal monarchs is born; and that he himself uttered with his "lion voice," "My births are now at an end; I wait the unchangeable body. I have come and gone for the salvation of all men, but now there is an end; thenceforth, there shall be no more birth."

The child grew up to learn all the wisdom of the age, and the chivalric skill and grace of a prince of good family.

Indulged in every delight, the boy nevertheless grew weary of the pomp and pleasures of his father's court.

It appears from the Laws of Manu that it was not unusual in the earliest times of Brahmanism for such as sought a superior life to turn hermits and to live secluded in the forest, engaged in the study of the Vedas, in abstinence, meditation, and prayer. The young prince's preceptors foretold that he would become a recluse. He himself appears to have entertained a larger idea than that of mere seclusion, and to have awakened to the belief that he was to stand forth among his fellow-men in the capacity of a saviour.

To the king it came as a great grief when his son, in the flower of his youth and the splendid worldly promise of his fine faculties of body and mind and his princely accomplishments, began to show signs of the rare unworldliness that marks the spiritual man.

The youth was no doubt for a long time going through deep experiences, and preparing for the transition that was to withdraw him once and for ever from the career of one of his rank, to a life shared in its externals at least by the mendicant and the anchorite.

He was married and had one child, a son named Rohula. Everything external betokened the likelihood of the usual settling down from the fleeting enthusiasms of youth to the shorter views of average mature life. But the spirit moved him too strenuously for this, and the evils of the world, which the most of us accept as a matter of course, pressed upon the keen sensibilities of the prophetic nature, and forced the youth's heart and brain into some attempt at a solution of the problem of mortal life.

The received account of his own personal final conversion from the gay routine of a prince's life to the arduous career of a seeker after truth, is in all probability a picturesque and artistically composed romance founded on facts.

Mounted in his chariot, drawn by four white steeds, Prince Sakya was on his way to his pleasure grounds, when his mind became drawn into serious thought by the appearance of a decrepit old man, grey-haired and toothless, tottering feebly along by the aid of a staff. The reflections aroused by this sight were none other than mournful, since man's subjection to decay is evidenced no less in the palace than in the highway, though it may be more nakedly manifest in humble life, where there are no artifices for hiding the ravages of time.

Four months later, Sakya's impressions were deepened by

encountering, while on a similar excursion to his pleasure gardens, a poor squalid wretch smitten with the horrible disease of leprosy. He returned again to the palace, only to brood over the fact that man is not only subject to the natural decay of old age, but to loathsome disease as well.

Four months more elapsed, and Sakya met on the same route a corpse being conveyed along by its bearers. He returned with the conviction—so heightened that it became a new and startling revelation—that man, no matter his station, is subject to decay, to disease, and to inevitable death. So came to his mind the sense of the vanity of what is existent, however well disguised by wealth and luxury and the conventional habits of life and modes of regarding it.

Again a period of four months, and he met a calm and cheerful recluse of a pleasant countenance, healthy, well and simply clad in the robe worn by those dedicated to religion, a man of few wants and no devouring anxieties or ambitions.

Here, in an air full of mortality and sorrow, in a state in which pleasures are fleeting, and nothing truly permanent or stable, was a being who seemed to have given up all, and to live in a world from which care was removed.

He pondered the matter. There could be nothing permanent but truth, the absolute eternal law that regulated existence. "Let me but discover that," he felt, "and I shall know the way of lasting peace for mankind, and become their deliverer."

He decided to go out from his life and never to return to it, until he should have attained to the sight of this divine law of life. So he quitted the palace and his native city, left behind him his wife and child, and, in spite of the opposition of his father, his wife, and his friends, exchanged the position of a prince for that of a mendicant friar. Some would think this an inhuman way of beginning wisdom ; but it was done for humanity, and, if he had not made such a complete change in his own life, the enervating influences of the palace (for it was not only father, wife, and child that he was leaving) might have insensibly overpowered the efforts of the young man whose course eventually affected the religious beliefs of half the human race.

So Sakya went forth on his wanderings in search of absolute truth. On his journey he cut off his long hair with the tiara of royalty still attached to it, and assumed the three simple garments of the friar, together with the begging pot, razor, sewing needle, and bathing cloth, which comprised the appointments of the homeless ascetic.

He was pursuing the orthodox plan of retirement and purification. Far away from home he begged, in the conventional manner, for alms and food, and retiring with the broken scraps that had been cast into his begging pot, he seated himself in a retired place, and, facing the east, ate without loathing (for his purpose and passion were strong) his first mendicant meal, so different from the repasts to which he had been accustomed.

He resorted for instruction, as was natural, to the Brahman priests, and hearkened to the exposition of their doctrines, but found little satisfaction therein; for to him, in his ardent state, they probably seemed cold and abstract.

As there are traditional records of Buddhas antecedent to Sakya, fragments of whose speech are incorporated with orthodox Buddhist scriptures, we may suppose it possible that the works of these earlier prophets were accessible to the new seeker after wisdom, and that what he may have studied meant more to him than it did to those of the learned class of the Brahmans who were without his enthusiasm.

As he pursued his pilgrimage, he acquired from certain Brahmans instruction in the faculty of silent abstraction and contemplation of the Supreme Being, but could not obtain from them the peace and certainty he sought—that deep interior tranquillity which, it is said, was at that time already called Nirvana.

Finding that by contemplation he arrived no nearer to the *bôdhi* or Buddhahood of which he was in search, he devoted himself to the vanquishment of Nature or concrete matter. Although not regarding as an end the austerities that subdue the force of the sense life, he spent six years in study and the practice of the utmost extremes of starvation and penance. At length, after dieting himself on a scanty allowance of seeds, and so reducing his body to a skeleton, he concluded that physical prostration, or any but a rational treatment of the body, was attended with debility of the will and no elevation of the mind; and, as the path of perfection evidently did not lie that way, he rejected the system of mortification of the flesh.

The years of privation had no doubt brought this fruit, that they had tested his earnestness and enabled him to vanquish any tendency to luxury or selfishness that his nurture in a palace might have implanted in him.

Being satisfied that Buddhahood was not to be reached through depravation of the body, but through enlightenment of the mind, he resumed his ordinary pilgrimages as a friar, and his simple but sufficient fare. On proper diet and a less unnatural mode of life, he regained both his bodily strength and mental vigour, but was deserted by the disciples who had been attracted by the amazing extreme of austerity which he had reached.

He now passed some time alone in his hermitage, or under divers trees, thinking out the problems which had disturbed him, and absorbed in deep meditation. Temptations assailed him, but his principles enabled him to withstand them, even the cowardly terrors of the Demon of Death.

Somehow his philosophy came to him, with the solid conviction for which he had longed. He was enabled to penetrate into the first principles of things, as it seemed, and so to lay the foundation of a practicable plan of life.

"Having attained this inward certainty of vision, he

decided to teach the world his truth. He knew well what it would bring him,—what opposition, insult, neglect, and scorn. But he thought of three classes of men: those who were already on the way to the truth, and did not need him; those who were already fixed in error, and whom he could not help; and the poor doubters, uncertain of their way. It was to help these last that the Buddha went forth to preach."

In himself he felt freed from the limitations of corporeal existence, but for the sake of promoting the emancipation of others, he did not pass away into his higher state, but directed his steps to the Deer Park at Sarnath, where he unfolded his principles, and first to those to whom he had been an offence by his departure from his course of consummate austerity. As they had followed him for his transcendent mortification of the flesh, so it is to be presumed that they were now attracted by the supremacy of his wisdom. By three months' kindly instruction he succeeded in converting them.

According to one legend, the father of Sakya attempted to allure his son from the life to which he had devoted himself, by all imaginable promises:—

"O son, I will bestow upon thee the elephant-drivers, the charioteers, the horsemen, and arrayed footmen, with delightful horses: I will also give thee the maidens adorned with all sorts of ornaments; raise up progeny by them, and thou shalt become our sovereign. Virgins well versed in dancing and singing, and perfected in the four accomplishments, shall delight thee with their attractions. What dost thou in this wilderness?"

The reply has a ring of early Buddhism: "O sire, why temptest thou me with perishing wealth, mortal beauty, and youthful bloom? O king, what is love, the pleasant look, present delight, anxiety in pursuit of wealth, sons, and daughters, and wives, to me who am released from the bonds? . . . I know that Death will not forget me; therefore of what use are pleasure and riches? . . . Return, return, O king! I have no desire for the kingdom" ("Incarnation of Booddhu," from the Burman, transl. F. Carey. W. Ward, *Hist. Lit. and Rel. of the Hindoos:* Serampore).

Another story of these early days is the following:—

Five Brahmans followed the Prince Gautama when he left his father's palace, into the forest of Uruwela. There they remained with him six years, hoping to see him obtain perfection through his austerities; but when, instead of increasing, his austerities ceased, and Gautama regained his health and beauty by eating sufficient food, they deserted him. When Gautama had become Buddha, he searched for these five Brahmans, and found them at Benares. To them he addressed this, his first discourse:—

"O priests! these two extremes should be avoided—an attachment to sensual gratifications, which are degrading and profitless; and severe penances, which produce sorrow, and are degrading and useless.

"O priests! avoiding both these extremes, Buddha has perceived a middle path for the attainment of mental vision, true knowledge, subdued passions, and the perception of the paths leading to the supreme good.

"O priests! this middle path has eight divisions—namely, correct doctrines, correct perceptions of those doctrines, speaking the truth, purity of conduct, a sinless occupation, perseverance in duty, holy meditation, and mental tranquillity" (Gogerly, "The First Discourse delivered by Buddha").

Buddha preached in many places, in forests and groves, in palaces, by rivers, in gardens, in cities. He visited Benares, and finally settled in the Jetavana at Sravasti, where a monastery was built for him. The late R. C. Childers specifies the provinces of Behar and Oude as being the "birthland of Buddhism." The great teacher's followers rapidly increased; he taught, by conversation only and precept, to the end of his life, which reached the span of eighty years.

Disciples had clustered round in great numbers in these

latter years, and wherever the preacher went there followed him a crowd. A general proclamation of the powerlessness of the world of sense to satisfy the soul, a simple code of deeply-founded morality, a continuous appeal to the law of kindness to all living things, an entire disregard of caste, and contempt for social distinctions as trivialities in the face of the great danger of continuance in wearisome transmigrations and ever unsatisfied unrest, these doctrines, proclaimed without ceremony, were intelligible to all. Women were enrolled as disciples, and no man was refused because he was a pariah of the lowest caste. "The Brahman is born of a woman, so is the outcast. . . . My law is a law of grace for all. My doctrine is like the sky. There is room for all without exception—men, women, boys, girls, poor and rich." This was a renovation of a truth proclaimed long before : " The man who has learned to recognize all beings in the supreme spirit, and the supreme spirit in all beings, can henceforth look upon no creature with contempt " (Isa-Upanishad).

It matters little whether the new teacher obtained hints of his philosophy from Brahman or Jain. His true legacy was the infusion of a new earnestness and reality into religion, so that one of the epithets that has become attached to him, or to any true follower of his, is, "He that hath life."

His doctrines all led in one direction—conduct. Knowing how much happier we are ourselves in our earnest and unselfish moments than when we are drifting down the heavy stream of *ennui*, or seeking for a new pleasure with an over-pleasured, enfeebled, and yet feverish taste, we need not wonder at the influence gained by such a teacher. He had earned the power to rouse his hearers out of apathy and formality into vitality, or even into a wholesome fear, and could succeed in stimulating them out of indulgence into the conviction that in the abandonment of selfish pursuits lay the certain way of peace, while, on the other hand, the poorest person by becoming a disciple might win an individual consciousness of power. Buddha did not expect anxieties to be laid down at once; he told his followers that progress was gradual. What he succeeded in impressing upon them was, that by adhering to the paths he pointed out they were on the right road to emancipation.

It has been somewhat too glibly assumed that because the Brahmanic conception of a God is represented as having been ridiculed by Sakya, and because he nowhere ascribes individuality to a Supreme Being, his system is an atheistic one. It is true that there is an avoidance of allusion to a personal deity, but it seems to be his reverence for his ideal of the universality of law that compels him to exclude any notion of personality. Personality, as the word is understood by the generality, would in his view imply a defect in that supreme ideal, a reduction to those lower elements wherein are limitations and impermanency.

If we trace the history of the word person, it would appear that we are more apt to employ it now to signify an integral entity than is warranted by its original use. The Latin word *persona*, from which we draw it, represents the very opposite of such a sense; it means a mask, a temporary manifestation, a mere appearance, an external show. The corresponding Greek word signifying person evidences the same dramatic idea at its root. To personify an abstract conception is to bring forward a thought into dialogue and dramatic form. The word means essentially outward appearance rather than inward verity. In Judæo-Greek thought, a respecter of persons is literally an accepter of faces—one who penetrates no deeper than the outward show.

To the Buddhist, in whose vision the supremely reverenced Law was that alone which is ultimate and eternal, it would have seemed profane to invest it with any of the selfish attributes of personality which by constant clash make up the seething drama of terrestrial existence, and the conquest of which is the way into heavenly emancipation.

Mr. D'Alwis says, in a Review of Müller's "Dhammapada:"—

"The Reformer of Brahmanism . . . did not ignore a first cause. He simply, perhaps qualifiedly, ignored Brahma's claims to omnipotence, and indeed denied his creative power; for it did not enter into Gotama's abstruse philosophy to assign a creative power to any being, when the great doctrine of 'Life,' which he propounded, denied (see Attanagaluwansa, p. 170) to everybody, including himself, the absolute power of final deliverance, or of recalling, even for a moment, the life which has once left this earthly tabernacle. Man is his own deliverer. He is a free agent—but an agent without a power over any one but himself. 'Self is the lord of self; who else could be the lord?' (Dh. v. 160)."

It has been poetically said of the reformer, in his relation to the existing Brahmanism: "Gautama made a new song for the old god."

A limited Pantheism—if so paradoxical an expression be allowable—would perhaps best represent the Buddhist conception of divine perfection. The soul released from its low conditions enters into a life that is one with the unconditioned Infinite; while the soul that dwells still in the weary whirl of selfish pursuit and the "orb of transmigration," is outside that Pleroma, which is too vast for man's heart to embrace, too inconceivable for the conditioned mind to define or explain.

The conception of a Love which by its very nature can, as it were, humble itself to sympathize even with the backslidings, impatience, and feebly renewed efforts of a stumbling soul, is the element lacking in the Buddhist theology, which, so far only as that negation extends, may be regarded as atheistic.

That the conception of divine love may subsist in a quasi-pantheistic religion may be argued from the following motto of the deity Vishnu: "As often as Right slumbers and Wrong raises up its head, I create myself" (Bhagavadgita, iv. 7).

With a conception of deity so exceedingly abstract as that of Buddha, it is little wonder that in minds tending to rigid intellectuality the doctrine should run on into negation or a kind of atheism. Similarly, as the idea of the eternal unchangeable condition of life was, intellectually speaking, and apart from its appeal to the feelings, arrived at mainly by the remotion of all the attributes of every-day life, it is natural that with many followers of Buddha the doctrine of Nirvana should lead to a blank prospect of utter annihilation. With another school, on the contrary, the idea became that of "restoration to the true condition of being," which is akin to the ancient doctrine of the Parsis, and in more or less sympathy with an element which is to be found deep in the heart of most religious faiths.

Buddha himself was probably content to leave something of mystery in his exposition of that unexplored land of restful truth. It was enough for him that he saw the way out of the inherent falsities of corporeal existence to be the vanquishment of the personal ambitions and fretful fevers of the untamed mind. A teacher, whose eyes were opened, might well have faith enough to leave undefined the undefinable, and yet hold it to be truth that inconceivable existence, when actually entered, might be positive, and not negative, life. But the logicians of the metaphysical schools could not be content with this. If the intellect by itself be raised to the throne, it ousts faith, hope, and finally charity. Whatever is not mathematically clear must be abandoned; the worship of the definite excludes the entertainment, even for a moment, of unrealizable dreams and of the glimmer of imponderable stars.

What it is that the contemplative devotee reaches is a difficult matter to solve. To the undeveloped soul that enters meditative life when the practical were the easier and more suitable school, the result may well be something apparently not far removed from imbecility; but what is it that the dreamer of the joyful countenance has found?

Warren Hastings, who can neither be regarded as an unpractical man nor as without opportunities of observation, thus wrote in 1784 upon the meditative faculty which is still an attribute of the Indian ascetic: "To those who have never been accustomed to this separation of the mind from the notices of the senses, it may not be easy to conceive by what means such a power is to be attained, since even the most studious men of our hemisphere will find it difficult so to restrain their attention but that it will wander to some object of present sense or recollection; and even the buzzing of a fly will sometimes have the power to disturb it. But if we are told that there have been men who were successively, for ages past, in the daily habit of abstracted contemplation, begun in the earliest period of youth, and continued in many to the maturity of age, each adding some portion of knowledge to the store accumulated by his predecessors, it is not assuming too much to conclude that, as the mind ever gathers strength, like the body, by exercise, so in such an exercise it may in each have acquired the faculty to which they aspired, and that their collective studies may have led them to the discovery of new tracks and combinations of sentiment, totally different from the doctrines with which the learned of other nations are acquainted; doctrines which, however speculative and subtle, still, as they possess the advantage of being derived from a source so free from every adventitious mixture, may be equally founded in truth with the most simple of our own."

Perhaps a man well accustomed to worldly ways is nearer to an appreciation of that Nirvana wherein the turmoil of selfish ambition is imagined to be stilled, than the merely intellectual critic can be. To the latter, Nirvana presents itself as a condition that must be defined with scientific exactitude; to the former it appeals without argument with the rude force of fact. Lord Bacon, who, like Buddha, had seen something of the world, wrote that "the long and solicitous dwelling in matter, experience and the uncertainty of particulars ... fixeth the mind to earth, or rather sinketh it into an abyss of confusion and perturbation, at the same time driving and keeping it aloof from the serenity and tranquillity of a much diviner state; a state of abstract wisdom!"

Many of the followers of Buddha who rushed in to define what with greater knowledge of the undefinable he had left indefinite, were doubtless holy friars from youth, and ignorant of almost everything in the world but devotion and metaphysics. They would naturally fail to appreciate his broad and simple notion of Nirvana. Hence arises the paradox that, to become a Buddhist after the primitive pattern, the best way is not to study Buddhism but to be first a man of the world.

And here we find the flaw of Buddhism as a system; it is like an exaggerated teetotalism. The young monk is withdrawn from the world before he knows what it is, and is kept by a rigid disciplinary system from the real teaching of causes and effects, which, tardy though its results may be, no religious leading strings can equal in efficacy :—

> "The mills of God grind slowly,
> But they grind exceeding small."

In the language of Ruskin, the temple devotee grows up "by protection innocent, instead of by practice virtuous."

The aim of Buddhism, or indeed of any monastic system, is to remove the individual as far as possible from the natural machinery of trial.

"Long is the night to him who is awake; long is a mile to him who is tired; long is life [transmigratory life, the constant revolution of birth and death] to the foolish who do not know the true law," says Buddha, according to the Pali Dhammapada; but so long as that kind of existence is not tedious to the individual immersed in it, the doctrine will take no hold on him. Better surely that he should be left to pass through the crucible of joys and pains than that he shoul' become a monk before he knows what it is that he seeks to escape.

"Few there are among men who arrive at the other shore; the other people here run up and down the shore." Here is a recognition of the truth that many undeveloped souls prefer that running up and down the shore, that common uncertain life with its epochs of birth and death, to the most certain passage across to Nirvana.

How strong is the tendency to nominalism, a state worse than having no religion at all, seems to have been a familiar thought with Buddha.

Here is his reply to a captious Brahman, in answer to the question, "Who is the true disciple?" "Not he who at stated times begs his food; not he who walks unrighteously, but hopes to be considered a disciple, desiring to establish a character (as a religious person), and that is all; but he who gives up every cause (karma) of guilt, and who lives continently and purely, who by wisdom is able to crush every evil (inclination)—this man is the true friar." "And who is the truly enlightened?" "Not he who is simply mute, whilst the busy work of his mind is impure—merely accommodating himself to the outer rule, and that is all; but he whose heart is without preference (indifferent), whose inward life is pure and spiritual (empty), perfectly unmoved and dead to this or that (person or thing)—this man is called an inwardly enlightened man (Muni)." "And who is a man of Bôdhi (an Ariya, or 'elected one')?" "Not he who saves the life of all things [this must mean by formality, as of the man who, on principle, would not destroy vermin], but he who is filled with universal benevolence, who has no malice in his heart—he is a man of Bôdhi. And the man who observes the law is not he who talks much, but one who keeps his body (himself) in subjection to the law (religion), although he be a plain, untaught man, always guarding the way without any forgetfulness—this man is an observer of the law." This passage is from Mr. Beal's version of the Chinese text of the Dhammapada.

If it is hard to attain this condition, so also, says Buddha, is ordinary life hard: "To aim at supreme wisdom and to give up sin is hard; but to live in the world as a worldly man is also hard. To dwell in a religious community on terms of perfect equality as to worldly goods is difficult; but difficult beyond comparison is the possession of worldly goods. To beg one's food as a mendicant is hard; but what can a man do who does not restrain himself? By perseverance the duty becomes natural, and in the end there is no desire to have it otherwise."

This recalls the precept which Bacon cites, "Optimum elige, suave et facile illud faciet consuetudo"—Fix upon that which is best, custom will make it easy and delightful. But even in this apparently perfect plan there is lurking danger, as an old gnomic philosopher, Publius Syrus, once discovered:—"Bonarum rerum consuetudo pessima est"—Customedness of good things is the very worst of things.

The Buddhist friar who had left all evil behind might as readily fall into spiritual dormancy in his good things as the worldly man in his worldliness, and end in a mechanical religion, removed from worldly activity not by being drawn into higher and nobler activities, but by having exchanged fever for nothing better than hibernation.

The Brahmans were careful not to make saints of unripe souls, for they had a law which has more than one humorous aspect, that, if a man at sixty years of age had not reached wisdom, it was his duty to return to his home and marry a wife.

There is a curious story of some Indian nuns which will show that the devotee is not always the most devout. They had sent to Buddha for an instructor, and he had responded by despatching an old mendicant of poor faculties who knew only one stanza of the law, but had learned its meaning thoroughly and could expound it. The party of nuns, learning who was to instruct them, began to laugh together, and laid a plot that when the old man came they should all repeat the verse backwards, and so confuse and put him to shame. Their agreement was frustrated by some minor miracle, according to the account as we have it; but the story at least shows that the nun of the time, even as seen by her own people, cannot have been much better than her less sanctified sisters.

Buddha again and again hurls himself with his full force against nominalism; the following saying of his, which was probably the corner-stone upon which the legend just quoted was constructed, is one evidence out of many: "Although a man can repeat a thousand stanzas, but understand not the meaning of the lines he repeats, this is not equal to the repetition of one sentence well understood, which is able when heard to control thought. To repeat a thousand words without understanding, what profit is there in this? But to understand one truth, and hearing it to act accordingly, this is to find deliverance."

The following is Buddha's definition of the true Brahman, which ancient term he adopted, with all its accumulated prestige, as a designation of his truest followers: "It is not by his clan, or his platted hair, that a man is called a Brahman, but he who walks truthfully and righteously, he is indeed rightly called a good man. What avails the platted hair, O fool! what good the garment of grass? Within there is no quittance of desire, then what advantage the outward denial of self? Put away lust, hatred, delusion, sloth, and all its evil consequences, as the snake puts off his skin, this is to be a Brahma-chârin indeed."

This passage is from the Chinese version of the Dhammapada, and it may be interesting to compare it with the rendering from the Pali, from which it differs very little. Max Müller Englishes as follows: "A man does not become a Brahmana by his platted hair, by his family, or by both; in whom there is truth and righteousness, he is blessed, he is a Brahmana. What is the use of platted hair, O fool? What of the raiment of goatskins? Within thee there is ravening, but the outside thou makest clean." We may add, also, the late Professor Childers's translation of the last paragraph, since it expresses a thought so familiar to Christendom : " Thou fool, what dost thou with the matted hair, what dost thou with the raiment of skin? Thine inward parts are full of wickedness, the outside thou makest clean."

Many a disappointment and rebuff must Sakya have experienced from the incurable frivolity of the generality before he could utter such words as follow : " Perceiving that the ignorant herd can never attain true wisdom, the wise man prefers in solitude to guard himself in virtuous conduct, not associating with the foolish ; rejoicing in the practice of moral duties, and pursuing such conduct as becomes this mode of life, there is no need of a companion or associate in such practice—solitary in virtue without sorrow, a man rejoices as a wild elephant escaped from the herd."

A man of the present age, one who in certain moods may almost be called a prophet, has expressed the same truth of baffling as that uttered by Buddha and many other spiritual men, in verses that rise to eloquence. They may help us to appreciate the meaning of the words of the solitary young Indian prince who quitted the life of a palace for that of a vagrant preacher, and was content to rejoice in his isolation.

> " Reformers fail, because they change the letter,
>   And not the spirit, of the world's design ;
> Tyrant and slave create the scourge and fetter,
>   As is the worshipper will be the shrine.
> The ideal fails, though perfect were the plan ;
> World harmony springs through the perfect man.
>
> " We burn out life in hot, impatient striving,
>   We dash ourselves upon the hostile spears ;
> The bale tree, that our naked hands are riving,
>   Unites to crush us. Ere our manhood's years,

We sow the rifled blossoms of the prime,
Then fruitlessly are gathered out of time.

" We seek to change souls all unripe for changes ;
    We build upon a treacherous human soil
Of moral quicksand ; and the world avenges
    Its crime upon us, while we vainly toil.
In the black coal-pit of the popular heart,
Rain falls, light kindles, but no flowers upstart.

" Know this !—For men of ignoble affection,
    The social scheme that is were better far
Than the orbed sun's most exquisite perfection ;
    Man needs not heaven till he revolves a star.
Why seek to win the mad world from its strife ?
Grow perfect in the sanity of life.

" Grow perfect ! bide thy time ! in thine own being
    Solve, by an actual test, the problems vast
That vex mankind ; and, if the years are fleeing,
    Wait patiently. Backward the shadow passed
Once at a prophet's word, and may for thee—
Nay, will, if thou from self art perfect-free.

" Be chaste ! be true ! be wholly consecrated
    To virgin right ! So shall thy soul unchain
The powers that for the perfect man have waited.
    Though thought and instinct fail, bear every pain,
Till thy resolving elements are free
From the dread curse thy fathers cast on thee.

" New heavens of light shall dawn, the mind enskying ;
    Age shall decease, and youth revive the frame :
And, from the desert, where men thought thee dying,
    Thou shalt return, flushed with celestial flame.
But even then, with gentlest motion, stir
The corpses of the world's dread sepulchre.

" Move as the air moves, rich with summer spice,
    O'er fields of tropic bloom, and wheresoever
Thou meetest hearts self-locked in Arctic ice,
    Know that they will repay thy kind endeavour
With many a shaft of malice, sent to kill
The gentle nations of thy innocent will.

" Seek only those who pine, in love's transfusion,
    To pour themselves into the world's great life,

As sunshine through the summer's green seclusion ;
  As music, when its haunting powers are rife,
Through all pure instruments and voices sweet,
Thou shalt attract them as the summer's heat

" Calls bloom into the woodlands ; but if none
  Rejoice at thy sweet coming, lift not up
Thy voice ; infold thy beams, thou human sun ;
  Pour not thy wine, O rapture-brimming cup.
God waits, and Nature waits, and so shouldst thou ;
Full oft thy silent presence is enow.

" What if thy tropic soul keep long in blossom !
  It feeds with spice the wild winds wandering by
God's breath, impulsing through thy sacred bosom,
  Shall stir full many a heart with ecstasy.
Not powerless thou, unheard, unseen ; for so,
Still and invisible, the angels go."

This is the difficulty in the way of many ardent souls ; themselves they can save, others they can only touch, and that not always. Having the power in themselves of living above the world, they cannot raise others to the same level by making of them monks and nuns. A shallow soul is not to be made a deep one, or a fool a sage, or frivolity turned into sympathy, by a profession of conversion or by any form of words, or even by service under the banner of the most inspiring master.

In his isolation as a prophet, Buddha was not contemptuous of mankind, but very full of pity for all. The assumptions of the Brahman caste were no doubt for him lesson enough for pride. The following words are among those attributed to him : " If any man, whether he be learned or not, consider himself so great as to despise other men, he is like a blind man holding a candle—blind himself, he illumines others."

Buddha in his earnestness went so much deeper than the orthodox formalist that it need cause no surprise that his doctrines had to be modified to suit minds less passionately real. He was such as he describes—the man who, in striving after true religion, forgets himself. In his revolt against the luxurious ideal of a heaven realizing all earth's most selfish gratifications without its pains, he taught that by the enlightened man not only were the sorrows of earth to be avoided, but the joys of heaven. We may remember another and an even more burning protest against spiritual selfishness: an affirmation that he that would save his soul must lose it; he must absolutely cast away himself. In the continuing alertness of the highest faculties to be for ever used for the good of others, lies the only way of arriving at a soul-quality worth saving.

The incessant cry of early Buddhism upon the inherent repulsiveness of the physical life tends to show how deep was the impression made upon Sakya's nature, when developing into manhood, by the disabilities of humanity. This tendency develops into morbid excess when a preference is shown for regarding ugly or revolting objects in corporeal life because of the support they bring to his doctrine. If we believe at all that the circumstances of life are adjusted to our truest needs, we are bound to concede that the immitigable facts of mortal life are lesson enough to those who are awake; while the constant repetition of depictions of the more hideous ills to which man is heir would tend to a dull and deadened habit of mind with regard to life in general, rather than incite it toward higher ranges of spiritual vision, such as might open themselves to the eyes of the patient seeker after truth.

"What room for mirth, what room for laughter, remembering the everlasting burning?" (This expression must not be regarded as anywise betokening our conventional notion of hell; it denotes rather that burning of selfish lusts and eager ambitions which is regarded as the cause of the ceaseless round of transmigration.) "Surely this dark and dreary world is not fit for one to seek security and rest in. Behold this body in its fashioning! What reliance can it afford as a resting-place, filled with crowded thoughts, liable to every disease? Oh! how is it men do not perceive its false appearances? When old, then its beauty fades away; in sickness, what paleness and leanness—the skin wrinkled, the flesh withered, death and life both conjoined. And when the body dies, and the spirit flees, as when a royal personage rejects a broken chariot, so do the flesh and bones lie scattered and dispersed. What reliance, then, can one place on the body?"

This passage, as rendered from the Pali, is even more striking in its mournful and ghastly effect: "How is there laughter, how is there joy, as this world is always burning? Why do you not seek a light, ye who are surrounded by darkness? Look at this dressed-up lump, covered with wounds, joined together, sickly, full of many thoughts, which has no strength, no hold! This body is wasted, full of sickness, and frail; this heap of corruption breaks to pieces, the life in it is death. These white bones, like gourds thrown away in the autumn, what pleasure is there in looking on them? After a frame has been made of the bones, it is covered with flesh and blood, and there dwell in it old age and death, pride and deceit."

In a sunny country, life is apt to turn to a gaiety that may become mere carelessness. Buddha, no doubt, knew the life of the wealthy princes to be rarely more than a gay round of thoughtless pleasure, taken often to the detriment of their subjects. It was necessary to show how close were the sterner facts of life to this unreasoning revel. We to whom the daily newspaper brings the record of all the pains and calamities that are befalling the world from one end of it to the other, can scarcely need so much to be reminded of the disabilities of mortal life and the impermanence of the condition of humanity. But in the days when Buddha proclaimed his gospel with frequent use of ghastly phrases, there were no newspapers to bring close to men the story of the mishaps of their brethren; and the meaning of the lesson of human imperfection is perhaps slowly brought home to the dweller in a crowded land where the individual is of small account, and, unless he be the head of a village community, passes away with but little disturbance to the ways of his fellows.

The kind of love which Buddha manifests is compassion—pity for the human race, which is blinded by the hood of self upon its eyes, and struggling vainly in the clinging toils of the immediate surroundings of its existence. Apart from this pitiful affection, which extends to the minutest thing that has life, Buddhism contains an abstract philosophy that conveys a sense of chill, as if a skeleton absolutely perfect in the order of its bones were our companion. We are told the only certain way of escape; it rests with us to pursue it. To reach it we must, so far as our mortal appetites are concerned, attain the Jesuit ideal, and become *perinde ac cadaver*. Thus—and thus only—by the conquest of the human frailties and selfishness that disturb us and keep us in the mesh of the lower elements, may we enter into the sight of the mystic promised land of Nirvana.

Man being in this world of sorrow and suffering, the question arises, How got he thither? This question, with its answer, is conspicuous in the Buddhist system. The belief on this point we may find in a popular form in the Pratyasataka (Century of Maxims):—

> "Not from the king that rules the realm proceed our ills and woes,
> Nor from the minister of state, our kinsmen, or our foes!
> Nor from the shining host of orbs that glitter in the sky,
> Descend the ills that compass us, and shall do till we die,
> And after. But the real source of all our woes on earth,
> Is merit or demerit earned within a previous birth."

The following is a fair exposition of such an ontology:—

"Uttering the sentiments of a Buddhist, a man might say, I regard myself as a sentient being, now existing in the world of men. But I have existed in a similar manner in many myriads of previous births, and may have passed through all possible states of being. I am now under the influence of all I have ever done in all those ages. This is my KARMA, the arbiter of my destiny. Until I attain NIRVANA I must still continue to exist, but the states of being into which I shall pass I cannot tell. The future is shrouded in darkness impenetrable." It may be questioned whether Sakya himself would not have defined the future as consisting of light impenetrable rather than darkness, but truly the idea of the developed negationist is rather one of darkness.

"It is the mind alone (spirit)," according to the doctrine of the Dhammapada (Chinese text), "that determines the character of (life in) the three worlds. Just as the life has been virtuous or the contrary, is the subsequent career of the individual. Living in the dark, darkness will follow; the consequent birth is as the echo from the cavern; immersed in carnal desires, there cannot be anything but carnal appetite; all things result from previous conduct, as the traces follow the elephant's step, or the shadow the substance."

The worthlessness of existence with the primitive Buddhist is not a doctrine of mere pessimism; what he means by existence is not pure being, but such life as is due to that quality in man or angel which Swedenborg called the *proprium*. Even the Dêvas, who dwell in higher worlds than man and in joys of long duration, eventually have to complain of their imperfect character, and to find that they are still in the net of transmigration. What it is to be absorbed into the universal life without loss of our own identity is a condition for us ineffable; but it is in the cutting off of every root of subjection to lower desire that, according to Buddha, the entrance into that sublime state of purity is to be found. In his creed, impurity is the cleaving to sensible objects; purity is the absence of such attachment. The substance of Buddha's doctrine is this: "That the spirit or soul is the individual, and the body is the habitation of the soul. As the spirit comes or goes, so the abode of the spirit (*i.e.* the body) is perfected or destroyed. It may be objected to this that in such a theory there is no room for real birth—it is merely the soul coming into a body; and also, in the case of death, it is merely the same soul going, and the abode falling to decay. But the fact is, men generally know nothing about this soul—they only think of their bodies—and so are led to desire life and fear death; and so their case is a pitiable one." Among the enlightened this ignorance vanishes; the knowledge of former existences is one of the specific attributes of possession of the supernatural condition. Among the Buddhist legends is one of a father who, after the death of a young son who had shown a marvellous grace and knowledge, was allowed, in answer to his prayers, to be admitted to a sight of his child, who was in a city of such heavenly spirits as sometimes dwell among men. He addressed the child as his own, when the boy upbraided him for using such a foolish term as father or child, and refused to return with him to the earthly tabernacle. The story has no doubt been made to illustrate the doctrine of Buddha.

In superficial thought it may appear that such doctrines end in indifference to all that is beautiful, alike with all that is evil. It is true that in developed Buddhistic doctrine there is an overhaste for emancipation, a lack of acknowledgment of the fact that the beauty we find on the way of our pilgrimage is a kind gift, so long as rightly used; that there is no harm in pleasure, so long as we do not become its slave; that transient attachments are better than self-withdrawal into loveless ice. It is true that we find also in Buddhism a tendency to a cold selfishness such as that of Lucretius; but it may be presumed to arise from the pronounced intellectualism of the Hindu character, rather than from any characteristic of Buddha's teaching with which it is so manifestly inconsistent. Though we find even in the Dhammapada such a sentence as "Climbing the terraced heights of wisdom, the wise man looks down upon the fools, serene he looks upon the toiling crowd, as one that stands upon a mountain looks down upon them that stand upon the plain," it does not follow that it emanated from Buddha himself, while it seems probable enough that it proceeded from some disciple who had become elevated by the new wine of a great teacher's words. And after all there is a truth in the crushing sarcasm of the Dhammapada : "If a fool be associated with a wise man all his life, he will perceive the truth as little as a spoon perceives the taste of soup." Buddha's own indifference may have been natural indifference, that is, disregard of what is physical and transitory, but he cannot be accused of spiritual indifference. The question suggests itself, whether, when the selfish passions that actuate mortal life are stilled, not by lapse of faculties as in old age, but through conquest of the lower by the higher, there does not arise a spiritual passion which fills the being of the truly earnest and enlightened individual with something that is very far removed from indifference, and that gives out a more potent influence than words. Buddha, who taught an indifference that would repel most persons who live strongly in the physical life, was a worker all his life for love.

A most striking passage in the Dhammapada we may speculatively attribute to Sakya as representing his feelings on the attainment of the gleam of vision for which he had so long striven, the illumination that sent him forth to preach with power for the remainder of his natural life. The passage requires to be studied carefully, for its expressions are otherwise apt to mislead. There is no antitheism in it, for there is no reference either to a divine creator or to a demiurge; the great architect in the parable is that in us which builds up this mortal life. It represents the cause of birth, discovered when the soul awakens to consciousness of itself, the building being the necessary expression of our state, the exact correspondence to what we are and have been in selfish desires. We give more than one translation of the text.

Mr. D'Alwis renders: "Through transmigrations of numerous births have I run, not discovering (though) seeking the house-builder; birth again and again (is) sorrow. O House-builder! thou art (now) seen. Thou shalt not again build a house (for me). All thy (rafters) ribs are broken (by me). The apex of the house is destroyed. (My) mind is inclined to *nibbana*. (It) has arrived at the extinction of desire."

Mr. Childers begins the passage: "I have run through the revolution of countless births seeking the architect of this dwelling, and finding him not; grievous is repeated birth."

Professor Max Müller has both these scholars against him in rendering the tense as a future, which also makes the passage unintelligible:—

"Without ceasing shall I run through a course of many births, looking for the maker of this tabernacle, and painful is birth again and again. But now, maker of the tabernacle, thou hast been seen; thou shalt not make up this tabernacle again. All thy rafters are broken, thy ridge-pole is sundered; the mind, being sundered, has attained to the extinction of all desires."

The following are variant versions:—

> "Through an endless circle of births
> Have I sought to end, to destroy the poison,
> Seeking the maker of the house;
> Again and again (have I known) the sorrow of birth.
> I have found the maker of the house;
> No more shall (he) make a house for me;
> All his grief is pulverized,
> And the poison is destroyed with the house.
> (My) mind is freed from the sanskâra;
> Craving is ended and (I) shall be no more."
> (*Jatakanidânam* [Tibetan version of the *Nidânakathâ*], 153, 154).

"Maker of the house, I have sought until now to find thee [I have gone again and again to draw thee forth, source of existence], going through the revolution of countless existences, and subject to the pain of ever-recurring birth. Maker of the house, having found thee out, and the great beams of the house being destroyed, and all the rafters hewn down, thou shalt not hereafter make a house (for me)" (Udanavarga, iv. 31. 6–7).

"This udâna, sung by all Buddhas," we have now at least the opportunity of making of more value than a thousand stanzas repeated without understanding, for the sense of the original can surely now be reached.

Another of the striking passages of the Dhammapada, designed, as it would seem, to stick to the mind like a bur to the garment, which is the prerogative of parabolic or paradoxical speech, is also worthy of special attention. It must be premised that among deadly sins are reckoned the acts of matricide, parricide, killing an Arhat or devout Buddhist who has attained sanctification, shedding the blood of a Buddha, causing divisions among the priesthood, following strange teachers.

"The true Brahman goes scatheless though he have killed father and mother, and two holy kings, and an eminent man besides" (Childers).

"The Brahman goes placidly, having destroyed mother, father, and two valiant kings; and having also destroyed a kingdom with all its subjects." "The Brahman goes placidly, having destroyed mother, father, and two venerable kings; and having also destroyed that which has the haunts of tigers for a fifth" (D'Alwis).

"A true Brahmana, though he has killed father and mother, and two valiant kings; though he has destroyed a kingdom with all its subjects, is free from guilt. A true Brahmana, though he has killed father and mother, and two holy kings, and even a fifth man, is free from guilt" (Max Müller).

The last-named translator takes it that these verses are either meant to show that a truly holy man who by accident commits all these crimes is guiltless, or that they refer to some particular event in Buddha's history. Mr. Childers gave it as his opinion that the verse was "intended to express in a forcible manner the Buddhist doctrine that the Arhat *cannot* commit a serious sin." Mr. D'Alwis argued that, although, according to Buddha, accidental homicide was sinless, accidental homicide is not here referred to. Accordingly, he advanced the theory that the depiction of the sanctified Brahman as going placidly after a murder was meant in a spirit of contradiction, and designed to startle and challenge discussion, whereupon the destruction of all that was held sacred by the Brahman society would be expounded as symbolic of the destruction of the germs of existence which are so fondly clung to. It may be open to question whether any satire is intended, especially if, as has been alleged, Buddha had adopted the revered word Brahman for his own followers. Mr. D'Alwis, however, appears to have been right in taking the various destructions as purely symbolic. Mr. Beal has discovered in the Chinese Lankâvatâra Sûtra the following exposition of the doctrine, which ought to help our occidental minds in the difficult work of appreciating the oriental parabolism :—

" Mahâmati Bodhisatwa addressed Buddha and said : ' According to the assertion of the great teacher, if a male or female disciple should commit either of the unpardonable sins, he or she, nevertheless, shall not be cast into hell. World-honoured One! how can this be, that such a disciple shall escape, though guilty of such sins?' To whom Buddha replied : ' Mahâmati! attend, and weigh my words well! . . . What are these five unpardonable sins of which you speak ? They are these—to slay father and mother, to wound a Rahat, to offend (*i.e.* to place a stumblingblock in the way of) the members of the Sañgha (Church), to draw the blood from the body of a Buddha. Mahâmati! say, then, how a man committing these sins can be guiltless ? In this way : is not Love [selfish attachment ought it not rather to read, not to profane the name of Love?] which covets pleasure more and more, and so produces "birth," is not this the mother of all? And is not ignorance (*avidyâ*) the father of all? To destroy these two, then, is to slay father and mother. And again, to cut off and destroy those ten "*kleshas*," which, like the rat or the secret poison, work invisibly, and to get rid of all the consequences of these faults (*i.e.* to destroy all material associations), this is to wound a Rahat. And so to cause offence and overthrow a church or assembly, what is this but to separate entirely the connection of the five *skandhas?** ["five *aggregates*," which is the same word as that used above for the "Church."] And, again, to draw the blood of a Buddha, what is this but to wound and get rid of the seven-fold body by the three methods of escape? [The seven-fold body, literally "the body with seven kinds of knowledge;" the three methods of escape are the same as the three "yânas," or vehicles.†] . . . Thus it is, Mahâmati, the holy male or female disciple may slay father and mother, wound a Rahat, overthrow the assembly, draw the blood of a Buddha, and yet escape the punishment of the lowest hell.' And in order to explain and enforce this more fully, the World-honoured One added the following stanzas:—

> "' Lust, or carnal desire, this is the mother;
> "Ignorance," this is the father;
> The highest point of knowledge, this is Buddha;
> All the "Kleshas," these are the Rahats;
> The five Skandhas, these are the Priests;
> To commit the five unpardonable sins is to destroy these five,
> And yet not suffer the pains of hell.'"

---

* The five skandhas are representative of the animal life. Probably originally employed in a more general signification, they became defined as (1) organs of sense and objects of sense; (2) intelligence or consciousness of sensation; (3) pleasure, pain, or the absence of either; (4) the knowledge or belief arising from names and words (which distract the attention from qualities); (5) passions, as hatred, fear, etc.

† Vehicles of escape from the possibility of birth, methods of salvation. The commentary belongs probably to developed rather than to primitive Buddhism, but it doubtless shows the true principle of interpretation of Buddha's paradox.

This paradox with its interpretation has a special interest, as reminding us of a more familiar paradox, that of a man's hating his father and mother, and of his enemies being of his own household, to wit, his own qualities.

In another part of the Dhammapada (Chinese) we find a parallel but variant treatment of one of the symbols interpreted above. Buddha says, "Learning first to cut off the mother, and to follow the one true guide (minister), dismissing all the subordinate place-holders. This is (the conduct of) the truly enlightened man." Whereon the commentary explains that Doubt is the Mother, the twelve causes and effects (*nidânas*) the subordinates, wisdom the one minister.

The following are parallel versions of the same original, from the Northern Buddhist Canon:—

"Having killed father and mother and two holy kings, having conquered their kingdoms with its inhabitants, a man will be pure."

"He who has killed father and mother and two pure kings, and who has conquered their kingdoms with the inhabitants, is without sin, is a Brahmana.

"He who has killed father and mother, and two pure kings, and who has killed an irresistible tiger, is without sin, is a Brahmana" (Udanavarga, xxix. 23; xxxiii. 70, 71).

Mr. Rockhill gives the note of the commentator Pradjñâ-varman, of the ninth century, A.D., as follows:—

"'Tiger' implies a being whose mind is solely bent on evil. As the tiger in its natural ferocity devours unhesitatingly flesh and blood, so likewise he whose mind is bent on evil or spitefulness devours all the roots of virtue [that appear in others?]. The five [persons killed] imply the five mental darknesses."

The "five mental darknesses" are represented as "lust, ignorance, pride, shamelessness, hardness of heart;" or, "lust, anger, ignorance, self-confidence and pride." These recall the "five hindrances" that exist outside of and beyond the "five categories of sense," viz. "covetousness, anger, sloth, restlessness, unbelief." The interpretation of the other symbols is to the effect that "king" means one of the *skandhas;* and "Râja," or "King," the region of passions, of form, and so forth. "Kingdom" signifies "the six senses;" "its inhabitants," "feeling and perception," the foremost of the six internal senses. In the *Arya Kâtyâyana*, "the mother" is "desire;" "the father" "corruption, existence, and deeds done;" the "king" "attachment and the other perceptions of the mind, the six senses which are lord of the abode;" "kingdom" "the region of sin," and "the inhabitants" "what accompanies sin."

It will be observed that, as in the case of the Christian Scriptures, the commentary is developed so abundantly as almost to smother the text.

One of the most interesting of the illustrative metaphors of Buddha is that of the wound: "He who has no wound on his hand may touch poison with his hand; poison does not affect one who has no wound; nor is there evil for one who does not commit evil." Max Müller says, "This verse can only mean that no one suffers evil but he who has committed evil or sin; an idea the very opposite of that pronounced in Luke xiii. 1-5." There appears to be a complete misapprehension here; the text seems to mean that a man free from any tendency to a particular evil cannot be contaminated by it. Evil is altogether relative; death itself is not an evil except when viewed from a physical standpoint only; there may be those who are glad to have their step. The man who has no wound on his hand represents, with regard to evil consequent on yielding to temptation, a person above the plane on which a particular temptation has force. Two men, for instance, shall pass by some vicious allurement, the one is conscious of struggle, of a drawing; the other is perfectly undisturbed in the spiritual state to which (after who knows how many warring years or lives?) he has attained. He has now, in this particular respect, no wound on his hand.

Two parables that seem to belong to primitive Buddhism, illustrate the positive ideal of Nirvana: they are known as the comparisons of the Guest and the Dust:—

"As a traveller takes up his quarters at an inn, and, having rested and refreshed himself, sets out again on his weary journey, and has no leisure to rest or remain fixed (so is man in his natural condition); whereas, the true master of the house moves not from the place of his abode. So, that which is impermanent and unfixed is like the traveller, but that which is fixed we call the Master of the House; this is the parable of the Guest."

"As in the case of a clear sky, when the bright sun is shining, a ray of light perchance enters through a crack in a door, and, spreading its brightness in the space through which it passes, exhibits all the particles of dust in commotion and unrest; but, as to the space in which the particles move, its nature is rest; so also is the condition of man in the condition of unrest and in that of permanency (Nirvâna)."

The parable of the water, from the Sutra of the Forty-two Sections, forms a pair with the last: "A man who cherishes lust and desire, and does not aim after supreme knowledge, is like a vase of dirty water, in which all sorts of beautiful objects are placed. The water being shaken up, men can see nothing of the objects therein placed; so lust and desire, causing confusion and disorder in the heart, are like the mud in the water; they prevent our seeing the beauty of supreme reason (Religion). But . . . the mud in the water being removed, all is clear and pure—remove the pollution, and immediately of itself comes forth the substantial form."

Again, the kingdom of heaven, and the obscuring influences of earth (to turn to more familiar imagery) are likened to water boiling in a pot upon a fire, into which if a man look he will see no image of himself. "So the three poisons [covetousness, anger, delusion], which range within the heart, and the five obscurities [envy, passion, sloth, vacillation, unbelief], which embrace it, effectually prevent one attaining (seeing) supreme reason. But once get rid of the pollution of the wicked heart, and then we perceive the spiritual portion of ourselves which we have had from the first, although involved in the net of life and death—gladly then we mount to the paradise (lands) of all the Buddhas, where reason and virtue continually abide." This at least is unspoiled Buddhism, and would seem to belong to the man whose disciples, to judge by the early sculptures, had no formal priestly tonsure, and who preached that no outward act or conformity was of any avail, but a new spirit only.

Other stories show the presence of the same man: "There was a Shaman who nightly recited the Scriptures with plaintive and husky voice, desiring to do penance for some thought of returning to sin. Buddha in a gentle voice addressed him thus: 'Tell me, my son, when you were living in the world, what did you practise yourself in learning?' He replied, 'I was always playing on my lute.' Buddha said, 'And if the strings of your instrument were lax, what then?' He replied, 'They would not sound.' 'And if they were too tight, what then?' He replied, 'The sound would be too sharp.' 'But if they were tuned to a just medium, what then?' He replied, 'All the sounds would then be harmonious and agreeable.' Buddha addressed the Shaman: 'The way of religion (learning) is ever so. Keep the mind well-adjusted, and you will be able to acquire reason.'"

Another caution, too, Buddha may have learned from his discovery that even the extravagance of asceticism formed no royal road to peace, "raw haste" being ever "half-sister to delay:"—

"The practice of Religion is just like the process followed in an iron foundry: the metal being melted, is gradually separated from the dross, and drops down; so that the vessel made from the metal must needs be good. The way of wisdom is likewise a gradual process; consisting in the separation of all heart pollution, and so by perseverance reason is accomplished. Any other cause is but weariness of the flesh, and this results in mental sorrow, and this leads to apostasy, and this leads to hell (Asura)." Very simple indeed is the doctrine of one of the most primitive of the Gâthas :—

> "Scrupulously avoiding all wicked actions ;
> Reverently performing all virtuous ones ;
> Purifying this intention from all selfish ends ;
> This is the doctrine of all the Buddhas."

The following, from the Vásettha Sutta, would seem to be a mixture of Buddha's teachings with the ordinary asceticism of Hindu religion. Many of the passages are almost identical with verses of the "Dhammapada :"—

"I call him alone a Brahman, who, having severed all fetters, does not tremble, and has avoided allurements, and remains unshackled.

"I call him alone a Brahman, who has destroyed enmity, attachment, scepticism with its concomitants, and has demolished ignorance and attained Buddhahood.

"I call him alone a Brahman, who, without anger, endures reproach, torture, and bonds ; and has for his army his own power of endurance.

"I call him alone a Brahman, who is not wrathful, (but) dutiful, virtuous, unenslaved (by lust), subdued, having attained his last body (birth).

"I call him alone a Brahman, who, like water on the lotus-leaf, or a mustard seed on the point of a needle, does not cling to sensuality.

"I call him alone a Brahman, whose knowledge is profound, who is wise, knows the right and the wrong paths, and has attained the highest good.

"I call him alone a Brahman, who mixes not with householders, or with the houseless, nor with both, who is freed from attachment, and is contented with little.

"I call him alone a Brahman, who, having laid down the club (of violence) in respect of movable and immovable beings, does not kill or cause them to be slaughtered.

"I call him alone a Brahman, who amongst the wrathful is not angry, who amongst the contentious is peaceful, who amongst those given to attachment is void of attachment.

"I call him alone a Brahman, from whom lust, anger, pride, and envy have dropped off like a mustard seed from the point of a needle.

"I call him alone a Brahman, who utters true and instructive speech, freed from harshness and offence to any.

"I call him alone a Brahman, who in the world takes nothing that is not given him, be it long or short, small or large, good or bad.

"I call him alone a Brahman, to whom there is no desire for this world or the next, who is desireless and unshackled.

"I call him alone a Brahman, who has no desire, who by his knowledge is freed from doubt, who has attained *nibbana*.

"I call him alone a Brahman, who in this world has thrown off his attachment to merit and demerit both, is freed from grief and sin and is pure.

"I call him alone a Brahman, who has gone past this difficult road, the impassable and deceptive circle of existence; who has passed through it to the other shore; who is meditative, free from desire and doubt, and released from attachments.

"I call him alone a Brahman, who abandoning sensual pleasures in this world, becomes a houseless ascetic, and in whom the desire for a sensual existence is extinct.

"I call him alone a Brahman, who, abandoning covetousness in this world, becomes a houseless ascetic, and in whom the desire for existence is extinct.

"I call him alone a Brahman, who, having cast off liking

and disliking, is passionless, freed from the germs (of existence), and is a hero who has overcome all the elements (of existence).

"I call him alone a Brahman, whose progress neither gods, demigods, nor men know, whose passions are extinct and who is a saint.

"I call him alone a Brahman, who has nothing, whether in the past, future, or the present, who has nothing (whatever) and is desireless.

"I call him alone a Brahman, who is fearless, eminent, heroic, a great sage, a conqueror, freed from attachments, one who has bathed (in the waters of wisdom) and is a Buddha.

"I call him alone a Brahman, who knows his former abode, who sees both Heaven and Hell, and has reached the extinction of births.

"What is called 'name' or 'tribe' in the world arises from usage only. It is adopted here and there by common consent.

"It comes from long and uninterrupted usage, and from the false belief of the ignorant. (Hence) the ignorant assert, 'that a Brahman is such from birth.'

"One is not a Brahman, nor a non-Brahman by birth; by his conduct (alone) is he a Brahman, and by his conduct (alone) he is a non-Brahman.

"By his conduct he is a husbandman; by his conduct he is an artisan; by his conduct he is a merchant; by his conduct he is a servant.

"By his conduct he is a thief; by his conduct a warrior; by his conduct a sacrificer; by his conduct a king.

"Thus the wise who see the cause of things and understand the results of action, know this (*kamma*) matter as it really is.

"The world exists by cause; all things exist by cause; and beings are bound by cause (even) as the rolling cart by the pin of an axletree.

"One is a Brahman from penance, chastity, observance of the (moral) precepts, and the subjugation of the passions. Such is the best kind of Brahmanism.

"Know, Vásettha, that to those who are wise, he who is accomplished in the threefold knowledge, is patient and has extinguished future birth, is even a Brahma and Indra.

"Therefore (a man) becoming possessed of presence of mind at all times, should abandon the longing for objects of sense. Having forsaken them, he should cross the stream, even as one baling out a ship is in the habit of reaching the furthest shore."

What has often been described as Christian meekness was taught even before Buddha, in the injunctions to the Brahmans:—

"Let not a man be querulous even in pain. . . . Let him bear a reproachful speech with patience; let him speak reproachfully to no man; let him not, on account of this frail and feverish body, engage in hostility with any one living. With an angry man let him not in his turn be angry; abused, let him speak mildly" (Inst. Menu., 161, 47, 48).

"If he who strikes him lets fall the stick which he is using, let him pick it up, and render it to him without a murmur" (Menu. cit. Jaccolliot., 301).

The idea of returning good for evil is conveyed with great beauty in the Aryan couplet upon the duty of a good man, even at the moment of his destruction, of "not only forgiving, but even desiring to benefit his destroyer, as the sandal-tree shedding perfumes on the axe, at the moment of its overthrow."

The following passage may be described as Buddhist with a gospel ring about it:—

"A man buries a treasure in a deep pit, reasoning thus within himself: 'When occasion arises, this treasure will be of use to me,—if I am accused by the king, or plundered by robbers, or for release from debt, or in famine, or in misfortune.' Such are the reasons for which men conceal what in this world is called treasure.

"Meanwhile all this treasure, lying day after day concealed in a deep pit, profits him nothing. Either the treasure vanishes from its resting-place, or its owner's sense becomes distracted with care, or Nágas remove it, or malignant spirits convey it away, or his enemies or his kinsmen dig it up in his absence. The treasure is gone when the merit that produced it is exhausted.

"There is a treasure that man or woman may possess, a treasure laid up in the heart, a treasure of charity, piety, temperance, soberness. It is found in the sacred shrine, in the priestly assembly, in the individual man, in the stranger and sojourner, in the father, the mother, the elder brother.

"A treasure secure, impregnable, that cannot pass away; when a man leaves the fleeting riches of this world, this he takes with him after death.

"A treasure unshared with others, a treasure that no thief can steal. Let the wise man practise virtue; this is a treasure that follows him after death" (Khuddaka Pátha, 8. Translated from the Páli by R. C. Childers).

From the same treatise comes the following fine passage, entitled "Good Will to all:"—

"This is what should be done by him who is wise in seeking his own good, who has gained a knowledge of the tranquil lot of Nirvana. Let him be diligent, upright, and conscientious; meek, gentle, not vainglorious.

"Contented and cheerful, not oppressed with the cares of this world, not burdened with riches. Tranquil, discreet, not arrogant, not greedy for gifts.

"Let him not do any mean action for which others who are wise might reprove him. Let all creatures be happy and prosperous, let them be of joyful mind.

"All beings that have life, be they feeble or strong, be

they tall or of a middle stature or short, be they minute or vast :

"Seen or unseen, dwelling afar or near at hand, born or seeking birth, let all creatures be joyful.

"Let no man in any place deceive another, nor let him be harsh towards any one; let him not out of anger or resentment wish ill to his neighbour.

"As a mother so long as she lives watches over her child, her only child, so among all beings let boundless good will prevail.

"Let good will without measure, impartial, unmixed with enmity, prevail throughout the world, above, below, around.

"If a man be of this mind so long as he be awake, whether standing or walking, or sitting or lying, then is come to pass the saying, 'This place is the abode of holiness.'

"He who has not embraced false doctrine, the pious man endowed with a knowledge of Nirvána, if he conquer the love of pleasure he shall never again be born in the womb."

Little need be said in connection with Buddha upon the supernatural. He professed to no more miracles than were believed to be within the power of any trained ascetic to accomplish. He claimed to no more than was open to his disciples. There was a regular plan of contemplation by pursuing which the patient disciple might at length perceive his physical body to be but "as a cloud or a shadow," and thus gradually attain to the different attributes of spiritual perfection. Abstract meditation is the first state, that of exercising the mind without disturbance from bodily influences, and thereby liberating the soul.

Among his mysterious gifts was reckoned the power of preparing and directing his wraith, so as to appear in another place than that where his body was. The expression invariably used is "to send off his appearance." The same power has been claimed by others.

The *trividyâ*, or triple knowledge, claimed to be acquired

by the Buddhist saint—ought we to say attainable by ourselves, also, provided the necessary discipline be undertaken?—consists of the faculty of memory of the conditions of preceding incarnations; the perception of the thoughts of others; and supernatural knowledge.

The first step in this disciplinary direction, one not yet wearied of "the orb of transmigration" would probably find sufficiently difficult to prevent his pursuing the way of emancipation any further:—

"Cut off the five (senses), leave the five, rise above the five. A friar who has escaped from the five fetters, he is called 'saved from the flood'" (Dh. tr. Max Müller, 370).

The abandonment of the five "desires of the flesh" must leave life, naturally speaking, somewhat naked and comfortless, for the five desires are of "beauty, sound, odours, taste, and touch."

In such recondite subjects it may seem presumptuous for one with no claims to sanctity to offer criticism, as the whole value of the Buddhist gospel depends upon the validity, so difficult for an outsider to substantiate, of the hypothesis, that once the terrestrial attachments are mastered and expunged, the mysterious art of liberating the spiritual nature is gained, and a new great world of Nirvana opens on the view:—

"When you have understood the destruction of all that was made, you will understand that which was not made" (Dh. tr. M. M., 383).

But, after an apology for ignorance of transcendental facts, one may timidly wonder why the soul cannot come to a decision whether to pursue or extinguish a transmigratory career, during one of the periods of disembodiment. Surely, during such a pause and quietude, upon any spiritual hypothesis, there should be clearness of perception to decide upon the next step of life. At least, it seems reasonable to suppose that the sight should be clearer then than when corporeal existence has again closed in upon the soul.

According to Tibetan ideas, "the intermediate state between death and rebirth," though of varying duration, does not exceed forty days. Of this breathless period after the five senses are cut off, we shall be reminded when we come to analyze one of the Christian parables—that of the Ten Virgins.

That Nirvana was not regarded as a negative repose due to annihilation after death may be seen from the references to its acquisition while still in life:—

"He who is a Muni and a Brahmana, and who is consequently wise, is delivered from the material (rûpa) and the immaterial (arûpa), and from all kinds of suffering.

"He who has reached the end and is without fear, is without pride and without sin; having left behind the pains of existence, he has a body for the last time.

"This is the chief [beatitude] of those who have reached the end, perfect and unsurpassable peace, the destruction of all characteristics, the perfection of perfect purity, the annihilation of death.

"The Muni having cast off the sanskâra of existence [and also] like and unlike, by delighting in perfect composure he has broken the shell of the egg of existence and goes out [of the world]" (Udanavarga, tr. from Tibetan by W. W. Rockhill, ch. xxvi., Nirvana, 29-32).

The "destruction of all characteristics" is rather a blow to the idea of identity, unless we take it to mean the vanquishment of earthly weaknesses and of national, local, or hereditary traits and prejudices.

It is interesting to compare the Nirvana which "is neither in earth, or in water, fire, or wind," with that "region without form" respecting which the orthodox of the day interrogated the Hebrew prophet, and were told, "The kingdom of God cometh not with observation: neither shall they say, Lo, here! or, There! for lo, the kingdom of God is within you" (Luke xvii 20, 21).

The nirvana of "final emancipation" and "life without end" is even closer to the Christian ideal: "The impermanency of the created, the visible, the made, the produced, the compound; the great torment of subjection to old age, death, and ignorance; what proceeds from the cause of eating: (all this) is destroyed, and there is found no delight in it; this is the essential feature of final emancipation. Then there will be no doubts and scruples; all sources of suffering [the five skandhas] will be stopped, and one will have the happiness of the peace of the sanskâra" (Udanavarga, xxvi. 24).

Harmonization of the respiration was considered necessary for truly meditative thought. The directions for this, and also with regard to food, sleep, and posture, are given in great detail. The harmony of the heart, and of the mental faculties, have also to be strictly attended to, to avoid anxiety, levity, excitement, or hysteria, when it is desired to secure the abstraction called "samadhi." Broken and uneven respiration will not allow of the passage of equable thought without interruption. The mind as an entity in Buddhistic thought probably corresponds to what we understand by soul or spirit. "The faculties have the mind for their leader; they hold it as their chief; they are made up of the very mind," is the sentence that begins the Dhammapada. Again we find:—

"As a fletcher makes straight his arrow, a wise man makes straight his trembling and unsteady thought, which is difficult to keep, difficult to turn.

"As a fish taken from his watery home and thrown on the dry ground, our thought trembles all over in order to escape the dominion of Mâra (the tempter).

"It is good to tame the mind, which is difficult to hold in and flighty, rushing wherever it listeth; a tamed mind brings happiness.

"Let the wise man guard his thoughts, for they are

difficult to perceive, very artful, and they rush wherever they list : thoughts well guarded bring happiness.

"Those who bridle their mind which travels far, moves about alone, is without a body, and hides in the chamber (of the heart) will be free from the bonds of Mâra (the tempter)."

Again, "Well-makers lead the water (wherever they like); fletchers the arrow; carpenters a log of wood; wise people fashion themselves."

The other mystic attributes or powers, besides the meditative faculty, are those of assuming any form at will, of clairaudience and clairvoyance, of thought-reading, of the extinction of desires, and of the knowledge of what took place in previous states of existence. The magical power enabling saintly sages to walk through the air is gravely accepted in the orthodox scriptures of Buddhism; and the same power is said to be found at the present day. But Buddha asserted that no man was a saint by outward acts. "I command my disciples," he said, "not to work miracles; but to hide their good deeds and to show their sins."

Of Buddha himself a pretty legend is told, that if he passed anybody in pain, the pain, however intense, ceased instantly; and when his foot touched the ground a lotus sprang up at every step." This belongs evidently to the period when a personal worship of Buddha had begun.

The way in which this worship accepts equally the man and his doctrine as its object is very curious, and throws some light upon the question how far a man may be reverenced as representing the ideal which is his legacy to humanity. Buddha, the law or doctrine, and the congregation of the Faithful, constitute the Triple Gem of the Buddhists. The following is from the *Kusa Jataka* :—

"Him who, all lusts uprooting through long-continued strife,
Became the BUDDHA, and proclaimed the bliss of heavenly life!
The true and precious DOCTRINE which through the world was shown
By him, shall I unceasingly with adoration own."

Buddhism is the most philosophical of religions, as the teaching of Jesus is the most full of love. But even Buddha felt that the human mind might easily lose itself in vagueness of thoughts too large to grasp; while, in taking conduct rather than thought as the true object to be attained, there was no such danger of aberration. So he left a caution (which his followers have not followed) against overmuch speculation. According to Mr. Childers, who made the Pali literature his special study, " Buddhism has four great problems; they are the First Cause (Karma), the Supernatural, the Origin of Matter, and the Attributes of a Buddha. These four subjects Gautama declared to be unthinkable, and he forbade his priests to dwell upon them, lest they should lose their reason."

The main principles of Buddhism are very simply summed up in its Four Truths, which are to be found in every compilation of the scriptures. These truths are: (1) the reality of misery, which is perceived in distinct marks of sorrow, such as birth, old age, disease, death, the removal of that which is loved, the presence of that which is disliked, the inability of obtaining what is sought; (2) the cause of the aggregation of misery; (3) the possibility of its destruction; (4) the means requisite.

"By rousing himself, by reflection, by restraint and control, the wise man may make for himself an island which no flood can overwhelm" (Dhammapada).

"Make thyself an island, work hard, be wise! When thy impurities are blown away, and thou art free from guilt, thou wilt enter into the heavenly world of the elect (Ariya)" (*Ib.*).

Even rebirths and resurrections are of no value, without the quality of the life is regenerated.

Buddha's reasons for his teachings show the result of his long years of earnest struggle and thought, for which we owe him a debt of gratitude; since there is much that the world may yet learn from him. Here is his golden rule: "As life is dear to one's self, it is dear also to other living beings; by comparing one's self with others, good people bestow pity on all beings." Again: "Victory breeds hatred, the conquered fares ill. He who has renounced victory and defeat alike, fares well." "Let a man overcome anger by love; let him overcome evil by good; let him overcome the greedy by liberality, the liar by truth." This is, in another form, "If any one smite thee on the one cheek, offer to him the other."

"The thoughtless man, even if he can recite a large portion (of the law), but is not a doer of it, has no share in the Sâmanna [priesthood], but is like a cowherd counting the cows of others" (Dhammapada, 19).

"Those whose mind is well grounded in the elements of knowledge; who, having abandoned attachment, cling to that which is free from attachment; they who have destroyed desire, and are full of light, become free (even) in this world" (Dhammapada, 89).

"Man torments his like as long as he is prompted to do so. And when others torment him, he torments in his turn. . . . Every murderer ends by being a murderer's victim, every victor a victor's, every slanderer a slanderer's, every man of wrath the victim of a man of wrath. So, by the revolution of acts, he who has been tormented, torments in his turn" (Sanyutta-nikâya, 1; Sâgatha, Kosala-Sanyutta, ii. 4, 5).

Perhaps the finest instance of splendid simplicity and loving truth for which we are indebted to India, is to be found in the following stanzas from the Dhammapada:—

"He abused me, he beat me, he defeated me, he robbed me—hatred in those who harbour such thoughts will never cease. . . . For hatred does not cease by hatred at any time; hatred ceases by love, this is an old rule. And some do not know that we must all come to an end here; but others know it, and hence their quarrels cease."

Here Buddha reached his highest range of inspired

thought. In this little morsel of language is crystallized all that religion can teach.

Not to speak of primitive Christianity, we may assert, without hope of disproof, that the world at large has not yet reached the level of primitive Buddhism.

THEISM AND ETHICS IN ANCIENT GREECE.

I.

So much more attention is paid in the schools to the poetry, mythology, and history of Greece, than to her gnomists and ethical philosophers, that one falls into the habit of regarding Hellenic glory as solely derived from consummate art and exquisite Pagan life, and of doubting whether it can be made to present on the spectrum of the mind any of the deep lines of religious thought. Of Plato it is true, with his wealth of ideal suggestiveness, his quasi-Christianism, something indeed is known, as also of Aristotle; but to the most distinctly ethical remains of the Hellenic sages less attention is paid than to the amours of an over-fabled Zeus, the brave battles with the Persians, or the political history of Athens.

Perhaps there has been a tinge of unworthy jealousy of sublime thought when found to antedate the Christian era. It has been convenient for sectarian purposes, or consonant with mediæval ignorance, to regard the heathen world as benighted in darkness, and remote from the love of truth or consciousness of immortality. Marcus Aurelius has been welcomed, but Pythagoras almost ignored; Plutarch has been preferred to Solon.

Perhaps also the door of the ancient philosophy has been too firmly closed against the impatient modern tourist who expects to see everything that there is to be seen in a day. No way into it has been widened and made easy for the multitude, so that the prying nominalist should enjoy the freedom of the shrine. It is not the way to bid for popular favour to say such unpleasant truths as :

> "Approach ye genuine philosophic few,
> The Pythagoric life belongs to you ;
> But far, far off, ye vulgar herd profane,
> For Wisdom's voice is heard by you in vain :
> And you, Mind's lowest link, and darksome end,
> Good Rulers, Customs, Laws, alone can mend."

The leaders of the Salvation army would prophesy smoother things than this to any one that would throw in his lot with them.

Even in respect of Plato, if we put out of count the comparatively few men of culture, and take into view the great reading masses, we might almost repeat, with a change of significance, the words of Jerome, now nearly a millennium and a half old : " Who is it that now reads Aristotle ? How many people know Plato's books, or even his name ? Perhaps in a corner some vacuous old man may be conning him over. But of our rustics, our fishermen, the whole orb is speaking, with them the entire world resounds."

The cause of this prejudice no doubt has been in the past, that we had derived, through another channel, our main stream of such spiritual wisdom as we had made our own. The cause of the comparative neglect of the higher Greek ethics at the present day, when philosophic studies are becoming broadened, perhaps lies in the fact that it is being discovered that the characteristics of the inmost Hellenic thought are rather drawn from foreign sources than originating in a national inspiration. In speaking of inmost thought we refer to the ethics of life, the faith as to heaven and man, and omit consideration of the phases of intellectual scepticism, or the progress of physical science.

But there is one reason why we should do well to turn more lovingly to the Greek thinkers, from the Gnomic Poet to the Stoic Sage ; and that is, that what they do think they think clearly, so that their expression is like the perfect carving of a statue, ample and well defined.

In case of question as to the neglect referred to, it may be sufficient to point to the fact that there is no lately edited text, and no recent translation whatever, published in this country of the literary remains of the school of Pythagoras; that the works of a voluminous English Platonist of a former generation are scarce in the book market, because when they emerge from old libraries they are demanded for America; that it is only within a few years that Epictetus has appeared in the series of translations that includes most of the works of the dramatists, the historians, and the orators of Greek-speaking tribes; that of the remains of Heraclitus, Empedocles, Menander, Epicurus, Cleanthes—to take names almost at random—there is no English version to be found; while Anacreon and Theocritus, as representing the gayest poetry of paganism pure and simple, have, notwithstanding the anomaly in a professedly anti-pagan land, enjoyed a considerable currency.

Linus is the name of the most ancient Greek poet, and is mentioned in the "Iliad." Not prose, but poetry only, was literature in Greece in his day: and the poet was the thinker. He is, according to one legend, son of Apollo and of the muse of choric dancing; according to another the son of Hermes, and of the muse of the azure robe; and the invention of the rhythm of verse and melody of music is ascribed to him. Hercules, blind Thamyris, and Orpheus are said to have been among his disciples. He is reputed to have written in Pelasgian characters, which Herodotus calls a barbarous, or extra-Hellenic, language. The probable date of the Pelasgian epoch is about seventeen centuries before our era, a time when Egypt was in the height of her glory, when India was at its Vedic period, and Moses was not yet born. The Pelasgian tribe (rovers, wandering "storks," as the name probably implies) is acknowledged to have brought into rude Greece a religious system and theology, to have established the Dodona oracle, and instituted the Cabeiric mysteries, which seem to have had a Phœnician origin.

The primitive character of the time is shown by its remains, — its massy walls, formed of polygonal blocks of stone, roughly wrought rather by friction than by chisel.

Though Linus himself is named in Homer and Herodotus, we only have fragments of his poems on the doubtful authority of collectors of fifteen to twenty-two centuries after his time; so that, although it would be pleasant to note with what optimism philosophy begins in the land that bore so much of beauty, we must doubt whether we have any evidence of the fact, or whether the following are veritable words of Linus:—

"In all things we must hope; for nothing at all is hopeless.
All things are easy unto God to perfect, and nothing is vain.
Mark how all by struggle is controlled throughout.
Never arrives an end, while always having ends.
What sort of source had this that is as it is?
Immortal death so wraps all with mortality—
All corruptible dies, and what subsists doth alter its guise,
With shows in circles of change and fashions of form—
That veiled is the sight of the whole. It will be incorruptible,
And ever-during, insomuch as it has reached what it is.
The seventh day is of the good, the seventh is the birthday:
Of the first things is the seventh, the seventh the consummation."

Tradition carries on his name as that of a song or lay, sung by a boy to the cithara, while the vintagers were at work. As the name has been found in Phœnicia, Cyprus, and Egypt, perhaps Linus is only a tradition of music; an embodiment of a soft, simple, plaintive melody. The Greek word *ailinos*, which represents a crooning dirge, is said to be derived from a cry signifying *Ah for me, Linos*.

In our word "linen" perhaps we hold the clue to the origin of the name "Linus," in the flaxen string of the cithara.

Early Greek history is a singular compound of the poetically mythic with probable facts. Inachus from Phœnicia, who builds Argos, and Cecrops from Egypt, who institutes the

Areopagus, stand in the list of early kings with Amphictyon, who is the offspring of a sort of Greek Noah. Cadmus introduces the alphabet from Phœnicia, Danaus brings a colony from Egypt, Minos brings from Crete laws that lasted a thousand years, and side by side with them is Eumolpus, reputed the son of Poseidon, the sea god. He migrates from Thrace to Attica, and is initiated into the Eleusinian mysteries of the mother goddess of earthly plenty, Demeter, of which he becomes hierophant. Of the family of Eumolpus, whose descendants presided over the spiritualistic mysteries and claimed from father to son the prophetic gift, was Musæus the bard, placed at 1426 B.C. in the Arundel marbles. From him, the servant of the muses, comes our word "museum." His words come down to us that for mortals of brief span of life the sweetest refuge is to sing.

How often from heroic times, when life is heartily enjoyed, comes an undertone of lament for its shortness, and consciousness of the necessity of a sturdy cheerfulness. In periods when the flower of national life seems overblown, the days are too full of surfeit for either young or old to cry so eagerly for more of them.

The following is among the fragments of Musæus :—

"For ever Art is better far than Strength."

In this single line, so trite in the midst of civilization, we see the progress of a young community. The following is more significant of an ethical bent :—

"Like as the fruitful earth produceth leaves—
Some on the ash tree die while others grow—
Leaves of the race of men, they eddy too."

And the following shows the belief in an encompassing cloud of spiritual vicegerents of God as having to do with the direction of men, or perhaps marks the position held by the oracle in the religious idea of the time :—

"Gladly to hear what the immortal ones
To men assigned, from cowards marks the brave."

It is significant how in times of simplicity of life in a beautiful climate, when men are in the perfection of physical health, and, therefore, on a materialistic hypothesis, there would seem no reason to expect an under-current of mystery, the problem of life with its spiritual solution is yet ever present. Musæus, though a priest, is a believer; it is a most arrogant and absurd assumption that the prophetic leaders of men were always laughing in their sleeves, and practising deceits for a wage. A servant of the oracle, he proclaims that to live in blind revel of animal existence is cowardly; but to open the eyes and ears, and to face what gleams and whispers of destiny may be caught from the undying world in its relation with men, is the clearest sign that marks a noble and brave man.

The name of Orpheus has so much allied with it, that we may fairly imagine it to have been borne by a line of hierophants, and to have been made sponsor for the mystical legends of a cycle. Clement of Alexandria records thus the opinions of his time: "Onomacritus the Athenian, who is said to have been the author of the poems inscribed to Orpheus, is ascertained to have lived in the reign of the Pisistratidæ, about the fiftieth Olympiad [the early part of the sixth century B.C.]; and Orpheus, who sailed with Hercules, was the pupil of Musæus. Amphion precedes the Trojan war by two generations . . . the *Crateres* of Orpheus are said to be the production of Zopyrus of Heraclea, and *The Descent to Hades* that of Prodicus of Samos. Ion of Chios relates . . . that Pythagoras ascribed certain works of his own to Orpheus. Epigenes, in his book respecting *The Poetry ascribed to Orpheus*, says that *The Descent to Hades* and the *Sacred Discourse* were the production of Cecrops the Pythagorean; and the *Peplus* and the *Physics* of Brontinus." This account is little more than hearsay to us, since a very large number of the books which Clement cites are lost—probably having perished in the library in which he wrote. But the confused rumours point at least to an Orphic traditional lore which was familiar to Pythagoras.

Plato refers to "what is called the Orphic life" as a discipline including among its tenets the doctrine of abstinence from all things that have life, which would point to a brotherhood of the Indian order, where bodily purification is an essential. The story of Triptolemus, the minister of the goddess Demeter, to whom Plato refers also as representing that period, is a legend showing a familiarity with speculation upon the relation of body and soul. Triptolemus is so favoured by the earth-mother, on a special ground of gratitude, that she feeds him with her own milk and places him on burning coals during the night to destroy the particles of mortality he had received from his parents. The natural mother, giver of that body which is being transformed, so marvels at the unearthly growth of her son, that she spies on Demeter and the process is disturbed.

The best known story of Orpheus is that of his descent into Hades. Having lost his wife, he gains, through the music of a lyre received from Apollo, an admission to the under-world, soothing even Cerberus, the dog-guardian of Hades, with his strain. The deities of that region consent to restore his lost bride, provided that on departing he forbears looking behind him until he exchanges their borders for those of earth. He promises, but either curiosity as to the process of the re-incarnation, or his pent-up love for his yet unseen wife, or a doubt whether she is actually following him, presumably gets the better of him. He sees her, but it is only for a moment; she vanishes in a dissolving vision, and can be found no more.

Such stories as these it has been the fashion of late years to take as mythological representations of natural facts; and some of the simply poetic impersonations of Greek fable no doubt are to be so accounted for. But the theory has been run to death, and has been too much of a mere theory. When we find in Egypt, long before the rudest beginnings of Greece, the religious doctrine of an under-world with its Typhonic beast, to which Cerberus corresponds, and find also in Aryan books accounts of a similar entry into Hades, we are bound to take such a Greek tradition as the above to be derived from these foreign sources, and to have been in its essence passed on from one priest to another as occult religious lore, rather than originating locally as the spontaneous outburst of a naturalistic poet.

What Orpheus is said to have known must constitute the body of learning of a whole period at least. He is supposed to have left metric writings on theology and cosmogony, hymns, epigrams, treatises on agriculture, physics, astrology, precious stones, botany, chorography, medicine, laws, and matters relating to Argos. What we have now under his name is but little, and probably most, if not all of it, of later date than that of the Orphic tradition. In fact, to such critical minds as Aristotle, Cicero, and Suidas, it appeared probable that no single versicle certainly attributable to Orpheus was then in existence. That there once were in existence true Orphic verses there seems little doubt; whether the Pythagorean or Egyptian school fairly represented the originals in what is given as Orphic it would be difficult to judge. The following are specimens :—

> " I will utter to such as have the right ; the doors
> Close ye forthwith on the profane ! "
> [*or*—" Close ye upon your ears, profane ! "]

> " But thou,
> Musæus, hark, son of light-bearing moon,
> For truth I will declare ; and let not things
> That formerly your bosom cogitated
> Amerce you of dear life. But looking toward
> The word divine, hang closely over it,
> Keeping aright the heart's perceptive frame.
> Yea, enter well the path without a turn,
> And gaze upon the universal King !
> He is one, self-proceeding ; from the one

> All that is born evolves ; circling therein
> He inly acts ; himself no mortal sees,
> But he sees all. To mortals are his gifts,
> Ill sequence after good, and bloody war,
> And tearful woes. Beside the mighty king
> There is none else, and him I may not see,
> For round about him is established cloud.
> Yea, every mortal's eyes a veil contain—
> A mortal pupil, powerless to perceive
> Zeus who hath guard o'er all. Within the sky
> That is as brass, upon a golden throne
> Is he set firm, and lights upon the earth,
> And stretches a right hand beyond the sea,
> Past ocean's every side : the mountains high
> Are of a tremble round, yea, rivers too,
> And depths of pallid-foamed cerulean sea."

Again—

> "Ruler of Ether, Hades, Sea, and Land,
> Who with thy bolts Olympus' strong-built home
> Dost shake ; whom demons dread, and whom the throng
> Of gods do fear ; whom, too, the fates obey,
> Relentless though they be. O deathless One,
> Our mother's sire ! whose wrath makes all things reel ;
> Who mov'st the winds and shroud'st in clouds the world,
> Cleaving wide Ether with thy lightning gleams,—
> Thine is the order 'mid the stars, which run
> As thine unchangeable behests direct.
> Before thy burning throne the angels wait,
> Much-working, charged to do all things for men.
> Thy young spring shines, all pranked with purple flowers ;
> Thy winter with its chilling clouds assails ;
> Thine autumn noisy Bacchus distributes.
> Decayless, deathless, by undying ones
> And none else utterable ! Greatest god
> Over all gods by mighty fate, come, dread,
> Unconquerable, vast, decayless one,
> Whom the blue ether as a chaplet crowns."

> " From Zeus all things proceed, Zeus is both male
> And maid immortal, head and midst is he,
> Earth's base and starry heaven's, the breath of all,
> The force of tireless fire, the wide sea's root,
> Sun and moon both, of all arch-fount and king,
> One force, one spirit, source immense of all."

These probably are much more modern than the date ascribed to Orpheus. Plato quotes a fragment or two, showing that there were Orphic collections existing in his day.

The first lines quoted under the name of Orpheus are perhaps more likely to be authentic than the rest, as belonging to the period when religious rites were jealously guarded from any but the initiated. The great ones were few—princes who were the centre of the community's wealth, and had ornaments and drinking vessels of gold, while the bulk of the people were in a state of almost savage simplicity, touched by bravery, poetry, and superstition. As the palace was inaccessible to the community, in whom the rich valuables might but awaken a passion of rapine, so was the shrine of religious studies also secluded, that no interloper should disturb the repose necessary for the commune of the priestesses with the invisible world, and that no one receiving truths within an unprepared mind should alarm the vulgar and destroy by force the only centres of profound wisdom.

Thomas Taylor, the Platonist, in his study of Orpheus, very fairly shows that the hymns bearing the name were at least destined for use by a line of ministering priests. They are, in fact, sacrificial invocations, and show a personification of natural powers within a wide poetic pantheism, which with the enlightened worshipper at least has a monotheistic centre. Though nymphs, demons, the muses, the furies, the fates—

"Unchanged, aërial, wandering in the night,
Untamed, invisible to mortal sight,"

and dwelling by the Stygian river, in Pluto's hidden realms where—

"White waters of the lake,
Falling into the sea with silvery whirls,
Burst from a fountain hid in depth of night,"

are treated each and all as individual powers, and there is a

host of powerful deities, to whom worship is due, yet Zeus—
"multiform deity"—is within and at the back of all, the root
and breath of all things. In this pervasive power, even the
subordinate deities share, as being manifestations of divinity.
In the address to Herè we have an example of this rather
complicated kind of pantheism:—

> "All things producing, for the breath of life
> Without thee nothing knows: since thou, with all
> Thyself in wondrous sort communicating,
> Art mixed with all."

In the invocation to Apollo, there is naturally a trace of
the ancient sun-worship:—

> "Whose lucid eye
> Light-giving all things views ... this plenteous earth,
> And ev'n beneath, through the dark womb of things,
> In night's still, gloomy regions, and beyond
> The impenetrable darkness set with stars."

Diana is addressed as "great nurse of mortals, earthly and
celestial," "dread universal queen."

Pallas, too, has universal attributes:—

> "Wisdom to the good,
> And to the evil, madness: parent of war,
> And counsel: thou art male and female, too:
> Multiform dragoness, famed enthusiastic."

The goddess Demeter is the "giver of all things,"
"supporter of all mortals;" blessing man with plenteous
means of life—mother Nature living yet. And in a
personification of Nature as a deity we may see how a
subordinate member of the Pantheon can be invested with
universal attributes to the extent of a particular sphere of
influence, without infringing upon the supreme unity of the
Father of Gods.

In the Orphic or pseudo-Orphic system we find, further,
a lower range of divine personages having relation to human

life, but not credited with the attribute of universal sway. "The Divinity of Dreams" is addressed as follows:—

> "Great source of oracles to human-kind,
> When stealing soft, and whispering to the mind,
> Through sleep's sweet silence, and the gloom of night,
> Thy power awakes the intellectual sight,
> To silent souls the will of Heaven relates,
> And silently reveals their future fates."

Phanes or Protogonos, the exemplar of the universe, is a divine emanation, an effulgence of the glory, and an express image of the substance, so to speak, of the Supreme. The Hebrew Angel of the Presence and the Gnostic Logos are similar personifications of the powers and agencies of God. The First-born is thus addressed:—

> "O mighty first-begotten, hear my prayer,
> Twofold, egg-born, and wandering through the air;
> * * * * *
> 'Tis thine from darksome mists to purge the sight,
> All-spreading splendour, pure and holy light."

Death is invoked in the same strain of poetical pantheism:

> "Thy sleep perpetual bursts the vivid folds
> By which the soul attracting body holds."

Thomas Taylor finds in Porphyry an explanation of the meaning here, and bases a comment thereon in a style almost purely Buddhistic: "Though the body, by the death which is universally known, may be loosened from the soul, yet, while material passions and affections reside in the soul, the soul will continually verge to another body, and as long as this inclination continues remain connected with body. But when from the predominance of an intellectual nature, the soul is separated from material affections, it is truly liberated from the body, though the body at the same time verges and clings to the soul, as to the immediate cause of its support."

The Homeric cycle of poems, whether the work of one or of a group of rhapsodists, is really the firstfruits of Greek literature. The Orphic writings claim to be earlier by some three or four centuries, and no doubt there was bardic tradition from the Argonautic times; but in all probability, in passing from the reputed Orphic remains to Homer, we pass up and not down the stream of time.

Homer being in mass of a hearty and vivid naturalism with what it has of the supernatural, clearly designed for the generality, whose superb bible it became, it would seem that little attention is its due from the point of view of either theism or sublime ethics. Pagan polytheism, with the rude morals of a barbarous, if heroic time, has for the most part been thought to be all to be expected from Homer. This, indeed, is to be found there, and many a contradiction is to be found within that external polytheism, as well as many a questionable example in the sphere of morals. But there is more in Homer than this. We find, in Indian works meant for the people, instances where an attractive narrative is designed as a thick coating of sugar for a small ethical pill. We find in Druidic tradition verses in which the memory is ingeniously cozened into taking up a morsel of moral counsel interposed between the easiest and brightest of stanzas. The traditions of primitive peoples, by whom moral aphorisms are prized more highly than among the over-cultured and sceptical, are wont to be transmitted in the form of pithy sententious maxims, which easily pass current amongst unstudious and simple folk and grow into a treasury of proverbial lore.

The Homeric singers wrought in this fashion; and scattered over the writings that have come down to us, are to be found by careful search a number of little fragments, which if gathered, would be recognized as an appreciable contribution to ethics.

Mr. Gladstone goes further than this when he says: "The morality of the Homeric man is founded on duty, not to the particular personages of the Olympian system, but to the divinity, *theos*, or the gods in general, *theoi*. Sometimes to

Zeus; not however as the mere head of the Olympian Court, but as heir-general to the fragments and relics of the old monotheistic traditions."

It is becoming generally recognized that in all religions two forces have been at work: one the effort of the more spiritual mind to cleanse the vision of the mental eye that has turned toward the great problem of existence, and to concentrate and deepen the impression of Heaven's relation to us. The other force is that of the unawakened minds disintegrating and distorting all grand conceptions, splitting up large ideals into small, and requiring even minor abstractions to be showily clothed before they could attract any heed. It is this complex form of popular demand, and attempt to satisfy it, that has led to the absurd and self-contradictory mythologies of polytheism. In Egypt the gods, to all but the eyes that could penetrate beneath the mask, were lost in the multiplicity of stony images that once were living symbols. In Greece the art faculty absorbed a nation's spiritual dreamings into beautiful visible forms, and tended to draw away the acute consciousness of the invisible beneath the comfortable veil of external things.

Mr. Gladstone says again: "If Homer can be exhibited as the father of Greek letters in most of their branches, there is one great exception, which belongs to a later development. That exception was the philosophy of Greece; which seems to have owed its first inception to the Asiatic contact established after the great eastern migration. The absence of all abstract or metaphysical ideas from Homer is truly remarkable. Of all poets he is the most objective, and the least speculative." It is perfectly true that Homer is most poetically free from mystical obscurities, and that the formal philosophy of Greece began after his time; but we ought scarcely to deny to the Homeric cycle of ballads the possession of a fair quantity of the current coin of a simple philosophy. Indeed, in the following, the same scholar supplements and so corrects his doctrine respecting Homer: "In this splendid work of art we trace the real elements of worship and of an ethical system, drawing its strength from obligations to an unseen Power; to a plurality, which is also to a great extent an unity, and which rules the world. Lastly, while some portions of the scheme point us towards an earlier and also a ruder state, and others in the direction of a later and corrupt civilization, a third portion reveals a primitive basis of monotheism, and ideas in connection with it, which seem to defy explanation, except when we compare them with the most ancient of the Hebrew traditions."

If the religious philosophy of Greece has been neglected, the error has lain the other way with regard to the study of Homer. However rich may be the philosophic element of this rhapsodic school, it was eminently a school of poetry, in which even theology was for the most part regarded from the side of the dramatic and the picturesque, and taken as it existed in the popular mind, rather than as arising from any earnest belief of the singer's own. Mr. Gladstone, as we have shown, sees in Homer the remains of primitive monotheism, but dares not go back further than to the Hebrews for its source. Whether this monotheism be primeval or merely prehistoric, there is in Homer comparatively little of it.

Seneca, some eighteen centuries ago, was laughing at the critics for disputing amongst themselves to which of the philosophic sects of their time Homer had belonged. He is discoursing (Ep. lxxxviii.) upon the liberal arts, as being so called because they enlarge the mind and become a free man; and he characterizes as puerile the stepping aside from the study of wisdom into the weighing of syllables and the scanning of verses. Especially he stigmatizes mere argumentativeness, and very wittily instances the discussions which had turned upon Homer. "For one while," he says, "they make him a stoic, in pursuit of virtue alone, and flying from pleasure, so as not to be drawn thereby from what is right and fit, even by a promise of immortality; at another time they represent him as an epicurean, highly extolling the state of a peaceful city, whose inhabitants spend their time in songs and banquets; at another time as a peripatetic, allowing three sorts of good; at another time as an academic or sceptic, affirming all things to be uncertain. Now to me he seems to be none of these in particular, because their several doctrines are all to be found in him."

This is as if we were to fight over Shakespeare, whether he were to be pronounced a ritualist or an evangelical, a spiritualist or a follower of Comte. The great minds, whether among poets or philosophers, are nowise sectarian, though their followers may strive often to constrain them to an appearance of support of cramped and dogmatic views.

Learned volumes have been compiled, and especially in the seventeenth and eighteenth centuries, upon the Hebraizing tendencies of Homer; upon the question whether he was a moral philosopher; and also upon his theology, gnomology, and psychology.

The theology of Homer is indeed most confusing. Representing the conceptions of his time by poetry rather than preachment, he has not the unifying consciousness of a religious man, which with glowing faith and spiritual instinct burns away minor external vagaries of belief, and fuses the stray centralizing tendencies he finds into one harmonious agreement.

The Greek poetic mind had a marvellous power of absorption from the more deeply religious thought of other peoples. Egypt, India, Phœnicia, contributed not only conceptions of deity, but cosmogonical plans and visions of the unseen. With large, easy, artistic hand, Greece wrought them all into her pantheon and her philosophy, as a modeller might blend wet masses of different clays, or a sculptor fit to his work alternate ivory and gold.

In the Homeric theology, divinity is seen in series after

series of diverse powers, in wondrous activities, on high, below, afar, anigh, in forces of aid, of comfort, of gloom and fear, in potencies both small and great.

There are the high Olympian deities, in whose king reside whatever monotheistic elements were called for by the higher consciousness of man, and whatever conceptions of majesty, rule, and justice remained from older revelations of heavenly things.

But Zeus, if to one Homeric singer he be true Lord of all, yet with another he is made to do ungodly things; and even Zeus, according to a decaying tradition of an older theology, is himself but God of God, being son of a careworn personification of Time. In the Olympian group, after Zeus of the bright sky, are Here, his sister-wife; Athene, queen of the air, or daughter of the sky, regarded generally as representing wisdom, and in harmony with Zeus, while being on earth the clear-seeing help of heroes. Phoibos, the god of arrowy rays, with his twin sister Artemis, is akin to the sun, but rather as moving in its far-darting beams than as attached to its bulk. Hephaistos is fire flame, a mechanical power, occupying a menial rather than an exalted position in Olympus. Ares is stormy turbulence personified, a confusing influence, belonging to the din rather than to the direction of war. Aphrodite is brightness rising from sea-foam, and flushing passion of love. Hermes is the intellectual faculty and the emblem of craft, with a messenger's office and a movement like the wind. In many respects he corresponds with the Egyptian Thoth, being, like him too, the guide of souls bound for Hades.

There are the earth-pervading deities, human-formed blossomings of Nature, representing rich wealth and summer, and the power and elevation of wine. There are the underworld deities, reigning over a world hidden from the sun, but with the power themselves of visiting the light of Olympus. Hades being localized beneath the earth, the under-world gods became the patron deities and guardians of the treasures of the mines. From the mystic Hades come the avenging lights, the Erinyes, who can see in the dark and discover evil deeds. The attendant ministers of the Governor of Hades are also Night, Sleep, Death, and Dream. Among lesser deities is Poseidon, the lord of the forces of the sea, in whose group of powers are water-dwellers and masters of sea monsters, and haunters of sea caves and whirlpools, river-gods, tutelary nymphs and deities of woods, wells, and mountains, flocks and herds, with the less gentle persons of the Sirens of blandishment and the Harpies of havoc and destruction. There are inspirers, messengers, servants, and poetic impersonations without end; Hours, Muses; Iris, the rainbow messenger; Themis, the oracular will of Zeus and dispenser of justice; Eileithya, the moon-ray loosener of day's tense and highly strung cords, and president over travail; the Charites who hold hands and dance around us, typifying graces and favours flowing to and fro, the Hearth-fire goddess, emblem of domestic truth and fair dealing; Aisa, the uttered word of Zeus and type of destiny. Among fates and powers were Atè—human folly and mischief becoming a fate or doom—Discord, Fear, Rumour, Uproar, Conflict, and Prowess.

The faith that sees God everywhere, and regards the various machineries of nature as provinces swayed by divine emanations, may be a more real and glowing one than that which chains its conception of deity within an iron cage of doctrinal bars and bolts; but, with such a crowd of divine persons as we find in Homer, and with the conception of Zeus as almighty ruler only here and there apparent, we can scarcely agree to regard the Homeric tradition in the light of a reaction against the belief in polytheistic agencies. It seems rather to constitute a poetic assent to a polytheism enhanced by pantheistic sympathy and occasionally inspired by a glimpse of the unity of the source of law.

In intellectual moods it is possible to shut out from view the occasions, too insignificant for scientific apparatus to note, in which circumstance seems to adjust itself to the individual—to become as it were confidingly personal; and this without any natural law that the scientific mind so coldly defines, being in the least degree shaken. From instincts left to themselves, and minds not set in the groove of specializing studies, it will scarcely be possible absolutely to exclude the sense of mysterious guidance; and we may ever expect a repugnance to the frigid theories that would condemn the universal ether never to vibrate beneath warning whispers, or subconscious currents of communion.

In Homer we find dim popular instincts of this kind enlarged into definite form, with a result that there are presented a motley crowd of anthropomorphic deities endowed with noble attributes, but mingling therewith human qualities not only of virtue but of vice.

When in the Iliad Zeus thunders, it is regarded as a providential sign; which is superstition, and even harmful to poetry if too largely introduced. A sign like this—which to the scientific man denotes that constant play of physical forces upon the equilibrium of which our natural lives depend—being so evidently addressed to no single individual, could only be made spiritually momentous relatively to each different superstitious mood to which it appeals. To a poet the coincidence of a calamity with an eclipse or a storm, or the flight of an ominous bird, might seem appropriate; but a priest who had to listen to a variety of human complaints and sorrows, would soon discover that there was no inevitable connection between the supposed cause and effect; save that darkness might produce dejection, a storm alarm, or the sudden entry of any unwonted thing a panic. Or, discovering that in certain parts of the earth an east wind, by reason of the harshness it gathers from the regions it traverses, frets the nerves of sensitive folk, and so may prepare the ground for quarrels; or that a thunderstorm is often heralded by a sense of discomfort affecting both men and brutes; priest, poet, and scientist might all be at one.

We must not attempt to find philosophic order or ethical centre in the Homeric tradition, for the singers of the epic did not profess to focus thought, but only to catch a gleam from each pencil of bright rays that attracted their imagination.

The stories that cluster round Zeus are evidence enough of the impossibility of proving Homer consistent. First there are generalizations not incompatible with a view of Zeus as the Supreme Being in a monotheistic sense. Events occur because the will of Zeus is being accomplished. If he nods assent to anything yet unfulfilled, the subordinate hierarchy may feel full confidence,—"for this from me is the greatest pledge with the immortals; for whatever is mine that I shall sanction by the nod of the head is not to be retracted, nor is it fallacious nor unfulfilled." He restrains all other immortal powers until that fulfilment. Zeus is the most powerful. Honour is from Zeus. Even a bodeful dream, and that which is to mislead, is from Zeus, and performs his fateful purpose. He calls all immortal powers whatsoever to council, and so becomes the supreme will, for there is no word of refusal.

There is a beautiful utterance put into the mouth of Hector: "Thou biddest me obey birds of far-sweeping wing, but these I nowise regard, nor care, whether they rush to the right toward both dawn and sun, or to the left toward the darkening west. But let us obey the will of mighty Zeus, who ruleth all, mortal and immortal. There is one augury, the best, to be a bulwark of our fatherland."

Of the great deity Phoibos Apollo, it is the subordinate attribute to declare to men the unerring counsel of Zeus.

The aged Trojan monarch Priam would have distrusted any order of earthly beings, even the heaven-commissioned prophet, soothsayer, or priest, but having had word and vision from a deity direct, and this only a bright little wind-footed messenger from Zeus, he follows implicitly the injunctions given him. It is not only because he has seen Iris and beheld her face to face that he obeys, but because she comes as ambassadress from Zeus, who, though remote, is full of care and pity.

Zeus fulfils not the intentions of all men. A well-meaning counsel is one "not without God." If a tyrant is hated, the fact is to be reverentially regarded, for the people may be following for their oracle the very voice of God. On the other hand, obedience is due to a ruler, because his sceptre is from Zeus. "God, if he be willing, can save a man from a distance." "A match for many peoples is the man whom Zeus cherishes in his heart."

These conceptions might be found in any monotheistic scriptures. There are in Homer passages closely akin to such expressions as the following:—

"God is with us at our head" (2 Chron. xiii. 12). "Let not the army of Israel go with thee; for the Lord is not with Israel . . . but if thou wilt go, do it, be strong for the battle: God shall make thee fall before the enemy, for God hath power to help, and to cast down" (2 Chron. xxv. 7, 8). "Out of the mouth of the Most High proceedeth there not evil and good?" (Lam. iii. 38). "Both riches and honour come of thee, and thou rulest over all; and in thine hand is power and might; and in thine hand it is to make great, and to give strength unto all" (1 Chron. xxix. 12). "I will lay thy cities waste, and thou shalt be desolate, and thou shalt know that I am the Lord" (Ezek. xxxv. 4).

The intense consciousness of an arbitrary ruling power manifested in the Hebrew Scriptures far transcends anything of the kind to be found in Homer, where the sense of God as a patriotic helper bringing resistless aid, or an angry smiter with terrible calamities in his hand, is largely modified both by pantheistic tendencies and the pagan revels of the Olympian circle.

But in current ethics there are many resemblances between

the Hebrew and the Greek. That the counsel of the Lord remaineth for ever; that God is a witness of covenants and oaths; that counsel is to be asked of God as to the prospering of the way; that he has knowledge of all things, and measures the actions of men; that he makes poor and rich, brings low and lifts up; that kings are his appointment; that he can turn an enemy's counsel into folly; that one man may put a thousand to flight if God will; that no man can see God's face and live ;—these are views that with very little difference in expression may be found in Homer. Both books manifest the same simple and resigned acceptance of circumstances as they are, the same belief in dream-warnings and in the inspired utterances of prophet and seer, the same recognition of the duty of honour to the aged and the stranger. Coupled with this pity for the foreigner when a defenceless unit, there is the same repugnance for aliens in mass, the "gentile" and the "barbarian" being equally outside the pale of reasonable sympathy. There is the same care to offer in sacrifice no blemished victim, the same honour of rectitude, notwithstanding the most serious lapses in both, though the subtlety of the Greek leads him to accord also a sly respect to the cunning that outwits. This quality is foreign at least to the ideal of the Hebrew, who obtained his results by a close perseverance, a marvellous aptitude for detail, a somewhat cold sobriety and far-seeing prudence, and a knowledge of the weaknesses of others—a combination which has enabled him to get the better of his competitors without any need to resort to gross fraud. Jacob deceives, but he is not a match for Odysseus.

There is manifest both in Homeric and Hebrew ethics the perplexity caused by the fact that the worser things have sway, and the wicked remain in power. There is in both a fatalism with regard to the duration, if not the main contour, of a man's earthly career. Even in the later Hebrew scriptures the death of one who is in danger does not occur when it might have been expected, for "his time had not yet come."

In both is the recognition of the prophetic power to foresee certain lines of the career, both of a man and of a people.

There are rare touches, even in the Hebrew scriptures, of a respect paid to the vigour of physical life which is very like gentile or pagan pride. Jehovah, like Zeus or Ares, makes the hands to war and the fingers to fight. David and Samson might both be Homeric heroes.

If the object were to compare the Homeric with the Hebrew traditions, a multitude of parallelisms might be produced; but the subject in which the likeness is manifested is most often outside the range of ethics or religion, and belongs rather to current proverbial worldly wisdom.

Besides the monotheistic view of Zeus, there is a less dignified conception, according to which he is one of three brothers, and has his supremacy only by the mortal law of birthright, and through his superior prowess. He is somewhat superior to the other deities, but different rather in degree than in kind. He can, if he so wills, make a golden cloud to overshroud himself, which even the sun-deity cannot pierce. He claims to be superior to Phoibos, "since I am older and know more." He is stigmatized by his sister-wife as cruel and overbearing. He is anxious while his purposes are tediously evolving themselves under opposition. He does not pervade the universe, for there are times when he is absent from Olympus, on a visit elsewhere! He shows irritation, he is deceived by blandishment.

If Athenè and Zeus together are on the side of a man, it is open to question whether that is enough. There are differences arising in Olympus, Zeus, and other deities ranging themselves obstinately on the one side, while all the rest oppose. Again, Athenè shows a weak side of personal feeling when she is pleased by the implied flattery of an only offering or a first prayer being made to her.

We find in Homer also the naturalistic view of deity, in which Zeus embodies in himself all shining splendour of sky, holds in his hand all force of thunderbolt, and terrifying roar of the elements. He is the whirlwind of retribution, the torrent of rain, the arouser of tumult, the sender down upon men of dewdrops, moist with blood. He is not the actual sun, for we find the address, "O father Zeus, and thou O Sun, who beholdest and hearest all things."

In the fourteenth book of the Iliad there is a beautiful picture, singularly paralleled in some of the Indian scriptures, of the divine earth gushing forth with new productiveness of herb and flower beneath his couch when the deity is under the influence of a fresh impulse of love.

Again, Zeus is part, an important element only, of a divine Pleroma. "All men have need of the gods." "The gods are bestowers of all things." "It was done against the will of the immortal gods, wherefore it could not remain perfect for any long continuance." "Zeus certainly knows this, and the other immortal gods." "It is easy for the gods to exalt and debase mortals."

There is also a system, or dynasty, or group of agents with which Zeus, under some aspects, is regarded as having little or no connection. By a very anthropomorphic imagination of deity, Sleep is invoked as "King of all gods and of all men," and is bidden to lull Zeus. Sweet Sleep, it is true, quails at her office, and affirms that she can only approach Zeus by his own command. Eventually she aids in subduing him. Night, in the same humanistic fancy, is styled "vanquisher of gods and men." Destiny is supreme. In another place Zeus is above Fate. But when it is said that a mortal's life is what Fate at his birth wove in the thread of his career, it is left unsaid whether Fate is an independent power, or one of the attributes of Zeus. And yet Pallas addressing him implies his power to undo fate: "O father, hurler of white thunder, gatherer of dark clouds . . . dost thou wish to deliver from sad death a man who is mortal and long ago destined to fate? Do it; but all we other gods will not assent to thee." Ocean is a primeval Titan, perhaps representing flowing Time. Zeus has warred with Titans, who are more ancient than himself. These hoary deities war among themselves as if rude elemental forces, owning no allegiance to the neoteric law-giver of Olympus. Ocean is the parent of the gods ; but the belief seems to have varied whether, when the question is fairly faced, these primitive perpetual powers are to be regarded as predecessors of Zeus. The Cyclopes, monstrous children of nature, have no laws, and trust in the immortals ; but, with some contradiction, they claim to care nought for Ægis-bearing Zeus or the blessed gods, by reason of being vastly superior to them. There is a certain similarity here to the anomalous position of the mythological Satan, who is of the creation of God, but becomes a rebel, and asserts his own independence. Such a conception has very naturally arisen : to us who behold so small a span of life at once, it easily seems as if eternal purposes were being frustrated by delays and oppositions that to a larger view might appear as appertaining even to the purposes themselves.

The following rather undignified picture is the Homeric way of settlement of the question of the divine headship of Zeus : " Thunder-rejoicing Zeus made an assembly of deities on the loftiest peak of many-topped Olympus. Himself haranguing them, the deities all gave subservient ear : 'Hearken to me, all gods and goddesses, that I may tell what the soul within my breast ordains. Let, therefore, no female deity, nor any male, attempt infringement of this my word ; but do ye all at once assent, that I may very promptly bring these businesses to issue. Whomsoever of the gods I shall discover gone apart and wishing to give aid either to Trojans or to Greeks, smitten so as to be no pleasant sight, shall he return to Olympus, or I will seize and hurl him into gloomy Tartarus, far, far from hence, where beneath the earth is a profound abyss, and iron portals, and a threshold of brass, as far below Hades as from earth is heaven ; then shall he know how far I am of all gods the mightiest. But come, deities, attempt it, that ye all may know. Get from heaven a golden chain suspended, all hang therefrom ye gods and goddesses; yet would ye not pull down from heaven to earth your supreme counsellor Zeus, not even were ye to exert yourselves in no trifling way. But when, in sooth, I should seriously wish to pull it, haply I could draw it up with earth and sea to boot. Then, indeed, would I bind the chain around the top of Olympus, and all these should hang in the high welkin. So far doth my power overlap both gods' and men's.'"

This is a curious, rude, early picture. With indisputable power resident in the king of the gods, none should have needed to be told of it. Coleridge very fairly remarks upon this fragment of barbarous theology: "Although the supremacy of Jove comes far short of the true conception of almighty power, the characteristic point which seems to be fairly established is that he is the active and ruling power of the popular mythology, the supreme and despotic chief of an aristocracy of weaker divinities, accustomed to consult them and liable to their opposition and even violence; yet, upon the whole, substantially aristocratic and independent of any recognized permanent superior."

Sometimes we find regard paid to deity in the general sense of spiritual power, and without any special reference to the Olympian Zeus: "Whenever contrary to deity (daimon) man would fight with a hero whom a god honours, swift upon him is vast destruction hurled."

Of the subordinate deities the attributes are as various and contradictory as of Zeus himself. When contention and "the worse things prevail," Hephaistos fears that his enjoyment of the banquet will be impaired. It takes two deities, one of them becoming wounded, to save one earthly warrior from another. Sometimes they seem to represent only special attributes; Here applies to Aphrodite when she desires a special gift of loveliness and allurement. When blundering

Ares, the representative of the din of war, is sulky and rebellious, it is the goddess of wisdom who, greatly fearing for the whole group of Olympians, leaps forth to prevent the danger by bringing Ares to his senses. The spite of unruly Poseidon punishes a tribe for a manifestation of human kindness in escorting strangers home. Pallas even stands in awe of this monstrous sea uncle of hers. Hermes is the unblushing representative of craft and deceit. Athenè becomes quite friendly with Odysseus, who has just prevaricated cleverly, on the common ground of that cunning of which he is an arch representative on earth as she in heaven. Poseidon reproaches other deities for leaving a fray without partaking of it. The deities can be wounded by mortals, but are unslayable. Phoibos said to Achilles, who was hotly pursuing him, "Thou canst not slay me, since I am not one doomed to die." Pallas passes like a breath of wind into a room with closed doors. Mortals are of a humbler size than deities. The subordinate deities often fulfil rather the functions attaching to the word *daimon* in its post-Homeric sense, that of attendant spirit or genius, than of the Divinity which the term originally implied. They are friendly to their heroic favourites, and have some control over any natural force with which they may be specially allied. Even Circe can see and predict a little way ahead of events. Earth-haunting deities can manifest themselves to one mortal only out of two, if they choose. The sight of a manifested god is attended with danger. Though "the race of the immortal gods and of men that walk on the earth is no wise similar," yet the spheres seem almost to touch. While deities manifest themselves daimonically, the more heroic mortals appear to develop into a race of demi-gods, with approximating attributes. Deities of both sexes are subject to passion, mingling with heroic men or lovely women. The offspring that results from sons of gods and daughters of men, or from daring hero mated with compliant goddess, is distinguished as being above the common.

A mortal cherished by a motherly deity is subjected to a chrism of ambrosia and fire intended to render him immortal and free from the lower necessities of mortal life, from subjection to injury and the corruption of age.

This is the beneficence of daimonic influence; the reverse is manifested in a number of ungainly and monstrous beings who are "an immortal evil, best to flee from." They seem to represent a mingling of the terrors of natural plagues and visitations with a notion of a debased sort of spiritual beings.

We might well expect that, with such heterogeneous notions of deity, the morals of the heroes would be somewhat various too. If the Iliad is meant to convey any lesson, it is that of the ruin wrought by blinding passion and the arrogance that becomes quarrelsomeness. Achilles addresses his goddess mother : "May I straightway die, since destiny would not have it that I should succour my comrade who is slain ; for he verily hath perished far from his native country, whereas he longed for me to be his doom's averter. But now, since I shall not return to my dear fatherland, nor have become any light of help to Patroclus or my other comrades who have been subdued in numbers by noble Hector; while I sit beside the ships an useless weight to the soil, though I am such as is none other of the brazen-mailed Achaians in war—howbeit, in council there are verily others superior :—Would that therefore contention might perish from among gods and men, yea, anger, which is wont to impel even the fully wise to bitterness, and which, sweeter far than dropping honey, rises like a smoke in the hearts of men ; thus but now did Agamemnon, king of men, put rage in me. But though sorely anguished, let us leave these things as past and done, controlling from necessity our dear passion in our breasts. But now I go, that I may find Hector, the destroyer of the dear head ; and for me I accept death whensoever Zeus shall please to accomplish it with the other immortal gods. For not even did the might of Herakles escape death, who was the dearest man to king

Zeus, Cronos-born; but fate subdued him, and the grievous wrath of Herè. So also shall I lie when I am dead, if a like fate have been my portion. But now may I bear away illustrious glory, and compel some one of the Trojan women and deep-bosomed Dardanians to heave frequent sighs, wiping away with both hands the tears from her tender cheeks; and may they recognize that I have had a long cessation from battle. Wherefore hinder me not from the combat, although loving me dearly, for thou wilt not persuade me." Here is self-reproach and the sadness of approaching fate, and yet an acknowledgment of the cleaving still to the course that has borne such bitter fruit, as the manliest way to end.

Agamemnon, a meaner character, throws his sins upon fate: "Often were the Achaians already telling this story to me and rebuking me, yet I am not to blame; but Zeus and Fate and shade-roaming Erinys, who during the assembly cast a sad injury into my mind on the day when I myself took back the reward of Achilles. But what haply could I do? for the deity accomplishes all things. Venerable daughter of Zeus is pernicious Atè, who injures all. She has tender feet, for she never approaches the ground; but in good sooth she makes her walks over the heads of men. Verily at one time she injured Zeus, who they say is the very chiefest of men and gods. . . . He straightway seized Atè by her head of shining curls, enraged in his mind, and swore a mighty oath that Atè, who injures all, should never revisit Olympus and the starry heaven. Thus saying, he cast her from the starry heaven, whirling her round with his hand, and quickly she reached the works of men."

A different opinion upon the conduct of man is put into the mouth of Zeus:—

> " Ye powers, how mortals do reproach the gods;
> From us, say they, proceed their ills, whereas
> Their own infatuate sins do bring upon them
> Woes that transcend the destiny of fate."

Ajax, a plain rough warrior of immense personal prowess, a man of large bulk, who is given an entire chine at the feast after a great battle, prays the manliest prayer in the book: "Zeus father, do thou but liberate the sons of the Achaians from darkness; make a clear atmosphere, and grant us to see with our eyes; then destroy us in the light, if thus it be pleasing to thee!" In the mouth of Hector we find the old proverb that we know in so many forms, but chiefly as "They that take the sword shall perish by the sword." "The war-god treats all alike, yea and slays outright the slayer." The same truth of retribution is expressed in another form: "Such word as thou speakest, to such shalt thou have to listen:" with which we may compare, "With what judgment ye judge, ye shall be judged; with what measure ye mete, it shall be measured unto you."

The Homeric warrior exults in his prowess, and has a mighty appetite for broiled lumps of flesh, being a very different man from those gentle beings, of whom there was a tradition in his time, who were "milk-nourished, of simple life, and most just men." But even the warrior, when he comes to consider life by itself, is represented as falling into a sober attitude of resignation. The theory of mortal life which the poet presents to us is rather sad than otherwise, not to say, pessimistic: "There is nothing any way more wretched than man, of all creatures that breathe and move over the earth," says Zeus. "The earth nourishes nothing weaker than man," says Odysseus, "of all things whatever that breathe and creep upon the earth." Of her son Achilles, Thetis says, "As long as he lives to me, and beholds the light of the sun, he suffers sorrow." Achilles himself says to aged Priam: "The gods destined to hapless mortals that they should live wretched while they themselves are free from care. There lie on the threshold of Zeus two cases of gifts, which he bestows, the one of evils, with the other one of good. To whomsoever thunder-rejoicing Zeus may mingle and give them, sometimes he falls

into evil, sometimes into good: but to whomsoever he gives
of the evil, he makes him exposed to injury; hungry calamity
pursues him over the bounteous earth, and he wanders about
in honour neither of gods or mortals." In the Homeric Epigrams, we find the cause of these gloomy views, they are the
tired opinions of a puzzled mind: "Although there are many
things obscure to mortals, yet nothing is more obscure to men
than their own mind." The state of things at the present
day would be terrible indeed for obfuscation and wretchedness, were we to carry forward to ourselves, in a mathematical,
rather than a poetical sense, and as the basis of our pedigree,
the saying of the Odyssey, "Few sons are like their father,
more are worse, but few are better than their father."

If we may define morals as a set of doctrines and customs,
and ethics as principles on which such doctrines and customs
may be founded, it is plain that in the Homeric traditions
there is more of the former than of the latter element. And
yet, though the deities are not infrequently of dubious
principles and conduct, and the men are as often little more
than blustering animals, the immortal voice of conscience
makes itself heard among them. Odysseus, shifty as he is,
appreciates what a good father would enjoin upon a son, and
exhorts Achilles in words probably impressed upon himself in
his youth, " My son, Athenè and Herè will bestow valour, if
they choose, but restrain within thy breast thy great-hearted
soul, because humanity is better." Achilles, when he opens
his mind, declares that "hateful as the gates of Hades is he
who hides one thing in his mind while he utters another."
Treaty-breaking is a term of reproach, and this amongst a
people prone by character to forget righteousness in subtlety.
The laws of hospitality, a breach of which would have entailed
infamy, show how, under the spell of an unwritten tradition,
unruly hatred, jealousy of the foreigner, and predatory instincts
could be curbed. A race, however rude, that holds to such a
maxim as that "all strangers and beggars are from Zeus," we

cannot ourselves afford to contemn, for though the saying may be too general, and mean bad political economy, its spirit is excellent, and it represents a humanitarian conception to which the modern rough and cad have by no means been enabled to rise, notwithstanding the constraining influences of a so-called Christian civilization.

Glory, in the Homeric religion, is a commission from above. Before a combat a prayer rises up to Zeus from one camp to grant victory to their own champion; but, if Zeus loves the hero of the hostile ranks, to grant equal might and glory to both. When "ten thousand fates of death" are pressing on them, a man cries to his friend, "Let us on; either we shall give glory to some one, or some one to us." This is not an ignoble spirit, though its manifestation is in bloodshed. The wife of long-absent Odysseus remains to this day an ideal example— the type of constancy; while his faithful and warm-hearted servant is a character that prouder peoples than the tribes of the Homeric ballads might be glad to own.

The other-world conceptions of the Homeric time deserve special notice. Though they are affected by ignorance of physical facts, there are more pretentious doctrinal systems in which such conceptions are not much more complete or consistent.

The earth, to the mind of the Homeric bard, was not spherical, but plano-convex, or, perhaps, convex above, concave below. The upper surface was only slightly rounded, like the broad back of the sea. In the midst is Mount Olympus, of indefinite height, and rising into ethereal regions unknown to man. Olympus is not in the sky, but above it; and yet it is not stated that it derives its light otherwise than from the sun of our system. Around the world flows the primeval deity Ocean, scarce distinguishable from the firmament or heaven. The spirit disembodied by death, according to the Egyptian faith, navigated this stream on its journey to the unseen world, or Hades. According to the Greek idea, the way to the infernal regions was round the verge by Ocean or by passage through a chasm in the earth. The sun, in the poem, threatens that he will cease shining upon the supernal regions, and will illumine this under-world. In his ordinary daily course he was regarded as enshadowed by this mighty ocean stream from the time of his setting until the dawn. Tartarus is a lower depth than Hades, and a place of punishment for the wicked and rebellious. Under Tartarus are the Titan gods, an ancient mysterious dynasty of force. Hades is as much above Tartarus as Olympus is above earth. But from every place on earth unto Hades there was an equal road, an inspired statement of a fact requiring a mystic and spiritual explanation.

The Homeric notions of the future state of the dead are most curious and interesting. The apparition of Achilles, when Odysseus says to cheer him, "Take it not sadly that thou art dead," replies, "I would choose to be on earth and a hired servant to another, a man of low estate without much livelihood, rather than to rule over all the departed dead." Achilles was a man of intense energy and passion, and in his mouth such a sentiment is very fitly put; but the conception is purely humanistic, and the thought proceeds from the dramatic sense of the poet rather than from any mystic message of the shade. The primary Homeric idea of the effect of the black cloud of death is evidently the blotting out of the life of the senses, and of that sane intellect which so well adjusts itself to the affairs of earth. Such a repugnance is most natural among men accustomed to see violent death threatening them in their prime, and in the very midst of vigorous interests of life. There is no priest at the elbow of the Homeric heroes to declare the reality of other-world life. And in fact there is no other-world life to speak of in a soul that is starving on the spiritual side, and finding manifestation in the sense delights and an animal energy only. We need not wonder, therefore, at the picture presented in Homer of the soul that flitters and flies away like a dream, of the spirits that go gibbering beneath the earth like thin smoke. This thing of wandering uncertain motion, when it appears to a mortal in a dream, is like unto the departed in all things as to bulk, voice, and eyes; it is an eidolon, the perfect image of the lost friend, but unembraceable by human arms, a weak and lamentable shadow. The "thumos" and the "phrenes"— the passionate vigour of earth life, and the capacity of the mind for earthly affairs, are both fled. The former element, in one instance, is described as renewed in Hades; but the "psyche" is the inherent unquenchable part that escapes and clothes itself in the phantom image of the body, the flitting emanational form. The Homeric psychology bears every evidence of being based upon traditions of visions of ghosts. Granted that there are appearances of ghosts, they are manifestly in such apparition remote from their own plane of life and dependent for their manifestation upon such thin tissue of material elements as they can attract to themselves. At least, the world's ghost traditions would favour such an idea, and the departed spirit of the Homeric bible is marvellously like those traditions. A belief is found in Homer and elsewhere that the presence of newly spilled blood will enable the shade to accrete to itself sufficient physical emanations or particles to enable it to speak. The presence of this piece of occultism in Homer rather tends to prove what we have advanced, that the departed soul is regarded there from the side he is supposed to present when pressing into the confines of matter, rather than from the side he might present to a seer who lived more or less in two worlds at once.

There is much that is instructive in the Homeric belief. Tiresias, who in life had been a prophet and necromancer, the infallible oracle of Greece, according to tradition, at the time of the Theban war, is invoked by Odysseus. This well-accustomed inhabitant of Hades seems to know his way about better than the inconstant, unsettled shades; he stands firm, and holds a sceptre in his hand, and has rather increased than diminished his knowledge. He tells Odysseus of things which are to come, which he sees in decrees of the gods that have not yet consummated themselves in the sphere of earth. He gives Odysseus a hint also that, if he would commune with a shade, he must not grudge his approach to the sacrificial blood; for, if this be suffered, it will enable truthful communication to be made; the spirit otherwise, it is to be presumed, being betwixt two worlds, powerless to act, and inclined only to return to his own. But even the departed soothsayer is represented as speaking of the realm of the dead as a joyless region; and the mother of Odysseus, who converses with him afterwards, expresses wonder at his having been able to come under the shadowy darkness, being alive, and warns him how difficult it is for the living to behold such things. The mother, being in Hades, seems to imagine that her son has come there to speak to her, and appears not to know that she has drawn nigh to him, rather than he to her. She shows intimate knowledge of what has taken place in her son's family, and looks back upon her own "sweet life" which has passed from her. In Hades, she tells her son, the fibrous nerves exist without flesh and bones, which are subdued, as it were, by a force of consuming fire.

There are four distinct aspects given of other-world life. There are Tartarus, the place of torment; Erebus or Hades, the place of gloom, from which the spirits speak as just described; the Elysian plains, or abodes of bliss; and the anomalous wold where wander the hapless wraiths of the unburied. Where the body was neither buried nor burned, it would seem either that some tie was held to bind the shade to wanderings on the confines of earth, or that until sepulture was accomplished, some element was lacking which, if it did not bring joy to the querulous and injurious shade, at least allowed its entrance into companionship with others, and its adoption of a settled existence. If we endeavour to penetrate to the philosophy of so obscure a matter, we may perhaps infer that, as the burning, or other reduction to gaseous elements, of articles of food was regarded as affording sustenance to parents passed among the shades, according to the rites of ancestor worship, so a similar resolution of a man's dismantled tenement of flesh might be supposed to provide him with some kind of corresponding absorption of the freed spirit of matter, and so with a more perfected establishment of his Hadean form.

The Homeric psychology gives to the living man two separate attributes—the mind in which he may desire to act, and the physical machinery of limbs which, if languid from overstress of labour, may refuse the bidding of the mind. Furthermore, in that mind there is a person's own perception, and also a faculty to or in which the deity suggests things. To this faculty comes prophecy or the divine communication of the immortals. A son of the King of Troy perceives in his mind the counsel which seemed good to the immortals when deliberating, and proclaims it as their voice. Heroes are represented as opened to a possession of this gift, just before they die, when the soul flies from their members bewailing its lot and relinquishing manliness and youth.

All the Homeric conceptions of the other world are not quite so dreary. Sleep, when lauded for its sweetness, is in the same breath described as so being nearest like death, and death and sleep are regarded as twin brothers. Though even the gods are represented as holding in loathing the squalid domains of the nether world, yet the picture of Achilles taking mighty strides through the meadow of Asphodel, in joyousness, is not a very grievous one. But it must be allowed that his joy is drawn from earth, because he has been told that his son is very illustrious. It is difficult to judge whether the after-death existence was ever regarded as identical in quality with immortal life. The favourite of a deity might be put through a process which would endow him with immortal strength and invulnerability; but it is not clear whether it was held that his veins would then run with the celestial ichor instead of blood, and that he would thenceforward be one of those that neither eat bread nor drink purple wine; or, indeed, whether after death he would be of the immortal race and not a vacillating shade. All we are told of the relation of immortal gods and earth-walking men is that they are in no wise similar; while at the same time an Olympian deity comes among men like a phantom, and a hero's wraith appears to his friend with recognizable characteristics, even to the beauty of his eyes.

The Elysian fields, evidently derived as to their name and quality from the flower-growing field of Aalu, of the Egyptian scriptures, are difficult to find, as good places often are. Perhaps—for there are diverse suggestions—that delightful region is situated in mid air, or in the moon or sun, or in the centre of the earth, or in the blessed islands far away. It was the place for mortals who did not die, heroes who somehow passed away and found themselves in those blessed plains on the boundaries of the earth. There dwelt Rhadamanthos of auburn hair (another Egyptian importation,—Rhotamenti, judge of the Amenti, the unseen or Hades), and there was the most easy life for men. There was there neither snow nor dreary winter, nor falling rain; but from the immeasurable ocean stream came ever gently blowing breezes of the west wind, potent to refresh.

This region is curiously like the Olympian home of the gods, but it does not appear to have been identified with it. That stable seat is described as shaken by no blast, nor ever bedewed by rain or approached by snow; but a cloudless serenity overspread it, and therein the blessed gods were delighted all their days. With them, however, as with us, the scene changes somewhat according to the quality of their mood. Perhaps the truest conception of the other world may be found in the Homeric proverb that "the deity ever brings the like to the like."

Dreams being regarded as bodeful, there is manifestly in and through them an opening into the world whence come prophetic thoughts and foresight and oracular wisdom. Dreams, according to Homeric fancy, afterwards elaborated by Virgil, constitute a double portal; the one is of horn, the other of ivory. Through the latter come fanciful and deceptive things, promises vague and not to be fulfilled. Through the gate of horn come forth to men dreams that accomplish what is true, whenever any one of mortals sees them. It has been suggested that ivory represents the teeth, and horn the substance of the cornea or membrane of the eyeball. The theory is plausible, inasmuch as what man sees he generally relies upon, while what he has by hearsay, or through the teeth of others, is not seldom deceptive. But to render thus is to destroy the poetry of the portals of dream, and in fact to abase them from their mysterious altitude and bring them down to being not dreams at all.

It is not unreasonable that the Homeric tradition, with the simple vigour of natural life that is displayed in its majestic ballads, the gallant heroism, the brave resignation of the characters, should have kept hold on the attention of the civilized world. If the spiritual pictures are somewhat childish or confused, we must bear in mind that we are looking on the work of a poet, not of a prophet; and furthermore, that no nation whatever has yet adopted an absolutely unimpeachable and consistent ethical and psychological system.

II.

Greece began her literary history by importation of foreign letters and alien lore. After Phœnicia, India and Egypt had contributed their stores, a long line of priestly mystics held the keys, and the oracles united the soul of the seeker after wisdom not only with heavenly inspiration, but with that earthly leaven of superstition which, when in excess, becomes corrosive rather than expansive in its effects upon spiritual life.

Great wars united clans, and gave tribes a sense of nationality; experience outside the narrow homestead fostered hardihood and enterprise. Colonies were founded, and rude barbaric individualism, grown out of the quasi-bondage of the old family government, learned to act its part as a factor in extensive popular movements. Homer gathers up the traditions of a time when barbarism and civilization mingled, when petty polytheistic superstitions went side by side with a not ignoble consciousness of the divine government of the world. From beyond the plane of the trifling potentates of Olympos, came glimpses of a power that saw and knew all things, and directed the aim of events, however apparently crooked in progress, to some foreseen goal; and however much Titanic nature-forces or rebel elements might wax turbulent and destructive, a nod of the supreme father of gods and men meant something altogether irrevocable, and absolutely certain to be fulfilled.

Within the Homeric university of ballads are gathered, too, the current ethics, morals, and proverbial worldly wisdom of the age.

The interval between Homer and Hesiod is brief as regards time, being but a century, or thereabouts; it is, however, wide as regards character. And yet amid the Homeric revel of naturalism there are to be found here and there touches that strike the peculiar religious note of Hesiod. "On account of their pernicious belly men take on grievous cares," we find it said in the Odyssey. "It is arduous indeed to redeem the race and offspring of man," says the Iliad. In Hesiod's verses the Muses address men contemptuously as mere slaves of the belly, who are even unfitted to have truth conveyed to them.

In the ideals Hesiod presents, we have neither the rude warlike vigour of the Homeric pattern, nor the basking, fawn-like carelessness of enjoyment that is wont to be regarded as the essential principle of Greek life. Hesiod is a religious man, equally painstaking in morals and agriculture. He may have been both farmer and priest, as many monkish communities have been in our own England. It is not unlikely, moreover, that more than one hand is responsible for the Hesiodic poems, seeing how different are the principal works that bear his name—the "Theogony," or birth legends of the gods, and the "Works and Days." The former is a rather reckless up-gathering of fables, by a careless poet who is apt to let the exigencies of metre decide for him questions of precedence, and makes his disposition in a manner at times resembling that of a child arranging a garland of wild flowers. Through the false dignity of age, which made them even less indicative of any original purport or inner meaning than they had been when their only partially apprehensive collector put them together, these fables, when systematized, became exalted and crystallized into a sort of doctrinal orthodoxy of polytheism; and being thus popularly regarded, they in course of time constituted a stumbling block to the more enlightened religious mind of Greece. "Plato deprecated and Xenophanes denounced" them. They contain noble beauties, and much theistic and ethical suggestiveness; but we should be very sorry to have to accept them in mass as containing all things "generally necessary to salvation."

Pythagoras was believed to have led the way in this contempt for romance-making about the forces and foibles of anthropomorphic deity. Diogenes Laertius cites the story of another writer to the effect that when Pythagoras descended to the shades below, he saw the soul of Hesiod bound to a pillar of brass, and howling in torture, and that of Homer suspended from a tree, environed with serpents, as a punishment for their assertions about the gods.

Very different from the "Theogony" is the "Works and Days," which contains a very simple and real morality, a high sense of religion, and some small superstition.

Hesiod's inspiration is poetical but not unspiritual. When he speaks of the Muses, it is not as of abstractions that may fitly adorn verse ; it is as of actual presences, who are in close relation with the man who will give them heed.

There is poetry about the Muses when they are pictured as guarding the sacred mount of Helicon, dancing nimbly with delicate, dainty feet in their choral ring around the violet-hued fount of Aganippe, or bathing their soft skins in the delicious spring of Hippocrene (Steedfount), which the mystic horse Pegasus was fabled to have evoked by a stamp of his magical hoof.

There is a spiritual reality in the conception of the Muses when we are taught that, so soon as air's deep mist shrouds them, and night makes covert, they sing sweet sounds and draw nigh to earth, to visit such mortals as are pure. In earlier ages the heaven-dwellers were deemed to have often held commune with men, and in open day ; but in the more worldly age they only came softly at night to a poetic soul or to a lonely prophet here and there.

Hesiod claimed to have learned a lovely song, as he fed his lambs beneath the sacred hill ; and he dreamed that the Muses addressed him with some such myth as this :—

> "Shepherds that tend the field folds, coward knaves,
> Mere glutton hungers ! we know how to tell
> Full many a fiction put in truthful guise,
> Yet know, at our good choice, how to place truth
> In hidden forms of fable."

Hesiod hailed gladly the eloquent damsels of the mystic world, who gave him a wonderful verdant rod, a staff of luxuriant laurel, whose leaves he might chew ; and imparted to him, by inbreathing, the gift of the divine voice, that he might sing of things to be as well as of things gone by.

These gifts were the simple apparatus and the faculties of the oracle.

Certain of the ancient writers ridiculed Hesiod for these spiritual communings; and modern commentators write scornfully of his gift of openness to the visitants whom he regarded as the Muses: "Hesiod's simple nature may have dreamed these visions, or have been wrought on by fancy, the Muse-haunted spot, and the plenteous laurel, their gift." But Hesiod has the belief of the old oracular mystics, and unless every form of faith in the contact of a supernal world with the borders of our own is pestilent moonshine, his laurel-chewing meant some method of dulling or quieting the external senses, and his openness to visions was something more than idle fancy acting on a too simple and credulous nature. At least he deserves whatever respect may be due to Buddhist adept or Hebrew seer. But whatever criticism the theory of inspiration may meet with, the gift of poetical genius, and its power to open men's eyes to visions of life that transcend our world of every day, has never been analyzed to its source. What a cruel mockery, explicable only on the most pessimistic theory possible, is this image-forming faculty, if the images be all baseless phantoms! The imaginative faculty seizes upon the fleeting visions of the seer, and works them into form with the manifest object of impressing man with the faith that the world he inhabits is not the all in all, but a region traversed by pathways of light that carry faint rays from a more wonderful unseen.

Granted that such suggestions as these be true, to the generality of us who dwell within an envelope sorely undiaphanous, they nevertheless seem difficult to catch hold of; and we have to be thankful to the poets who can bring them nearer home to our senses by the aid of pure art, and an appeal to that romantic element which still abides deep down in our nature, and perchance is a relic of some Eden-realm whence we have strayed.

The poetry of Hesiod is not ruined in its artistic attributes by didacticism, but interspersed with it. "Poetical genius" in Hesiod, says O. K. Müller, is regarded as "a free gift of the Muses, imparted to a rough unlettered man, and awakening him from his brutish condition to a better life. ... This gift of the Muses is to be dedicated to the diffusion of truth."

In judging of the theism of Hesiod we must, as in the case of Homer, accept the fact that the many gods are not God, as we understand the word, but are manifestations or servants of his. Some are high daimonic influences, intermediate beings forming a vast hierarchy of life between ourselves and the Supreme. Step by step does the ladder extend from the true wielder of fate, through Olympian deities, demigods, muses and heroes, down to man.

Of the Homeric Zeus Sir G. W. Cox ("Manual of Mythology") says, he "is described in ways so different that we should rather say that there were two gods called by that name. Sometimes he is represented as partial, unjust, fond of rest and pleasure, changeable in his affections, and unfaithful in his love, greedy, sensual, and impure. But in hours of real trouble and grief, Achilles and the other Achaians pray to a Zeus who is not only irresistible in might, but also just and righteous." "How," the question is asked, "is this contrast to be accounted for?" "As the Indian word Dyaus seems originally to have been a name for the One only God, so it was retained by the Greeks and other kindred peoples to express all that they felt towards God. But, as the word also meant the visible sky with its clouds and vapours, some of the phrases which described its changes came, when their meaning was forgotten, to denote shameful actions. Thus the earth had been spoken of as the bride of the sky, and the sky was said to overshadow the earth with his love in every land; and all this, when applied to a deity with human form and passions, grew up into strange stories of lawless licence." "While in Hesiod," says the same writer, "the descent of the gods, their earthly loves, and their gross actions are brought out even more prominently, yet the poet can turn sharply away from all such things to the thought of that pure and holy Zeus who looks down from heaven to see if men will do justice and seek after God." "How," he asks, "was this contrast felt by the poets and philosophers of a still later age? By some the thought that the gods must be good was regarded as a sufficient reason for disbelieving all stories to their discredit; by others these tales were considered to disprove their divinity, as Euripides said—" If the gods do aught unseemly, then they are not gods at all." But others rested content with the knowledge that Zeus was a mere name by which they might speak of him in whom we live and move and have our being; but which is utterly unable to express, as our mind is to conceive, his infinite perfection."

From Hesiod may be drawn instances of exceedingly diverse conceptions of Zeus and of deity. We have the naturalistic use of the name, showing the Sanskrit Dyaus, the firmament, still to linger in it. In early spring, "let Zeus rain three days, and not cease, in measure neither exceeding nor falling short of the depth of the hoof-print of your ox," and a late sower may reap a plenteous harvest. In winter, "haul ashore your ship, and cover it thick with stones on every side, to keep off the violence of wet-blowing winds . . . that the rain of Zeus may not rot it."

In the following, Zeus represents a partaker in elemental strife, the mightiest factor in a very materialistic chaos. We roughly translate:—

> " No longer then did Zeus
> Suppress his power, but in his soul at once
> There rose expansive force; and putting out
> His fullest strength, he then stepped forth, from heaven
> And from Olympus lightning ceaselessly :
> Forth from his sturdy hand the bolts outflew
> Thick with thunder and flash, making a whirl

Of sacred flame, no rift between the showers.
On every side life-giving earth on fire
Put forth a roaring, while with mighty flame
Huge forests crackled. All the land did boil,
And Ocean's streams, yea and the desert sea.
Round and around the Titans, earthly born,
Hot vapour circled, the incessant blaze
Streamed up to swathe the atmosphere divine,
Whilst flashing sheen of bolt and lightning's flame
Blasted their eyes in spite of all their power.
The preternatural burning fixed its hold
On Chaos' depths, and to the eye and ear,
So far as sense could grasp, it suchwise seemed
As if the earth and firmament so wide
Met hurtling in mid air, for such a crash
Might only come of ruined nether earth
Borne down beneath wrecked heaven's supremacy."

Zeus triumphs by his immortal faculty over his father Cronos (afterwards identified with Chronos, Time), and claims fealty from the elements his servants. The notion of a divine rule and order superior to aught else, and reducing all else to an obedient harmony, is here foreshadowed.

Then, again, we find the personal Zeus the member of a family of deities, generally outwitting the rest, and ruling by a very human kind of superiority.

But the same Zeus is capable of being deceived, though as it is lamely argued he was not really cheated, but only sought an excuse for his contemplated severity to men. When gods and mortals were contending, Prometheus laid a trap for Zeus by asking him to choose between two divisions of a slain ox. On the one hand was good flesh covered up by offal, on the other the bones subtly disposed beneath white fat. Zeus reproaches Prometheus for the unfairness of the division, but is asked, nevertheless, to choose whichever portion the better suits his inclination:—

"Musing deceit he spake ; nor did Zeus fail,
    Of counsel incorruptible, the fraud
    To know and grasp ; and in his inmost thought

> Much evil he foredoomed to mortal man
> Which time should bring to pass. With both his hands
> The white fat he upraised from earth. Then wrath
> Possessed him ; yea, his very soul was wroth,
> When laid with cunning artifice he saw
> The whitening bones. Thenceforth the tribes of earth
> Consume such whitening bones, when the smoke climbs
> Wreathed from their fragrant altars. Then again
> Cloud-gatherer Zeus with indignation spake :
> 'Son of Iäpetus, most deeply versed
> In counsels, dost thou then remember yet
> Thine arts delusive ? So to wrath incensed,
> Spake he of wisdom incorruptible ;
> And still the fraud remembering, from that hour
> The strength of unexhausted fire denied
> To all Earth's denizens. But none the less
> Benevolent Prometheus baffled him ;
> The far-seen splendour, in a hollow reed
> He stole, of quenchless flame. But thereupon
> Resentment stung the Thunderer's inmost soul ;
> And his heart chafed in anger, when he saw
> The fire far-gleaming in the midst of men.
> Swift, for that flame, devised he ill to man."

Finally, we may turn to a picture of a Zeus who has Justice for a daughter, and is the watchful father of all men :

> " Ye judging kings, ponder for your own selves
>   This Nemesis, for close at hand within
>   Men's borders are immortals who declare
>   How many one another waste and grind
>   By crooked laws, aloof from all regard
>   To the god's retribution. For there dwell
>   On many-nurturing earth ten thousand told
>   Thrice over of immortals Zeus ordained
>   For watchful guardians over mortal men.
>   These, be ye sure, maintain within their charge
>   Both upright judgments and injurious deeds,
>   As clad in air they walk earth every way.
>   Yea more, there is the maiden Justice, sprung
>   From Zeus himself, noble and reverend held
>   Before the gods who in Olympus dwell.
>   Whenever any wight brings wrong on her
>   By crookt disparagement, she takes her seat
>   Forthwith by father Zeus, old Cronos' son,

And cries out on the impious mind of men,
So that the people's body may atone
For kings' infatuate deeds, who by their schemes
Pernicious twist the judgments from their path
By crookt forthtellings. O ye kings of law,
Guard ye against these things, make straight and fair
What words your mouth delivers, hungry maw,
For bribes ; and put warped judgments out of sight.
He harms himself who plans another's harm,
And evil counsel serves its author worst.
The eye of Zeus that sees all and perceives,
Yea now, if so he will, these things regards,
Nor him escapes the nature of this justice,
Whatever kind a city's walls enclose."

. The proverb in the above, which reminds us of the truth, "They that take the sword shall perish by sword," is repeated in another form as, "If you have spoken ill, haply you will yourself hear worse."

The most valuable part of Hesiod, from a philosophical point of view, lies in those deeper words of his where he manifests a monotheistic tendency, and in the ethical sentences which he intersperses through his works, and especially enshrines in the "Works and Days."

The following might be found under the name of a Hebrew prophet :—

"With ease he maketh strong, with equal ease
The strong abaseth ; the illustrious
He minisheth, and him that is obscure
He raiseth up ; yea, more, great Zeus, who wields
High thunders and in mansions dwells above,
With ease makes straight the crookt, and blasts the proud.
Hear and behold and heed, and righteously
Make straight the way of oracles of God."

Here again is the old honest faith that our hearts so deeply cling to, our lives so oft ignore :—

"'Tis plainly in thy power to make thy choice
Of evil, yea abundantly, with ease ;
For smooth the way, and lying close at hand.
But virtue's road the deathless gods did set

> With toilsome sweat for entrance; long and steep
> And rugged at the outset is the track
> That leads thereto, but when the peak is gained,
> 'Tis thence of ease, however harsh before."

Of this passage Cicero said, "Our dear Lepta must learn Hesiod, and have by heart 'The gods have placed at virtue's threshold the sweat of the brow.'"

The following comparison of the original and earnest thinker, the conventionally good, and the utterly careless, is of high interest, and evidences an advanced state of mental and moral development:—

> "Best every way is he who brings his mind
> To bear on all things for himself, and broods
> On what were best for after and the end;
> He too is good, who yields to good advice;
> But when a man thinks neither for himself,
> Nor takes into his heart another's word,
> Far else it is, a worthless fellow he."

The following contains much of a sort of trite proverbial wisdom:—

> "Both gods and men are rightly wroth with him
> Who lives a sluggard's life, like stingless drones
> Whose temper is to lazily consume
> The meat the bees' toil wins; thy pleasure be
> To set in order works of seemliness,
> To fill thy barns with seasonable store.
> Through work, men gain increase of flocks and wealth;
> Toil thou, thou shalt be dearer thus by far
> To deathless ones, yea, and to mortals too,
> For sluggards meet with an exceeding hate.
> Work is disgrace no whit, 'tis idleness
> That is reproach. . . . An evil kind of shame
> Attends the needy man—shame which is found
> To be great aid or injury to men.
> Shame verily haunts wretchedness, but near
> Prosperity dwells confidence. But mark,
> Goods must not be to evil rapine owed;
> But what the gods give, these are far the best.
> If with his very hands, by violence,

> One shall have seized great wealth, or by his tongue
> Shall have made prize of it, as happens oft,
> So soon as gain beguiles the mind of men,
> And shamelessness comes suddenly on shame,
> Then easily the gods make him obscure;
> Unto that man his house is brought to nought,
> And no long time his wealth his comrade bides."

Hesiod does not rise, it will be seen from the following, to Christianity; or rather, lest we wrong him, and to speak more exactly, he does not reach the level of the teachings and life that formed the original basis of what was afterwards turned into conventional Christianity:—

> " Invite the man that loves thee to a feast,
>   Thine enemy leave alone; especially
>   Ask to thy board the man that dwells near by,
>   For at thy house if any trouble hap,
>   Neighbours stay not to gird, but come forthwith,
>   While kinsfolk might delay for travelling gear."

This is simple and not unwholesome worldly wisdom, and takes us into a careful country life, where no imperial centralization overshadowed the self-protecting villagers.

A curious custom is shown, which was also common among the Hebrews, that of a feast to which each guest brought his own quota of provision: " Be not uncourteous in a feast of many guests, where the arrangement is of a contribution from all; for the pleasure then is greatest, the expense least." The observation marks an early time very different from the profuse modern style, which must add a spare set of best rooms to a house to be ready for guests, and holds in readiness ever a more than common provision of food and apparatus for them. The Homeric visitor not seldom slept, covered by some wild beast's skin, in the porch. In Hesiod's day there was no doubt great pleasure in the feast, when all were free and equal contributors, and no host or hostess was kept anxious by responsibility for the whole. With the rudeness of primitive style, perhaps has been lost some of its gaiety.

Again we find the note struck that reminds us inversely of the Sermon on the Mount :—

> "Love him that loves thee, draw thou nigh to him
> That draweth nigh to thee ; to him that gives
> Give thou ; to him that gives not give not thou.
> To givers some give, to withholders none."

In the following is a curious mixture of high morals with worldly wisdom :—

> "Measure right well in borrowing from a neighbour,
> And duly pay him back on the same scale,
> Or better, if thou canst, so if in want
> In future days thou mayest find in him
> One to depend on. Gain thou not base gains.
> Gains that are base are equal to a loss."

Though Hesiod's simple morality and religion speaks for itself in its evidently genuine character ; yet we must allow for a certain amount of personal prejudice in him, which prevents his being, like Homer, a gleaming mirror of the notions of life of his time. Hesiod appears to have been wronged by a brother, and by means of the bribery of the judges who tried the cause. Though he afterwards befriended this brother when he came to him in want, yet we see a slight tinge of gloom, scarcely deep enough to be called morbidness or pessimism, overshadowing his reflections. By K. O. Müller he is thus compared with Homer : In Hesiod "we miss the powerful sway of a youthful fancy, which in every part of the poems of Homer sheds an expression of bright and inexhaustible enjoyment, which lights up the sublime images of a heroic age, and moulds them into forms of surpassing beauty. The abandonment of the thoughts, with heartfelt joy and satisfaction, to a flow of poetical images, such as came crowding on the mind of Homer—how different is this from the manner of Hesiod! His poetry appears to struggle, to emerge out of the narrow bounds of common life, which he strives to ennoble and to render more endurable. Regarding with a melancholy feeling the destiny of the human race, and the corruption of a social condition which has destroyed all serene enjoyment, the poet seeks either to disseminate knowledge by which life can be improved or to diffuse certain religious notions as to the influence of a superior destiny, which may tend to produce a patient resignation to its inevitable evils. At one time he gives us lessons of civil and domestic wisdom, whereby order may be restored to a disturbed commonwealth or an ill-regulated household; at another, he seeks to reduce the bewildering and endless variety of stories about the gods to a connected system, in which each deity has his appointed place. Then, again, the poet of this school seeks to distribute the heroic legends into large masses, and, by finding certain links which may bind them all together, to make them more clear and comprehensive."

In the cosmogony of Hesiod, to which, where the inclination is towards pantheism, we have to look for the scheme of theology, there is occasional suggestiveness, but more confusion. Some of the stories are badly arranged, as if incorrectly handed down from some earlier original.

The Hesiodic conception of life strongly recalls alike the Hebrew and the Aryan sacred writings. There is a notion of a lower or fallen state, and of a pre-existent and superior condition. There are golden and silver ages of innocence, the origin of which, with that of other legends of Eden or Elysium, we may take the hint from the Rabbis of tracing to reminiscences of seers of a pre-corporeal or spiritual state, or to conditions of "open vision" affecting the present existence with some glimmering consciousness of that higher plane which is to most men as a far-away dream.

The beings representing life of the order described as the Golden Age die easily, as those would to whom death was only a passage from one state to another. As Hesiod most suggestively expresses it, "they used to die as if subdued by sleep." And after they had pleasantly passed away from earth, in the manner, as expressed by a modern poet, of one—

> "Who sinks to rest
> Like a tired child upon his nurse's breast,"

they dwelt near it—" kindly haunting earth, spiritual guardians of mortal men . . . wrapping themselves in air," with the kingly functions of watching over justice and conferring wealth and honour upon men.

While on earth they had lived as gods, with a life void of care and free from labours and troubles. All good things were theirs, and the land yielded up its fruits spontaneously for them to gather in quietness. They did not give way to quarrels and competitive strife, as is the way of mankind; all blessings were theirs; they were in harmony with the gods. What a strange dream this for men to have had if evolution be true! It could only have found its way from dreamland, or from some hidden paradise. On this everyday earth of ours we find no traces of a time—

> "When every brute
> Had voice articulate, in speech was skilled,
> And the mid-forests with its synods filled.
> The tongues of rock and pine-leaf then were free;
> To ship and sailor then would speak the sea;
> Sparrows with farmers would shrewd talk maintain;
> Earth gave all fruits, nor asked for toil again.
> Mortals and gods were wont to mix as friends."

The picture is essentially the same as the prophet's vision of a future, when—

> "The wolf shall dwell with the lamb,
> And the leopard shall lie down with the kid;
> And the calf and the young lion and the fatling together;
> And a little child shall lead them.
> And the cow and the bear shall feed;
> Their young ones shall lie down together;
> And the lion shall eat straw like the ox.
> The suckling child also shall play on the hole of the asp,

And the weaned child shall put his hand on the viper's den.
They shall not hurt nor destroy in all my holy mountain :
For the earth shall be full of the knowledge of Jehovah,
As the waters cover the sea" (*Isaiah* xi. 6-9.)

We must not despise these seemingly so illusive dreams of a harmony of man with deity, and of the consequent pacification of subordinate nature ; they imply an aspiration in man which is at present unrealized, and, implying that, argue also the existence of a faculty which is either rudimentary or obscured.

By a weaklier race those of the golden age are succeeded. The link between earth and heaven would seem to have become precarious, and the mortals of the silver age, while they have lost the secret of spiritual strength, yet have not learned the rude strength and vigour of a lower earth life, dissociated from the angelic worlds. They are poor weak creatures, of a prolonged infancy and a brief imprudent manhood, and the earth meetly takes them into her bosom, to become the "blessed mortals" of the under-world.

The third and brazen race suits the earth right well ; they have no troubling dreams. They do not eat wheaten food only, but have turned to flesh also.* They are a sturdy set, but, earth-born, they fight with one another, and, subdued by one another's hands, pass out of the bright sunshine into a squalid, chilling, inglorious Hades.

Then succeeds upon earth a hero race, half divine; but they perish in great wars; they are given life and settlements in the Isles of the Blest, apart from men, and yet not with the true immortals. Then Hesiod bemoans himself that he had not at least died among these, or been born in the remote afterward, instead of mingling with the race of iron, which, with a touch of personal experience, he says will never cease from toil and wretchedness, albeit some good shall be

* This notion of a progress towards earthliness, marked by increasing grossness of food, is more fully manifested in the Parsi scriptures.

mingled with their ills. These are men such as history tells of; and their perversities, which are so many, there is no need to recount, for we know the men of this age not by hearsay only.

The theogony of Hesiod, says Paley, "might seem to contain traces of what appear to be primitive and nearly universal traditions of the human family; obscure reminiscences relating to the creation of the world, to ancient races which had long passed away, and generally to a state of mankind higher, more godlike, more exempt from sin and toil, such as we used to contemplate man when first placed on the earth, as represented in the Mosaic accounts." The opposition to the conclusion that the theogony of the Greeks was derived from either the Persians or the Indians, or from Egypt, is also referred to, while it is urged that it was "an Hellenic development of the same common traditions, traditions so immensely ancient, that all traces of anything like a history of them had long before Hesiod's time been utterly and irretrievably lost. The coincidences between the earliest known traditions of mankind and the Mosaic writings are much too numerous and important to be purely accidental, and much too widely dispersed to have been borrowed solely from that source." This was written in 1860, and since that time the great discoveries of ancient records have placed beyond doubt the inference that Greek and Hebrew religious traditions alike are in great part fragments of the lore of an earlier epoch.

Religious aspirations have characterized the hero men of every age of which we have any record. There are among nations cases of arrested development; degraded races may be found; perhaps even spheres of humanity representing in some sort an infantine growth; but, so far as the remotest whisper of history makes itself heard, there has ever been a bearer of the divine torch in the world. Indeed, from what records tell us, it is plain that five to ten thousand years ago there were men living on earth of a spiritual and mental altitude equal at least to our own. And as there are at the present day races of men as low as any of which we can form a conception or have heard of in history, there is a certain reason in the inference that, if traces of very low races be found in the remotest past to which we can reach, there may concurrently have existed also groups occupying a higher plane.

The study of Hesiod's book of genesis in the light of modern discoveries, affords an enviable example to those who are seeking a solution of their doubts with respect to more modern systems of religion. It is in his case comparatively easy to combine and make fruitful the double process of scientific analysis and poetic rehabilitation. The parted strands into which his webs divide under examination, could be reunited in a solid and beautiful fabric.

The reason why this is so with the Hesiodic myths is, that their foundation is usually naturalistic. The phenomena of the elements, viewed imaginatively and raised to the heights of poetry, have become deities of the sacred hill, and part and parcel of the group of Olympians. Where the symbolisms of religious myths are not confined to personifications of physical actualities, but represent passages of the occult life of man, the analytic process is infinitely more difficult: and its result is less generally acceptable in a world in which the senses and the external life hold undisputed pre-eminence over, and manifest a strong repulsion towards, any interloping mystery.

It would be difficult to decide whether it is from legends and symbols of naturalistic or of spiritualistic basis, when degraded or obscured, that the more dangerous superstitions arise. Who shall say which shall the more terrify a child, a story of Furies, Gorgons, and Harpies, or a story of an everlasting brimstone sea of hell? As the child grows into a man, certainly the bogies that resolve themselves into physical facts are the most easy to face, whilst the uncanny remoteness of the others constitutes their irremovable dread.

A familiar aspect of the physical myth is that in which we see the patent fact of some daily marvel of nature—when seized upon by the imagination, and in process of absorption into the poetic mind—being met half way by some interior fact of consciousness which seems to delight in entering into correspondence with it. Given, for instance, some physical disturbance, some elemental terror; and a guilty conscience is most pathetically ready to ally itself with it, to hide in it, as it were; to clothe itself in the darkness or the storm, as its own appropriate and destined garment.

We know the truth of the saying, "Every one that doeth evil things hateth the light, and cometh not to the light, lest his deeds should be convicted." Turning to the Greek mythology, we find a fearful worship given to certain stern and inexorable deities, the Erinyes. Grim and terrible, with winged feminine forms, bearing burning torches and whips of scorpions, and having serpents twining in their hair, they are the ministers of the vengeance of the gods. They punish the guilty alike on earth and in Hades. The people pay them worship, and yet scarcely dare call them by name or gaze on the temples dedicated to them, for their attendants are Terror and Wrath, Pallor and Death, and their subtle influence is to deprive of his crafty reason the manslayer, the perjurer, the undutiful, the cruelly treating, the presumptuous, and to drive the evil man to distraction and fury. From without come the chastisements of these avenging deities, in wars, pestilence, and dissensions; and from within, in sore stabs of guilty conscience.

In spite of all these horrors, their name Erinyes was most often left unsaid, and the name Eumenides, or kindly disposed, was given to them, as being venerable goddesses whose anger was just. And poets and artists who celebrated their festivals were wont to see that gentler side of them, and so to depict them as beautiful and young.

What is the original secret of such a two-sided personification, a secret which was apparently unknown to Homer and Hesiod? And how come these Furies to be so like that conception of the terrible convicting light which is hated by evil? —a conception which was expressed in a country that followed a different worship from that of the Eumenides, and which, moreover, must draw so clear a response and verification from general human experience.

We have to go to India to find a clue that joins the religious with the imaginative conception, and makes of them two aspects given by the conscience of man to a single simple natural truth. The Erinys of the Greek mythology is the Saranyû of the Vedic,—a mythical being whose name is an equivalent for the morning light. The swift flash of the dawn comes forth from the grove of gloom, and is the pursuing fury of darkness and evil. The irresistible light is the fury that finds out sin and convicts the sinner. The light is implacable by very justice, and yet is ever beautiful and young to the eye of the righteous poet. The origin is thus made clear of an ideal vengeance that is alike to be feared and to be worshipped, a power lovely and ghastly at once, and that acts with equal sureness from without and from within. The light from without discloses the darkest deed; what we call light breaks upon the mind from within and probes our most deeply hidden motives. The Furies are ever at our doors.

"Every sin and blasphemy shall be forgiven unto men, but the blasphemy of the spirit shall not be forgiven" (Matt. xii. 31).

"Who sins against the light is hurt beyond the hope of cure" ("Works and Days," 281).

The identity of the Indian Saranyû and the Greek Erinys might be open to question, and the resemblance might be regarded as a mere coincidence, were it the only one between the myths of the Veda and Hesiod. But Eos, the dawn, resembles the Indian Ushas; Eros, the child Love, is the Indian Arusha, a name for the sun, regarded as a beautiful child beginning his course; Daphne is Dahana, Argynnis Arjuna. Hesiod's fabled monster Echidna, half-nymph, half-serpent, dwelling in a cavern, insensible to age, and giving birth to destruction, finds her prototype in the Indian Ahi, or snake. Her offspring, Orthros, and Kerberos the dog of hell, are similarly represented by the great dragons of the Veda, and powers of darkness, Vritra and Sarvara. The Olympian deity Ares or Mars, the god of war, is presumably akin to the Maruts of the Veda, the gods of the storm-winds, deriving their origin from the root "mar," to grind.

In a similar way, other mythological heroes of Greece can be traced to their origin in Egypt. Themis, the goddess of justice and mother of judgment and peace and law, is the Egyptian Thmei, or *truth*, and the Hebrew *Thummim*, an expression which the Septuagint renders by *truth*. Rhadamanthus, the mythical ruler on earth and fabled judge of hell, is Rhotamenti in ancient Egypt, the King of the Amenti, or the unseen. The gloom of Erebos is drawn from the associations of the Egyptian with Ereb, the west; and our Europe shows the same derivation without the accompanying notion of gloom. Hecate is akin to Heka, a name of Isis. Harpocrates, the deity represented with finger on the mouth, is from Hor-pi-krut, the infant Horus. Kharu, an archaic Egyptian deity, possibly associated with a root signifying silence, appears as Charon, the Greek boatman of the dead, and Acheron, a river of the unseen world.

Ocean, in the Hesiodean mythology, is more than the deep, the main, or the barren salt sea, which was a separate personification, and was represented as only a child of earth. The deity Okeanos is child both of Earth and of Heaven, a being stretching round earth and constituting its mystic boundary, just as the Egyptian Ur-nas, which makes the great vague water-way from earth to the unseen worlds.

In these mythological conceptions, a marvel almost beyond analysis is the fusion of a natural fact or physical

theory with a spiritual faith. The latter seems sometimes to
have expanded beyond the former, and to have used the
metaphorical form as a ladder by which to raise itself into
a conception appreciable in the world of sense. A materialist
might plausibly argue that our whole belief in a world of
spirit was but a poetic fancy evolved during long ages from
a custom of the Egyptians to bury in the west, to which end
they had to cross their river, which hence grew to be the type
of an imaginary pathway of the soul into the regions of the
unseen. It might even be claimed that from such beginnings,
and from such alone, a complete soul-theory had developed
itself. But equally well might it be argued that there could
be no such faculty as conscience before some poet saw that
light frightens darkness, and thencefrom drew a fanciful
picture of a pure spiritual element in man before which his
lower nature shrinks back abashed.

Such arguments are difficult to answer save in two ways.
One is by the production of antecedent records of man, in
which the same old interest and belief in a preternatural
world exhibits itself, changed only in the imagery in which it
is clothed. The other is by retreat into the stronghold of
the very consciousness itself, the fact of whose absolute
existence is impugned. That dim spiritual consciousness,
ever present and ever active in more or less degree, must, if
we grant its existence, be the motive power that is endeavouring to find expression, and ever clothing itself in the
symbols that best represent or enshrine it. Sometimes perchance the oft-used symbols will lose their outline and become
deteriorated by change and misconceptions, while concurrently
with the obscuration of their original physical sense, their
inner meaning may also have become dull. Nevertheless,
in spite of all defects, which perhaps are inherent in the
attempted representation of one sphere of life on the plane of
another, they may continue expressive of a true idea in a form
that man may convey, or pass on, to man.

There is no reason to doubt that a number of poetic personifications, even such as have become included among religious types, and were of the most high and sacred regard, were simply naturalistic in their origin. There is no more reason to doubt this than to doubt the possibility of a crafty man originating such a proverb as "Honesty is the best policy," with the accent on policy, and of this subtle maxim being read by an honest man in a higher sense.

Among the mythological conceptions of Hesiod that may fairly be deemed simply naturalistic, notwithstanding any poetic apotheosis, may be classed such as that of the Harpies, who accompany the wind-blasts. They are named in Homer, and in later mythologies appear in hideous forms. They are very reasonably taken to be personifications of pestilential breaths that accompany winds blowing from infected quarters. The Graiæ, born of a monstrous deity of the sea, and of the abyss, have fair faces and gray hair, and are supposed to represent waves with white crest and grayish spume; or to personify some effect of the gloaming when light and darkness cross each other. The Gorgons, again, who come from the remote nightward quarter beyond Ocean, with their terrible faces, have been thought to symbolize the huge and fearful ocean rollers which, when driven over a long wide stretch of seas by a hurricane, are enough to inspire even the seafaring man with something like fear. On the other hand, as of these dire sisters one is mortal, the others immortal, the former has been thought to be the sky of a starlit night, which is doomed to vanish and die at sunrise, while the latter represent that remote and absolute darkness which it was supposed the light of the sun could not penetrate, and which might therefore be regarded as impregnable and immortal.

To judge of symbolic religions we must draw into comparison with our own times a picture of races unperturbed by the manifold distractions that a complex civilization brings, races of men living by what their hands can draw from the earth, rather than by commerce and the aid of steam machinery; races living mainly out of doors and sheltered by tents or simple walls and roofs instead of by the wonderfully fitted structures of the present day that make indoor life quite a busy sphere of its own. To the old rural men, the gigantic play of the elements, the alternations of the seasons, the ceaseless steps of night and day, must have had a significance that we cannot now recall.

To imaginations fostered by long winter glooms which enforced comparative idleness, and fed by the superstitions which lonely life in remote districts engenders, not to name the frequent shocks accruing from the casualties by storm and many kinds of danger to which barbarian life is exposed, it is no wonder that the processes of nature should appeal with startling vividness, and readily assume even a personal shape. To the shepherd contemplating from a hillside the sky blood red after a storm, and then seeing the evening setting in with ghostly shadows marshalled in the lowlands, which ever encroached upon the spear-wielding armies of light till these seemed to mount the hills and vanish, with front still towards the foe; the combatants may well have seemed to wear heroic forms, spectral, and associated in his mind with vanished ancestors. And when, after the pause and hush of night, during which the shapes of blackness reigned supreme, or were feebly attacked by the silver-clad pigmy host of stars, how gladly must he have welcomed as a strenuous deity and friend the deathless lord that rushed into the sky, gave battle, and put to flight all ghastly dreams and terrors!

What a charm must poetry have possessed in those days of unmurdered simplicity! What magical delight, "in a season of calm weather," to witness over again by the aid of graphic story some mighty struggle of wind with rain, or sun with cloud, or day with night, realized in the persons of heroes and monsters who were but shadows made definite and immortal! Bellerophon on winged Pegasus slays the monster dragon Chimæra, type ever of haunting mysterious dread. The Firmament, an ancient mighty god, hates the fierce turbulent Titanic children of earth, and imprisons them. Their mother forges a sickle of white iron and gives it to a child called Time. When the Firmament came down with Night and stretched brooding over earth, by Time he was shorn of his strength, but his divided powers fall in blood drops upon earth, and breed furies and giants and nymphs, while prolific emblems fall into the sea, and from their white foam comes tormenting Aphroditè, at whose footstep blooms verdure, as at her touch the heart of man becomes elate.

Time, being set up for sovereign, swallows his offspring so soon as born, poor short-lived babes, who seem to represent the days that vanish one after the other down that hungry maw we call Eternity. But Zeus, whom we must perhaps here regard as essential life, eludes the devouring deity, who swallows instead a huge dead stone, which he afterwards disgorges together with the once-swallowed children, who now typify perhaps the return of the days and seasons. As to this stone, we should perhaps be too subjective if claiming to regard it as the symbol of matter, which we now know to be chemically swallowed and disgorged again in new transmuted form. The poetic imagination in seizing upon its romantic food was wont to overleap itself, and the eventual form of fancy sometimes veils rather than manifests the original idea from which it started.

Of deep import in another direction is the legend of Sisyphos—the overwise, if the etymology of the name be correct. He was so cunning that he sought to outwit fate, and when his time was come to die, he constrained his wife to promise to leave his body unburied, which was an offence against the custom of the time, and was thought to restrain the shade to forlorn wanderings in an outer Hades. When he had arrived in those regions, he put in action his subtle plan of getting back to earth, by craving permission to return for the purpose of punishing his wife for her shameful neglect. Reaching earth once more, he ignored the condition of his having been allowed the visit, which was his solemn promise to return, and was accordingly most ignominiously captured and taken back to Hades by Ares. His punishment, which evidences a moral conception of retribution, was to roll uphill a huge stone that for ever rolled down again—a fine metaphor of the injurious project that recoils upon its prime mover.

The story of Prometheus gives promise of being pregnant with meaning, but the legend is somewhat defaced, as if drawn from an imperfectly understood original. Iäpetus, a mystical personage whose name is equally akin with Japheth and Iao-pitar or Jupiter, has four sons: broad-backed Atlas, a doomed Titan, who supports the vault of heaven, and would seem to represent endurance; Menœtius, who represents overweening arrogance, hurled down to Hades; Prometheus, representing providence or forethought, and identical with the Indian Pramantha, or instrument for churning out fire from pieces of dried stick; and Epimetheus, afterthought or blindness.

Inapprehensive Epimetheus, laggard in wits, careful after the event, receives from Zeus a very dangerous gift, an inextricable snare. Water and earth were mingled by the order of the derisive deity. The compound was endued with voice and strength as of a man, and with a maiden's loveliness like in countenance to the immortal goddesses. Pallas was bidden to teach her spinster's work, and Aphrodite to endow her with grace and allurement, with a spell to produce woeful desire and cares that waste the limbs, while Hermes was allowed to bestow a winning quality of voice, an impudent mind, and tricksy ways. With mien like a modest maiden, decked with every grace, hung with Persuasion's golden chains, and crowned by the fast-fleeting fair-tressed Hours (the seasons) with blossoms of spring, apparelled with every ornament, this incarnate mischief is ushered forth. She is called Pandora, because every Olympian deity bestows on her a gift.

Prometheus had warned his brother not to accept a gift from Zeus, but to return it, for fear of its containing insidious hurt to mortals. They had obtained the advantage of fire ; they were now to receive disadvantage in countervail, the pernicious race of woman, who is represented as no aid in poverty, but a helpmate of surfeit. There is evident prejudice in the legend, though the kind of woman pointed at may be deemed still to exist.

Either the same writer in a more agreeable mood, or some other writer, corrects this partial view by picturing the pernicious old age of the celibate, the distant kindred partitioning his goods at his decease ; and on the other hand, the lot of marriage when it comes with a good congenial wife, a happy chance that may now and then recur, since the original evil has good ever contending with it.

Pandora would seem to be a late arrival in an old legend. The Homeric tradition is that two caskets of gifts are at the bestowal of Zeus, the one containing evils, the other goods. In giving, Zeus mingles these opposites, but sometimes presents evil alone.

According to the version of Hesiod, the casket of evils is closed, but the beautiful caprice, through prying curiosity no doubt, as befits a Greek Eve, removes the great lid from the vessel, and disperses these imprisoned banes, which are thus outpoured upon men. The legend is again somewhat confusing, for evils having become disseminated by being let loose, Hope, which is surely not an evil, is allowed to be bestowed upon man, which boon is accomplished, not by that sweet solace being permitted to fly forth and accompany the troop of ills, but by the lid being shut down again before Hope, in flitting forth, had passed the vessel's verge. The only quality in the box, which, fallacious though it may often be, can fairly be deemed a good quality, is not allowed to go forth.

To these confusions or contradictions may be added another, that Pandora would not have been led to open the box of baneful things if she had not already been endowed with a harmful quality called curiosity.

Finally, the conception of mankind as composed of males, lonely "Adams" living wretched without the boon of fire, then blessed with furtive fire, and afterwards dowered with woman and a box of woes, is contradictory to the story which makes the Golden Age the first period in the cosmogony according to Hesiod. If, however, we take the Golden Age to be a dim representation of a visionary pre-existence, and the evils let loose upon man to be such as are inseparable from existence on a corporeal plane, the inconsistency becomes less glaring.

In Prometheus is the conception of a benefactor to men standing midway between them and a jealous god,—a Zeus who, in the aspect which he wears in this story, is to be frustrated rather than trusted. He binds Prometheus in inextricable bonds, with galling chains, which are attached to a column, and incites against him an eagle which daily preys upon his liver; this organ, however, being immortal, makes up its loss by new growth during the night.

There is much that is attractive in the picture of Prometheus, the Titan who wrests from an unwilling deity (who in modern view might be deemed unwilling only because gifts have to be won before they can be truly held) the gift of fire, without which the progress of mankind would be impossible. Perhaps, in too modern a spirit, we might interpret the eagle's gnawing as the pain of the anxious taking thought which so eats into the joy element in the life of humanity, the gnawing fret of the state in which, as embodying Prometheus in ourselves,—

> "We look before and after,
> And pine for what is not."

Again, there is a chain that binds down this Titan counsellor: foresight is constrained and limited in life as we know it; worldly wisdom is content with very short views: in life beyond ours we may indulge hope that the Prometheus is more loosely chained, and allowed a more extended view of life. In Hesiod, at any rate, he is a strange, dim, heroic figure, who seems to afford us some misty mystic revelation of ourselves.

III.

Of the oracular poets before Homer we know so little that poetry distinctly objective may be claimed as the firstfruits of Greece. In Hesiod the grand careless naturalness of the old pagan ballad is crossed by a strain of care, and the free, almost reckless, ideal of the Homeric heroes is succeeded by a moralism quickened by the recognition of the irresistible, irreturnable buffets which proceed from no mortal foe, but from the heavy hands of worldly experience. If there were any young illusion that life is a jovial revel in which the day of the feast never fades into the day after, in Hesiod it is vanished.

After Homer, the broad pictures of artless life are seldom found in their primitive simplicity; the poetic mind has turned inwards, and in that introspection finds querulousness come to mingle with joy; or else is outside of what it depicts, and uses artifice to give a show of reality to its conceptions.

Few outside the student rank have much knowledge of the poets of the period immediately following Hesiod. Nevertheless, we are their debtors, for if to the Homeric age we are to ascribe the invention of a metre which is found not very suitable to our own language, we must credit to a poet who came afterwards, a metre, without which as a model, so familiar a home product as Gray's "Elegy," with probably some thousands more of English poems, would scarcely have been written in their present form. Archilochus, the poet in question, an unfortunate and exasperated man, lived in the earlier part of the seventh century before our era. As the story runs, a girl who was betrothed to him jilted him for a wealthier man, and the passionate wretch in return drove both her and her father to desperation by his stinging iambics.

His verse is more severe, less simply æsthetic, than that of the poets of a ruder period; his metrical specialty lies as much in a style of versification as in the iambic rhythm. Before his century, the continued ballad, or the epic, was the only kind of poetry, the heroic the only measure at all general. Soon after him sprang into existence a small crowd of minor bards.

The best-known poem by Archilochus is a brief and philosophic address to his soul, a piece of advice to himself that perhaps may seem old and trite to us, but if interpolated among the dramatic narratives of Homer, would suggest a comparatively modern mood. Several English translations have been made of the poem.

It is fair to a writer to give more than one translation of his work, if such exist. One may help to throw light upon him where another does not; and they are unlikely all to maim him in the same limb, so that some notion of him can be gained from the very clash of the paraphrases. The following are some of the versions of the little poem:—

> "My soul, my soul, by cares past all relief
>   Distracted sore, bear up! with manly breast,
> And dauntless mien, each fresh assault of grief
>   Encountering. By hostile weapons pressed,
> Stand firm. Let no unlooked-for triumph move
>   To empty exultation; no defeat
> Cast down. But still let moderation prove
>   Of life's uncertain cup the bitter and the sweet."
>   (COLONEL MURE.)

> "Spirit, thou spirit, like a troubled sea,
>   Ruffled with deep and hard calamity,
>   Sustain the shock: a daring heart oppose:
>   Stand firm, amidst the charging spears of foes:

If conquering, vaunt not in vain-glorious show :
If conquered, stoop not, prostrated in woe :
Moderate, in joy, rejoice ; in sorrow, mourn :
Muse on man's lot : be thine discreetly borne."

(ELTON.)

"O soul, my soul, though tost by care,
Whence chance of rest is hard and rare,
Keep up, protect thyself, and throw
A manly breast to meet thy foe.
Where worst his arms and ambush threat,
Possess thee, firm and fearless, yet ;
To no proud boasts, when victor, borne,
By no despair, when vanquished, torn ;
Joy not too loud when life is glad,
Nor sink too low when days seem bad,
But still preserve the proper mean
Each perilous extreme between."

(MAJOR R. G. MACGREGOR.)

" My soul, my soul, careworn, bereft of rest,
Arise ! and front the foe, with dauntless breast ;
Take thy firm stand amidst his fierce alarms ;
Secure, with inborn valour meet his arms.
Nor, conquering, mount vain-glory's glittering steep ;
Nor, conquered, yield, fall down at home, and weep.
Await the turns of life with duteous awe ;
Know, Revolution is great Nature's law."

(MARQUIS WELLESLEY.)

We have attempted a more doggedly literal version :—

O soul, O soul, mazed by resistless cares,
  Up ! stem thy woes by putting forth thy breast ;
When the spears menace, stand in sturdy rest.
If victory thine, show no inflated airs ;
  Come loss, then skulk not, making gloom thy guest ;
Vaunt not success, nor grieve 'neath evil's ban,
Too much, but learn what rhythm encloses man.

Two poets mark the former part of the seventh century before our era ; Alcman, the intense enthusiast for the beautiful, and father of erotic minstrelsy, and Terpandros, who brought elocutionary perfection to the recital of Homer's verses, and has the fame of having added three new strings to the lyre, which first had but four. His great invention, however, is that of characters for musical notation.

Alcman, if we may trust a fragment found in a tomb in Egypt, and edited by M. A. Canini, held to a simple poetical mythology and the old nature worship. "Love, Fate, and Force are of all daimons the most ancient. Deity makes man happy by the gift of the Graces. From the Divine ones comes vengeance also."

Alcman's epithet for memory is well worth making a mental note of; it is "that which has sight within the mind."

Before we pass from the elegiac poets, the fathers of the subjective school, to the division of the literary stream into lyric and gnome, a word is due to the fabulists. Archilochus is said to have woven fables into his verses, but the ancient school of fable is ranked under the familiar name of Æsop.

Æsop, it is said, was born a slave, but such was his talent that, following the mode of expressing moral instruction then prevailing in Attica, he was able to baffle the tyrannical projects of an autocrat by a fable, reminding us of the relations of Nathan and King David and the parable of the ewe lamb. But, according to report, his usual manner was to say pleasant things. A conversation with Solon is given in which Æsop exclaims, "Solon! either we must not speak to kings, or we must say what will please them." Solon replies, "We should either not speak to kings at all, or we should give them good advice, and speak truth." What a touchstone of politics lies in this essential difference!

The kind of fable associated with the name of Æsop can scarcely be described as religious; it constitutes a branch of literature adjoining rather than coincident with the loftier region of parable. It is as much the father of the modern novel, as in their several ways are the epic and the drama. But though, through being a teacher of worldly wisdom, fable may not take the highest rank as an instructor, yet it may not rightly be thrust outside the sphere of ethical instruments.

By the ironic flash in which it exposes human motives, by the stream of piercing light which it throws upon subtle phases of human conduct, rays which it is impossible to evade, fable may claim to be a divine agent in an equal degree with a sermon.

The chief use of the fable, however, seems to have been political. "The Belly and the Members" contains the essence of the best republicanism; "The Sick Lion and Fox" shows the subtlety of a tyrant and the wit of his victims; "The Eagle and the Fox" might have been a caution to some proud potentate that he was not so absolutely impregnable but that some unexpected attack might yet be made to reach him. "The Horse and the Stag" was deftly used to warn certain citizens who were debating whether they should assign a bodyguard to their ruler, by which they would have given him the power of bit and saddle over themselves. "The Old Man and Death," which is regarded as one of the oldest and most authentic fables of those that bear the name of Æsop, is a fine commentary on the difficulty felt by mortals of knowing what they want most: "A poor, feeble old man, who had crawled out into a neighbouring wood to gather a few sticks, had made up his bundle, and, laying it upon his shoulders, was trudging home with it. Wearied with age and the length of the way and the weight of his burden, he grew so faint and weak that he sank under it, and as he sat on the ground, called upon the death-deity to come once for all and ease him of his troubles. Death no sooner heard him than he came and demanded what was wanted. The poor old man, who little thought Death had been so near, and was frighted out of his senses by his visitor's grim aspect, answered him, trembling, That having, by some mishap, let fall his bundle of sticks, and being too infirm to get them by himself on his shoulder, he had made bold to call for help; which, indeed, was all he wanted." This fable is generally supposed to be referred to by Euripides in the *Alcestis*, and is a good example of the peculiar province of fable, which we have endeavoured to define. Certain fables of Æsop are also referred to by Aristophanes, Demosthenes, and Aristotle, and he is named by Herodotus. But since in Hesiod may be found a fable afterwards included with those bearing the name of Æsop, the question of actual authorship becomes very obscure.

It is pleasant to think of Socrates, as is recorded by Plato, versifying some of the fables of Æsop to relieve the tedium of prison.

The history of the Oracle, as it winds in and out of the history of Greece, has not yet been written. That in its uncorrupted period its influence was not unlike that of the prophetic voice among the Hebrews, we may fairly infer. The principle of it seems to have been the purification of the natural senses, so that they should open themselves to influx from a higher range of faculties. The following from the Anthology, entitled "Oracle of the Pythia," is a fine instance of the ancient symbolism of baptism :—

> " Enter the pure God's Temple sanctified
> In soul, with virgin water purified.
> One drop will cleanse the good ; the Ocean wave
> Suffices not the guilty soul to lave."
>
> (H. WELLESLEY, D.D.).

Our own version runs :—

> Be clean in soul, O stranger, and laved in vestal spring,
> The Deity's pure precincts if e'er thou wouldst draw nigh :
> One drop for worthy men suffices everything ;
> To cleanse the vile would make the ocean's streams run dry.

As, according to the Hebrew record, there were times when the written word was precious, or inspiration was lacking ; times when there was no mystic faculty to be found in any one, " no distinguishing open vision ; " so also there are times when poetry vanishes and prose takes its place. The soul is no longer led by eager feeling, but, as it were, requires shafts to support it, a whip to stimulate, and orderly rather than spontaneous work. There is a subsidence from bright and elevating emotion into calmness of thought. The gnomists of Greece show two sides, the one a wisdom which has not lost the spiritual glow, and so may truly be called philosophy; the other an intellectual frigidity degenerating into dogmatism, and so producing the peculiar arrogance of the sage.

The true seer is inspirationally gifted; the true poet is affectionately and humanly wise; entering upon regions less celestial than the one and less romantic than the other, we find a class claiming the title of sage, and busying themselves upon the evolution of good mundane truth in the practical form of maxim and apophthegm. A class of utmost political benefit if its sound sagacity can be worked into the basis of law; a class very dead if it miss alike the practical stimulus of real life and the ideal fervour of the earnest prophet. A sage evolving even with mathematical accuracy a sententious perfection of thought, shall be of less import to mankind than a man of but half his intellectual ability who, whatever he has to give, savours it with love's earnestness.

Synchronous with the gnomic period in Greece was the beginning of physical speculation and study; and we have to thank the men of that time for influences recognizable in very different provinces of life;—in wonders of physical science, in the undying wisdom of proverbial lore, and in the dulness of sermons.

Thales is regarded as the father of Greek philosophy, not because he introduced much that was truly majestic to the world, but because he made of physical research a study apart from that of mystic cosmogony, which perhaps had grown somewhat chaotic. Instead of the physical universe being regarded as a link in the chain of a great moral conception of life, its substances began to be scratched and laid bare to discover whether in them could not be found the true beginning of things. When Thales and his followers sought in water, fire, or air—substance rather than spirit—to find what had hitherto been sought in the power and purpose of Deity, they were beginning that terrible disruption which has broken the old homogeneous philosophy into the two discordant schools of theology and materialism.

The Seven Sages, according to Diogenes Laertius, a writer of the second or third century, were Thales, Solon, Periandros, Kleoboulos, Cheilon, Bias, Pittakos. But some of these must hold a doubtful place, or there were more than seven in this constellation of wisdom, for there are added also Anacharsis the Scythian, Myson, Pherekydes the Syrian, Epimenides the Cretan, and Peisistratos. It is curious to mark the differences of nationality amongst men professedly Greek, denoting that Greece was a sort of focus to the intellect and culture of the time, the centre not only to Asia Minor and the islands, but even to more distant regions. Thales himself, born at Miletus, is said by Herodotus to have been Phœnician by origin, and both Diogenes and Plutarch allege that he learned his philosophy in Egypt.

Thales being a natural philosopher, as well as a moralist, an astronomer, a geometrician, and a believer in the soul, may well have found himself with enough to occupy him to the full. Indeed, his pursuits so fully absorbed him that, as the story goes, when his mother urged him to marry, he replied that it was not yet the time. When years had passed, and his youth was gone, she pressed him again, and he changed his reply, now saying, "It is no longer the time."

Thales has been described as the first person who affirmed that the souls of men were immortal. This is an absurd position to assume with regard to an instinct which has manifested itself in one form or other in every nation known to history. That he affirmed the soul to be "moveless yet ever moving," as otherwise recorded, seems more probable.

A tripod was, it is said, drawn up in a net by some fishermen of Miletus, and became the cause of dispute. They sent to the Oracle at Delphi, and received as answer:—

> "You ask about the tripod, to whom you shall present it;
> It's for the wisest I reply, that fortune surely meant it."

It was accordingly given to Thales, but he passed it on to some one else, and eventually it came to Solon. He said that it was the Deity himself that was the first in wisdom, and so sent the tripod to Delphi again.

Among the recorded sayings of Thales may be found the following:—

"Beautify not the appearance, but be beautiful in practice." This is a literal rendering, and not so well polished by use as "Handsome is that handsome does."

"Be not enriched in an ill way." "Be not idle, even though you be rich." "If you rule, order yourself." "Be at one with yourself." "Have a care of life."

"All things are full of the gods." "What is the eldest of things? God, for he had no birth. . . . What is the wisest? Time, for what it has not found out already, it yet will find. What is the most common? Hope, for though one have nought else, this is near by. What is the most serviceable? Virtue, for this by right use makes other things of service. What is the most harmful? Vice, for there are few things which its presence does not harm. What is the strongest? Necessity, for it alone is unconquered. What is the easiest? That which is according to nature; since even in pleasures men often grow weary."

"An adulterer asked of him whether he should swear that he had not committed adultery. 'Is not perjury,' he replied, 'worse than adultery?'"

"He used to say that death differed nothing from life. 'Why, then,' said some one, 'do you not therefore die?' 'Because there is no difference,' he replied."

"When some one asked him whether a man's sin escapes the notice of the gods, 'No, not even his intent,' he replied."

"When asked how we may best and most justly live, he said, 'If that which we blame in others, we never do ourselves.'"

Some of these sayings seem very trite, but we must bear in mind the reason why they are so, that they have come down to us almost unconsciously to ourselves, and form part of our own proverbial tradition.

Certain truths seem to be so assured as to have become the inalienable property of man, and to be ready ever to take root in a new form. It would be difficult to discover which among the following most nearly represents the earliest or original expression:—

"Harm seek, harm find."

"Curses, like chickens, come home to roost."

"He that is an object of dread to many, let him dread many."

"Gains that are base are equal to a loss."

"Ill got, ill spent."

"He harms himself who plans another's harm; and evil counsel serves its author worst."

"If you have spoken ill, haply you will yourself hear worse."

"Such word as thou speakest shalt thou have to hearken to."

"Give, and it shall be given unto you."

"With what measure ye mete, it shall be measured unto you."

"They that took sword shall perish by sword."

"If any one is for captivity, into captivity he goes; if any one will slay with the sword, he must be slain with the sword."

"He that striketh with the sword shall be beaten with the scabbard."

"Hoist by his own petard."

"Pain comes after anger."

"He who smites will be smitten; he who shows rancour will find rancour; so likewise from reviling comes reviling, and to him who is angered comes anger."

"To evil sinks who evil thinks."

The result of the speculations of Thales, leaving the celestial contemplations of the ancient bards for the scrutiny of the obscurities of nature, was that all things had their origin in water; that earth was flat, and floated on the water: a kind of discovery that does not greatly enlarge or deepen our conceptions of life. The morals of Thales are much to be preferred to his science. However, as an astronomer, he progressed so far as to note the fact of the solstices and equinoxes: he could measure the height of a pyramid; and is said to have been able to predict the time of an eclipse within a year.

Solon, who divides with Thales the honour of being the first of the seven sages, is popularly known as a lawgiver rather than a poet or ethical teacher; but he was all three. As a lawgiver, he inclined to what would now be styled paternal government; he enjoined that if any one did not support his parents he should be accounted infamous; that the man who squandered his patrimony should be equally so accounted, and that the sluggard was liable to prosecution by any one who chose to impeach him, while an annual inquiry was permitted into the manner in which each citizen maintained himself. These were sharp, if wholesome enactments, but milder than Draco's code, which had assigned to idleness a penalty as severe as the punishment for murder. The laws of marriage Solon revised, so as to make that union so far as possible one of affection and tenderness, rather than a mercenary contract. His laws were evidently framed to protect the poorer citizens, and such was the wisdom with which they were adapted to the need, that they remained in full force for over four centuries.

Solon recognized the virtue of really conscientious compromise ; when asked if he had made the best laws for the people, he replied : The best that they would have accepted. He had great power moreover as an orator, charming a large audience by his verse. But, like every reformer, he found his plans disturbed by offended faction. Born in Salamis, he died self-exiled from Athens in Cyprus, at the age of eighty. Solon, though a poet, had a lack of imagination. Had he possessed this quality, he would have been able to discern and foster the good uses of the stage. As it was, he expressed his indignation at the dramatic representations of Thespis, sternly observing that if fiction (which he regarded as falsehood), were tolerated on the stage, untruth would find its way into the common occupations of men. Truly it does so find its way, but its impetus cannot be said to be due to any form of imaginative fiction.

Some of the words of Solon may well put us to the blush, for we can no more come up to their level in practice than we can transcend it in thought. "When he was asked how men could be most effectually deterred from injustice, he said, If those who are not being injured feel an equal indignation with those that are."

Among his maxims we may instance the following : "Nothing in excess." "Flee from such pleasure as brings forth sorrow." "Adhere to moral probity as more trustworthy than an oath." " Make friends slowly, but once made, do not hastily repudiate them." " If you expect others to give correct accounts, be ready to submit your own." " Counsel not what is pleasantest, but what is best." "Conjecture the obscure from the manifest." "Worship God, reverence parents, succour friends, envy no one, sustain the truth." "The end of every matter must be considered, in what direction it will tend." "Consider your honour as a gentleman of more weight than an oath." " I grow old finding ever much to learn."

Here is a truth which is as manifest now as it was in

Solon's day: "Laws are like cobwebs, which hold fast anything light and insignificant, but when anything greater comes in, it bursts through them and is gone." The following appeals to personal sympathy: "When he was shedding tears over a son that had died, he was told that he was effecting nothing. It is because I effect nothing, he said, that I weep."

The following seem to be based upon Solon's experience as a statesman:—

"In great matters it is difficult to please all.

"As much as iron can effect in war, so far can well-handled speech prevail in a state."

Another apophthegm shows one reason of his for the protection of the persons of the poor, namely, that the over-rich become injurious to the state. "Satiety," he said, "is generated by wealth, and insolence by satiety." He gives a caution too, which illustrates his experience of the rich: "Be not idle, even if thou art wealthy." The same saying is also ascribed to Thales.

The following is told of Solon: "When he was spat upon by some one and bore the affront with equanimity, and was blamed by some one else on that account, he replied, 'Are then fishers to abide being sprayed by the sea, to catch a koby, while I am not to be patient to endure the same, to be fisher of a man?'"

This resembles what was afterwards known as Stoicism, but with heart in it; it even transcends the triumph over externals enjoined by Confucius: "A scholar whose mind is set on truth and who is ashamed of bad clothes and bad food, is not fit to be discoursed with."

Solon said: "When thou hast learned how to obey, thou wilt know how to rule."

There is an unwritten tradition which supports this maxim: a boy at a public school who on his entrance is placed in a class above those junior forms, whose members fulfil the useful office of "fag" to the seniors, will be told by his comrades that when it comes to his turn to have "fags" of his own, he will not know how to treat them, through not having been a "fag" himself.

One of Solon's ordinances, in the inferences to which it leads, has been reduced by modern acuteness to something of a dilemma. His law is, "Whosoever shall put out the eye of him that hath but one, shall have both his own put out for so doing." What, the modern critic asks, shall be done in the reversed case, where a man having but one eye happens to thrust out one of his neighbour's two? Shall he lose his sole eye by way of retaliation? If so, he would suffer double penalty for his offence.

Pittakos was a general and lawgiver of Mitylene. In a very naïve manner he gives his experience of life: "It is a difficult thing to be a really good man." The same elevation of motive, which constitutes virtue, marks him that characterizes the others of the group of this period. "Forbear," he said, "to speak evil, not only of your friends but also of your enemies."

His sentence "The half is of more account than the whole," is paradoxical. Does it mean that moderation is better than surfeit, or self-control than licence, or that the first half of most things is the pleasantest part, or that a good abstract is better than a diffuse compilation? The saying is also found in Hesiod, and was probably an ancient proverb. It is generally believed to originate in the advice to accept a friendly compromise, rather than launch on the sea of litigation even to win everything.

An apophthegm attributed to Pittakos is also ascribed to Thales: "When asked whether the committer of an evil deed escapes the sight of the gods, he replied, No, nor even of an evil thought." One of his enactments was, that if a man committed an offence when drunk, he should be visited with double the ordinary penalty. Modern lawgivers who allow drunkenness to count as an excuse, must settle this point with Pittakos.

Bias was a barrister of an almost extinct school; he would only give his talent as a pleader to the side which seemed to him to be in the right. With this fact in view, the manner of his death is beautiful to contemplate. He had pleaded a cause when he was extremely old, and after he had finished speaking, he leaned back with his head on the bosom of his grandson. The business of the court went on; the advocate on the opposite side made his speech; the judges gave their decision in favour of the client of Bias; and when the court broke up, the old man was found to have passed out of mortal life unperceived.

All his apophthegms are in harmony with the upright and religious nature of the man. "Unhappy he who cannot bear unhappiness" is an epigrammatic saying of his. "Good men," he said, "are easily deceived;" but he was by no means without shrewdness himself, for this is an observation of his: "It is preferable to decide a question between enemies than between friends, for of the friends the one against whom it goes is sure to turn enemy, while of the enemies one is sure to become a friend."

"When he was asked which was the most pernicious amongst animals, he replied, 'Amongst wild ones the tyrant, amongst tame ones the flatterer.'"

"An impious man asked him, what kind of thing might piety be? He was silent. When the other asked him the cause of his silence, he said, 'I am silent, because you are asking of things with which you have no concern.'"

"He was asked what was the best counsellor, and replied, 'The moment itself.'"

Of Bias, Cicero tells the story, that when his native place Priene fell into the hands of the enemy, and the citizens were taking flight and carrying large quantities of their property with them, Bias was admonished by some one to do the same.

"But I am doing so," he replied, "for I am carrying with me all that I have."

Periandros was an absolute ruler, and might well have been omitted from the constellation of sages. Indeed it is wonderful how he should have been placed there, in face of the recorded but almost incompatible elements in his character—wisdom, cruelty, and wickedness. There is a question, however, whether there were not two of the name. The only noticeable saying among those ascribed to him, is that "When asked, what is the greatest thing in the smallest, he replied, 'A good soul-faculty in the body of a man.'"

Perhaps Periandros, like Solomon, saw the good, but found evil present with him. The saying ascribed to him, "Pleasures are mortal, virtues are immortal," may be that of a man who had tried the one, but only longed for the other.

Cheilon was a son of Sparta, and is a fair exemplar of the Spartan sobriety and manliness.

"The story runs that when he was asked by Æsop what Zeus was doing, he said, 'He is humbling the high and exalting the lowly.'" This story, by a mistranslation of the Greek, has been told the reverse way, that Cheilon asked the question of Æsop.

The world has altered little these twenty-five centuries. The same answer as Cheilon's might yet be made to the question, "What is difficult?—To keep silence upon secrets, to dispose well of leisure, and to be able to be bear unjust treatment."

"When Cheilon saw the corpse of a miser being carried forth, he said, This fellow lived a lifeless life, and has left behind his life for others."

How easy it seems, how difficult it is, to conform in spirit and in truth to the following maxim of Cheilon: "To the banquets of friends come slowly, but to their misfortunes with speed."

Cheilon was evidently a man of foresight, consideration,

and patience. His ideal was of virtue, and was a sound one; many a lofty profession of religion, if bared to its real basis, would show a less worthy range of motives. Cheilon taught: "To prefer punishment to disgraceful gain; for the one is painful but once, but the other for one's whole life." "Not to laugh at a person in misfortune." "If one is strong, to be also merciful, so that one's neighbours may respect one rather than fear one." "Not to dislike divination." "To obey the laws." "To love quiet."

There are few relics of Kleoboulos, and some of those, such as "Go more quickly to the misfortunes of friends than to their good fortunes," seem confused with the sayings of other sages. "What you hate, do not to another" is his approximation to the standard of the golden rule. "Every prudent and wise man," says Kleoboulos, "hates a lie."

He may be claimed as an early supporter of the education of women. "He used to say that daughters should be given in marriage when girls in age, but women in sense, as indicating that even girls ought to be well educated."

Anacharsis was of royal birth and of a Scythian father, his mother being Greek. He was brought up to know the language of either parent. He chose the study of wisdom in preference to wealth and position, and in the time of Solon came to Athens, where he spent his time in learning, and was initiated into the Eleusinian mysteries. This honour was unique for a barbarian, and had such weight with him as to make him almost forget his own country. But when his friend Solon died, he returned.

One of the sayings of Anacharsis might be the origin of Ruskin's expression, "necessary play," or the phrase, "recreation a religious duty;" he says: "You must play, in order to do serious work." "When asked for what cause men are always unhappy, he replied, 'Because they are unhappy not only about the ills of their own, but also about the good things of others.'"

The seventh and sixth centuries before our era are marked by an effervescence of ethical wisdom; one country perhaps communicating the impulse to another, for a comparison of dates and histories points to a general revival of religious thought as taking place about this period. The sages of our race seem ever to have dowered us with fully as much wise lore as we can absorb or make a good use of. In Greece, wisdom was so plentiful, that after seven had been fixed upon as a perfect number of sages, it was found difficult to confine those who deserved the honour within the limits of it. They now mostly seem like lesser lights showing the way to the philosophic luminary Pythagoras.

One marked as *proxime accessit* to the constellation of sages is Epimenides, whose strange history has been exposed to doubt, apparently on the ground that he was of Crete, and the Cretans were liars.

Epimenides is the original of Rip Van Winkle, whom Washington Irving and Jefferson have made so fabulously and dramatically real to us. It is told of Epimenides that once, when he was sent by his father into the fields to look for a sheep, he at midday turned out of the road, and lay down in a cave and fell asleep. Whether the cave was impregnated with gas such as helped the priestesses of the oracle into their trance, tradition does not say; but Epimenides slept for seven-and-fifty years. It is curious to think of this in connection with the fact that at the present day scientific theories should be put forward upon the possibility of prolonged suspension of animation by refrigeration, desiccation or otherwise. When we think of the various animals that hibernate, and of those that are dormant for indefinite periods, we may reasonably allow that the suspension of physical functions on the part of a human being of exceptional characteristics may, however extraordinary, be yet an occurrence on the believable side of the marvellous. When Epimenides awoke, he went on looking for the stray sheep, thinking he had been taking a brief noonday nap; but, as he could not find that long defunct animal, he went back through the field, where he found everything changed, and the estate in another person's possession. In great perplexity he came back again to the city, and, as he was going into his own house, he met certain folk who inquired of him who he was. At last he found his younger brother, who had now become an old man, and from him he learned all the truth.

The theory must have been, that such a sleep betokened the prophetic faculty, and that Epimenides had been a visitor to the Olympian halls while his body lay sealed from his use; for so soon as he succeeded in identifying himself, he became regarded as a person especially beloved by the gods. He was reputed, as K. O. Müller gathers from the ancient sources of information, "A man of a sacred and marvellous nature, who was brought up by the nymphs, and whose soul quitted his body as long and as often as it pleased; according to the opinion of Plato and other ancients, his mind had a prophetic and inspired sense of divine things."

The average commentator, however, unable to conceive of a prophet not of the Hebrews, expresses himself thus about Epimenides: "All that is credible about him is, that he was a man of superior talents, who pretended to intercourse with the gods; and, to support his pretensions, lived in retirement on the spontaneous productions of the earth, and practised arts of imposture; perhaps in his hours of pretended inspiration had the art of appearing totally insensible and entranced, easily mistaken by ignorant spectators for a power of dismissing and recalling his spirit." It is instructive to compare with this the view usually taken of the prophetic ecstasy when it happens to have fallen upon a Hebrew. Stochius, an expositor of a few centuries ago, describes the state as "A sacred ecstasy, or rapture of the mind out of itself, when, the use of external senses being suspended, God reveals something in a peculiar manner to prophets and apostles, who are then taken or transported out of themselves." And a writer in "Kitto's Cyclopædia" follows with the note that "the same idea is intimated in the English word trance, from the Latin *transitus*, the state of being carried out of one's self . . . the nearest approach we can make to such a state, is that in which our mind is so occupied in the contemplation of an object as to lose entirely the consciousness of the body—a state in which the highest order of ideas, whether belonging to the judgment or imagination, is undoubtedly attained."

Are we, then, to refuse Epimenides a place "among the prophets," and not to allow it as possible that Greek wisdom, as all truly spiritual wisdom, may be drawn secretly from supernal worlds, as well as acquired by deductions from the commonplaces of materialized life?

Epimenides is credited with a considerable bulk of literary work; the titles of the subjects which he treated are, however, all that remain to us in this department. They are evidence of his mystical bent: he wrote on Minos,[*] the fabled Cretan lawgiver, who, like himself, is said to have loved retirement in a cave, wherein each time he stayed there a new law was communicated to him by Zeus. With Zeus he was, as Clement of Alexandria reads the tradition, as a familiar friend, discoursing with him after the manner in which Jehovah is said to have once conversed with Moses, "as one speaking with his friend." The work treats also of Rhadamanthus, to whom a Cretan birthplace is given, a king whom legend relates to have become one of the judges of Hades, and whose name is now traced back to that of the Egyptian Deity of the Amenti, the regions of the unseen. A poetic theogony also is ascribed to Epimenides, and a treatise of his *Of Oracles and Responses* is referred to by Jerome, and is supposed to be the work from which quotation is made in Paul's Epistle to Titus (i. 12).

---

[*] *Cf.* Egyptian "Men," Hindu "Menu." The root still lives in the English word "mind."

The history of Epimenides is not without evidences of other than literary activity. When the Athenians about 597 B.C. were in a state of discord and disorder, and were troubled by certain sacrilegious acts which had occurred, and the Delphic priestess had enjoined upon them to purify their city, they invited the Cretan prophet and sage to come and take means to rid them of the pollution. His ministrations allayed the despondency of the people, and they offered their benefactor a talent of gold, but he refused money and accepted instead a little branch of the sacred olive tree which grew on the Acropolis. He became acquainted with Solon, whom he is said to have privately instructed in the proper methods for the regulation of the Athenian Commonwealth. Another story is, that he was assisted by Solon, from which two accounts we may perhaps fairly infer that each learned from the other, as one great man cannot but learn from another. Plutarch states that Epimenides was accounted one of the Seven Sages by those who would not admit Periandros into the number.

There was high culture in Greece even at the early date of Epimenides, a hundred years before the time of the first great dramatist. The wit and poetry combats, as well as athletic contests, of the Olympian games, had been long established; and there was friendship with Egypt, and colonization there.

It was still the heroic age; national life had scarcely built itself up in Greece out of clan and family life; the village patriarchal household and the city commune were the simple forms of society, and the kindly laws of hospitality shed a grand nobility over the rudeness of the time.

As civic life expanded, caste became more marked, and the people of the Attic states were divided into classes whose provinces were severally war, agriculture, the shepherd's trade, and handicraft; while there were also classes of serfs attached to the soil, which they held by payment of rent, mostly in kind and according to their status, to the classes in power.

Of whatever degrees the social scale was formed, Greek life extended itself with rapid growth, until, half a millennium before our era, the Mediterranean was a sort of Hellenic lake, adorned with the manifold results of the work of the artist, the sage, and the artificer: forms of beauty in stone, metal, pottery, and in colour; forms of strength in law, order, and government; forms of mental art embodying inner glow and healthfulness in poetry and philosophy; results of well-trained labour in the harbour, the vessel, the temple, and the house. Frequent wars, it is true, there were, but rarely without some flash of virtue or stainless honour in them redeeming the Greek faults of deceit and corruption.

Pherekydes has been cited as one of the earliest Greeks who wrote in prose, and as having been a teacher of Pythagoras. A number of verified predictions are attributed to him. As to his doctrines, some among ancient writers suppose that they were derived from the sacred books of the Phœnicians; others that he studied in Egypt, and learned there the symbolical method. These beliefs at least show that in the days before thoughts were circulated by printing it was deemed no marvel for the lore of one country to penetrate and influence another.

Anaximandros is one of that group of Greek philosophers who had ceased to look to interior, occult, or oracular revelations for the secrets of the laws of life, and searched instead into the facts of the external world. Both methods must result in the same story where they meet; spiritual explanations are liable to become spoiled and confused in passage through unperceptive minds; external details are more generally comprehensible, but seem to lead the mind a long way round before it can find a direct path through them to the secrets of the universe.

Anaximandros, whom Cicero styles the fellow-countryman and crony of Thales, but who is otherwise regarded as rather his disciple and successor, avoided the pitfalls of ascribing to water, air, or fire the source and origin of life, and took refuge in infinity as the starting-point and head of all things. Infinity, not in the sense of exhaustlessness of pervading Deity, but as denoting the unlimited range of physical nature, out of which all things visible come into being, and into which they fall by decay. Worlds, he thought, spring out innumerable in youth from that mighty bosom, and into it fall again, converted once more to that enduring seminal element which itself changes not, however mutable its developments. The earth, he supposed, was a globe, placed midmost the "vasty deep" as a centre; the moon, he had learned, shone by a false light, borrowing her splendour from the sun. The sun was so vast as to be at least no smaller than the earth, and was composed of the purest fire.

No ignoble conception this of the physical framework of the universe; inadequate only, if it should seek to supplant the ethical consciousness of the meaning and divineness of life. There are two attempted solutions of the problem of human existence: man's nature is matter's supreme secretion; or he is a spiritual entity, fitting itself with the best suit of plasm that is available, and making of it not only clothing fit for the terrestrial life, but even an individualized shape and beauty, and an instrument for many purposes and passions. Anaximandros shows his preference for the former blunt hypothesis, when he defines the origin of animal life as taking place in moisture, the creatures being covered with prickly coats, which later are ruptured, when the animals pass to existence in a drier state, and man develops from them; his proof being that other animals speedily find pasture for themselves, while man, for a lengthened period from his birth, requires constant nursing. He could not therefore have been kept alive in the beginning of things, and must be the descendant of fishes, which, like whales, must have learned to suckle their young before being cast upon the shore to learn dry-land existence.

This sage also taught the use of a sundial, and the meaning of the phases of the moon.

Anaximandros is accounted the first who made public a concise statement of his views and opinions upon the nature of things, a course which had been foreign to the etiquette of the time. Previously, these speculations were reserved for private discussion amongst the sages, or formed the stock-in-trade of the schools and the matter of the oral tradition.

The following may be quoted from the very few fragments that remain of the works of Anaximandros: "All things that exist are either the beginning, or derived from the beginning; of the infinite however there is no beginning, for otherwise it would have a termination. It is, moreover, uncreate and incorruptible, by reason of being the beginning; for that which comes into being must needs come to ending, and termination is a property of all the corruptible."

Anaximenes, a reputed disciple of Anaximandros, instead of finding the primordial something in the unnamed infinite, took it to reside in eternal, infinite air. Our soul, because it is air, guards and rules us, and the whole universe is begirt by spirit and air. Limitless in its kind, this creative air is bounded by such things as are produced of it. All things are made of air that is become dense, or made rare. The gods he regarded not as the authors of air, but as themselves sprung from it.

Anaxagoras was a sage of an uncompromising stamp. Of noble birth, he relinquished his patrimony to travel in pursuit of knowledge, and when he returned from his wanderings and found his possessions lying waste, he said, "I should not have been safe myself if those had not perished." When his relations blamed him for neglect of his estate, he replied, "Why, then, do you not take care of it?" When he had made his final choice to give up the cares of worldly life, and to devote himself to philosophic study, and had decided to leave even politics to others whose minds were more decidedly bent upon busy affairs, he was reproached for having no affection for his country. His reply shows how large his estate and province was, and how he felt himself to be a member of a humanity that reaches beyond the markets of commodities and the arenas of power. He said, pointing the while up to heaven as the symbol of that life of ours that stretches beyond the merely mundane, "Be silent, for I have the greatest affection for my country." We must be careful not to confound a saying like this with the same words if uttered to-day. When said, it might have come fresh from the deep well of profound conviction. Now, it would be borrowed, and possibly have degenerated into a merely sentimental and superficial, or canting expression. Real feeling, true emotion, ever finds a perennial freshness of speech.

Anaxagoras came to Athens when a young man, and studied and taught there for a long period, numbering among his hearers Pericles, Socrates, and Euripides.

In natural philosophy the doctrines are ascribed to him, that wind is due to local rarefaction of air by the sun; that the rainbow is the effect of the reflection of solar rays from a rain cloud; that the moon is an opaque body, illumined by the sun; and that the primary elements of everything were founded on similarity of parts, the beginning of any substance being a mingling or cohesion, the end a separation, of parts. He practised astronomy, calculated eclipses, travelled into cultured Egypt for improvement, and used to say that he preferred a grain of wisdom to heaps of gold.

In metaphysical philosophy he abandoned the petty systems of his predecessors, and instead of regarding some elementary form of matter as the origin of the universe, he taught that mind was the principle of motion, and that Supreme Intelligence, distinct from the visible world, imparted form and order to what would otherwise be the chaos of nature.

Strange to say, these innovations afforded the Athenians

a pretext for indicting Anaxagoras on the ground of impiety, the very quality that he would seem to have been trampling upon. There was, however, probably the bias of political faction underneath the impeachment, owing to the connection of Anaxagoras with Pericles, who belonged to a definite political party. When news was brought him of his condemnation to death, and at the same time, as with Job, the news arrived of the death of his children, he said, " Nature has long since pronounced the same condemnation on both them and me ; " and of his children he specially said, " I knew that I had become the father of mortals."

When he was thrown into prison for his opinions, and was awaiting judgment, Pericles is alleged to have come forward and challenged accusation against him respecting his course of life—an interesting example of discrimination between freedom of thought and licence of life.

Anaxagoras is said to have been the first to read the Homeric poems, not as the literal accounts of heroes which they seem to be, but as allegoric pictures, not only of virtue and justice, but of the processes and vestiges of order in nature. When he was dying, the governors of the city asked him what he would like to have done for him, and he replied begging the favour that they would keep the anniversary of his death as a play day for children. This happy suggestion was followed, and the *Anaxagoria* were held as a festival of recreation.

Something of his doctrines we may gather from fragments. He regarded plants as possessed of soul or intelligence after their kind, as beings endowed with life.

Sleep, he taught, was an affection, not of the soul, but of the body.

" Everything but mind contains parts of universal matter ; mind itself is infinite and its own master, and is combined with nothing, but alone is itself of itself."

What are left of his teachings are mostly physical speculations: we turn therefore to such suggestive sayings of his as that uttered when he saw the prodigious tomb of Mausolus, "A costly tomb is an image of a petrified estate."

When death in a foreign land was spoken of, as a matter of grief, he made comfort of the fact that, "The road to the other side of the grave is the same from every place." The same thought is given in the Anthology, as of uncertain authorship: "The road down to Hades is straight, whether you go from Athens or depart from Meroë, a corpse. Let it not vex you that you have died at a distance from your country. There is one wind that carries you from everywhere to Hades." There is not a very dissimilar epigram attributed to Plato, referring to the position of the underworld.

Xenophanes, a philosophic writer in hexametric verse and elegiac couplets, who lived about the close of the sixth century before our era, was iconoclastic, a great protestant against the popular religion, defaced as no doubt it was by polytheistic corruptions. His objections to accepting the Olympian deities as perfect divine ideals are reasonable and true:

"Sad things are ascribed to the gods by Homer and Hesiod, such as would be shame and disgrace among men; adulteries, deceits, thefts, and iniquities."

His own ideal is a higher one, holding "One God, among gods and man supreme, neither in body nor spirit like mortals."

He protests against anthropomorphism. His conception of deity is rather of an immovable principle of physical life than a spiritual source of love. A sort of blue infinite vault was God, a spherical form, remaining in the same state, requiring never to move from place to place, moving all things without effort of mind. This universal being could see and hear, but was without the very symbol of life, respiration; and was in all its parts intellect and wisdom and eternity. But Xenophanes said, "Surely never hath been, nor will be, a mortal well knowing such matters I treat, of the gods and the all. Though by chance he may utter the true and the perfect, it is not of knowledge; opinion presides over all things."

The argument against taking the finite human form as a representation of deity is cogently put, as follows:—

"Mortals opine that gods are created like unto themselves, and endowed with perception, voice, and form like their own. If oxen or lions had hands, whereby they could depict and do works like men, horses would portray forms of gods like horses, oxen like oxen, each making representations of bodies just like their own."

Perhaps the criticisms of Xenophanes were rather frigidly intellectual; a lover of the poetic deity of the rainbow might rebel against being told he must confine himself to the scientific fact—

"That which men call Iris, it is but a cloud,
In purple and crimson, and pallor of green."

Xenophanes possessed a spice of humour; when Empedokles said to him that the wise man was undiscoverable, he replied, "Very likely, for it takes a wise man to discover a wise man."

G. H. Lewes—who had not passed away when the following quotation was made from his work on philosophy—gives a rather enthusiastic account of Xenophanes:—

"He wandered over Sicily as a rhapsodist. . . . He lived poor, and died poor. But he could dispense with riches, having within him treasures inexhaustible: his soul was absorbed in the contemplation of grand ideas, and his vocation was the poetical expression of those ideas. He had no pity for the idle and luxurious superstitions of his time; he had no tolerance for the legends of Homer, defaced as they were by the errors of polytheism. He, a poet, was fierce in the combat he perpetually waged with the first of poets—not from petty envy, not from petty ignorance, but from the deep sincerity and enthusiasm of reverence. He who believed in one God, supreme in power, goodness, and intelligence, could not witness without pain the degradation of the Divine in the common religion. Alive to the poetic beauty of the Homeric fables, he was also keenly alive to their religious falsehood."

There may be very different reasons why philosophers are sometimes obscure. A very obvious cause is that their thought does not always run clear : but this will not account for studied obscurity, parabolism, or paradox. It is no doubt a fact that a great thought, if passed through a narrow and vulgar mind, is shorn of its noble proportions, clouded over as to its deepest meanings, dwarfed, distorted and made commonplace. It is possible to imagine a thinker so disgusted at seeing the far-flying birds of his mind taken hold of by rude hands, and set to strut about with clipped wings in the guise of farm-yard fowls, that he should prefer to give them no feet by which to alight among the dwelling places of the grovelling multitude. Leaving to others to be, if they will, the "wing of unwandering birds," he makes straight for the ether, clearing a glorious track in the full delight of unchecked, unlimited energy, and leaving to him to follow who can dare to fly.

Upon Herakleitos was bestowed the nickname of the "dark master," by men of his own race ; and, as symbolism is in part conventional, and dependent like language itself upon a concurrence of acceptation, we may expect it to be difficult to penetrate to the inner secret of his utterances now.

Herakleitos was pre-eminently an idealist, so far unsuited to grapple with practical life and its compromises, so far from being able to share the satisfaction with which the worse than even the second-best is greeted in the world, that the contemplation of the lives of men inspired him with sadness, and even made him weep. He must also have fallen into some degree of pessimism, for, when requested to make laws for the inhabitants of his native city Ephesus, he refused on the ground that the city was already committed to a polity, and that an altogether vicious one. He had probably seen places and emoluments played for under the guise of policy in the game of worldly life, and, as the story runs, after his refusal to make laws, he retired with some children and began to play at dice with them. When the townsmen came round him, he said, "Wherefore marvel you, folk of the basest? Is it not better to do this, than to turn to public affairs along with you?"

Of an ancient royal house, to which belonged the founder of Ephesus, he relinquished to his brother all his titles and privileges, retaining to himself thus the independence of a lofty spirit, as the truest and best of royal prerogatives.

His satire is of a scathing kind. The Ephesians had banished Hermodoros, a friend of his, because his life and example filled them with shame, and they desired to be all on a footing of equality in profligacy of conduct. Herakleitos said, "The Ephesians deserve to be all put to death in their prime, and those who are younger to be banished,—such of them as have thrust out Hermodoros, the best man among them, with the words, Let none of us be pre-eminently good, and if any one be so, let it be elsewhere and among other persons."

The manifest intention of Herakleitos so to express himself that only those should penetrate the enigma of his style who could grasp the fulness of his thought, brought its natural consequence in the jealous indignation of those who could not comprehend him. The vulgar mind loves to believe that it possesses all things, and shades off all that is beyond its apprehension into a twilight of obscurity and unimportance. When a sage presents a casket as containing a pearl that only a sage can discover, the vulgar mind receives an affront —something is being concealed from it. The critics revenged themselves on Herakleitos by telling absurd stories about him, and attacking him with nicknames and opprobrious epithets.

Our philosopher, at war with the compromising world, which even his tears could not inspire with an effort towards a higher standard, appears to have become something of a misanthrope. His place of residence was a mountainous retreat, his food the grasses and plants of the district; meditation became his life. Unfortunately, such a manner of existence brought him to a dropsy, of which it is not certain whether he died or no. He is said to have humorously asked the physicians, in reference to his complaint, whether they could bring a drought out of wet weather; and to have shut himself up in a shippen and covered his body with the droppings, forestalling, in his effort to produce perspiration, the doctrine of modern advocates of hot-air bathing.

Herakleitos must have found his way to deeper springs of life than his worldly minded compatriots knew of to make him express a thought thus: "Abundant learning does not form the mind, . . . there is one wisdom, which consists in knowing that inner will which is able to regulate everything throughout all."

To the political intriguer, the wire-puller of a corrupted power, what interest was there likely to be in such a conception of the divine order which underlies all things, although often so deeply overlaid with confusion, or in the most philosophical dream of a perfect standard, to be approximated to as closely as the great poet makes idea and form correspond? What wonder that the writings of Herakleitos remained long in the Temple of Diana, where they were deposited, until an interpreter came? And then it was said of the book that one needed to be a pearl diver not to be drowned in it. A sect, however, arose in consequence of the reputation it achieved, and bore the name of the author. Of his style it is said, "Sometimes in his treatise he expresses himself with brilliancy and clearness, so that the most stupid can easily understand and receive an elevation of soul; while his conciseness and weighty power of speech are incomparable!"

We need not dwell upon the cosmogonical doctrines of Herakleitos. He regarded a primeval fiery force as the mainspring of all life by its intrinsic power, and all things as in motion by actions and reactions through its energy. This primary fire is deity, and all existing things are harmonized and made to agree together by opposite tendencies. War or discord is the parent of life with its vicissitudes, peace or concord leads to a conflagration which terminates a cycle; and either is alike in harmony with fate.

We may judge what Greece owed to her philosophers by calculating the steadying effect upon a rude people of such maxims as this: "The people ought to fight for law as for their city wall."

But no doubt the style of Herakleitos was too fine for the comprehension of the generality, as, for instance, when he says: "Whatever is said in the presence of listeners without comprehension, is a testimony that people can be present and absent at once."

Some minds have an inability to appreciate metaphor. In the year of grace 1885, a man applies to a Clerkenwell magistrate for protection, "going in fear of his life," because he had received a letter: "I give you fair warning that if I find you aspersing my character in any way; if you are worth powder and shot, I will make you pay for it."

The following brings before us the unworldly recluse gazing on the passions of men, as something outside himself: "Those who search for gold dig a great deal of soil, and find merely a little metal."

The symbolic style seems to be natural to unearthly communications all the world over. Herakleitos recognizes the genius of parable when he says: "The king whose oracle is in Delphi, neither speaks out, nor conceals, but gives significant indications."

In the following passages is much suggestiveness:—

"No one twice can step into the selfsame stream, or twice

catch mortal nature in one particular state; but the sharpness and fleetness of change is dispersing and again gathering it together, or rather there is no former or latter [backwards or forwards, upstream or downstream], but simultaneously it forms and falls away, approaches and recedes. Wherefore, that which is born of it never arrives at a consummation in absolute existence, because of the fact that creation never either leaves off or stands still."

"Though men step into the selfsame rivers, the waters stream onward different and different again."

"The way above and below is one."

The sense of Herakleitos of an essential stability of things, such as makes the circumstances of an actual moment a detail only, is humorously manifested as follows: "If all things that are, into smoke were turned, noses at least would sniff what was burned." A difficulty, however, must arise with regard to the survival of the noses in a day in which "the heavens shall pass away with a great noise, and the elements shall melt with fervent heat." This, however, Herakleitos has met by urging that souls are possessed of scent and perception in Hades.

The idea of Herakleitos of a general conflagration, a cyclic conception of purification and resurrection, seems to be akin to early Aryan doctrines; it made his apophthegms in favour with Clement of Alexandria and others of the Gnostic school, who are fond of quoting him. The following are mystical enough :—

"Death means such things as we see when up and awake; dream such as we see when asleep."

"Both life and death are in our life and in our death."

"Gods are mortal and men immortal, in the sense of living the others' death and dying the others' life."

"There await dead men such things as they neither hope nor think."

Bacon quotes with favour a maxim from Herakleitos, of which the following passages are the original:—

"When a man is drunk, he is led by a beardless boy, tottering, and does not know whither he is going, having a wet soul."

"The dry light is the best soul, kindling fire throughout the body, as lightning through a cloud."

There is a reminiscence of these words of Herakleitos in Clement of Alexandria, when he says (Pædag., ii. 2): "Thus shall our soul be pure and dry and luminous; for the dry soul is the wisest light and the best, and thus, too, it is fit for contemplation, and is not humid with the exhalations that rise from wine and form a mass like a cloud."

The following opens out deep thought: there is no morality in nature, but in that which wields nature: "The merely human character is without essential morals, but the divine possesses them."

Here, again, is the peculiar obscurity of Herakleitos:—

"Man at night kindles a light for himself; but at his death is quenched. While he is alive he touches upon one who is dead, in his sleep; as awake, if he shuts his eyes he touches upon one who is asleep."

"A foolish man heard from a spirit (daimon), just in the same manner as a child from a man." That is, one may presume, without comprehension.

"Herakleitos, as having effected something great and holy, said: I have sought the meaning of myself, and that 'know thyself' would seem to be the divinest thing in the literature of Delphi."

"Listening not to me, but to reason, it is wise to allow that all are the development of one."

"They know not how that which differs agrees with itself; just as there is a contrary harmony of lyre and bow."

"Poor witnesses unto men are the eyes and ears of those who have barbarous souls." In other words, the senses are fallible, unless a reasonable mind is acting behind them to steady them.

"All things are full of souls and spirits (daimons)."

We have quoted but few of the fragments of Herakleitos, for some seem imperfectly recorded, and are indeed difficult to follow. And the modern mind is not quite so readily appreciative and charitable as Euripides is said to have been, when, in replying to the question what he thought of the dark master's works, he said that what he understood was noble, and he thought that even what he failed to understand was noble also.

An epigram which Diogenes Laertius quotes as having been written upon him is as follows:—

> "Be not too hasty skimming o'er the book
> Of Herakleitos; 'tis a difficult road,
> For mist is there, and darkness hard to pierce,
> But if you have a guide who knows his system,
> Then everything is clearer than the sun."

The name of Parmenides reminds us that in our brief review of Greek wisdom-lovers we are reaching the age of Pythagoras, who, however, is of too large a presence to include in a group and must occupy a chapter to himself. Parmenides, as a youth, heard the words of old Xenophanes, but it was to the Pythagoreans that he afterwards became addicted. He was of noble family and of great wealth, living in splendour; and disposed towards a political career; but the society of two poor and virtuous Pythagoreans led him to withdraw to some extent from public life, and to embrace the tranquil career of the seeker after wisdom. To one of these gentle students he felt so grateful for his own introduction to the sacred recesses of philosophy, that when Diochartes, the Pythagorean, died, Parmenides erected to his memory a shrine, such as was dedicated to heroes. The withdrawal of Parmenides from political labours was not absolute; certain laws which he made for his native town of Elea were so good that the magistrates annually swore in the citizens to the observance of them. These were days when philosophy was young in the districts to which Greece was a centre, and it was a grateful task, when it was not a dangerous one, to sow the seeds of knowledge, which thinker after thinker was struggling to effect wherever circumstances afforded opportunity, introducing to the remotest cities higher ideals of life and the virtues of civilized order.

Parmenides wrote of philosophy in verse, which seems not its proper vehicle, for abstract thought and the picturesque imagery of poetic visions do not readily come into unity. Prose writing was, however, not yet very common in Greece, and it was not until afterwards that poetry and prose occupied well-marked provinces, the lyrist, the idyllist and the dramatist occupying the one, and the historian and the philosopher the other.

The muse of Parmenides thus addresses him :—

"O boy, by immortal consorts of thy chariot companied,
On horses that bear thee drawing nigh to our home,
Good cheer, if it be not ill fate forth sent thee to wander
This way (for 'tis far from the worn tracks of mortals);
But justice and right. Thou hast need to learn all things,
Both precision of heart for truth that is full of persuasion,
And mortal opinions, wherein a true faith is not found.
But at any rate learn this much, how things in their seeming
Thou must warily prove, by finding all thoroughfares through them.

"Come now, I will tell thee, thou giving good ear to my word,
What ways of enquiry alone there are to be minded of :
The one, the existence, and how non-existence exists not,
The way of persuasion, for truth stands close on the threshold ;
The other,—there is and there must be a thing of nonentity ;
I tell it thee plainly, this is an incredible road ;
For that which is not, neither mind nor can word e'er attain it,
It cannot be reached. To think and to be are identical."

Ambiguous, hesitating mortals with fluctuating minds, who confuse being and not being, and whose way is doubtful and retrograde, these the sage is to avoid :—

"'Tis to me of no personal moment,
    Whence I spring, being bound to get thither again."

Of multiplex science he is also to beware, the plying of sightless eyes, deaf ears, and a tongue ; but is to judge by reason. But Parmenides lands himself in merely metaphysical subtleties, such as, " How can be hereafter a future existence, or how should there have been existence before ? If there were, it is not in being, nor is it in being if it is but to be in the future: so its birth is destroyed, and its death incredible. . . . Being is not without end, nor is it lacking of aught, for, if it were, it would lack all things."

A Daimon governs the universe, but with Parmenides the word means no more than Fate, such as forces man to woman and woman to man ; he seems to have studied the physical world and to have found therein all of what he calls being, intellect the power of it, and all else nonentity, and therefore only an emptiness, and to be let alone. Things merely absent, however, are not nonentity, and can be made present in the mind and held there firmly for contemplation.

Epicharmos unites the apparently not very congruous qualifications of Pythagorean philosopher and comic poet. He is even credited with being the inventor of comedy, that is, of the Greek development of comedy. He is said to have given to comedy a dignified and poetic form, and to have raised it from mere *bon-mots* and *facetiæ* to something nearer the level of mind in which a wise man might take delight. In other words, he instituted high comedy, as opposed to low. The history of his turning to it is interesting. He believed that of all disciplinary pursuits philosophy was the queen, the sole master of life and expeller of vices. But the ruling despot of the day stood in the way of public profession of the Pythagorean tenets, so Epicharmos brought his poetic faculty to his aid, and took to the stage as a means for bringing the teachings of his master in philosophy before the world with safety. In framing his comedies, he took care to open out in fabling manner the causes of good and evil, and to lay bare the manners and minds of men even to their most secret recesses, and this in a mode in which the excellence of the doctrine spoke for itself, and the charm of the style softened the gravity of the utterance.

Giving something to please the senses and tickle the humour of men, he at the same time insinuated an appeal to the eyes of the mind. As he says—

"Mind sees, mind hears, all else is deaf and blind."

His humorous description of going home from a banquet is worthy of Hogarth's pencil, as well as his tirade against a chattering extravagant wife, whom he describes as "an ornamental misfortune."

He reminds us of the satire of the Hebrew Isaiah of the Return, when he says in one of his comedies—

"From any log may be made both a dog-collar and a god."

We may imagine the character in the comedy who should plausibly urge: "A mortal must give his mind to mortal things, not to immortal;" and a play written to illustrate the maxim, "His disposition is man's good daimon and his bad," might be discovered, and found to be not unlike Macbeth.

The following might have been meant to apply to all morbid people, pessimists and proselytizing crotchet-mongers :—

"You are no lover of your species,
You have a disease, and are glad when you give it."

Some of Shakespeare's broad, fearless, and equal acceptance of real life and ghostly life may be seen in the following :—

"It was compounded, then dissolved away,
And thither whence it came, it went again,
Earth unto earth, and spirit up on high,
Which is there grievous of these facts ?—Not one."

Perhaps Epicharmos found he could compose comic business best in sunny daylight, with the real world buzzing around and making unconscious comedy-scenes; but when the bodily faculties are more stilled, and the hidden nature wakens, the faculties are differently balanced; he says:—

"All serious things are best found out by night."

The following are among the extant fragments of Epicharmos:—

"If a pure mind thou hast, 'tis sure
In thy whole body thou art pure."

"A pious life's man's greatest stay,
And best provision for his way."

"Endowed with pious mind, you will not, when you've died,
Suffer aught ill; the spirit in heaven above will abide.'

"As destined long to live, as but a while,
So set thy mind."

Of this he has to share the authorship with Bias and Demokritos, among the fragments attributed to whom it is found in a slightly varied form.

"Wretch, covet not luxuries, lest hardships fall to your lot."

"Nothing evades the Divine; this it behoves thee to know,
He is our overseer, there is nought God cannot do."

"All the good things the gods sell us for our labour."

"I experience a sense of suffocation when any one speaks evil words to bring noble-mindedness to nought, and is ignoble in his own manners. What connection is there between a blind man and a looking-glass?"

"There is in man reasoning; and a divine reason:
Reason is implanted in man to provide for life and sustenance,
But divine reason gives an universal eye to the arts,
Teaching men always that which it is advantageous to do.
It was not man that discovered art, but God brought it,
And man's reason derives its origin from the Reason Divine (Logos)."

Diogenes of Apollonia is another of those who on the physical plane have sought the origin of the universe. He came to the conclusion that, as air seems to penetrate everywhere, and nothing is withheld from it, air is the creative material. In warm air he found the basis, or rather the parent, of all life; without discerning that, unless he could account for the presence of air, or of heat in it, his speculative physics had not yet brought him to the discovery of the supreme origin of life. The breath of life that fills our lungs, and the manifold fire that makes warmth and growth and colour, are indeed the noblest factors in created existence, but not the most pregnant wave of air, or keenest ray of light, or pulse of heat, can reveal the whole secret of life. Nature is voiceful, but not explanatory.

Diogenes says: "To me it seems that what men call air is that which contains intelligence, and that thereby all things are controlled, and it rules all things. From this it seems to me that mind proceeds, penetrating all things, constituting all things, and dwelling in everything. For there is nothing in existence which is not a partaker in air, while nothing else can be found which has to an equal degree that relation of partaker; but the modes are many both of air itself, and of intelligence. For air is of many modes, hotter, and colder, and dryer, and moister, and more stationary, and subject to sharper motion, and has many other dissimilarities with endless varieties both of smell and colour. And the soul of all living creatures is the same, being air, hotter indeed than the outer air in which we live, but much colder than that about the sun." It is to be feared that Diogenes has not here quite fulfilled the first condition of his treatise, in which he says, "It appears to me that he who begins any treatise is bound to lay down principles about which there can be no dispute, and that his exposition of them ought to be simple and dignified."

Archelaos, a pupil of Anaxagoras, bent upon physical speculations, such as whether animals are generated out of hot mud, meddled with moral philosophy so far as to affirm that there is no justice or baseness in nature, but that those qualities depend upon opinions and positive institutions; all actions are thus indifferent until law pronounces upon them—a doctrine which the conscience of man can scarcely acquiesce in without uneasy doubts. Nevertheless there is enough of merely conventional morality in the world to mislead a philosopher who forgets to inquire for a moment what is that glimmering consciousness which prompts to any moral system whatever, however blundering and confused.

Melissos conjoined literary studies with the serious profession of arms, and was distinguished in both. He shows a laudable clearness of logic in the treatment of metaphysical questions: "If being be infinite, it is one; for if there were two, they could not both be infinite, but would have boundaries against each other. . . . If it be one, it is also immovable . . . nothing beside the *ens* existed from all eternity, therefore, it cannot be moved." Melissos has bequeathed us no ethical lessons, and little but clear, cold reasonings.

Of the philosopher Demokritos it is difficult to write, so contradictory are the accounts and theories respecting him. He is a fine and suggestive moralist, as serious as any other, and yet tradition has given him the name of the Mocker, as of one who found sport in the follies of mankind, in opposition to Herakleitos, who was nicknamed the Weeper.

Demokritos is written down a Sadducee, on grounds much too slight, and probably erroneous. Lucian tells a story that, when the philosopher was busy writing in a cave at night, some youths dressed up as ghosts to frighten him; but he remained quite unmoved, and without even looking at them bid them end their game. From this it is deduced that it was his conviction that when souls passed out of bodies they were nought. A better conclusion is that the philosopher very quickly recognized that whether ghosts existed or not, a pack of masking boys were not of ghostly order. The man who one day saluted a young damsel who came with his friend Hippokrates, with "Good morning, my maid," and the next day changed his mode of salute to "Good morning, madam," the girl having in the interval altered her state, was not one likely to be deficient in closeness of observation, or easily imposed upon by mountebanks.

The other reason for the traditional presumption that Demokritos was a materialist is found in his physical theories, to which we will afterwards refer. But, having regard to the whole of his work that is left to us, it would seem more probable that Demokritos and Democrates are separate persons, than to set up the theory that the more spiritual work of Demokritos was done before his views had been developed into materialism by physical research. This is indeed to measure a steady old philosopher by the standard of the mental fluctuations of the nineteenth century.

Demokritos was born in a little city of Thrace, probably about the middle of the fifth century before our era. He was the youngest son of a wealthy family, so wealthy that it was able to entertain, not only King Xerxes, when, on his return from Asia, he visited Abdera, but also, as the story goes, his army.

When is father died, Demokritos divided the patrimony with his two brothers, taking a smaller portion than the others, because he wanted it in ready cash, as he proposed to spend years in travel. These wanderings are described with perhaps a tinge of boastfulness: "I have travelled over the most ground of any man of my time, investigating the most widely distant regions. I have seen the most skies and lands, and listened to the largest number of learned men; in the setting together of lines, with the working out, no one has surpassed me, not even those of the Egyptians who bear the name of Harpedonaptai; with these, moreover, I sojourned during five years' absence from home."

Doubtless the Chaldeans were among those whom this wanderer visited, but we cannot follow Lewes when in his

"History of Philosophy" he says that Xerxes left some of his Magi to instruct young Demokritos; seeing that he fixes the lad's birth at 460 B.C., while Xerxes died about four years previously.

His story shows how thought in the ancient world was not without its communications. Without the aid of printing, or the power of steam, ideas travelled, for the scholar was eager to carry them himself.

An interesting story is told by the Emperor Julian of Demokritos, and Darius the successor of Xerxes. The king's wife had died, and he was inconsolable. The philosopher promised to restore her to life, if the all-powerful king would provide him with certain necessaries. After some delay Demokritos reported that he had everything prepared, with one exception, which surely the king of all Asia could easily provide: he required the names of three men who had never experienced sorrow, to inscribe on the queen's tomb, when she would return from the under-world. Darius could not find one such man, and the moral of the story is obvious. It is a pair to the story of the shirt of a happy man, which was to be worn to bring back joy to a jaded king. When a happy man at last was discovered, he turned out to be a vagrant, who never wore such a thing as a shirt.

When Demokritos returned home from his prolonged wanderings, he was reduced to the utmost destitution, having consumed all that he took with him. But he had brought home a vast stock of knowledge. For a time his brother supported him, but he astonished the natives so much by foretelling future events, meteorological or connected with the harvest, that he soon became famous. There was a law, however, that any one who had made away with his patrimony should be denied funeral rites in his own country; Demokritos, therefore, to avoid calumny on this score, recited in public his greatest work, as a tribute to the power of which he was presented with a large sum of money, and honoured by the erection of brazen statues. He was offered the highest political position, but whether he accepted it is doubtful.

The remainder of his life was quietly passed in the study of nature and of letters. He lived to a very advanced age, and a story told about the manner of his death, if true, evidences a marvellous unselfishness on his part. When he seemed on the point of death, his sister was lamenting that he would die during a festival, at which she did not wish to be prevented from discharging her duties to the goddess. He wished her good cheer, and ordered hot loaves to be brought him each day, by applying which to his nostrils he succeeded in keeping himself alive over the three days during which his sister was busied in her religious observances. An epigram upon him runs, that "he kept off Death, though present, for three days, and entertained him with the steam of muffins."

It is not to be wondered at that the commentators should have found it hard to reconcile such noble sentences as the following, with the mind of a narrow physicist, who had discovered the secret spring of the universe to be atoms and a vacuum :—

"The felicity or infelicity of the soul resides not in flocks, or in gold ; for the soul is the abode of Divinity."

"Evil springs up into men out of good, whensoever one knows not how to administer the good things, or to support them easily. It is not just, however, to reckon such among evils, but amongst good things, for it is possible to use even good things for evil."

"From whatever source there arise to us good things, from the same we gather evil things also ; but from the evils it is within our power to be free. Deep water, for instance, is useful for many things, but it may have its evil side, too ; for there is danger of getting drowned. For this the remedy is found : it is to learn to swim." There is indeed here the solution of the problem of life, in a nut-shell.

"The gods give unto men all good things, both of old and

now, and not such things as are evil and hurtful and useless. These indeed, neither of old nor now, do gods bestow upon men, but men run upon them by blindness and ignorance of mind."

The following belong to a plane of thought more in relation with everyday affairs :—

"Many who seem to be friends are not so, and many who seem not to be, are."

"Not every relation of yours is your friend, but those who unite themselves with you for mutual advantage."

"As the sword cuts, so calumny separates friends."

"If you can do a good turn, do not delay, but give, knowing that no state of things is permanent."

"In prosperity it is easy to find a friend, but in adversity the most difficult of all things." Time has shortened this to the well-known proverb, "A friend in need is a friend indeed."

"To a wise man every land is viable, for the whole world is the fatherland of a noble soul."

"Magnanimity lies in the mild tolerance of fault or failure."

"It is not fitting for instructed people to reason with uninstructed, as it is not for sober people to argue with drunken."

"He who is about to rule others ought first to rule himself."

"Men have imaged a spectral form of Fortune as a pretext to cover their own imprudence; for Fortune makes small resistance to prudence, and the perspicacious soul gets the better of most things in life."

"Shouldst thou open thyself interiorly, thou wilt find a certain varied and impressionable storehouse and treasury of evils, not of influx from without, but containing as it were, native and indigenous sources, which vice lets loose, when widespread and liberal to the passions."

The following may represent the ideas of Demokritos upon education :—

"The virtue which is proper to nature is corrupted by easy indifference, while depravity is rectified by training ; easy things escape the neglectful, whilst difficult things come within the reach of diligence."

"Neither art nor science is to be reached without devotion to learning."

"Nature and training are very near neighbours; for though training transforms a man, yet in that transformation it is moulding a second nature."

"Youths who cannot willingly give themselves up to tasks, will learn neither literature, nor music, nor athletics, nor what contains the main part of virtue—modesty; for modesty chiefly grows out of such things."

With all his love for education, Demokritos can have been no pedant, or he would not have expressed himself as follows:—

"Those who possess varied erudition are sometimes altogether lacking in mind."

"Abundance of sagacity, rather than quantity of learning, is what one ought to strain for."

"There is such a thing as wisdom in youth and folly in old men; for time does not teach intelligence, while nature herself is nurture in due season."

How thorough his principles were, the following will stand for evidence:—

"Even stories about vile deeds ought to be declined."

The daily newspaper had not become an institution in the days of Demokritos.

"It is good not only to abstain from wrong, but never to will it."

"Not only is he that does one wrong, a foe; but he that is minded to."

"Penitence for base deeds is the salvation of life."

Demokritos may have given Epikouros a hint of value to him in arriving at a philosophy. Moderation in pleasure, and symmetry of life, these are the ideal of Demokritos, and from them, he avows, springs tranquillity of mind, while either lack or surfeit creates disturbance. The philosophy is plausible, but average human nature seems to require "the slings and arrows" in view to keep it at its best. However, the moderation signified by the philosopher is that arising from command over one's self, and is a thing quite distinct from the uneventfulness of circumstance: "Where any one exceeds moderation, the sweetest at once becomes least sweet." "The equal is beautiful in everything; but excess and deficiency appear to me to be the reverse."

The following, as well as one or two sentences already cited, might have come from the Buddhist Dhammapada: "As medicine heals the diseases of the body, so wisdom frees the soul from perturbations."

There is ethical beauty and loving truth in the following :—

"Men as we are, it beseems us not to laugh at, but to grieve for, the calamities of men."

"A charitable man is he who looks not for return, but deliberately purposes to do well."

"I count him who loves no one as loved by no one."

"He that inflicts wrong is more ill-starred than he that suffers wrong."

"The laws would not prevent each person from living with individual independence, unless one had a way of injuring another."

"There is disease of house and of life, just as there is of the bodily tabernacle."

Demokritos is ordinarily quoted as the author of the doctrine of atoms. Cicero regarded atoms as being, according to this doctrine, indivisible particles of matter, the first element of the universe. Not venturing to oppose so high an authority, or the dictates of the whole German school, we will nevertheless see how the apophthegms of Demokritos will read, on the hypothesis that he is a misunderstood prototype of Berkeley, and not a materialist at all. The term employed by Demokritos, and usually translated atoms, is *atomoi* or *atoma*. Leukippos, who is supposed to be the master of Demokritos, taught that the universe, being infinite, is in part a *plenum*, in part a *vacuum*, the former containing innumerable corpuscles or primary atoms. Let us suppose that Demokritos, instead of being an adherent of this doctrine, which explains nothing, and only touches the scaffolding of the physical universe, relinquished the pursuit of the atom, or indivisible thing, in *nature*, to the division of whose particles there would appear to be no end, and found the true indivisible in the *mind* of a living being, that is, in an *individual*. Aristotle, it may be observed (Anal. Pr. 2, 27, 9, Part. An. I. 4, 4), employs the term *atoma* in a sense of "individuals."

Quotation will now help us to judge whether Demokritos has been persistently misunderstood or not. If we follow his proposition that mind is the only fact, and so say that all sensation is subjective, then we must hold that the void, or vacuum, is all that is not mind, that is to say, is the apparent phenomenal universe, which is to be regarded as objectively void and only a resulting appearance, the fact of which is an impression made on the mind. This would be a very different conception from the vacuum of Leukippos, which was a sort of emptiness made for the atoms to sport in and arrive at variety of form.

"Assuredly either nothing is true, or what is, is not evident to us. While, however, sense-perception is entirely due to an under-support of intellectual faculty, and this sense-perception is an aberration, that which is made apparent is of necessity true relatively to sense-perception." (*I.e.* so far as sense-perception is concerned, the phenomena are truly seen; the mind alone can detect how erroneous are the uncorrected impressions which it receives through its sense-faculty.)

G. H. Lewes translates the passage we have rendered above so as to present a very different purport: "Demokritus says, that either nothing is true, or what is true is not evident to us. Universally, in his system, the sensation constitutes the thought, and, as at the same time it is but a change [in the sentient being], the sensible phenomena (*i.e. sensations*) are of necessity true."* If sensation did fully constitute thought, we should be conscious of no lack whatever.

Lewes, again, says that Demokritos, as a hypothesis to explain perception, "supposed that all things were constantly throwing off images of themselves (εἴδωλα), which, after assimilating to themselves the surrounding air, enter the soul by the pores of the sensitive organ. The eye, for example, is composed of aqueous humours; and water sees. But how does water see? It is diaphanous, and receives the image of whatever is presented to it."

The account we have of the view entertained by Demokritos respecting these *eidola* is probably a confused one, but it seems to convey the notion of vague spiritual entities, which can draw near to man and convey impressions to his mind:—

"Demokritos says that there are certain eidola in propinquity to man, and that some of them are beneficent, others maleficent; wherefore he goes so far as to pray that he may meet with propitious eidola. These beings are great and monstrous, and not readily subject to corruption, though not incorruptible. Moreover, they signify to men things that are coming to pass, by making themselves seen and emitting sound. Whence, when the ancients received an impression of these very beings, they suspected them to be deity, on the supposition of there being none other god beside these that has an incorruptible nature."

Seeing that Demokritos believed in elemental beings who could communicate subtly with man, it would be strange if

---

* It is well to give the original text: Ἤτοι οὐθὲν εἶναι ἀληθὲς ἢ ἡμῖν γ᾽ ἄδηλον. Ὅλως δὲ διὰ τὸ ὑπολαμβάνειν φρόνησιν μὲν τὴν αἴσθησιν, ταύτην δ᾽ εἶναι ἀλλοίωσιν, τὸ φαινόμενον κατὰ τὴν αἴσθησιν ἐξ ἀνάγκης ἀληθὲς εἶναι (Aristotle, Metaphys. iv. 5).

he did not connect their influence with the problem of the mode in which those impressions are received which appear to come to us from external images. The title of one of his books which are lost is, "Concerning eidolon, or concerning foresight." The fact of such a title, coupled with his allusions to eidola as individual beings of a shadowy æonic character, would seem to show that he had a very different view of them from that presented by Lewes, of emanational spectres being thrown off from things, as it were photographs made in air. The word "eidolon" is of very indeterminate signification even yet: in the following lines from "Dreamland," Edgar Poe uses it in a sense not very unlike that of Demokritos :—

> "By a route obscure and lonely,
> Haunted by ill angels only,
> Where an Eidolon, namèd NIGHT,
> On a black throne reigns upright,
> I have reached these lands but newly
> From an ultimate dim Thule—
> From a wild weird clime that lieth sublime
> Out of SPACE, out of TIME."

The essential meaning of the word "eidolon" is visible shape, and we are familiar with it in a limited signification in the term "idol."

"Demokritos, in abrogating those things which are an appearance to the perceptions of sense, goes so far as to say that nothing of these appears in accordance with verity, but only in accordance with opinion; whereas the element of underlying truth in things is the existence of individuals (*atomoi*) and a void. 'For,' says he, 'sweet is sweet because conventionally so regarded, and bitter is so by conventionality; heat, cold, colour, have their subsistence in opinion: whereas in reality what exists is individuals (*atoma*) and void.'

"In his 'Works in Support,' although undertaking to set up the mastery of argument for the sense-perceptions, he is nevertheless found giving judgment against them. For he says: 'We actually know nothing of exact truth, but perceive something that changes according to the posture of the body, both of things which fall across us and things which press against us.'

"And again he says: 'In reality now, that we know not whether each thing is such, or is not, has been often made plain.'

"In his book concerning Ideas, 'Man ought to know,' he says, 'by this rule, that he is many removes from real truth.' And again: 'This reason assuredly proves, that in real truth we know nothing respecting anything; but share each in the popular belief.' And further he says: 'And indeed it will be plain, that to know in real truth of what each thing is, we are quite at a loss.'

"In these works, indeed, he does away with almost every kind of apprehensiveness, and only specially fastens on the sense-perceptions. But in the Rules he says that there are two kinds of cognition, the one through the sense-perceptions, the other through the intellectual faculty. The cognition through the intellectual faculty he brings down as genuine, testifying to its credibility for the determination of truth; whereas he calls the cognition by the sense-perceptions obscure, denying its unerringness for the investigation of truth. I give what he says, word for word: 'Of cognition there are two kinds, one genuine, the other obscure; to the obscure belongs the whole group of sight, hearing, smell, taste, touch; while that is genuine which is distinctly separated from this.'

"Then, preferring the genuine to the obscure cognition, he adds a word thus: 'Whenever the obscure cognition can no longer in its smaller degree either see, or hear, or smell, or taste, or perceive by touch, why then one must resort to the property which is more subtle.'"

The passage just given, with its quotations from Demokritos, is found in the works of Sextos Empeirikos; the following is from Diogenes of Laerte: "Demokritos disregards quiddities, where he says, What is cold is cold in opinion; hot, hot in opinion; but individuals and void exist in reality. And again: In reality, we know nothing, for truth lies in a deep."

These are the reverse of what we might expect as the dogmas of a confident atomist; but misunderstanding of Demokritos has been so general that we are afraid to add to it.

It is possible that Demokritos is not the author of all of the following:—

"The nobility of cattle lies in the fine strength of the bodily frame, the nobility of man in the well disposedness of the character."

"Beauty of body, without basis of mind, marks animal nature merely."

"The harmony of man consists in making account of the soul rather than of the body; for a highly perfect soul gives uprightness to a mean state of the tabernacle, whereas strength of the carcase without rationality renders soul better no whit."

"It is the mark of a divine mind to be always dwelling on what is noble."

"The world is a scene, life a passage; thou camest, sawest, and didst depart."

"The world is an estrangement; life in it an interruption."

"Whatsoever things a poet writes when under inspiration of holy spirit, are beautiful exceedingly."

If these apophthegms, however, some of which have not fallen under suspicion of spuriousness, do not prove Demokritos something more than a mere atomist, the title of one of his lost works, "Concerning those that are in Hades," may do so. We may pass by as fabulous the story that he put out his eyes with a burning glass in order to become more intimately a student of the reasoning faculties through the minimizement of the disturbances of the external senses; the theory, however, he may perhaps have speculatively advanced. But if he wrote of existence in Hades, either there are two of the name, or Demokritos did not find the supreme source of life in the molecule.

THE SCHOOL OF PYTHAGORAS.

IT is not certainly known whether an Athenian boy named Aristocles, better known to the civilized world as Plato (broad), earned his nickname from the burly size of his shoulders, the width of his forehead, or the eloquent breadth of his expositions. It is scarcely surprising, therefore, that a mystery should lie upon the name of one Pythagoras, who lived over a century before him, and, although less widely read by reason of having left us doubtful fragments instead of unmutilated treatises, is at least as great a man.

If about a hero himself there is no obscurity—though indeed the world can generally make but little of him in his own time—mystery is wont to accumulate around him after he is gone. In the case of Plato, whose ancestry went back in the sword-line to the last king of Athens, and on the spindle side to Solon the sage, wonder came out in fable, and gave him a virgin mother, and god Apollo for his father.* The relations of Pythagoras to our planet have almost as ethereal a vagueness of outline. First, and almost incredibly (did we not know another instance), seeing that he founded a sect great in both politics and religion, no one knows with certainty the date of his birth, or how long he lived. Calculators fix

* "The report was that Plato's mother, Perictione, was very beautiful, and that Ariston endeavoured to violate her but did not succeed; and that, after he had desisted from his violence, he saw a vision of Apollo in a dream, in consequence of which he refrained from approaching his wife until after she had brought forth" (Diogenes Laertius, "Lives of Philosophers," Plato, i.). Plutarch also (Conviv., viii. 1, p. 715 E) refers to this dream of Plato's father.

his birth variously from 640 to 570 years before our era, his death from 550 to 466, allowing him thus a margin of life of from twenty years to nearly a century and three-quarters. We may roughly fix 575 to 495 as most probably containing his period. With regard to his birth, almost the same story is told of him as afterwards of Plato :—

> "Pythais, fairest of the Samian tribe,
> Bore from embraces of the god of day,
> Renowned Pythagoras, the friend of Zeus."

With respect to the meaning of the name Pythagoras, also, there is some difference of opinion; the theory has been advanced, in view of his reputed travels in India and other eastern countries, that it is of oriental origin. And the theory is very plausible. Pythagoras is Sanskrit—*Budha*, wisdom; and *guru*, or venerable father, the title given in the "Institutes of Menu" to the teacher who confers the benefit of sacred learning. Or, it is *Budha*, wisdom, and the Greek *agoreuo*, to explain, or announce. The first woman who entered the order founded by Pythagoras, or, according to another account, his wife, was Theano; Sanskrit, *Dhyana*, devout contemplation. And of this mystical marriage a daughter is named Damo; Sanskrit, *Dharma*, virtue or practical morality. Two early Pythagoreans also, the celebrated Damon and Pythias, have names that fit in with the Sanskrit derivations. So also does that of Pythanax, reputed mother of Theano. Curiously enough, the root *Pyth* has its own sacredness in Greece, as *Budh* in India.

Unfortunately for this alluring etymological hypothesis, which is due to a distinguished Indian general officer, the reduction of the proper names to Sanskrit words signifying qualities, however seemingly applicable to the character of the work of Pythagoras, can have no special reference to him. Theano, whether originally derived from Sanskrit or not, is a proper name in Homer, several centuries before the time of Pythagoras; and Pytho in Homer and Hesiod is the name of the site of the Delphic oracle, with which the legend and title of the Pythian Apollo are associated. From the similarity of the names Pythagoras, Pythaïs, Pythanax, Pythias, it would seem most likely, however, that they are not simple patronymics, but were introduced by the biographer of Pythagoras for some symbolic purpose. Iamblichos says that the father of Pythagoras, Mnesarchos, was informed by the oracle that his wife Parthenis (or virgin) would bring forth a son of exceeding beauty and wisdom, a benefit to his race in all pertaining to the life of men, through a rare prerogative and divine gift. Thereupon, as the story runs, he named his wife Pythais and her son Pythagoras, which might be supposed to signify, Declared by the Pythian deity. "And indeed," says Iamblichos, "no one can doubt that the soul of Pythagoras was sent to mankind from the empire of Apollo, either being an attendant on the god, or co-arranged with him in some other more familiar way; for this may be inferred both from his birth, and from the all various wisdom of his soul." The latter quality is truly a fair reason for his having proceeded from some sphere of divine quality, whether styled Apollonian or not. But, as to the name Pythagoras, though it may have been used with special significance in the case of the philosopher, it appears to have been shared with several more commonplace mortals of about the same period, among them an athlete and trainer, a statuary, an orator, and a physician.

The most generally adopted tradition is, that Pythagoras was born in the island of Samos. Another account is that he was a native of Tyre, or at least of Phœnician origin. The trade of his father tends to countenance the story of Tyrian race, for, according to some, he was an engraver of gems, according to others, a rich merchant, both of which occupations might well have gone together, the quest of precious stones and sale of valuable engraved gems necessitating travel and a busy commercial life.

His father's profession is thought to add probability to the legends that Pythagoras himself visited many lands. He might have been taken abroad by business for his father, and at the same time have fed his inquiring mind with such knowledge as made it thirst for more. Miletos, Crete, Delphi, near home, Phœnicia, Judea, Egypt, Persia, Babylon, India, Gaul, abroad, he is said to have visited, making acquaintance with learned priests, getting at their symbols and secrets, absorbing into his mind their sacred lore, even becoming a partaker in their rites. As we learn more of Egyptian, Zoroastrian, and Buddhist teachings, we shall see more clearly how far Pythagoras may have drawn from them. It will probably be recognized that Greece had a great power of assimilation, and that as from the strong but straitened sculptures of Egypt and the intaglios of Phœnicia and Babylonia, she evolved her own perfection of work in marble and gems, so also in the province of philosophy she fostered into a new and developed grace of form the thoughts of races before whom she was but a child in point of antiquity. In the exquisite poetical expressions of her bards and sages, we may not always know to how large an extent we are receiving, according to Bacon's fine metaphor, "sacred relics, gentle whispers, and the breath of better times, from the traditions of more ancient nations, conveyed into the flutes of the Grecians."

Pythagoras was fortunate in his early life; instead of his mind being crushed by having to commit to memory burdensome stores of detail, his education was one that fulfilled the signification of the term, the leading out and expansion of the young faculties. Development and grace formed the high Greek ideal, and the boy who, in "the dim magnificence of legends," was long-haired and beautiful as one under divine inspiration, was instructed in gymnastics for his body, in the music of the harp, and in painting from life, as exercises for the spiritual and mental nature. With the lyre went the verses of Homer, so that the inspiring suggestions of poetry went hand in hand with the stricter training of musical art. Afterwards came the study of philosophy under the great sages of the time, and with a mind well tempered by such training he resorted to the priests of the oracles to learn their arcana. There is probably imaginative excess in the legends told of his studies of the mysteries, for there is an evident tendency to hero-worship on the part of his biographers. But, as the practical sense of Lewes puts it, "wherever we find romantic or miraculous deeds narrated, we may be certain that the hero was great enough at least to sustain the weight of this crown of fabulous glory." Pherekydes, who is cited as one of the teachers of Pythagoras, may have helped to link philosophy with mystical theology in his pupil's mind. He taught the continuance of the soul, notwithstanding external change called death; and this as an indispensable part of his philosophic doctrine. Besides the lessons of the philosopher of Syros, Pythagoras is credited with initiation into the mysteries of Byblos and Tyre, and with making a considerable sojourn in the retreat of the prophets in Mount Carmel. Here the fame of Elijah and Elisha yet lingered, but the wooded hill was probably a resort rather of Phœnician and Syrian than of strictly Judæan hermits, especially at this time, when the Hebrew nationality was little more than a straw drawn this way and that on the great opposing streams of Egypt and Babylonia.

The portrait drawn by Iamblichos of Pythagoras while yet a youth, if it represents a being too flawless to have existed, and is presumably unhistorical, at least presents an ideal which it is suggestive even to gaze on from afar: He was the most beautiful and godlike of all that have been celebrated in the annals of history. His aspect was most venerable, and his habits most temperate, so that he was even reverenced and honoured by elderly men. He was adorned by piety and disciplines, by a mode of living transcendently good, by firmness of soul and by a body in due subjection to the mandates of reason. In all his words and actions he discovered an inimitable quiet and serenity, not being subdued at any time by anger, or laughter, or emulation, or contention, or any other perturbation or precipitation of conduct; but he dwelt at Samos like some beneficent daimon. He confined himself to such nutriment as was slender and easy of digestion. In consequence of this, his sleep was short, his soul vigilant and pure, and his body confirmed in a state of perfect and invariable health.

From Anaximandros at Miletos, and Epimenides in Crete, Pythagoras is also said to have received instruction, being conducted by the latter to the sacred cave where the priests of Cybelle treasured the legislation of the revealer Minos.

The Phœnician coast is said to have been the starting-point of Pythagoras for Egypt. There is a pretty legend of this passage of the sea, which is the diametrical opposite of the fable of Jonah. "The sailors gladly received him, foreseeing that they should acquire great gain by exposing him for sale. . . . He ascended the ship, and sat silent the whole time of the voyage, in that part of the vessel where he was not likely to interfere with the occupations of the sailors. He remained in the same unmoved state for two nights and three days, partaking neither of food, drink, nor sleep, unless perchance, as he sat in that firm and tranquil condition, he slept for a short time unobserved by all the sailors. When the sailors considered how, contrary to their expectations, their voyage had been continued and uninterrupted, as if some deity had been present; putting all these things together, they concluded that a divine daimon had in reality passed over with them from Syria into Egypt. Hence, speaking both to Pythagoras and to one another with greater decorum and gentleness than before, they completed, through a most tranquil sea, the remainder of their voyage, and at length happily landed on the Egyptian coast. Here the sailors reverently assisted him in descending from the ship; and after they had placed him on the purest sand, they raised a certain temporary altar before him, and heaping on it from their present abundance the fruits of trees, and presenting him as it were the firstfruits of their freight, they departed from thence, and hastened to their destined port."

Pythagoras, according to Plutarch, found his way to Heliopolis, the university town of Egypt, where he found a master in Œnouphis. In those spacious halls, adorned with mural sculpture, appropriated to the use of the priests, in the temple with its long alleys of stony sphinxes, its avenues of inscribed obelisks, what illustrious visitors had been seen! Moses, the Hebrew lawgiver, was an alumnus there, in all probability; one old tradition says, a priest; Solon, the Greek lawgiver, had discoursed with those taciturn scholars of Egypt; subsequently to Pythagoras, Plato also went to study there. In Heliopolis, Jews, Greeks, and Egyptians met on equal terms, as befitted the breadth and tolerance of the city of learning. As a matter of comparative chronology, we may note that about half a century before the visit of Pythagoras, Jeremiah, the Hebrew prophet, against his will, was in or near Heliopolis; and though finding himself among a large number of fellow-countrymen resident in the land, the prophet looks with the eye of a sore-hearted patriot rather than that of an artistic appreciator, upon "the images of Beth-Shemesh."

Pythagoras was prepared for the Egyptian learning, says Iamblichos, by the fact of his previous instruction in the mysteries of the Phœnicians, which were derived from the sacred rites of Egypt. The tendency of a people to regard its own doctrines as the only orthodoxy is pleasantly confronted by evidences of the opposite and nobler tendency, that of sympathy and communication of one religious philosopher with another. On a lower plane, an almost comic effect may follow such amities. In Nubia some pious "Vandal" paints the figure of apostle Peter with his key over that of the original patron deity of the temple, so that Rameses II. is represented as making offerings to a post-existent saint; and there are to be found the most apparently incongruous evidences of harmony between the religious symbols of different races, as in an Egypto-Syrian combination such as "Osiris-Eloh," or a Phœniko-Judean title such as "Adonai, the Baal of Heaven."

Pythagoras managed to become on friendly terms with the priests and prophets of Egypt. According to Iamblichos, he was both admired and loved by them, so that we need not wonder at their being communicative when he asked it of them. And, according to tradition, he was one with them in this, that he never wrote—revealed no mysteries, never communicated a truth to one unprepared to receive it.

Polykrates, the despot of Samos, is well known for the story of the ring which he flung into the sea. It was one of his most highly prized possessions, but his prosperity was so excessive that he was led to fear a reverse if he could not substitute for it some voluntary deprivation. The next day a present of a fresh-caught fish was made him, in which was found his inalienable ring. To Amasis (Aahmes), the King of Egypt, who had given him the warning respecting his prosperity, Polykrates is said to have given Pythagoras a letter of recommendation. This sovereign was a man of enlightenment, who opened his country to the stranger, and during his reign many eminent Greeks visited Egypt.

This introduction, little as it may seem to consist with the story of the departure of Pythagoras, as an unprotected wanderer, from the coast of Phœnicia, may help to account for his friendly reception among the priesthood, of whom the king for the time being was always the nominal head. According to another story, Pythagoras made and took over to Egypt three silver goblets, as presents for the priests.

The hypothesis has been mooted that the travels of Pythagoras are a fable, and have no reference to an individual man, or to actual voyages, but are designed to represent the growth or progress of some quality. If we take it that a Greek priest were tracing the history of the transcendental conception of life, as developed in his own mind and doctrine, he might say, the idea came from an old philosopher at home, Egyptian lore fostered and enlarged it, it was deepened by a knowledge of the mysteries of the oracle, in Babylonia an element was added to it, to India could be traced one of its germs. It is true that the ancients were given to such personification of abstract generalizations, but in presence of the fact that learning in those days could only be acquired orally, and by personal contact of one student with another, there seems no reason to resort to the hypothesis of myth as the origin of the tradition that Pythagoras, the son of a wealthy father, was a great traveller. Proclus asserts that Pythagoras was initiated by Aglaophamus into the mysteries brought from Egypt by Orpheus.

According to Iamblichos, Pythagoras spent so long a period as two-and-twenty years in Egypt, gaining admission to the various temples, and learning geometry, astronomy, and divination. If he was eighteen when he left home, and spent three years in learning from Greek and Phœnician teachers, at the close of his stay in Egypt he would have reached the age of forty-three. The beneficent ruler of Egypt had lately died, and Psammenitus (Psamtek III.), his son, was reigning in his stead, when Cambyses (Pers. Kabujiya; Egypt. Kambat), the Persian king, flushed with conquests, came thither with his army, and vanquished the Egyptian forces in a single battle. The date of this event is known, it is 525 B.C.: the only question is whether its relation to Pythagoras is historic fact or doubtful legend. According to the tradition, he was taken captive and conveyed to Babylon, where he soon came into friendly association with the Magi, and received instruction from them in arithmetic, music, and divine rites. Plutarch cites the name of his Persian master as Zaratas, which seems clearly to point to Zarathustra, or

Zoroaster. But that prophet having long passed away, it is probable that a member of the order of priests or mages bearing that name is the true teacher in question. Ten or eleven years before, the Babylonian empire had broken up before the Medes and Persians, and such of the Hebrew tribes as desired to return to their own country had left Babylon. But a number remained, and there is a tradition that Pythagoras conversed with their rabbis, and learned the Jewish law. Twelve years, says Iamblichos, Pythagoras remained with his magian associates, and then returned to Samos.

Pythagoras gave a new sense to the word philosopher, which probably signified beforetime one devoted to some art, craft, or special knowledge. He used it in the larger sense of lover of wisdom, or, as Plato understood it, one zealous after all wisdom. When asked his art or craft, he said, "I have none, I am a philosopher." And when asked the difference between philosophers and others, he defined it as follows: "Life may be compared to the festival of the games: some persons are there to contend with bodily prowess for glory and the crowns; some seek gain by traffic in mercantile wares; others, more noble, resort thither neither for applause nor gain, but solely as spectators of all that passes, and observers of the manner of it. So also in the present life, men of all-various pursuits are assembled. As a merchant on business intent travels from town to town, we quit another life and come into this world, where some are born hunters after glory, others greedy of gain, others influenced by desire of power, or luxury. There are a few who, reckoning all else of no account, are earnest seekers after truth in the nature of things. These I call philosophers, for, as the most liberal position at the games is that of the person who is only a spectator, and has no acquisitive function, so in life the contemplation of things, and knowledge, far transcend all other pursuits." Pythagoras did not despise the practical—the essential difference of his ideal is the elimination of selfish personal motive.

Upon his return to Samos, where the prophet was in his own country, he found himself remembered by a few, but there was little disposition to attend to the disciplines he desired to introduce.

A pretty legend is told of an artifice which he employed to get disciples, after he had set up his school. "Happening to observe a certain youth, who was a great lover of gymnastic and other corporeal exercises, but otherwise poor and in difficult circumstances, playing at ball in the gymnasium with great aptness and facility, he thought the young man might easily be persuaded to attend to him, if he were sufficiently supplied with the necessaries of life, and freed from the care of procuring them. As soon, therefore, as the youth left the bath, Pythagoras called him to him, and promised that he would furnish him with everything requisite for the support of his bodily exercise, on condition that he would receive from him gradually and easily, but continually—so that he might not be burdened by receiving them at once—certain disciplines which he said he had learnt from the barbarians in his youth, but which now began to desert him through forgetfulness and the incursions of old age. The young man immediately acceded to the conditions, through the hope of having the necessary support. Pythagoras, therefore, endeavoured to instruct him in the disciplines of arithmetic and geometry, forming each of his demonstrations in an abacus, and giving the youth three oboli as a reward for every figure which he learnt. This also he continued to do for a long time, exciting him to the geometrical theory by the desire of honour; diligently, and in perfect order, giving him (as we have said) three oboli for every figure which he apprehended. But when the wise man observed that the elegance, sweetness, and connection of these disciplines, to which the youth had been led in a certain orderly path, had so captivated him that he would not neglect their pursuit though he should suffer the extremity of want, he pretended poverty, and an inability to give him the three oboli any longer. But the youth on hearing this replied, 'I am able without these to learn and receive your disciplines.' Pythagoras then said, 'But I have not the means of procuring sufficient nutriment for myself,' adding, that as it was requisite, therefore, to labour in order to procure daily necessaries and mortal food, it would not be proper that his attention should be distracted by the abacus, and by stupid and vain pursuits. The youth, however, vehemently abhorring the thought of discontinuing his studies, replied : 'I will in future provide for you, and repay your kindness in a way resembling that of the stork ; for I, in my turn, will give you three oboli for every figure,' and from this time he was so captivated by these disciplines, that he alone of all the Samians migrated from his country with Pythagoras."

If in his school in the Hemicycle Pythagoras failed to win over his Samian neighbours to enter upon his profound and uncompromising system of discipline, yet the citizens laid claim to his assistance in the administration of public affairs. Certain obscure references also make it probable that his fame reached the Greeks who lived on the Hellespont, and were therefore within the range of the influence of the priests of the Getæ—heroes who contemned earth life, and also of the magic-loving Scythian prophets of the Hyperborean Apollo.

Pythagoras appears to have been out of his element in Samos. He longed to realize his educational ideal, and, by the thorough training of individuals, to make wisdom a power in the State ; he did not wish to spend his time in the petty detail of home politics. There is a story that a citizen of Crotona in Italy had assisted him in redeeming himself from his captivity in Persia. There is also a tradition that he had accompanied his father on a voyage to Crotona, which was a thriving republic, a Greek colony on the southern coast of Italy. Whatever may have been his inducement, he journeyed to Crotona, and there hoped to find a people more open to enlightenment than the negligent folk at home. Perhaps

Democedes, the first physician of Greece, was there at this time, who also was acquainted with Samos, and intimate with its despot Polykrates. It is probably about the year 522 that Pythagoras reached flourishing and populous Crotona, Tarquin the Proud being at that time ruler of Rome.

The constitution of the city seems to have been a mingling of aristocratic with democratic institutions. A council of a thousand held the reins of power, composed of the nobles and of the wealthy burgesses, who may be considered representatives of trade and of the everyday interests of the people at large.

How the influence of Pythagoras affected a community so constituted, we shall see better when we follow out the plan of his work. He founded an institution that may be described as a secret society, with nothing to hide or be ashamed of, and thoroughly open as regards its external acts, and those alone.

Were Pythagoras a spiritual being, and not a man, the plan of his society is just what we might expect. It was a hierarchy of perfection, and if Pythagoras could have commanded a constant supply of embodied angels, both to rule and to be ruled, it might be in existence now.

As a commencement individuals must be attracted. Pythagoras began in Crotona by being a preacher and teacher. Crowds flocked to hear his persuasive eloquence; he selected the most earnest among them. Earnestness may be only for the moment, emotional and spasmodic rather than continuous and fruitful. He appointed tests that should eliminate those unfit for his purpose. Membership of his society was a prize as difficult to win as was his own initiation into the symbolic secrets of Egypt, to attain which, it is said, he did not shrink from circumcision. For five years the novices were condemned to silence—awful trial of constancy of purpose and reality of earnestness. During this time they did nothing but listen to discourses, and never saw Pythagoras. After approval by this test, and a diagnosis by him of their habits, associations, converse, passions, employment of leisure, physique, physiognomy, even to the mode of walking and the body's movement, which he regarded as manifest signs of the unapparent nature of the soul, the probationers were allowed to advance a step farther. Their property became common to the guild, and was committed to the care of the appointed managers or economizers. They themselves were permitted to see as well as hear Pythagoras; they were within the veil.

Such as were rejected received double the wealth they brought—a most uneconomic proceeding if many were rejected, and enough to prompt unbelievers to enter upon temporary probation—and a tomb was raised to them by their comrades. They were presumably "dead in trespasses and sins." One of these rejected ones was Kylon, a magnate of the neighbouring city of Sybaris, of whom more anon.

For a backsliding Pythagorean we must needs have pity, considering the arduousness of the ordeal. A true disciple writes retrospectively: "It will be well to consider what a great length of time we consumed in wiping away the stains which had insinuated themselves into our breasts, till, after the lapse of some years, we became fit recipients of the doctrines of Pythagoras. For, as dyers previously purify garments, and then fix in the colours with which they wish them to be imbued, in order that the dye may not be washed away, and may nowise be evanescent; after the same manner also that divine man prepared the souls of those that were lovers of philosophy, so that they might not deceive him in any of those beautiful and good qualities which he hoped they would possess."

Pythagoras was one that did not "infuse theorems and divine doctrine into confused and turbid manners. Just as if some one should pour pure and clear water into a deep well full of mud; for he would disturb the mud, and destroy the clear water. A similar thing likewise takes place between those who teach and those who are taught after this manner. For dense thickets and full of briars surround the intellect and heart of those who have not been purely initiated in disciplines, obscure the mild, tranquil, and reasoning power of the soul, and openly impede the intellective part from becoming increased and elevated."

The disciples, as admitted, were divided into classes, as men are naturally dissimilar. They were led into all the paths of erudition which his genius and experience had opened to Pythagoras. But he was not merely an intellectual teacher; he was a "healer of souls," possessing an almost magical influence and power of attracting friendship, and whenever he found any one having any community of symbolic understanding with himself, he at once strove to make a companion of him. With the members of his college he was like an intimate companion of lofty speech and gentle dignified manners; and the evident unselfishness of his purpose, with his devotion to his ideal, that of the formation of excellent men, must have exercised a rare charm.

The morning was begun by music, and in the community it was realized that music may be of evil tendency or good, of perturbing or tranquillizing, awakening or soothing effect according to its quality. Music appears to have been regarded as an influence equally affecting body and mind; rhythms, melodies, and incantations were an enchantment by which to treat both psychical and corporeal passions. "The disciples performed their morning walks alone, and in places where there happened to be an appropriate solitude and quiet, and where there were temples and groves, and other things adapted to give delight. They thought it was not proper to converse with any one till they had rendered their own soul sedate, and had co-harmonized the reasoning power. They apprehended it to be disorderly to mingle in a crowd as soon as they rose from bed. On this account all the Pythagoreans always selected for themselves the most sacred places. After their morning walk they associated with each other, and especially in temples, or, if this was not possible, in places that resembled them. This time, likewise, they employed in the discussion of doctrines and disciplines, and in the correction of their manners." They seem to have realized the influence of a sort of cathedral awe, and the elevating effect of noble and poetic surroundings. But they did not remain in meditation only; "after an association of the kind described, they turned their attention to the health of the body. Most of them used unction and the course; a less number employed themselves in wrestling in gardens and groves; others in leaping with leaden weights in their hands; others in mimetic gesticulations, with a view to the strength of the body, studiously selecting for this purpose opposite exercises. Their dinner consisted of bread and honey or the honey-comb; they did not drink wine during the day."

After their meal, the students turned to more external work, such as administrative details and the reception of guests. In the evening they grouped themselves into walking parties, for discussion and mutual improvement. After the walk came the bath, and after this they assembled, ten together, for certain religious rites. Then they took supper, which was finished before sunset. Their food was simple—wine, bread, and boiled herbs or fresh salads, with certain kinds only of animal meats. They were as careful not to injure the higher varieties of plants as the useful orders of animals; and were specially trained to avoid certain flatulent and noxious foods, particularly such as are "an impediment to prophecy, or to the purity and chastity of the soul, or to the habit of temperance, or of virtue."

Pythagoras "rejected all such things as are adverse to sanctity, and obscure and disturb the other purities of the soul, and the phantasms which occur in sleep." It will be observed that the value of this discipline rests on the faith that, when the body is brought into the best and purest state, mystical senses and consciousness, or spiritual gifts, will be found to be opened normally.

After supper, the eldest of the group fixed some passage for reading, and the youngest read it aloud. Music closed the day, as it had begun it. As Iamblichos puts it, in a somewhat high-flown way, "In the evening, when his disciples were retiring to sleep, he liberated them by these means (appropriate medicine of melody) from the day's disturbances, and purified their intellective power from the influxive and effluxive waves of a corporeal nature; rendered their sleep quiet, and their dreams pleasing and prophetic."

Pythagoras seems to have had a science of music, viewed as purification. Certain melodies disposed the circle which joined in them to elegance and orderly manners; others were remedies against despondency; others against rage, anger, desire. The lyre, rather than the pipe, he deemed the true instrument for his purpose. But there is a story of his making the pipe useful in a wonderful way. It is said that once, "through the spondaic song of a piper, he extinguished the rage of a Tauromenian lad, who had been feasting by night, and intended to burn the vestibule of his mistress, in consequence of seeing her coming from the house of his rival. For the lad was inflamed and excited to distraction by a Phrygian song, which, however, Pythagoras promptly suppressed. He was astronomizing, and happened to meet with the piper at an unseasonable time of night, and persuaded him to change his Phrygian for a spondaic song, through which the fury of the lad being immediately repressed, he returned home in an orderly manner; though shortly before he could not be in the least restrained, and would bear no admonition; and even stupidly insulted Pythagoras when he met him." The Phrygian music, if we are to judge by what Catullus tells of the Galli, must have been maddening, and was probably akin to the frenzied chorus of the devil-priests in oriental countries.

It was doubtless the personal presence of Pythagoras, as much as any musical charm, which acted as a gentle corrective of the disturbed moods of the members of his college. "By his later disciples," says G. H. Lewes, "he was venerated as a god. He who could transcend all earthly struggles, and the great ambitions of the greatest men, to live only for the sake of wisdom, was he not of a higher stamp than ordinary mortals? Well might later historians picture him as clothed in robes of white, his head crowned with gold, his aspect grave, majestical, and calm; above the manifestations of any human joy, of any human sorrow; enwrapt in contemplation of the deeper mysteries of existence; listening to music and the hymns of Homer, Hesiod, and Thales, or listening to the harmony of the spheres. And to a lively, talkative, quibbling, active, versatile people like the Greeks, what a grand phenomenon must this solemn, earnest, silent, meditative man have appeared."

That a man's ears should catch the music of the spheres as they circle round in their grand harmonious courses sounds like a rare piece of poetic hyperbole; but Simplicius not only asserts it as a fact, but gravely argues for it, giving reasons: "A harmonic sound is produced from the motion of the celestial bodies, which may be scientifically collected from the analogy of their intervals." Jupiter, we might presume, ought to play the bass,* and Mars a warlike tenor, the shrill chorus of asteroids not having then made itself manifest. With regard to this faculty of Pythagoras, Simplicius argues as follows: "Perhaps the objection of Aristotle to this assertion of the Pythagoreans may be solved according to the philosophy of those men, as follows: all things are not commensurate with each other, nor is everything sensible to everything, even in the sublunary region. This is evident from dogs who

* Saturn was really credited with the deepest note.

scent animals at a great distance which are not smelt by men. How much more, therefore, in things which are separated by so great an interval as those which are incorruptible from the corruptible, and celestial from terrestrial nature, is it true to say, that the sound of divine bodies is not audible by terrestrial ears. But if any one like Pythagoras should have his terrestrial body exempt from him, and his luminous and celestial vehicle and the senses which it contains purified, either through a good allotment,* or through probity of life, or through a perfection arising from sacred operations, such an one will perceive things invisible to others, and will hear things inaudible to others." It seems probable, however, that what Pythagoras really meant was, that the ratios between the intervals of the planets betokened relations of number, which is the mathematical constituent of music. Pythagoras was acquainted with the fact that our earth is not a stationary body, a fact of which many Christians long afterwards showed themselves most dogmatically ignorant.

The reverence amounting almost to adoration which Pythagoras inspired is only accounted for on the presumption that he actually possessed certain preternatural qualities, or in default of that we must suppose that his admirers had the consummate faculty of conceiving a thing which is not known to exist. Empedokles, himself a sage, spoke of Pythagoras as a man "transcendent in knowledge, who possessed the most ample stores of intellectual wealth, and was in the most eminent degree the promoter of the works of the wise. For when he extended all the powers of his intellect, he easily beheld everything, as far as to ten or twenty ages of the human race." The theory seems to have been, that Pythagoras was conscious of his spiritual as well as his terrestrial being, and had the faculty of awakening this dormant consciousness in others. Iamblichos says, " If we may believe in so many ancient and credible historians as have written

* Cf. Wisdom viii. 20.

concerning him, the words of Pythagoras contained something of a recalling and admonitory nature, which extended even so far as to irrational animals." Legends are told of Pythagoras gently stroking a most dangerous bear, and conjuring it to touch living beings no more; to an ox he is said to have given counsel in whisper, counsel which was followed; and an eagle he is said to have allured from the sky to his hand, afterwards letting it go. We are reminded in these legends of the traditions attaching to Orpheus.

Pythagoras was "the cause to his disciples of the most appropriate converse with divine beings, whether while awake or asleep; a thing which never takes place in a soul disturbed by anger, or pain, or pleasure, or by any other base desire, or defiled by ignorance, which is more unholy and noxious than all these. By all these inventions, therefore, he divinely healed and purified the soul, resuscitated and saved its divine part, and conducted to the intelligible its divine eye, which, as Plato says, is better worth saving than ten thousand corporeal eyes; for by looking through this alone, when it is strengthened and clarified by appropriate aids, the truth pertaining to all things is perceived."

The main original feature in Pythagoras as a teacher seems to be his high consciousness of harmony, whether in actual existence, or as a treasure to be earnestly absorbed into the mind. This harmony he saw, in the interdependence of the parts of the universe, in the amity between divine beings and men, between one doctrine and another, between the soul and the body, the rational and irrational part; he desired to see the same harmony made more sure in the relations of man to man, of husband to wife, of brothers one to the other, of the mortal body, with all its contrary powers, to its pacificator, the mind. Friendship, using the word in its widest sense, as implying relations even between things inanimate, was his vision of life.

The rules of the community administered by Pythagoras

must have been very rigid ; or rather the atmosphere which he breathed was so rare and pure that a man failing to live up to the high ideal presented to him by the master would almost of necessity find himself outside the societary life. And, so far as may be judged by the traditions remaining, there was no arbitrary enforcement of membership, but the association was wholly voluntary.

Mathematics was made one of the early studies in the Pythagorean school, as being the first step towards wisdom. For a science which deals with that which lies in the middle region between things appreciable to the senses and spiritual and divine facts, enlarges the mind and renders it the more elastic for the reception of supersensual ideas. In other words, that which has to do with abstract and intangible properties, is a fit preparation for the study of what is spiritual. What the students learned, they were trained to learn thoroughly, and the strength and accuracy of the memory were maintained by constant exercise. The student before rising from his bed was led to review the actions and studies of the preceding day in the minutest detail. This was done methodically and in the right order ; and one day's events resumed, the Pythagorean proceeded to recall to himself the transactions of the day before that.

The late Dr. Mozley asserted that the simple apprehension of a spiritual world is by itself no preservative whatever against moral obliquities. This may be true, though the enlargement of the vista of life due to such an apprehension should not be without an effect at once steadying and elevating. The acquisition of spiritual knowledge might possibly modify the standard by which moral questions are judged in the world. What the world calls right, might when analyzed resolve itself into expediency ; what the world calls wrong might be found to be only an imperfect use of what is right. Tyndall urges that "what is really wanted is the lifting power of an ideal element in human life." "What's the best thing in the world? Something out of it, I think," says Elizabeth Barrett Browning. If it is in this best thing that the true ideal is found, it is of little moment on the score of marvel, but of the greatest on the ground of fact. Pythagoras painted no vague or startling picture of life in Hades, but he staunchly asserted that to be injured one's self is better than to murder another, for in that unseen life is judgment, and the soul there finds its proper estimation and level. Retributive justice he very ingeniously associated with the symbol of the right-angled triangle. That figure may be composed with an infinite number of variations of its sides, but it will ever contain an equal demonstration of power. Whatever the relative proportions of the sides of the triangle, the square of the side subtending the right angle will invariably be equal to the combined squares of the two sides containing the right angle. Circumstances vary, the law abides.

A man raised, strengthened, and purified by earnestness and culture has a double duty—to himself and to others. He is bound to exercise his faculties for his own sake lest they perish of inaction; he is constrained by the law of his being to exercise them not only for himself but for others. It is an almost necessary consequence of the growth of a community to strength, that it should be called upon to do practical work. If it has dealt kindly with those who are without its rules, it will have won respect, and will be besought to contribute its experience and power.

In the order founded by Pythagoras, there were the listeners who passed on into classes for mathematics and physics. Among more advanced students we find the division into exoterics and esoterics. There were members given to contemplation, to science, to politics. And outside these divisions there were others founded on the relations of the disciples to the master. There were personal friends, direct disciples, who were called—probably not in his lifetime—

Pythagorics; the disciples of these, Pythagoreans; while those who lived outside the community, but emulated its life, formed the class of Pythagorists.

Everything of the Pythagorean tradition betokens a volunteer hierarchical order, in which by the conquest of unruly ambitions and passions, each found his true place. Two considerations suggest themselves: that an organization so formed must prove one of great power; but that when it came to extend its influence publicly, there would be a lack of homogeneity, tending to disruption, between a group of persons trained to absolute self-control and a common accord, and a mass of citizens priding themselves on the most they can acquire of individualism and freedom from restraint.

The late Lord Lytton speaks thus of Pythagoras in reference to the external and political development of his Order. "He selected the three hundred, who at Croton formed his Order, from the noblest families, and they were professedly reared to know themselves, that so they might be fitted to command the world. It was not long before this society, of which Pythagoras was the head, appears to have supplanted the ancient Senate, and obtained the legislative administration. In this institution Pythagoras stands alone; no other founder of Greek philosophy resembles him." Even Plato was content to have his ideal Republic on paper.

The ideal of a community of perfect order, each having his place, learner at the feet of teacher, novice gladly subordinate to sage, when carried out into the political world, means a hierarchical aristocracy. An aristocracy, with one proviso, is the most perfect type of government conceivable. It must ever maintain the condition of its title by being an administration conducted by such as are, at the time being, the noblest souls, and the fittest to rule, of the whole community. Such a government possessed of absolute power would raise life to its highest possible perfection.

But in this world, even if the maintenance of an unimpeachable and trusted body of administrators could be ensured, the system will not always work so well in practice as in theory. We seem to need to live by actions and reactions, rather than by the placid perfection which wise theory would dictate.

Questions difficult to answer arise : whose choice decides who are the aristocracy ? what is to be done when corruption follows the temptations of power ? These do not seem to have arisen to complicate the political problem on which the Pythagoreans were labouring. They came into power of their own inherent force ; their discipline was not impaired by the exercise of power for its own sake.

But the system is too perfect to work. There are jealousies and discontent among the masses, to whom to be free is a more intelligible ideal than to be orderly. A democracy, if it suffer, has no one to blame but itself, it can but supersede individual officials, grumble and go on. Under aristocratic rule there is a ready target for the vials of the popular wrath to accumulate themselves against. The masses are like children, they love their own way, and that way is not always the way of wisdom. The ardour of inharmonious life, the sway of popular caprice, Pythagoras meets by a system as rigidly perfect as that of the steps of his disciples' initiation. His standard is too high, his ideal of life too solemn and religious, too much like the life of the Egyptian priests in the temple. The higher natures cannot always allow for the lusts and loves and self-will of the lower ; they would tranquillize those who prefer to retain the prerogative of not being wise until they want to be. It is easy to understand how a restless, pleasure-loving community might baffle the benevolent schemes of a calm philosopher, and how he would vainly seek to remedy the difficulty by relaxations of one kind, restrictions of another.

The late Lord Lytton, a man of statesmanlike mind, comments thus: " Pythagoras committed a fatal error when, in his attempt to revolutionize society, he had recourse to aristocracies for his agents. Revolutions, especially those influenced by religion, can never be worked out but by popular emotions. It was from this error of judgment that he enlisted the people against him; for by the account of Neanthes, related by Porphyry, and, indeed, from all other testimony, it is clearly evident that to popular, not party, commotion his fall must be ascribed. It is no less clear that after his death, while his philosophical sect remained, his political code crumbled away. The only seeds sown by philosophers which spring up into great States, are those that, whether for good or evil, are planted in the hearts of the many."

The good influence of the Pythagorean school must have been considerable. From great luxury and licentiousness, the community was in great part converted to sobriety and order. The original constitution of the city appears to have been aristocratic; the Pythagoreans held in especial respect existing laws, but probably they consolidated, and made more theoretically perfect the aristocratic system.

Jealousies arose; party spirit developed, and with that the calm rule of wisdom, such as we may imagine to hold good amongst angels, or perfectly trained Pythagoreans, must at once be impaired. On the one side was the strong tumultuous agitation and excitement of a popular movement; on the other, calm, beneficent, impassive philosophy, impressed with the religious conception of the moral utility of obedience! To Pythagoras the licence of a mob must have meant servitude to passion.

Excuses were not long wanting among those who sought to throw off the strict, but kindly Pythagorean yoke. Trifles or monstrosities of well-marked colour, these please savages and mobs. It was urged that the members of the order had a separate life from that of the other citizens; that they gave their right hand to those of their own sect alone (it was probably the secret grip by which members recognized one another); that they shared their possessions with each other in common, but excluded their relations from this fellowship, as if they were strangers. Every citizen, it was advanced ought to be eligible for the magistracy, and the rulers were bound to render an account of their conduct to a committee elected by lot from the multitude. A democratic impulse this, and an absolute inversion of the perfect ideal of hierarchical rule.

Kylon, who had been found unfitted to go through with the Pythagorean training, on account of his violent, undisciplined character, delivered long harangues against the society. Another individual followed suit with a garbled and calumnious version of certain of the maxims of the order. In fact, it was discovered by their opponents that their whole system of pretended philosophy was a mere plot and conspiracy against popular rights!

These articles of impeachment, industriously circulated, produced their natural effect. The people for whom the right to magistracy was claimed, took the law into their own hands, set on fire a temple where a number of Pythagoreans were assembled, or, according to another account, the house of Milo, and all but two of those within were burned or massacred. It is not known whether Pythagoras himself was among the number present; and whether he went into sorrowful exile or was killed is a matter of doubt. A simultaneous wave of democracy was advancing in Greece herself, and Pythagorism, as a political rather than a philosophical institution, was crushed for ever.

Pythagoras had imbued his followers with a high spiritual influence, and his doctrines were such as would be engraven upon the heart rather than set as dogmas upon a skin of parchment. When the democratic revolt had succeeded in breaking the bands and casting away the cords of the Pythagorean order—a constraint that was irksome because too noble, and therefore too exigent—the influence of the brotherhood was not wholly upset, but only changed in character. The political organization was finally broken up, or in other words the endeavour to force wise and sober action upon unfit people, whose ambitions craved the wide exercise of freedom, was frustrated. The Pythagorean medicine for humanity might be the true one, and yet not the true one for individuals who had not yet traversed the early and perhaps necessary lessons of personal emulation and life's natural activities. By the suppression of its political proceedings, the Pythagorean order, so soon as the protracted civil dissensions were pacified, was able to devote itself with a single heart to its true pursuit of religion in philosophy and harmony in science. Having journeyed through the fires of adversity, the members might well have passed out of discipleship into the serenity of the realization of truth. And now they were able to communicate of such things as they had in the old and peaceful way to such alone as were earnest and willing to receive them. The organized attempt to make heaven out of earth by a quasi-paternal control had fallen through; the purpose remained the clearer of fostering the divine spark little by little and wherever it might present itself. As a philosophical sect, after the political feud was healed, the Pythagoreans were re-admitted to the very cities from which they had been expelled. We are reminded of the jealous fear lest Jesus of Nazareth, tolerated as a humble spiritual teacher, should set about making himself a king; a fact which may be taken in support of a doctrine we may advance, that the generality would rather be ruled by a tyrant than by an angel; their bodies might bend before the violence of the one, their inmost souls would tremble before the mild perfection of the other. The Pythagoreans were in all probability far from being angels; they probably gave way to an elation in their early political successes, which no magical music of their master could altogether free from the taint of partisan pride.

It was a beautiful dream, the noblest chimera in the world,

not only to render God the things that be God's, but to render to God also the things that be Cæsar's; but even for the completeness of the contour of the life of Pythagoras, we may be glad that he died in the tumult that purged his institutions from their error, rather than that he should have found an apotheosis in the triumph of that which was to be proved untriumphant in the sequel. We may say in fancy that the difficult lesson of Ithuriel is to learn that his fine-pointed delicate spear has to refrain from the touch that will crumble even manifest evil, when that evil has to bide its time, and become in some manner, even beyond Ithuriel's ken, good in the making. The way to the blessed life shown by Pythagoras was not a way that a mob could walk in, nor was it the true mode of preparation to constrain them by laws wielded by a brotherhood who were unconstrained and volunteer workers themselves. The most certain way of all to irritate the surging democratic factions was to govern them straitly by an exclusive oligarchy, whose members lived apart and had a secret bond of brotherhood among themselves, a spring of sympathy which was closed to those without the pale of the order.

Too much, perhaps, has been said of constraint. It is probable that for a time the influence of Pythagoras was such that even the bustling masses of the great Greco-Italian city were eager to follow him, even in directions demanding a higher ideal than they were wont to follow. And some hundreds of the noble and wealthy classes had become converts, and were enrolled in the exoteric club which represented Pythagorean politics. But of ignorant enthusiasts, as of revival converts, few possess staying power. A French writer upon Pythagoras (A. Ed. Chaignet), speaking of human nature where he should rather be speaking of mediocre human qualities, says that, "while in the intoxication of a beautiful sentiment of perfection it believes itself capable of so many sacrifices and so sublime an effort, it relapses quickly indeed into prosaic and vulgar reality." A relapse of this kind, which, from the democratic point of view, seemed not a reaction but a struggle for political rights, gave birth to the revolution, to whose blind fury was due the death of the leading associates of Pythagoras.

The master himself had occupied no official post in the administration, and it is probable that the action of the inner circle of the order was rather that of latent influence than of any public exhibition of power. It was the more easy, therefore, after the turmoil had calmed down, for the brethren to resume their position as students of the mathematics of this world and the rhythmic perfection of the next. After worldly failure, they were the better able to succeed as initiators into a mode of life which endeavoured after purification from mundane dross, and opened an entrance into the higher spheres by way of self-mastery, self-denial, and the exchange of a sensual view of things for one æsthetically pure.

Among the many suggestions designed to account for the peculiar acquirements of Pythagoras when in his youthful stage, is one that he derived the greater part of his ethical doctrines from Themistoclea, the Priestess of Delphi. If he received from a woman, he well returned the gift to the sex. He instituted reunions of ladies who were attached to the order, while youths and children were also brought under the influence of his ideal. The individual he knew how to help on the way of reform; the State might also be reformed with mathematical certainty by the improvement of individuals, were it not for one ascertained fact. This is that parents of inferior qualities of mind and even of inferior constitution are more prolific than those who, from their own high qualities, might be expected to bring into the world children of genius, or at least, a progeny of superior parts, ready to carry forward rather than fling into the mire the splendid torch of progress. And, moreover, the system of reform by units must be a volunteer system, to be of any value; and consequently can never be completely undertaken until all are of one mind.

Meanwhile, the heroic efforts after the reform of the State by wise laws had failed, and magistrates, descending from the *rôle* of fathers and tutors, arrived once again at the position of executors of the will of the people ; or, if they were like the generality, effected the most of appearance of performance of that august will with the least contravention of their own judgment that the popular surveillance would allow. It is reasonable to suppose that the private and individual lessons and labours of the brotherhood may have been carried on the more earnestly for the collapse of their administrative scheme. Their faith had been tried and not found wanting. They at least succeeded in initiating a way of life which no doubt helped many a brother that came after them to "take heart again."

"Have those who delighted in the conversation of Homer," asks Plato, "handed down to posterity the tradition of any Homeric way of life, in the same way that Pythagoras was himself much beloved on this account, and from that day to this those that bear his name and follow the Pythagorean habit are accounted conspicuous beyond others?" (Rep. X. 600 a).

We may bear in mind the notable differences which exist between the Pythagorean brotherhood and monastic communities, such as those of the Buddhists, Therapeuts, and Christian ascetics. The Greek wisdom-seekers were not celibates, they did not hold in morbid contempt and fear the principle of beauty, or the exercise of the functions of life, but strove rather to refine and cultivate the perceptions and the uses of art. Their ideal being perfection, they could not reasonably neglect any of the many roads by which the human spirit may rise into glimpses of that ideal. This concord of the spirit of the universe, they typified as the choir of the muses, who they said subsisted in conjunction with each other, and were always one and the same, comprehending in themselves symphony, harmony, rhythm, and all things whatsoever which lead to concord. "Sweeter than Sirens are the muses," said Pythagoras.

Women in the community were called to life and activity, and not to intellectual activity alone, but by a separate and frequent instruction, to the practice of the virtues and duties proper to their sex and position. They were to be taken as from a vestal hearth by their husbands and brought home by them in such spirit as if both were in the presence of the gods. The pair were to be true to each other, the wife being taken into association, not as a subordinate, but as the companion of life. And as other compacts were engraved in tablets and pillars, so the conjugal compact was to find its seal and writing in the offspring themselves. The divulsion of parents and children from each other, Pythagoras also regarded as the greatest of injuries. To him who saw that no project for improvement was of any avail which did not make the individual its sole ground and only test, it must have seemed like expecting to add gentleness to life without the spells of music, to look for good progress in children without their knowing the warm touch of the love of their parents.

If, in presence of their philosophic dignity, we regard the Pythagorean ladies as abbesses, we must not forget that they were married abbesses, equal with their husbands, and mutually sharing with them the love of their children. And the simple purpose in life, which all the brethren were taught to hold before them, was, To be such in reality as they wished to appear to be to others.

How pure was the ideal of the marriage relation among them may be judged from the following, which is of more import if considered in its relation to a then prevalent conception of ceremonial purity than can be well understood now. It puts to shame the petty precautionary precepts of Rabbinism. "Theano was asked in how many days a woman becomes pure after intercourse with a man. She replied : If it be her own husband, she becomes pure at once ; if it be another's, never." This is as the story is told by Diogenes Laertios and Stobaios ; in Clement of Alexandria it is given with the added implication that the purity is to be such as to entitle the women to join the festival of Thesmophoria, which was in honour of Demeter, the laws of nature, civil order, and especially the institution of marriage. By Iamblichos the observation is ascribed to Pythagoras himself; but between his wife and himself there is no need to debate the authorship.

The influence of Pythagoras is in no way shown to better advantage than in its effect upon the women, whom, like Buddha, he admitted among his disciples. To his daughter Damo it is said that he entrusted his Commentaries, and charged her to divulge them to no one outside the circle, Though she might have sold these discourses for money, she faithfully fulfilled her trust and would not abandon them, deeming obedience to her father's serious injunctions to be, even in face of poverty, something more valuable than gold.

It was long ago remarked that the Greek schools were schools of philosophy and not of languages, and that it is in the knowledge of things, and not of the mediums by which a knowledge of them is conveyed, that true learning consists. Modern scholars are perhaps in danger of losing sight of the light of truth that inspired ancient writers, by placing it under the bushel of scientific criticism and the apparatus of philology.

The pre-existence of the soul, which is said by Herodotus to be originally an Egyptian doctrine, and by Philostratos to have been learned from the Brahmans, Pythagoras appears to have believed in, with all seriousness and earnestness as a fact ; the modern tendency is to regard such a view historically, as an interesting philosophical speculation ; to hold it off as at arm's length by the intellect, and by no means to entertain or reject it with any warmth of personal interest. "He reminded many of his familiars," says Iamblichos, " by most clear and evident indications, of the former life which their soul lived before it was bound to the body." With regard to the memory which Pythagoras claimed to have of the sojourning places of his own soul in its past transmigratory life, there is a tradition tending to show that, if it were a madness, there was at least sane method in it. It is quite possible that the stories, according to which Pythagoras specified the historic individuals whom he identified with himself, may be the inventions of his followers, in supposed accordance with the theory. Pythagoras is said to have asserted that his soul found its presentment as the chieftain Euphorbos at the epoch of the Trojan war; and in the six hundred years between that time and the then present, his soul had passed through several bodies before it came into that in which it then tabernacled. But the theory itself, left in its proper indefiniteness, deserves respect. We may remember the Water of Oblivion into which a mortal was believed to be dipped while on his journey from Earth to Hades. Conversely, we are bound by fact to recognize that, if we adopt a theory of pre-existent life, we have somehow let the realizable memory of it be washed away. If we picture to ourselves a soul entering material existence from some other life, it will be evident that the memory of that existence does not reside in the new material tabernacle, but, if anywhere, in the spiritual entity which by degrees is availing itself of, informing, and actuating the wondrous physical machinery that is placed, with new openings at every stage of growth, at its disposal. If, now, the spirit be fully attracted into that external life, finding all its interests therein, receiving all its impressions therethrough, and leaving no unabsorbed part of itself still opened to the life unseen, there is no likelihood of any spiritual consciousness or reminiscences asserting themselves. The faculties of the spirit are all applied to its physical activity.

But if a spirit should come to be incarnate, which is too

large in its proper actions to be wholly drawn into terrestrial life, there will remain a part not closed in by the corporeal bars, but reaching above them or into a ken beyond them. A gateway will remain open, a vista along which in meditation or emotion, by vision or by effort, the spirit may gaze on or wander toward that sea which brought it hither, bearing it along, as it were fluid particle becoming nucleated cell, within the infinite circulation of the veins of God. Through that hidden channel, when the soul is conscious of its partial enfranchisement, will come scarce intelligible whispers, broken messages of strange memories, stimulating sub-consciousness of spirit; these may make the routine of earth seem comparatively small, and either draw the soul into the deep recesses of what seems to be mere contemplation, as viewed from the earthly plane, or sting it into large dreams of such actions as mark heroes, and make the marvel of pettifogging men.

Of this gift of Pythagoras we have the account in poetic form; that Hermes, who among the Egyptians was accounted the conductor of souls in the unseen world (a doctrine which Pythagoras also explicitly teaches), had desired him to select any gift he pleased, with the exception of immortality; such immortality, that is, it must be presumed, as was deemed to appertain to deific beings; the hierarchical order, according to Pythagoras, being gods, daimons, heroes, men. He accordingly requested that, whether living or dead,[*] he might preserve his memory. He therefore retained it on his transmigratory road, preserving consciousness of his soul's Hadean experience, and a recollection of the hap of other souls. As Ovid (Metamorph.) puts into the mouth of Pythagoras:—

> "Souls dispense with death; and their last abode left behind,
> For aye, in new homes received, a dwelling and life they find."

---

[*] It is difficult to decide in what sense the words are used; whether "living" must here mean terrestrial living, or the opposite condition, as implied in such phrases as "to live is death, to die is gain." Socrates says (Gorgias, 492 e), "I should not wonder if Euripides speaks the truth when he says: 'Who knows whether to live is not death, and to die, life?'"

In this consciousness of pre-existence Pythagoras manifested what the Brahmans and Buddhists regarded as the sign of the true prophet. "I call him alone a Brahman, who knows his former abode, who sees both heaven and hell, and has reached the extinction of births," has "attained his last body" or birth (Vaseṭṭha Sutta). Sakya Muni says of his own corporeal embodiments, and their cause in selfish longings: "I have run through the revolution of numerous births, seeking the architect of this dwelling (the body), and discovering him not; grievous is repetition of birth. O, architect, thou art now seen; thou shalt not build me another house; thy rafters are broken, thy ridge-pole is sundered; the mind being detached has attained to the extinction of desire."

There is very good reason for this doctrine being unfamiliar and incredible to the most of us, who in all probability, if the hypothesis be true, have not yet arrived at the state when the soul begins to stir mightily within the husk of its final infleshment: our body, therefore, is for the time being the best one possible, and, being suited to our state, gently veils our eyes to obviate the disturbance which a too early vision of enfranchised life might produce.

Those who care to discover whether Pythagoras was alone in cherishing a seeming chimera, or rather whether, among any traditions more familiar to us than the doctrines of Hindoo ascetics, there are any traces of acceptance of the theory of pre-existence, may ponder in all reverence such instances as the following:—

"Jesus said . . . before Abraham was born, I am" (John ix. 58). That is, Before Abraham was in terrestrial existence, I possessed essential existence.

"Glorify thou me with thine own self with the glory which I had with thee before the world was" (John xvii. 5). The expression "the world" denotes terrestrial existence; and we may be reminded of such an expression as "all the tribes of the earth will mourn" as denoting the depression and overthrow of the bodily powers when the spirit leaves them to their inherent nothingness.

The Pharisees, it is known, held the doctrine of preexistence; of the disciples of Rabbi Jesus the following is told: "His disciples asked him, saying, Rabbi, who sinned, this man or his parents, that he should be born blind?" Glanvil in his "Lux Orientalis" advances the theory that "there were doubtless many doctrines entertained by the apostles and the more learned of their followers, which were disproportioned to the capacities of the generality, who hold but little theory. . . . There was strong meat for the more grown and manly Christians, as well as milk for babes and weaker constitutions. Now Scripture was designed for the benefit of the most, and they could little understand, and less make use of, a speculation so remote from common conceit as pre-existence." Jerome states that the theory was propounded among the early Christians.

The following shows the popular Jewish doctrine on the subject, blindly and superstitiously held:—

"Who do men say that the son of man is? And they said, some, John the Baptist; others, Elijah; and others, Jeremiah, or one of the prophets!" (Matt. xvi. 14).

"Herod, the tetrarch, heard of the fame of Jesus, and said unto his servants, This is John the Baptist; he was raised from the dead; and therefore the mighty works are active in him" (Matt. xiv. 1, 2).

It is probable that the doctrine of corporeal resurrection is an offshoot of this belief in reincarnation, having sprung from the difficulty of the realization by the mind, while relying upon corporeal senses for its information, of any but terrestrial embodiment. It was probably in this materialistic sense that David Hume pronounced transmigration to be "the only system of immortality that philosophy can listen to."

Pythagoras asserted that the soul went a necessary circle of transmigrations; but we hear nothing of his expressing any expectation to be embodied again, after his decease as Pythagoras. We may recall Buddha's apostrophe of the cause of repeated birth which he had discovered in his own nature, and at last had overcome. It seems to be the quality which later theologians described as " the will of the flesh."

The writer of the Book of Wisdom expresses himself thus as to the reason why he was able to find a body that served him well : " I was a witty child, and had a good spirit. Rather, it was through being good that I came into an undefiled body." Spenser appears to be following this when he writes :—

> " So every spirit, as it is more pure,
>   And hath in it the more of heavenly light,
> So it the fairer body doth procure
>   To habit in, and it more fairly dight
>   With cheerful grace and amiable sight.
> For, of the soul, the body form doth take,
> For soul is form, and doth the body make."

But Spenser goes a step further when he says the soul makes the body. The body is prepared for it, and may be chosen by it. The stronger the tenant, the more it may modify and transfigure that tabernacle. But can we, with the facts of life before us, say more than this ?

Having shown that there were adherents to the doctrine of pre-existence in the ages succeeding Pythagoras, we may ask the question how far they are indebted to him as the father of the tradition. From Pythagoras to Plato is a short and certain step; from Neo-Pythagorism and Neo-Platonism was drawn much that, however we may disown the source, we have absorbed through our own traditions. But the doctrine of pre-existence has for the most part shone with broken rays, like a light floating on the wave of a troubled and misty sea. In India alone has it held a central place among definite and accepted dogmas.

One great secret of the wide influence of Pythagoras seems to lie in the fact that he was not a fanatic or sectarian. With a spiritual creed visionary enough to carry a man off his natural balance, he yet deliberately wedded to that faith the practical truth that "the first attention which should be paid to men, is that which takes place through the senses, as when some one perceives beautiful figures and forms, or hears beautiful rhythms and melodies." He strove to make the natural life pure, and sane, and strong, conceiving that a well-developed and wholesome man would better receive the higher truths of life in their season, than one narrowed and crippled by frantic asceticism. Virtue, he realized, is not a plant of sudden growth, but one requiring careful and patient development. His followers starved no part of their nature, but strove to regulate all their faculties, whether corporeal, emotional, or intellectual.

The philosophy of metempsychosis is subtly conveyed by the late Prof. F. D. Maurice as follows ("Mental and Moral Philosophy"): "This soul, which can look before and after, can shrink and shrivel itself into an incapacity of contemplating aught but the present moment. Of what depths of degeneracy it is capable! What a beast it may become! And if something lower than itself, why not something higher? And if something higher and lower, may there not be a law accurately determining its elevation and descent? Each soul has its peculiar evil tastes, bringing it to the likeness of different creatures beneath itself; why may it not be under the necessity of abiding in the condition of that thing to which it has adapted and reduced itself?"

We find among the relics of Xenophanes a story which is understood to refer to Pythagoras: "It is said that as a passer-by he was touched with pity on account of a dog that was being beaten, and spoke the following words: 'Stay thine hand, and do not strike, since it is the soul of a dear man which I recognize by perception through its cry.'" This is a clear trace of Indian philosophy; but it is probable that Pythagoras, if he uttered the words recorded, only meant to startle, and thus to attract men's minds into a broader sympathy with living beings. The claim to distinguish the voice was, it may be imagined, a bit of fiction, and it reminds us of the methods of the Hebrew rabbis when they wished to fledge the arrow of a recondite thought.

The Golden Song of the Pythagoreans concludes with the assurance, "When thou hast left behind thy body, and art come to the Ether, free [or to the free Ether], thou wilt be deathless, an imperishable god, no longer a mortal."

This will remind readers of the Hebrew scriptures of the expression (Gen. iii. 5), " Ye shall be as Elohim ;" and (Gen. iii. 22), "The man is become as one of us, to know good and evil." The word *Elohe*, plural *Elohim*, is however not confined to the Supreme Being, but applied to supernal beings, and also to mortals as vicegerents of Deity.

The following story argues the possession by the Pythagoreans of a calm and orderly mind, even in regard to occult powers: "When Pythagoras was asked by a certain man what was indicated by seeming in sleep to converse with his father who was dead, he answered that it indicated nothing. ' For neither,' said he, ' is anything portended by your speaking with me.'"

From Pythagoras was derived the impetus to so large a wave of thought, spreading in different directions with distinctive tendencies, but not absolutely accordant doctrine, that, since he did not write, it is impossible to differentiate the exact teaching of the master himself. The problem is further complicated by the fact that other kindred influences commingled with his. As K. O. Müller states : "An extensive Orphic literature first appeared about the time of the Persian war, when the remains of the Pythagorean order in Magna Græcia united themselves to the Orphic associations."

But some of the ethical sayings ascribed to Pythagoras are so simple and of such deep religious feeling, that they seem rather to have emanated from him than to be the formal utterances of a philosophic school.

He forbids men to pray for anything in particular for themselves, because they do not know what is good for them. He pronounces against oaths, on the high ground that every man ought so to exercise himself as to be worthy of belief without an oath. He proclaimed the beautiful rule, far too high apparently to be generally followed among men, that people should associate with one another in such a way as not to make enemies of their friends, but to make friends of their enemies. The spiritual nature of the man is also evidenced by his teaching his disciples that they should think nothing exclusively their own. The nature which is opened to nothing beyond earth life cannot dare to relax its grasp even upon the lowest form of property. Pythagoras says, "Esteem that to be above all things good which in being communicated to another will be the rather increased to yourself."

"Despise those things which, when liberated from the body, you will not want; and exercising yourself in those things of which when liberated from the body you will be in want, invoke the gods to become your helpers" (Stobæi Sent.). "It is not proper to despise those things of which we shall be in want after the putting aside of the body" (Sexti Sent.).

The souls that belong to the orders of daimons and heroes, from whom dreams come to men, make, according to Pythagoras, this most excellent affirmation, that man's most important privilege is the being able to persuade his soul to either good or bad. The soul of man, he taught, possesses intuition or instinct, mind,* and reasoning faculty, whereas other animals lack the last division.

The following may serve as examples of the symbolic

---

* In the sense in which the word is used in the phrase, "I had a mind to," which includes will and even passion.

sayings of Pythagoras; which are said to be analogous to prophecies, to the Pythian oracles, and to seeds, small in bulk, which produce manifest and extensive effects:—

"It is not good to walk in the dark without any clothing." In obscure or hidden matters do not lay bare your thought.

"Do not sleep in a grave." The current interpretation of this is, When your parents have left you money, do not grow idle. But this version can, perhaps, be bettered by those who call to mind the injunction, "Let the dead bury their own dead." Plato, too, calls the body a grave of the soul (Crat. 400 c), probably drawing his doctrine from a Pythagorean source. Philolaus (as recorded by Clem. Al., Strom. iii. p. 403) says, "The ancient theologists and soothsayers testify that the soul is conjoined with the body as a punishment, and is, so to speak, buried in this body." Socrates says (Gorgias, 492 e), "We, perhaps, are really dead, as I have heard from one of the wise, that we are now dead, and that the body is our sepulchre."

"Do not touch the lyre with unwashed hands." The teacher must himself be what he teaches.

"Sing not your song before a four-footed thing." Cast not your pearls before swine.

"Do not hold discourse in a reedbed." Do not confide in men who are like reeds shaken by every wind. "Do not write on snow."

The following ethical maxims are from a Pythagorean collection ascribed to Demophilos, and entitled "Similitudes; or Life's Medicining":—

"Life, like a musical instrument, becomes sweeter by a system of both relaxation and tightening up.

"As a harbour is a refuge to a ship, so is friendship to life.

"Ridicule, like salt, should be sparingly used.

"Garments down to the feet impede bodies, property in excess impedes souls.

"Pleasures must be passed by as if they were sirens, by one who is earnest to look on virtue as a fatherland.

"As in plants, so in youth, the first growth foretokens the future fruit of virtue.

"Of life, as of a statue, all the parts ought to be comely.

"Neither should the altar be removed from the temple, nor compassion from human nature.

"A loquacious and brutally ignorant man in prayer or sacrifice casts a slur on that which is divine; the wise man then alone is priest, alone is god-lover, alone knows how to pray.*

"Whatever, if thou shouldst acquire, thou canst not retain, ask not this of God; for God's gift is inalienable; wherefore he will not confer that which thou canst not retain.

"Be sleepless with regard to thy mental part, for sleep in respect of this is akin to veritable death.

"God misleads, not from anger, but from our want of perception; wrath is foreign to God, for wrath is excited by things not in accordance with one's will; but with God there is naught not in accordance with his will.

"Naked was a wise man sent forth, in nakedness will he call upon him that sent him; for to him only that is not burdened with alien matters is God a listener.

"Other gift greater than virtue it is impossible to receive from God.

"Oblations and sacrifices convey no honour to God; votive offerings are no adornment to God; but the God-inspired mind enduringly conjoins itself to God, for like must needs continually advance to like.

"It is more grievous to be the slave of passions than of tyrants.

"It is better to argue more with yourself than with your neighbours.

---

* "Pythagoras announced that sacrificers should approach the gods, not only with a body purged from all practice of iniquity, but also with a soul that kept itself pure" (Diod. Sic., Exc., p. 555).

"If you always bear in mind that in whatever place your soul may be, and your body accomplish its work, God is present as inspector; in all your prayers and actions you will be in awe of the spectator from whom nothing can be hidden, and will, moreover, possess divinity as an indweller with you.

"We ought to seek such husband and children as will abide after the departure of this life.

"Lives like unto divinity as truly as may be, the independent and property-less philosopher, and deems the greatest wealth to be the having gained possession of naught of what is another's, or of what is not necessary. For the fresh gain of money expands the lust thereof ever; but the independence of true well-living is to do no one wrong.

"Esteem those to be eminently your friends who advantage your soul rather than your body.

"Desire rather that thy comrades should respect thee than fear thee; for veneration is akin to respect, but hatred to fear.

"Be aware that no false pretence lies hidden for long.

"It is not safe to say a word concerning God to those who have become the prey of opinion; for in sooth to speak truth or falsehood before them brings equal danger.

"Deem that to be fine training, by which you are enabled to bear the boorishness of the ignorant.

"A stranger, provided he be righteous, surpasses not only a citizen, but even a kinsman."

We may call to mind the outcry of the opponents of Pythagoras at this introduction of the higher law; the following, also, presented too stern an ideal of freedom for the democratic factions who threw off the yoke of Pythagoras:—

"No one is free who is not master of himself.

"Every goodly thing gotten is preceded and led up to, by labour with self-mastery.

"Do what you judge to be morally beautiful, even though by doing it you incur ill-repute; for a mob is a bad judge of a virtuous deed.

"Do great things without making promises of great things.

"Since we have our roots, and grow forth out of God, let us cling to our root; for verily, streams of water, and the plants of the earth also, if cut off from their root, grow withered and rotten.

"Vigour of soul lies in temperance; for this is the light of a soul unaffected by passions; nay, it is much better to die, than through ungovernableness of body to make dark the soul."

The following are from miscellaneous collections:—

"About the life of the uninstructed, as on a play-actor, are many wrappages that have to be pulled off—wrappages of cloudy conceit.

"The arms of Achilles will not fit Thersites, nor the goods of the soul a fool.

"As with an obliging friend, it is sweet to grow old in fellowship with goodly thought.

"Have confidence in virtue like a chaste wife, trust fortune like a fickle jade.

"We should take nourishment from the contemplative pursuit of wisdom, up to what measure we may, exactly as from ambrosia and nectar. For undefiled is the sweetness that proceeds therefrom, and it has the power of making the divine element large-souled, and if not eternal, at least versed in eternal things.

"We render reasonable worship to God, if we make the mind that is in us free from all depravity as from a spot.

"We should adorn a temple with offerings, but the soul with lessons.

"As before the great mysteries we have to receive and hand down the small, so before philosophy comes training.

"The hopes of virtue are own children of the soul, but those of vice bastards.

"Vain the word of the philosopher, if no mischievous

affection of man's nature be cured. For as medicine is of no service without it drives out diseases from bodies, so with philosophy, unless it expel the vice of the soul.

"Men become the best of themselves, when they are walking towards the gods.

"All things of friends are common, and friendship is equality.

"It is grievously difficult to walk in many ways of life at once."

"On being asked in what act men can be like gods, Pythagoras replied, 'In speaking the truth.' The mages indeed declare with regard to the greatest of the gods, whom they call Oromagdes (Ahura-Mazda), that in his body he is like unto light, in his soul unto truth" (Iamblichos).

"Pythagoras affirmed that there enters into cities first luxury, thereupon satiety, then insolence, and thereafter perdition.

"The origin and basis of all good order in states is a righteous disposition of domestic affairs, for states consist of houses.

"Exact not punishment from those who have done unjustly, for it is enough for them to be brought low by their own evil."

From these ethical and practical precepts, small as they are in number of words, something may be learned of the religious and moral system of Pythagoras.

A RAY FROM THE SPHERE OF PLATO.

IF we seek to "unsphere the spirit of Plato"[*] we undertake a large task, for every great spirit is sphere-like, and cannot be seen all round at one view. Nor can such an orb be rightly unsphered by being unwound like a cocoon, and woven with an alien warp into a critical and analytic web. The silvery threads have their perfect shine, only when they lie entwined in their own organic order and purity.

But, if on any side we can touch a sphere, the great law of sympathy allows us to enter at that point of contact into its precincts; and now, if we clarify our own atmosphere, we can catch the beautiful colours of a radiance which is shining in upon us.

In this country we are professedly Christian; there is said to be a Christian element in Plato; here, then, should be an avenue into which Plato's road and our own converge, and in which we might reasonably expect to find a green and pleasant spot abounding in pasture for the pilgrim mind.

If we enter into Plato's thought by means of such a comparison, we may be sure that, if the result proves satisfactory under such a test, there will be other regions in Plato's mind which we may safely infer to be worth visiting. And into these at any time we may enter at will, if provided with the passport of interest and appreciation.

Dr. C. Ackerman, archdeacon at Jena, wrote, in 1835,

[*] Milton, "Il Penseroso."

words which those who look upon Christian doctrines as something different in kind from the religious utterances of noble Gentiles would do well to ponder: "The deeper we penetrate into the writings of the ancients the less can we ward off the conviction that, on the side of doctrine, they truly stand but little behind Christianity. They contain, not only almost all the moral doctrines and sublime sayings which the gospel has given us, but many of these are even more sharply conceived and more beautifully presented in the former than in the latter."

For the purpose of the present comparison we shall take any words put in the mouth of any of Plato's characters, which are not merely controversial, as Plato's own; and this on the ground that, whatever the origin of each thought, he would not give expression to any (apart from the momentary necessities of controversy) with which he was not in more or less sympathy himself.

It has been said that "Plato finds his highest joy in the whole and the unit; Aristotle in the mass and abundance of sharply defined particulars;" and that all philosophizing leans to the Platonic or to the Aristotelian school.

We must, therefore, be prepared, in touching upon the sphere of Plato, to put aside for a while the plodding methods of science; to turn away from the minute certainties of the senses, and to unchain the mind for a more daring and extended sweep. We must seek the faith which was in Plato;—that the ideal is not mere subjective phantasy; that there is a something, called truth, which the mind may not only grasp, and find substantial and organic, but recognize as being its own birthright and sustenance.

Whether our "builder and maker is God," or is Protoplasm; whether man is Nature's secretion, or the spirit of a higher plane, bent beneath a yoke for education, and for a growth which he is free to retard; on these great questions Plato is never for a moment in doubt. His conception of man in polar opposite states—the ideally perfect, and the fallen condition, is embodied in one of his most sublime passages:—

"Through many generations, so long as the God's nature within them was yet a sufficiency, they were heedful of the sacred laws, and bore themselves with loving mind toward the kinship of divineness, for their uttermost motives were real and true, and in everywise great; so that they dealt with meekness conjoined with wisdom in regard to the contingencies of fortune, and in their relations one with another. Wherefore, overlooking all but virtue, they little esteemed circumstances as they presented themselves, and bore lightly as a burden the weight of gold or other possessions; nor were they drawn beneath the intoxication of luxury, or rendered intemperate through opulence; but with soberness they clearly perceived that out of their common love, combined with virtue, all these things would proceed with increase; whereas to bestow earnest pains and marks of esteem upon material things, would result not only in their decay, but in the ruin of virtue and affection with them.

"It was owing to such reasoning and to the steadfastness of the divine nature, that they gained increase of all things as we have related.

"But when the God's portion became extinct in them, through admixture again and again with the prevalence of what was mortal, and the human nature gained the upper hand, then at length they became unable to bear circumstances as they presented themselves, and fell into deformity of life, and wore an aspect of baseness in the sight of him that can see, losing the fairest of what they had of most honourable, while unto those powerless to discern true life that leads to blessedness, they then bore the appearance most especially of being all-noble and happy, filled though they were with selfish lust after unfairness and power"* (Critias).

---

* The following would seem to be a modern reflection from Plato's luminous picture:—" . . . A human intellect originally greatly gifted, and capable of high

The doctrine is here conveyed that a community of persons, who act wisely and temperately and kindly one to another, and possess steadfastness of character, will find little difficulty in supplying their physical needs. It is, no doubt, an economic fact that waste of force is a consequence of rivalries and contentions, and that a community which could agree and work in harmony might become rich in the supply of every need. Indeed, there are instances which prove the fact. On the contrary, where the religious spirit ceases to be a devout attitude governing every act, and loses itself in ceremonial vagaries, where wholesome life is despised, and bodily needs are treated, not with cheerfulness, as a light burden, but with contempt, the very reverse will be the case. It is also true that over-anxiety about circumstances is not the way to improve them; for it paralyzes the natural powers. Viewed in this light, the teaching of Jesus is at one with the ideal of Plato, as represented in the quotation above made. Jesus declares a principle; it is for us, if we desire, to discover its application and verify its basis :—

"Fret not for the life (soul), what ye shall eat; nor yet for the body, what ye shall put on. . . . Your Father knows that ye have need of these things. But seek his kingdom, and these shall be added unto you. Fear not, little flock; for it is your Father's good pleasure to give you the kingdom" (Luke xii. 22, 30).

"Fret not for your life, what ye shall eat, or what ye shall drink; nor yet for your body, what ye shall put on. . . . Seek first his (your heavenly Father's) kingdom and righteousness, and all these shall be added unto you" (Matt. vi. 25, 33).

---

things, but gone utterly astray, partly by its own subtlety, partly by yielding to the temptations of the lower part of its nature, by yielding the spiritual to a keen sagacity of lower things, until it was quite fallen; and yet fallen in such a way, that it seemed not only to itself, but to mankind, not fallen at all, but wise and good, and fulfilling all the ends of intellect in such a life as ours, and proving, moreover, that earthly life was good, and all that the development of our nature demanded" (Nathaniel Hawthorne, "Septimius").

It may seem impossible to apply so ideal a principle to worldly circumstances already in existence, but it is really simple enough. The whole secret lies in the injunction "seek first God's kingdom." That kingdom is love, the true relationship of divineness. Were two people only, who are isolated in the worldly struggle, to join hands, and help each other by affectionate thoughtfulness, and a constant sympathy and willingness to give mutual aid in any and every way, there is no doubt whatever that the burden of both would be lightened to an extent beyond anticipation. The blind man can carry the lame, and in return be kept in the right way.

Plato puts in the mouth of Socrates an appeal which we cannot but regard as own brother to the words of Jesus quoted above: "I go about doing none other thing than persuading you, young and old alike, to take no care for the body, nor for riches, prior to or as zealously as for the soul, telling you how that virtue does not spring from riches, but riches and all other human blessings, both private and public, from virtue" (Apol. 30 a).

The apostolic character of Socrates is even more clearly shown in the following: "Oh, Athenians! I cleave to you and love you; but I shall rather obey God than you, and, so long as I breathe and am able, I shall not cease the pursuit of philosophy, and exhorting you, and making myself clear to any one of you with whom I may ever happen to come in contact" (Apol. 29 d).

Again we find:—

"To be excessively rich and good at the same time is impossible" (Laws, v. 742 e).

"A rich man will hardly enter into the kingdom of heaven" (Matt. xix. 23).

"To make much of riches, and, at the same time, fairly win the palm of a temperate life, is an impossibility; for one or the other must of necessity be held in little care" (Rep., viii. 555 c).

This will remind us of the more pointed utterance: "No man can serve two masters; for either he will hate the one, and love the other, or else he will hold to one, and despise the other. Ye cannot serve God and mammon" (Matt. vi. 24).

But Mammon, as Plato shows, is very readily taken for God: "Do you think that any one, when brought from the below to the middle, imagines anything else than that he is brought to the above; and when he stands in the middle and looks down to the place whence he has been brought, will he imagine that he is anywhere else than above, while he has not even seen the true above? . . . Such as are without experience of wisdom and virtue, and are always taking part in banquetings and such like things, are carried, as it appears, to the below, and back again to the middle, and there they wander throughout life, but they never pass beyond this and look up towards the truly above, or are drawn to it; nor are they ever filled with real essential being" (Rep., ix. 584 d, 586 a).

The comparison between the spiritual and the corporeal is continued still further by Plato. The following passages declare the supremacy of the soul over the body, and of virtuous purpose over untoward circumstance. After referring to the inherence to each particular of the physical world of a something which is injurious, as blindness to the eyes, disease to the body, rust to the metal, he turns to the soul: "Is there not something which renders the soul evil? Yes— injustice, intemperance, cowardice, ignorance. . . . Let us at no time say that the soul shall be ever a whit the nearer brought to destruction through burning fever, or any other disease, or by slaughter, not even though the whole body be cut into the smallest parts possible, until some one prove that through these sufferings of the body the soul herself becomes more unjust and unholy" (Rep., x. c. 10, 610 b).

"That which is divine is beautiful, wise, good, and everything of this kind. By these the wing of the soul is most of all nourished and increased, while by what is base and vile and the other contraries, it is brought to decay and perishes" (Phædr., 246 e).

"A man's soul is, after the gods, the most divine of all his possessions, a possession which is most his own. . . . The third is the honour of the body according to nature" (Laws, v. 726, 728 d).

"With respect to things just and unjust, and honourable and base, and good and evil, concerning which we are now taking counsel, ought we to follow the opinion of the multitude, and to pay respect thereto, or the opinion of the one, whoever it be that professes knowledge, whom we ought to reverence and respect rather than the whole mob of others? One whom, if we fail to follow, we shall corrupt and maim that part of ourselves which would be made better by justice, but is ruined by injustice? . . . Do we think that to be of less value than the body, whatever part of what is ours it may be about which injustice and justice are concerned? . . . It is not mere living that ought to be made of much account, but living well" (Crito, vii., viii., 47 c, e, 48 b).

"Suffer any one to despise thee, as without understanding, and to fling at thee the mud of contumely if he pleases; and by Zeus, cheerfully let him strike that ignominious blow; for thou wilt suffer nothing terrible, if thou art in reality honest and good, and a practiser of virtue" (Gorgias, lxxxiii. 52 c).

"Is there any one whom it avails . . . to take gold unjustly, supposing something of this kind befalls, that in taking the money he is at the same time enslaving the best part of himself to the worst? . . . But if he enslaves the most divine part of himself to the most godless and polluted part, is he not wretched, and taking a gift of gold to far more dreadful ruin than Eriphyle when she received a necklace for her husband's life?" (Rep., ix. 589 d).

We scarcely need quote the obvious parallels: "Be not afraid of them that kill the body, and are not able to kill the soul; but rather be afraid of one able to destroy both soul and body in a gehenna" (Matt. x. 28).

"Whosoever would save his soul, shall lose it; and whosoever shall lose his soul for my sake shall find it. For what shall a man be profited if he shall gain the whole world, and forfeit his soul? or what shall a man give in exchange for his soul?" (Matt. xvi. 25).

The following goes further in its assertion of the supremacy of the inward part, in its triumphant carelessness as to nominal stigmas and the conventional appearance of evil: "Blessed are ye when men shall hate you, and when they shall separate you from their company, and reproach you, and cast out your name as evil, for the son of man's sake" (Luke vi. 22).

"Amongst a multitude of arguments, whilst the rest are being refuted, this one alone remains unshaken, that we ought to beware of committing wrong rather than of being wronged, and that above all a man's care ought to be not to seem to be good, but to be good, in private life and public life alike" (Gorgias, 527 b).

"He who commits injustice is ever more wretched than he that suffers it, and he that is not punished than he that is" (Gorgias, 479 e).

According to the teachings of Jesus, a man may not only choose to be wronged rather than to wrong another, but may rejoice in being wronged, provided the evil said against him is false.

The comparisons between Plato and Jesus suggest very forcibly the difference between the slow and reasoned manner of the philosopher and writer, and the impassioned abruptness and poetry of the preacher and seer.

"One who is injured ought not, as the multitude thinks to return the injury. . . . To do evil in return when one has been evil-intreated, is that right or not? . . . It is not right to return an injury, or to do evil to any man, however one may have suffered from him" (Crito, x.).

This is a logical deduction from the broad principle that to do evil is not right. The sacred passion of the Christian spirit transcends even this lofty standard, and perhaps by disclosing the gleam of a more heavenly ideal, enables some to come up in practice more nearly to the level of virtue than would have been the case had a higher peak of aspiration never been revealed :—" Ye heard that it was said, Thou shalt love thy neighbour and hate thine enemy. But I say unto you, love your enemies and pray for them that persecute you."

There is a curious parallel between the Platonic and the Christian respect for established law, as a correspondence to perfect law. Jesus says, " Think not that I came to destroy the law or the prophets ; I came not to destroy, but to make full " (Matt. v. 17). [Cf. " Love is the making full of the law," Rom. xiv. 10]. Plato personifies violated earthly laws, as indignant with their violator, and saying, " Our brothers, the laws in Hades, will not receive thee kindly, knowing that thou didst endeavour so far as in thee lay to destroy us " (Crito, xvi. 54 c).

The following passages, taken in pairs, are mutually illustrative :—

" Blest are they that hunger and thirst after righteousness ; for they will be satisfied " (Matt. v. 6).

" They who have a yearning according to the soul—for there are those who yearn in their soul still more than in their bodies—find their object in whatever it is meet for the soul to have conceived and to swell with. What is it that is thus meet ? Thoughtful character and every other virtue " (Symposium, xxvii. 209 a).

" They were good by being sprung from the good " (Menexenus). Cf. Horat. " Fortes creantur fortibus."

" Every good tree brings forth good fruit " (Matt. vii. 17).

" Men are willing to have their feet and hands cut off, if their own members seem to them to be an evil " (Sympos., xxiv. 205 e).

"If thy right hand causes thee to offend, cut it off and cast it from thee; for it is profitable for thee that one of thy members perish, and not that thy whole body go away into a gehenna" (Matt. v. 30).

"That which is not seen continues always the same, but that which is seen never continues the same" (Phædo, xxvi. 79 a).

"We look not at the things which are seen, but at the things which are not seen; for the things which are seen are for a time, but the things which are not seen are eternal" (2 Cor. iv. 18).

"Holding the soul to be immortal, and able to bear all evil and all good alike, we shall always persevere in the road that leads upwards" (Rep., x. 621 c).

"Set your mind on the things that are above, not on the things that are upon the earth" (Col. iii. 2).

To the impassioned peace of the primitive Christian ideal, as to the reasoned calm of the philosophic spirit, the carping of wavering minds, the uncertain murmurs of selfish dissatisfaction, the nagging of argumentativeness, and the protrusion of an irrepressible personality are foreign and objectionable. "Be not of unsettled mind ... but seek God's kingdom" (Luke xii. 29, 31). "Why were ye reasoning on the way? They held their peace; for they were disputing one with another on the way, who is the greater" (Mark ix. 33, 34). "Why reason ye among yourselves, ye of little faith?" (Matt. xvi. 8). "What reason ye in your hearts?" (Luke v. 22). "Do all things without murmurings and reasonings, that ye may become blameless and simple, children of God" (Phil. ii. 15).

With Plato's hero, the Truth is that which stills the unquiet personality, the Truth is the haven of the kingdom of peace:—

"Whenever any one should believe in any argument as being true, being a person that has no skill in the art of reasoning, and then directly afterwards it should appear to him to be false, at one time being so, and at another time not, and so on different and different again;—and this is especially the case with those who keep up a discussion over mere controversy; you know that they end in thinking that they have become exceedingly wise, and are the only people that have remarked how in things and reasonings alike there is not a particle of soundness or stability, but all things that exist are swaying up and down, and remain for no time in any state of permanence. . . . These wranglers, when they are arguing any point, care nothing about the real condition of the subject under discussion, but are sedulously exerting themselves to make what they have themselves advanced look well to those that are present. . . . I shall not be anxious to make what I say appear true to those present, except as a result by the way, but I shall be anxious above all to make it seem to have such a basis to myself. . . . For yourselves, if you will be guided by me, pay little heed to Socrates, but much more to the truth" (Phædo, xxxix., xl. 90 b, 91 a, b).

The concluding paragraph here affords a gleaming glimpse of the enfranchisement from personal anxiety which a sincere motive empowers; the full sense of the glory of release from conventional responsibility is conveyed in the words, "Ye will know the truth, and the truth will make you free" (John viii. 32).

The following passages seem to reflect light upon one another, in regard to the acknowledgment of the legacies of forerunners, the accumulation of experience, and the new extraction of its essence, as being factors in the elevation of man :—

"Verily I say unto you, that many prophets and righteous men longed to see those things which ye behold, and did not see them; and to hear those things which ye hear, and did not hear" (Matt. xiii. 17).

"The saying of Epicharmos, 'What two men said before, I by myself am able to say'" (Gorgias, lxi. 505 d).

"The elements themselves cannot be defined or known, but only appreciated by the senses, whereas compounds of them can be both known and expressed and apprized by true judgment. . . . Science is true judgment in conjunction with reason. . . . Have we then thus, on this very day, discovered what of old many a sage did seek, and grew old before he found?" (Theætetus, 202 b).

Perhaps this view may help to clear up the meaning of a somewhat obscure passage: "The law and the prophets were until John; since that time the gospel of the kingdom of God is preached" (Luke xvi. 16). A new inspiration revives what preceded it, and by so doing, and enlarging it as well, makes a new creation greater than anything that has preceded it.

We have referred to the differences between philosopher and seer in handling great subjects. The following is an excellent illustration of such a comparison:—

"Those who are found to have lived a holy life are emancipated and set at large from the regions in the earth as from a prison, and make their way upwards to the pure abode. . . . For the sake of these things we ought to use every endeavour to acquire virtue and wisdom in this life: for the reward is noble and the hope great. To affirm positively, however, that these things are as I have described, does not become a man endowed with mind; but that either this or something of the kind takes place in relation to our souls and their habitations—since the soul appears to be assuredly an immortal thing—this appears to me to be a seemly belief, and worthy the hazard for one that deems that so things are: for the hazard is noble, and one should allure one's self with such things as with enchantments" (Phædo, lxii., lxiii. 114 b, c).

This is the reasonable hope of the philosopher, expressed

with the glow of real feeling and belief. But, as a poet has pointed out, "Hope itself is fear viewed on the sunny side." Jesus never expresses hope, never teaches hope; the heart is not either to allure or to trouble itself with hope in matters of spiritual certainty. "Let not your heart be troubled: have confidence in God, and have confidence in me. In the house of my Father there are many mansions: were it not so, I would have told you" (John xiv. 1, 2).

The philosopher is like a kindly brother talking with brothers; the prophet is like an angel speaking tenderly to children.

Plato stretches out his arms as far as philosophic certainty or reasonableness can go; his mind is strongly convinced that the ideal is not a castle in the air, but a city having foundations. But one who can see the spiritual city is certain in quite another way; he speaks with glowing simplicity and assurance that needs no proof, with the boundless trust of a fond child saying, "I love my mother."

In the following there is no more question of the existence of spirit than of flesh: "That which has been born of the flesh is flesh, and that which has been born of the Spirit is spirit. . . . Ye must be born from above [or, afresh]. . . . We speak that which we know, and testify to that which we have seen" (John iii. 6, 7, 11).

The calm philosophic argument will compare with this fervid assurance: "As to the possession by the dead of some sense of what goes on here—the best souls divine, while the worst deny it. Now the divinations of godlike men are more authoritative than of those who are the reverse" (Epist., ii. 311 c).

Plato cannot be regarded as a philosopher only; he is of the godlike men who divine what is beyond earthly philosophy. As Goethe presents him, "Plato is related to the world as a spirit of the blest, who is pleased to be its guest for a time." When he speaks of the soul, it is not with the cold assurance of reason only but with some serious sense of reality, a sense full of glow or full of awe. Of "the soul's ascent," he says, "God knows whether it be true" (Rep., vii. 517 b.).

Plato, with the simplicity of religion, sympathizes with good wherever he finds it, as when he quotes the words of an old poet, a prayer of far-seeing faith: "King Zeus, give us good things, when we pray for them, and when we do not; and keep from us evil things even if we pray for them."

Plato, in the mouth of Socrates, relates a fable of the primeval time before the division of the divine sovereignty, according to Homer, between three elementary deities—sky, water, and earth. "A very beautiful tale it is," says Socrates, "which you will consider a fable (myth), as I think, but I a tale; for what I am about to tell you, I tell you as being true." The fable is, that during the reign of Cronos, the lives of mortals were judged while they were still in the flesh, on the very day on which they were about to die, and by living judges. This led to injustice, and Zeus introduced a new rule, thus: "Sentences are badly awarded, because those in process of judgment are judged clothed, inasmuch as they are judged while living. Many, therefore, whose souls are depraved are clad about with beautiful bodies, nobility of birth, and riches; and whenever the judgment takes place, many witnesses come in their behalf, to testify that they have lived justly. Hence the judges are awed by these environments, and moreover they too pass sentence when clothed, for over their soul do their eyes, ears, and whole body hang like a veil. . . . Men ought to be judged unclad of all these things; they must be judged after they are dead: the judge, too, must be unclad and dead, and must examine with his soul the soul of each immediately after death, forsaken of all his kindred, and leaving behind upon the earth all that which is ornament, in order that the judgment may be just" (Gorgias, lxxix. 522 e).

This fable, which recalls the task of the assessors as set forth in the Egyptian Book of the Dead, must remind us also of a later fable which conveys the very same moral, that of the possible absolute reversal in Hades of earth's judgment upon a man. In the fable of Dives and Lazarus, the rich man has many friends who, for the sake of his sumptuous entertainments, would have been ready to give excellent testimony to his virtues before any human judge. But Dives seems to have done nothing else but make merry, and in the pursuit of selfish pleasure could not even find time to consider whether the fragments from his table might not well be given to a poor helpless creature who lay outside his gate, on whom even dogs took compassion. When the angels come, representatives of the judgment which is not blinded by earthly advantages, they bear away the soul of Dives to a Hades as painful as the life of poor Lazarus had been, who in his patient endurance of trial has developed a soul worthy of a lofty place, and has accordingly been borne to a Hades of comfort.

The cry of Dives to Lazarus has in Plato an extended suggestiveness. Many have believed that the penance prepared for evil doers is the slow and arduous process of undoing their own work, and of obtaining a hearty and willing forgiveness from those they have wronged.

As to those who have led wicked lives, when they reach the Acherusian lake, the general receptacle of souls, "they call on those whom they injured, and entreat and implore these to permit them to go out into the lake, and to receive them, . . . and they do not cease from their sufferings until they have won over those whom they have injured" (Phædo, 114 a).

"You will never be neglected by the judgment of the gods; yea, though you were so small as to sink into the depths of the earth, or so lofty as to fly up to heaven; but you will suffer from them the fitting punishment, whether you abide here, or depart to Hades, or are carried to a place still more wild than these" (Laws, x. c. 13).

Punishment in Plato's view was not arbitrary, or for punishment's sake, but natural and appropriate sequence to crime. If you sow wild oats, you must live on the porridge. "The greatest punishment is the becoming similar to bad men" (Laws, v. 728 b). The belief in a retribution closely allied with the crime has taken a strong root in the popular mind. Plato cites with evident feeling "the account, which many of those who are earnestly interested in the rites of the initiates concerning such matters have heard, and strongly believe, that for such persons [murderers] punishment comes in Hades, and that the necessity is on them to come hither again and pay the full penalty according to nature, namely of suffering from another the very thing each one himself did, and under such a destiny to find the termination of his then life" (Laws, ix. 870 d).

"We must not let the poet say that those are wretched who are suffering punishment, and that it is God who does these things. But if it were to be said that the wicked deserved correction, wretched beings indeed, and in suffering punishment were being benefited by the deity, we must let the assertion pass. We must, however, by all means oppose its being said that deity, who is good, is the cause of ills to any one" (Rep., ii. 380 a).

To the woman taken in adultery, Jesus says "Nor do I condemn thee; go, and sin no more." (John viii. 11. Doubtful text.) To the man made whole, he says, "Sin no more, lest something worse befall thee" (John v. 14). In Plato (Critias, i.) we find the same beautiful appreciation of punishment as discipline, in the prayer to God to inflict on us suitable punishment: "The right punishment for one out of tune is to make him play in tune."

The following carries faith still further: "Shall we not agree that whatsoever from the gods befalls the god-beloved man, all befalls as the best possible, unless there attach to him some necessary ill from prior sin? ... If the just man comes to be in poverty, maladies, or any other of seeming evils, these things will issue to him in something good, either living or dead " * (Rep., x. 612 e).

Side by side with this may be set the familiar words in which so many have found comfort: "We know that all things work together for good to them that love God" (Rom. viii. 28).

Here is a brighter picture still, philosophy ascending into faith, and reason into spiritual instinct :—

"While we live, we shall thus, as it seems, draw nearest to knowledge, if to the utmost we hold no intercourse or communion with the body, saving for absolute necessity, nor become overcharged with its nature, but purify ourselves therefrom, until God himself shall loose our bonds. And thus being pure people far removed from the foolishness of body, we shall, we may reasonably expect, be with people like unto ourselves, and learn through our very selves the absolute, and that probably is the truth; for it is not in law for the impure to reach up to the pure. . . . The journey into the far country which is now appointed me is set out upon with good hope, as it would be by any man who thinks that his mind is

---

* An ill-appreciated modern thinker has thus expressed the same, if not a larger faith :—

"I do not doubt interiors have their interiors, and exteriors have their exteriors; and that the eye-sight has another eye-sight, and the hearing another hearing, and the voice another voice;

"I do not doubt that the passionately wept deaths of young men are provided for; and that the deaths of young women, and the deaths of little children, are provided for;

"(Did you think Life was so well provided for—and Death, the purport of all Life, is not well provided for?)

"I do not doubt that wrecks at sea, no matter what the horror of them—no matter whose wife, child, husband, father, lover, has gone down, are provided for, to the minutest points;

"I do not doubt that whatever can possibly happen, anywhere, at any time, is provided for, in the inherences of things;

"I do not think Life provides for all . . . but I believe Heavenly Death provides for all " (" Passage to India ").

brought into a state of something like purification. . . . Would it not be ridiculous for a man who, during his life, kept himself in such a state as to live in the closest proximity to death, when this death comes up to him, to be disturbed? . . . Shall one who in reality loves wisdom, and strongly grasps this very hope, that he shall nowhere else obtain it in any way worthy of the name save in Hades, be disturbed at dying, and not go thither with joy? One must needs think that it would be with joy were he in reality a philosopher; for he will strongly hold this opinion, that he will nowhere else but there attain wisdom in purity; and if this be so, would it not be highly irrational if such a man were to be afraid of death?" (Phædo, xi., xii., 67 a, c, d, 68 a).

Plato's picture of the State within man is full of instruction, and leads us on to an appreciation of the meaning of the kingdom of heaven within us :—

"When a man has the form of that which is most excellent, naturally weak in his soul, so that he is unable to govern the creatures within himself, but ministers to them, he is able only to learn what flatters them. . . . In order then that such an one may be governed under a like rule with the most excellent man, we say that he must be the subject of the one who is most excellent, and who has within himself the divine governing principle. Not at all with the idea that the government should be to the hurt of the subject, but on the ground of its being best for every one to be under the governance of one divine and wise, above all if he possess that ruler as his own within himself. But if not, then as a superintendent from without, in order that so far as possible we may all be alike and friends, as under one and the same government. Law itself, too, plainly shows that such a thing is in its design, for it comes to the aid of all in the city; as is likewise the case with the government of children in not allowing them to be free until we have established in them a proper government, as in a city; and after tending that which is best in them, by the same quality in ourselves, we establish, instead of our own rule and government, a like guardian and governor in each of them, and then at length we set him free. . . . It is by looking to the State which is within himself, and taking care that nothing of what is there be moved out of its place through fulness of possession or through scantiness, and by governing in such a way, that a man will add to his possession and spend out of it to the extent of his ability.

"Having regard to honours likewise in the same manner, of some he will willingly partake and taste, whichever he may judge will render him a better man. But as for those which he thinks would dissolve that soul which subsists within him, from them he will fly both in private and public.

"He will not be willing then to take a part in political affairs, if he really cares for this?—Decidedly, in the State which is in his own, but verily not equally so in his fatherland, unless on the contingency of a peculiar divine fortune.—I understand: you mean in the State we now went through the building of, which exists in our conversations, but I think is not to be found on earth.—But perhaps in heaven its pattern is in being for any one who desires to see it, and seeing, to establish his own self.—But it matters nothing whether it does or will exist anywhere; for he would perform the duties of this State alone, and of none other" (Rep., ix. 590 c, 591 e).

With Jesus, the State or kingdom within is the kingdom of heaven: "Being asked when the kingdom of God was coming, he answered, The kingdom of God comes not by close observation, nor will folk say, Lo here! or, There! for behold, the kingdom of God is within you" (Luke xvii. 20). If that vision is become dull, which once for a while was made so bright, we must console ourselves with Plato's wise observation, that "the idea of the good is the ultimate object of vision, and hard to be seen" (Rep., vii. 517).

The position of mediator taken up by Jesus, as one under

the chrism of the Spirit of God, is thus understood by Plato: "The whole daimonkind is between God and Mortal. . . . It interprets and plies with messages to gods of men's matters and to men of gods' matters, bearing from men supplications and sacrifices, from gods commandments and requitals of sacrifices. Being in the middle between both, it makes the completion, so that the universe is reciprocally bound together with itself. Thereby proceeds every kind of prophecy, . . . for god is not mingled with man, but by the medium described is carried on all intercourse and the commune of gods as brought unto men, whether waking or sleeping alike. He that is wise in respect of such things is a daimonic man, while he that is wise in anything else, or in respect of certain arts or handicrafts, is mechanical merely" (Sympos., 202 e). The philosopher is not the man who is prophetically or daimonically wise; "those who philosophize are those between the wise and the ignorant" (Sympos.).

The following passages present this daimonic element within us, as seen in different aspects, in relation to the body, to the exit of the soul, to character, to dream, to divination, to transmigration, to angelic incarnation :—

"When a large and soul-overpowering corporeal part becomes conjoined with a small and weak mental part, . . . the motions of the more powerful province prevail and enlarge what is their own, and by making the region of the soul dull, unteachable, and oblivious, induce that greatest of diseases, ignorance. There is one safety for both, not to move the soul without body, nor body without soul, that the twain by mutual requital may become equilibrated and healthy" (Tim., 88 a).

"He who neglects his soul, will make a lame passage through life, and again come into Hades ineffectual and without understanding" (Tim., 44 c).

"There is nothing, but the soul, that causes each and all of us to be in this life the very thing that we are" (Laws, xii. 959 a).

"Giving the soul at night a course of life of a modest character, with the power of divination in dream, to make up for its lack of reason and wisdom" (Tim., 71 d).

"No one in his ordinary senses participates in inspired and true divination, but only when fettered in the force of his wisdom either in sleep or by some disorder, or when distraught by some ecstatic passion" (Tim., 71 e).

"Whatever bad habit it had acquired, the soul, according to the analogy of the original birth of the habit, should pass into a brute nature corresponding thereto, and in its changes should not cease from labours, until by following up the course in itself of the same and corresponding quality, and mastering by reason its turbulent and irrational part, . . . it should arrive at the form of its first and best disposition" (Tim., 42 c).

Clement of Alexandria (Strom., i. 15) alleges that, according to Plato, the barbarians "think that good souls, on quitting the super-celestial region, submit to come to this Tartarus, and assuming a body, share in all the ills which are involved in birth, from their solicitude for the race of men." These are the Messianic individuals who make laws and divulge philosophy, "than which no greater boon ever came from the gods to the race of men, or will come" (Tim., 47 a).

The history of the battle ground in the soul is thus presented by Plato: "Sometimes . . . some of the cupidities get destroyed, while others are dethroned, because of the coming into play of a certain modesty in the youth's soul, and once again he gets restored to order. And, again, there are other cupidities, allied to the dethroned ones, that gain secret nurture, and, for lack of experience of a father's tending, grow numerous and masterful. They are wont then to draw him towards the same intimacies as before, and, through their secret connections, they give interior birth to a multitude. Eventually, I think, they are wont to seize upon the citadel of the youth's soul, since they perceive it to be vacant of discipline, virtuous pursuits, and true principles—the best watchmen and guardians over the rational part of men dear to God. And, then, indeed, false and vagabond considerations and opinions rush up in the stead of these, and take possession of the identical region in such a man," (Rep., viii. 560 a).

There is the most singular similarity, not only in the idea, but even in the metaphoric form of expression, between the passage just quoted and the following parable of the inmates of the house or citadel of the soul: "When the unclean spirit is gone out of the man, it goes through dry places, seeking rest, and finds it not. Then it says, I will return into my house whence I came out; and having come, it finds it vacant, swept, and garnished. Then it goes and takes with itself seven other spirits more evil than itself, and they enter in and dwell there; and the last state of that man becomes worse than the first" (Matt. xii. 43).

"To conquer one's self is the first and most excellent of all conquests, while to be worsted by one's self is the most infamous and base of all things" (Laws, i. 626 c).

This is in special harmony with early Buddhist teachings. If we read metaphorically the saying "A man's foes are they of his own household" (Matt. x. 36), we may find the same thought.

As the stream of life is ceaseless, so must judgment or spiritual adjustment be incessant. It is always a judgment day when an individual turns decidedly to the right or to the left. But as we are familiar with number, yet know not infinity; as our eyes can apprehend the stages of time, while they can perceive only as in a mist the vast gliding flow of eternity, our pictures of the judgment are local, temporal and made up of numbers. The after-death realization of one's self and one's purposes must form an important moment, a new and exacting condition of judgment. Of the more familiar conception Plato presents the following pictorial embodiment:—

"Er,[*] the son of Armenios, by descent a Pamphylian, happening on a time to die in battle, when the dead were on the tenth day carried off, and already corrupted, was taken up sound: and being carried home, as he was about to be buried on the twelfth day, and was laid on the funeral pile, revived; and when he was come to himself, he told what he saw over there. He said that after his soul had gone forth, he went with many others, and they arrived at a certain ghostly place, wherein were two chasms in the soil, contiguous to each other, and others in the heavens up above over against them, and the judges sat between these. And when they gave judgment, they commanded the just to go on the right hand and upwards through the heaven, having invested with certain signs on the forefront those that had been judged; but the unjust they ordered to the left and downwards, and these had behind them in like manner the marks of all they had done" (Rep., x. 614 b).

With this we may compare the symbolism of the great Assize, as follows:—

"And thou Capernaum, shalt thou be exalted unto heaven? thou shalt be thrust down unto Hades" (Matt. xi. 23).

"When the son of man shall have come in his glory, and all the angels with him, then will he sit upon the throne of his glory, and before him will be gathered together all the nations; and he will separate them one from another, as the shepherd separates the sheep from the goats; and will set the sheep on his right hand, but the goats on the left" (Matt. xxv. 31).

The disciples of Jesus cry out for fear of an apparition (Matt. xiv. 26); Plato also has a certain ghost-belief. If the soul's way of light be toward the heavenly heights, the dark way is back again towards earth, or lower still:—

"Can the soul in sooth, the invisible part, that which goes to some such different place, goodly, pure, invisible, unto

---

[*] This Er is said by Clement Al. (Strom., v. 282) to be Zoroaster. The story is probably derived from the Zoroastrian book of Arda.

Hades to say true, beside the good and wise deity,—can this soul of ours, being such as it is and with such endowment, on its liberation from the body be forthwith dissipated and destroyed, as the generality of men affirm ? Far from it. . . . If the soul is detached from the body polluted and impure, as having constantly held communion with the body, and having served and loved it, and been bewitched by it, through lusts and pleasures, so as to think that there is nothing real save what is corporeal, which one can touch and see, and drink and eat, and employ for sensual purposes ; but as regards what is dark and invisible to the eyes, which is intelligible and apprehensible by philosophy, if it has been accustomed to hate, fear, and shun this, do you think that a soul in such a state can depart from the body by itself, and uncontaminated ? It will, I opine, be clasped round with the corporeal, which the intercourse and habitual association with the body, through the constant linking together of the two and the great care paid to the body, have made second nature to the soul. We must opine that that is ponderous and heavy, earthly and visible, by the possession of which such a soul is weighed down, and drawn again unto the visible plane, through fear of the invisible and of Hades, wandering to and fro, as it is said, around the monuments and the tombs, about which, moreover, certain shadowy phantoms of souls have been seen, being such images as such souls produce as have not purely got free, but partake of the visible, on which account also it is that they become seen. Not that these are the souls of the good, but of the worthless, which are compelled to wander about such places, paying the penalty of their former way of life, which was evil ; and they continue wandering until, through the desire of the corporeal nature that closely accompanies them, they are again immured in a body" (Phædo, xxix. 80 d ; xxx. 81 b).

"In consequence of the soul's forming the same opinions with the body and taking pleasure in the same things, it is compelled, I imagine, to become addicted to the same habits and the same nurture, so that it can never pass into Hades in a state of purity, but must invariably go forth infected by the body, so as soon again to fall into another body, and to grow up as if it were sown" (Phædo, xxxiii. 83 d).

"The soul comes to Hades possessed of nought else than its education and nurture, which, even at the very inception of its migration thither, are said to be of the greatest benefit or detriment to the dead. For it is said that each person when dead is accompanied by the particular daimon that was assigned to him during life, who proceeds to conduct him to some place where people have to be gathered together and submitted to trial, and thereafter go on to Hades with that guide, whose instructions are to conduct them hence thither. . . . The well-ordered and wise soul both follows on and is not ignorant of its present, but that which by reason of lusts clings to the body, flutters about it and about its visible place for a long time distraught, until after much resistance and with much suffering, it is led away by force and with difficulty at the hands of the appointed daimon. It wanders to and fro oppressed with every kind of helplessness, until certain periods of time have elapsed, and when these are fulfilled, it is carried of necessity into the abode that is proper for it. The soul, on the other hand, that has passed through life with purity and control, meets with gods for companions and guides, and dwells in the place fitted for its particular self" (Phædo, lvii. 107 d, 108 a).

There is a curious half-confused reference, probably the refracted ray of some mystical utterance, to a mission of Jesus to spirits in prison: "In the flesh he was put to death, in the spirit he was made living, in which he went and preached even unto the spirits in prison." It is interesting to compare Plato's notion of a spirit in prison: "The saying in the mystical doctrines that we men are in a kind of prison, and that one ought not either to break himself loose or escape from it, appears to me something great and yet not easy to see through " (Phædo, vi. 62 b).

Plato's reference to the "mystical doctrines," as to a sort of corpus of divinity then accessible, is somewhat perplexing. But the traditions, whether oral or literary, of the religious mysteries of Greece form ground upon which there is not a very clear light. There is a curious blending of an Orphic and Pythagorean stream of spiritual lore, and it may be that its most considerable part was so jealously guarded as to have become lost. In any case, Plato's relatedness to the Hebrew oracles was a standing puzzle to the Church fathers, the explanation of which was sought in an acquaintance made during his Egyptian sojourn with Hebrew Rabbis and their scriptures. An "Atticizing Moses" was a name given to him, and contrariwise Celsus averred that Jesus borrowed his best sayings from Plato, and that the whole system of Christian doctrine consists of Platonic dogmas, in part misunderstood, and in part perverted. Plato avowedly derives one of his ethical illustrations from a Phœnician myth, and the most satisfactory solution of such knotty points is to believe that there was a much fuller sympathy between the guardians of the lamp of faith of ancient times, much less jealousy between the enlightened of different races, than the prevalence of the more modern exclusiveness and arrogance in matters of religion, or of a sectarian and disputatious spirit, would permit.

The Christian fathers could not resist the fascinations of Plato. Clement of Alexandria, in his gentle catholic way, says, "We do not, if you have no objection, wholly disown Plato" (Exh. VI.). By several of the fathers, Plato is regarded as exhibiting a conception of a trinity in deity. The following are the passages to which attention has been most distinctly drawn on this account :—

"Adjuring the God who is the Governor of all things both that are and that are to come, and the Lord who is the Father of the Governor and cause, whom, if we philosophize truly, we shall all know as clearly as is in the power of men under a good genius" (Epist., vi. fin.).

"From essence indivisible and always the same, and from that which is divisible and comes into being in reference to bodies, he composed, by a union of both, a third and intermediate form of essence" (Tim., 35 a).

"It is not possible for two things alone to cohere, without the intervention of a third, for a certain bond is necessary between the two. And the best of all bonds is that which, as nearly as possible, unites into one both itself and the natures bound with it" (Tim., 31 c).

"Gods of gods, of whom I am the creator (demiurge), and father of works. All things that have come into being through me are indissoluble so long as I will it not. . . . As ye have been generated, ye are not immortal nor wholly indissoluble, yet ye shall never be dissolved, nor shall the destiny of death befall you, because my will is your portion" (Tim., 41 a).

"Around the King of all, all things are, and all things are for his sake; and the same is the cause of all that is beautiful. But around a second are the second things, and about a third, the third. Now, the soul of man is eager to learn respecting these things, of what kind they are, looking towards things allied to itself, of none of which it possesses enough. Now, respecting the king and those of whom I spoke, there is nothing of this kind. But it is of what is after this that the soul speaks" (Epist., ii. 312 e).

There is certainly a tendency in these passages, taken together, to a subdivision of deity; and Plato may very reasonably be regarded as affording a link in the evolution of the trinitarian conception.

Plato's ideas of deity and of the creation and support of the universe are still worthy of attention. We have but to drop out the errors in his explanations of physical phenomena, into which the state of science in his day allowed him to fall.

"Working out according to his plan that just as fire to air, so air to water; as air to water, so water to earth; he thus linked together and co-established a heaven visible and tangible. Wherefore also from such elements, which are four in number, the body of the world was generated by a postulation of proportion; and derives thence such a sanction, that its parts aptly cohere and are indissoluble, except by him that linked them together. . . . He gave to it also a figure becoming and cognate. To the living being destined to embrace the whole of living beings within itself, the most proper figure that could be is that which comprehends all others within itself—the spheroid. . . . By art it is made to afford its own nutriment out of its own decay, as well as to suffer and do all things within itself and by its own operation . . . a blessed god he generated. . . . The body of the heaven has been made visible, but unseen is the soul, which partakes of reason and harmony, being made the crown of created things by him who is the crown of intelligent and eternal things" (Tim., 32 b–36 e).

The universe, then, is "the image of its fashioner, a sense-appreciable god, greatest and best, most lovely and most perfect, this one only-begotten heaven" (Tim., 92 c).

In the mind of Plato, the Spirit that inspires this lovely universe is Love. Here we turn to a poet—Shelley—for the rendering of the "winged words" of the great idealist:—

"Nor can I restrain the poetic enthusiasm which takes possession of my discourse, and bids me declare that Love is the divinity who creates peace among men, and calm upon the sea, the windless silence of storms, repose and sleep in sadness. Love divests us of all alienation from each other, and fills our vacant hearts with overflowing sympathy. . . . Before the presence of Love all harsh passions flee and perish; Love is the author of all soft affections; the destroyer of all ungentle thoughts; merciful, mild; the object of the admiration of the wise . . . the father of grace and delicacy, and gentleness, and delight, and persuasion and desire; the cherisher of all that is good, the abolisher of all evil; our most excellent pilot, defence, saviour, and guardian, in labour and in fear, in desire and in reason ; the ornament and governor of all things human and divine ; the best, the loveliest ; in whose footsteps every one ought to follow, celebrating him excellently in song, and bearing each his part in that divinest harmony which Love sings to all things which live and are, soothing the troubled minds of gods and men " (Agathon, in the " Symposium," 197 c).

Concerning the springs and sources of life which are too deep to be discovered by the trembling hazel wand of human science, Plato discourses in another place :—

" The supercelestial region no poet here has worthily hymned, or ever will. . . . For Essence, as it really exists, is colourless and formless and intangible, only to be beheld by the guiding intelligence of the soul ; and around it the family of true science has this abode. As, then, the mind of deity is nourished by intelligence and pure science, so that of every soul, in so far as it is destined to assume its relative condition, seeing after a time that which really is, is well pleased, and contemplating truth is nourished and thrives " (Phædr., 247 c).

It might almost be thought that these words of Plato's had been condensed and heightened into the sentence, "Things which eye saw not, and ear heard not, and which entered not into the heart of man, whatsoever things God prepared for them that love him " (1 Cor. ii. 9). But these words are mostly a quotation, the original (" From of old men have not heard, nor perceived by the ear, neither hath the eye seen, O God, beside thee, one which worketh for him that waiteth for him," Isai. lxiv. 4) having been written perhaps about 541 B.C., while the date of Plato's work (he lived 429–347 B.C.) is more than a century later. There are evidences of the influence of ancient thought upon Plato, as in the reference lately cited to the mysteries, and as, for example, in the words put in the mouth of Socrates : " This is a certain old-time saying, which we have in mind, that there are souls which pass away and go thither (Hades) from hence, and again pass and come hither, and come into being from among the dead" (Phædo, xv. 70 c). We may compare with this the doctrine of Pharisaic orthodoxy as evidenced, to take a single instance, in the reference to prenatal sin on the part of a man born blind.

On the consideration of such a dread subject as the after-death course of the soul, supervenes, perhaps, some pardonable human fear; philosophy finds a remedy for this: "To dread death is nothing else than to appear to be wise, without being so; for it is to appear to know what one does not know. For in good sooth no one knows but that death is the greatest of blessings to man; but men fear it, as if they well knew it to be the greatest of evils.... But to do injustice, and to disobey a superior, whether God or man, I know to be evil and base. Before evils, then, which I know to be evils, I shall never fear or shun things which, for aught I know, may be good" (Apol. Socr., xvii. 29 b).

The following we may regard as the humour of the subject: "'Both you and Simmias appear to me ... to be childishly afraid, lest when the soul departs from the body, the wind should blow it away and disperse it, especially if one should happen to die not in a calm, but in some sort of violent storm.' Whereupon said Cebes with a smile, 'Endeavour to give us conviction, as if we are afraid, or rather not as if we are afraid, but as if there be perchance in us some kind of a boy that is afraid of such things. Let us then endeavour to persuade him not to be afraid of death as if it were a hobgoblin.' 'But you must sing charms to him every day,' said Socrates, 'until you have charmed him away.' 'Whence, then, O Socrates,' he rejoined, 'shall we get a good charm-singer for such a purpose, seeing that thou art leaving us?' 'Greece is wide, O Cebes,' he said, 'and therein are somewhere to be found good men, and there are many, too, of the races of the foreigners, all of which ye ought to search through in looking for such a charm-singer, sparing neither money nor toil, for there is nothing on which you could more reasonably spend your money. You ought, too, to seek him amongst one another, for maybe you will not easily find any better able to do this than yourselves'" (Phædo, xxiv. 77 d).

The following is in the same key, though coming from Socrates at a time when he knew he had so soon to die—and this for striving to better his fellow-creatures :—

"Crito: 'In what manner are we to bury thee?' Socrates: 'Just as ye please, if only ye can catch me, and I do not give you the slip.' And at the same time smiling gently, and looking round on us, he said, 'I cannot persuade Crito, my friends, that I am that Socrates who is now conversing with you, but he thinks that I am he whom he will in but a little while behold dead, and inquires forsooth how he is to bury me. But that which I some while since argued at length, that after the poison-draught is drunken I shall abide with you no more, but shall be gone hence and depart to some happy state of the blessed, this I seem to have told to him in vain, though I meant at the same time to console both you and myself. . . . Ye must be of good cheer, then, and say that ye bury my body, and bury it in such a manner as is pleasing to you, and as ye consider most consonant with our laws'" (Phædo, lxiv. 115 c).

Such as can enter the spiritual world through the gate of the poet and the prophet, are conscious of an angel's joy. It is earthly motives and retardations, which allow only the gate of the charnel-house to be seen, that make the road seem so drear.

"It does not appear to me that it is for grief that birds sing, or swans in their last song. But in my opinion it is because they belong to Apollo, and are prophetic, and presage the blessings that are in Hades, that they sing and revel in delight on that day more excellently than in the foregoing time. Now I, too, deem myself to be the fellow-servant of the swans, and votary of the same God, and possessed, at the hands of the master, of prophetic power no whit inferior to theirs, and no more down-hearted than they are at being set free from this life " * (Phædo, xxxv., 85 b).

The following strikes a note still more purposeful and assured, manifesting an undisguisable elation, the joy as of one that is going home : " Now I am going unto him that sent me. . . . Now I come to thee ; and these things I speak in the world, that they may have my joy made full in themselves " (John xvi. 5 ; xvii. 13).

This is effortless, the joy of consciousness of the life eternal ; the following manifests a victory after a struggle against fear: " I have no longer a fear of death, but already even a desire, and that I too may say something expansive in imitation of the orators ; and for a long time I have been thinking of things on high, and going through the eternal and divine course, for out of my weakness I have collected myself together, and am become a new man " (Axiochus, 370 e). The book Axiochus, though bearing Plato's name, is regarded as the work of one of his school.

The following manifests a very happy and desirable mean between Calvinistic gloom and the opposite pole of thoughtless frivolity: " This is surely a proverb, bruited amongst all, that life is a kind of sojourn in a strange place, and that we reasonably ought to pass through it in a good-tempered way, all but singing glad songs on the road to fate. On the other hand,

* The following is a modern song upon the same theme of emancipation :—
> " At the last, tenderly,
> From the walls of the powerful, fortress'd house,
> From the clasp of the knitted locks—from the keep of the well-closed doors,
> Let me be wafted.
> Let me glide noiselessly forth ;
> With the key of softness unlock the locks—with a whisper,
> Set ope the doors, O Soul !
> Tenderly ! be not impatient !
> (Strong is your hold, O mortal flesh !
> Strong is your hold, O love) " (*Passage to India*).

to conduct ourselves in a spiritless manner, and so that it is difficult for us to be torn away, is to exhibit, like a child, a period of life of a kind not overwise" (Axiochus, 365 b).

Plato, like other great teachers, must have felt keenly the pestilent stupidity of humanity on its lower planes: "To find the Creator and Father of this universe is a task indeed, and having found him it is impossible to describe him to mankind at large" (Tim., 28 c).

If he required any reminder of the ungrateful reception the highest efforts are likely to meet with, he had but to turn to his unextinguishable memory of the fate of his friend and master, Socrates.

Speaking of persons unwilling through intemperance to relinquish a bad mode of life, he says: "Is not this pleasant of them, to deem him the most hateful of all men who tells the truth, namely, that till one abandon drunkenness and gluttony and sexual excesses and idle neglect, neither drugs, nor caustics, nor surgery, nor charms, nor amulets, nor any other such things as these will be of any avail? That, was the reply, is not very pleasant, for to be angry with one who speaks us well and fair has no pleasantness in it" (Rep. iv. 426 a).

The following is an instructive thought, the fact advanced being as true in matters physical as no doubt it is in all things else: "It would, perhaps, not be a difficult thing to prove how that the gods are not less careful for small things than for those of surpassing greatness" (Laws, x. 900 c).

The corresponding moral we may find in the following: "He that is faithful in the least is faithful also in much; and, he that is unjust in the least is unjust also in much. If, therefore, ye were not faithful in the unjust Mammon, who will commit to your trust the true good?" (Luke xvi. 10).

As to what is true gain and true life, Christianity and Platonism are clearly at one. The grain that, instead of being sown in good earth, fell among thorns, represents those that heard of spiritual things, but in whom the pursuit of them is choked by anxieties and riches and pleasures of life, so that no fruit comes to perfection (Luke viii. 14). And the warning runs: "See and keep yourselves from covetousness; for not because one has abundance does his life consist in his possessions" (Luke xii. 15).

With Plato we find a consciousness of the same fact of the evil of possessiveness: "Through the love of wealth making the whole of time to be without any leisure for the care of anything other than private property, upon which every soul of a citizen is hanging, it can have no care for aught else than daily lucre; and whatever learning or pursuit leads to this, every one individually is most ready to learn and to practise, but he laughs down all the rest" (Laws, viii. 831 c).

We borrow from nature portions of its elements only as things to be one day restored. And rightly we ought to have dominated them by our spiritual part as soon as maturity is reached. The great waves of nutrition, and the advance of external sensations, according to Plato, which constitute the bodily life of youth, disturb the resolutions of the soul, which consequently shows no intelligence of its own; "but when the stream of growth and nutrition invades it to a less degree, then once more the orbits of the soul restored to tranquillity resume their own path, with gradual increase of steadiness . . . . and agreeably with the orbits of nature" (Tim., 44 a, b). Neither orbit can be done away; our work is to harmonize them. Proper food and proper discipline are the necessaries for this combination which we call life.

But when the career is over, the body is but a "mass of flesh:"—"It cannot be right for one to ruin a family by extravagance on the score of an opinion that the mass of flesh which is being buried belongs to him, but rather to hold that the son or brother or whomsoever he laments the most and thinks he is burying, has departed, consummating and fulfilling his destiny" (Laws, xii. 959 c).

Plato's conception of righteousness is "that harmonious and proportional development of the inner man, by means of which each faculty of the soul performs its own functions without interfering with the others." He makes the fullest allowances for the state of darkness and imperfection in which the majority of mankind are floundering :—

"When the soul supports itself upon that which truth and real being irradiate, it understands and knows it, and appears to be possessed of intelligence; but when on the other hand it leans upon that which is blended with darkness, which is born and dies, it then has to do with mere opinion, and becomes dim-sighted, changing about in ups and downs of opinion, and seems to be unpossessed of intelligence" (Rep., vi. 508 d).

A reflection of Jesus is that "the sons of this world are wiser with respect to their own generation than the sons of the light" with respect to theirs. And he advocates as busy an ardour in making friends outside the unrighteous Mammon, as its subjects manifest in its selfish service. Plato notices this staunchness in the pursuit of worldly interests, and converts the fact into a hope that the principle will remain when the pursuit is changed for the higher and more difficult one :—

"Have you never yet noticed, in the case of those accounted wicked but wise, how keen is the sight of the little soul (*psycharion*, soullet), and how acutely it perceives those things upon which it is turned, showing that it has no dulness in the power of vision, but is compelled to be so far the servant of vice, that the more acutely it perceives, so much the more evil it perpetrates.

"As regards this part of such a nature, if from childhood upwards it should be docked and stripped of the affinities of its birth as if they were plummets cut away from it—affinities which by means of feastings and pleasures and lickerish things of this kind become second nature, and turn the vision of the soul to the things that are below; if from these the soul can free itself and turn itself toward truth, the very same principle in the same individuals would not less acutely see truth than it saw those things upon which it was but lately turned" (Rep., vii. 519 a).

Holding a belief in a progress which may extend over an indefinite period, Plato finds support to that belief in the differences that exist between men in the present world: "In the greatest dangers, when men are in peril, in wars, or diseases, or storms at sea, they behave towards those who have power in each several case as towards gods, looking up to them as their saviours, though these surpass them in nothing whatever but knowledge" (Theætetus, 180 b).

With the belief in eternal progress must be held another without which that belief would be void: "If the soul is immortal, it requires our care not only for the present time, which we call life, but for all time" (Phædo, lvii. 107 c).

The metaphor of a race fits well the earthly career viewed in its immediate results: "Do not men who are both cunning and unrighteous act as those in the race who run well at the beginning but not at the end, for at the first they briskly leap forward, but end by becoming ridiculous . . . and run off without the crown. But such as are true runners reach the goal and receive the prizes and the crown" (Rep., x. 613 b). With this we may compare the following variation on the metaphor: "Ye were running well; who hindered you from obeying the truth?" (Gal. v. 7).

The spiritual sense of light and darkness, expressed by symbolic use of the terms, is to be found alike in Plato and the Gospels: "There are two disturbances of vision arising from two causes—when we turn from darkness to the light, and from the light to darkness. And when one considers that this is so too with regard to the soul, he will not give way to silly laughter, when he sees it disturbed and unable to make sure of its perception, but will rather give his attention to the question whether it is in coming from a brighter existence that it has been darkened by unaccustomedness, or whether it is on emerging from gross ignorance into a brighter state, that it is overpowered by more dazzling splendour" (Rep., vii. 518 a).

In Plato's story of the cave are to be found his most suggestive pictures of light and darkness, viewed in reference to the clear vision, or shadowed imperfect straining, of our spiritual eyesight :—

"'Compare our nature, as regards instruction and the want of it, with such a condition as follows : Picture men, as it were, in an underground cave-like dwelling, having an entrance open to the light, the width of the whole cave. Within it imagine persons, who from childhood upwards have had their legs and necks in fetters, so that they do not stir, and only look at what is right in front, unable to turn their heads by reason of the bonds, their light proceeding from a fire burning above, and far off, behind them. And between the fire and the fettered folk is an elevated roadway, along which may be seen a low wall built, like conjurers' screens are put up in front of the people, above which they exhibit their marvels. . . . By the side of this low wall, picture to yourself men carrying all sorts of articles which overtop the wall, statues of men, and images of other animals in stone and wood, and all kinds of materials, and, as probably would be the case, some of the bearers talking, others silent.'

"'You are describing an out-of-the-way comparison, and out-of-the-way fettered folk.'

"'Such as resemble ourselves ; . . . for think you that such persons as these would have seen anything more of themselves or of one another than the shadows which are thrown by the fire upon the part of the cave that is right opposite them?'

"'Why, how can they . . . if they were compelled through life to keep their heads immovable?'

"'But what of the articles that were being borne along? would not this be the same? . . . Now, if they were able to hold conversation with one another, do you not suppose that they would think fit to give names to what they saw before them, as if present? . . . And if the prison had an echo from the opposite part, as often as one of the passers-by spoke, do you suppose that they would regard the voice as anything else than the shadow that was passing by? . . . Undoubtedly, then, such people would regard truth as the shadows of manufactured articles. . . . Consider, then, their release from their fetters and the cure from their folly, what it would be like, if it was by nature that such things were befalling them. Whenever one was set loose and compelled suddenly to rise and to turn his neck round and walk and look up to the light, would he not feel pain in all these acts, and on account of the dazzle be unable to discern those very things, the shadows of which he saw before? What do you suppose he would say if any one told him that what he saw before were fooleries, while now he was seeing something much nearer to the reality, and was turned towards much more genuine things? And then if any one were to point out to him the passing things, one by one, and question him, and oblige him to answer what it was; do you not think that he would be at fault, and would suppose that the things as seen before were more true than as now pointed out? . . . Therefore, even if some one were to force him to look at the light itself, would he not feel pain in the eyes and shun it, turning aside to those things which he could really discern, and reckon them as clearer in reality than those that were pointed out? . . . And if . . . any person should drag him thence by force by the rugged and steep ascent, and not stay until he had dragged him to the light of the sun, would he not be in distress and angry at being dragged? and, when he came to the light, would he not, through having his eyes full of splendour, be unable to see a single thing of those that are now accounted to be the true ones? . . . He would require, then, some practice if he were about to look at the things above, and first he would discern shadows most easily, and after that the images of men and of other things in water, and the things themselves afterwards. For the same reason he would behold the things that are in the sky, and the sky itself, by night, gazing on the light of the stars and moon, more easily than by day the sun and daylight. . . . Last of all, then, he would be able to perceive the sun, not in water, nor by its images in any out-of-the-way place, but itself by itself in its own station, and to contemplate its nature. . . . And after this he might now reason concerning it, that it is this that brings the seasons and the years, and is the steward of all things in the visible sphere, and in one sense the author of all that they saw. . . . If the man calls to recollection his first habitation and the wisdom that was there, and his companions in captivity, would he not congratulate himself on the change, and pity the others? . . . And if they had amongst themselves honours and praises and rewards for him that had the acutest vision of what passed by, and the best memory as to which of these things were wont to go before and after and together, and from such observations was best able to presage the future; do you think that he would be desirous of such marks of pre-eminence, or envy those honoured by them and possessing influence, or would not rather experience what Homer describes, and ardently desire—

> "As a day labourer for some needy man,
> To do another's work for wage,

and rather endure anything than hold those opinions and live in that manner? . . . And . . . were such a man once again to descend to the same sitting-place, and be seated there, would not he have his eyes full of darkness in consequence of coming suddenly from the sun? . . . As for those shadows, again, if he were constrained to form judgments and enter into contentions about them with those who had always remained in fetters, from the time when he was short-sighted, before his eyes were set right (and this period of habituation would be by no means a short one), would not he afford food for ridicule? and would it not be told concerning him, how, since he had gone up, he had returned with his eyesight destroyed, and that it was not meet that he should even attempt to go up, and as for the one that took it in hand to loose him and take him up, they ought to put him to death if they could get him into their hands?'" (Rep., vii. 514 a–517 a).

This famous parable deserves some study, as conveying the bitter truth how slavish natures that "sit in darkness and the shadow of death" clamour against those whom the truth and the light have made free.

It has been adduced also in illustration of the idea of beings living in the perception of two dimensions only, endeavouring to judge of more advanced existences who like ourselves live and move and have our being in three dimensions; and has suggested the obvious question, How far could we three-dimensional folk make shift at judging of and discussing beings existing in a state one power higher?

This question leads us into the mystic region at once, and we conclude, with some humility, that we see only according to our state. This truth is reiterated among the Christian records. "The light shines in the darkness, and the darkness apprehends it not" (John i. 5). "This is the judgment, that the light is come into the world, and men loved the darkness rather than the light" (John iii. 19). Jesus is the man who came out of the world where the sun was seen in direct vision: "I am the light of the world: he that followeth me shall not walk in the darkness, but shall have the light of life" (John viii. 12). "I am come a light into the world, that whosoever believeth on me may not abide in the darkness" (John xii. 47). And the world turned to its conventional view of the worshipful shadows on the wall, and got into its cruel hands the man who taught the mischievous doctrines of the upper world. "For now we see in a mirror, darkly [in a riddle,— the shadow-pictures of the cave]; but then face to face"— in the light (1 Cor. xiii. 12).

"Mortal nature, ... irrationally avoiding pain and pursuing pleasure, will set both these before what is more righteous and more excellent, and by producing a darkness in itself eventually fill both itself and the whole city with every ill. Wherefore, should any man, strong by nature, born with a divine destiny, be competent to comprehend this, he would require no laws for the government of himself. There is no law or order superior to knowledge, ... but it exists nowhere except to a small extent; therefore we have to choose the second in rank, namely, order and law" (Laws, ix. 875 b).

"If the light that is in thee be darkness, how great the darkness (that is in thee)!" (Matt. vi. 23).

"Among intelligibles, the last and the difficult one to be seen, is the idea of The Good. When beheld, it has to be inferred from reason to be the cause of all that is right and beautiful, giving birth in the visible to light and the lord thereof, and in the region of perceptions being itself the sovereign providing truth and intelligence" (Rep., vii. 517 c).

"Where there is no light in the ways of one with another, but a darkness, there no one ever rightly meets with the honour that is his meed, nor ... even with the justice that is seemly" (Laws, v. 738 e).

"He that doeth the truth cometh to the light, that his works may be made manifest, that they have been wrought in God" (John iii. 21).

"So let your light shine before men, that they may see your good works, and glorify your father which is in heaven" (Matt. v. 16).

The following afford an interesting parallelism:—

"Life is the outcome of fire and spirit [breath]" (Tim. 77 a).

"He will baptize you in holy spirit [a holy breath, or wind] and in fire" (Matt. iii. 11).

"The mouth ... as Plato says, is the entrance of mortal things, and the way of exit of things immortal. For into it there enter food and drink, corruptible foods of a corruptible body. But out of it proceed expressions of thought, immortal laws of an immortal soul, by means whereof the rational life is regulated " (Philo de Mund. Opif. xl.).

"Not that which enters into the mouth defiles the man, but that which goes out of the mouth, this it is that defiles the man. . . . Everything that enters the mouth goes away into the belly and is cast out into a sewer. But the things that proceed out of the mouth come forth from the heart, and it is they that defile the man. For out of the heart come forth evil designs, murders, adulteries, harlotries, thefts, false witness, blasphemies " (Matt. xv. 11, 17-19).

Plato has no doubt which is the responsible part of us: " Which answer is more correct, that we see with or by our eyes, and hear with or by our ears?—By which we receive each sensible impression, it seems to me, rather than with which.—For surely it would be strange if many senses resided in us . . . and they did not all tend to one certain archetypal principle (*idea*), whether it be soul, or whatever it be right to call it, with which, by these as instruments, we are sensible of all objects of sense " (Theætetus, 184 c).

The following discloses a view of what, Platonically speaking, is the daimonic plane of being :—

"See that ye despise not one of these little ones ; for I say unto you, that their angels in heaven do always see the face of my Father which is in heaven " (Matt. xviii. 10). That is to say, there is a part that is of them and not yet of them, the unseen part which, unconsciously to the physical faculties, touches on the angelic spheres, and therein finds its sympathy and guidance. The following is Plato's conception of our spiritual link and strengthener :—

"With respect to the most authoritative element of the soul that dwells with us, we should conceive as follows : that God has assigned it to each of us as a daimon ; that part, namely, which we affirm, and most correctly, resides at the body's loftiest border, and raises us from earth unto our kinship in heaven ; being, as we are, a plant not of earth but of heaven ; and proceeding from that quarter from which the primal genesis of the soul had its being, the divine nature, raising aloft our head and root, gives uprightness to the whole corporeal frame " (Tim. 90 a).

Plato's vivid consciousness of the substantial existence of " that which truth and real being irradiate," if transferred to the religious plane, would become what is called faith : " Precisely as essence is to genesis, so is truth to faith " (Tim: 29 c).

As creation to the essential quality that rules it, so is human conjecture to absolute truth! Did Plato's suggestive saying never come before the eyes of the writer of the words ? —" Faith is the substantiation of things hoped for, the induction of things not seen " (Heb. xi. 1).

The following is a test of sincerity and unworldliness, which, allowing for the difference of style, might have been found in the Gospels : " The righteous man, according to Æschylos, is simple and high-minded, not wishful to seem to be good, but to be so. . . . He must take away the seeming, for if he seem to be righteous, he will have gifts and honours as seeming to be of such a sort ; and so it will be uncertain whether he be righteous for righteousness' sake, or for the gifts and honours. He should be stripped of all but righteousness " (Rep., ii. 361 b).

The doctrine here expressed takes us very near to the moral of the fable of the Pharisee and the Publican, and also to the injunction not to do works of compassion or righteousness so as to be seen of men.

But the passage goes further, and contains a singular kind of prophecy, the application of which will be obvious. The position in the world of the truly righteous man is thus portrayed : " Without doing any unjust thing, let him have the utmost reputation of injustice, in order that he may be put to the test for righteousness, so as not to be moved by reviling and its consequences, but rather be unchangeable till death, seeming indeed to be unjust through life while really righteous. . . . The just man, thus situated, will be scourged, tortured, bound, will have his eyes put out, and lastly, will suffer all manner of evils, and be crucified."

Another passage illustrates further the despite which an unworldly unselfish man is likely to meet with at the hands of his fellows:—

"How can this be wise, Socrates, that any art should deteriorate a man of native ability whom it has seized upon, rendering him unable to help himself, or to preserve himself or any one else from the greatest dangers, and suffering him to be plundered of all his substance by enemies, and to live in the state utterly without honour? Such a man, to speak rudely, one may buffet on the cheek with impunity. . . . Employ yourself in what will give you a reputation for wisdom, leave to others these clevernesses, whether they ought to be called nonsense or fooleries, by which you will come to dwell in an empty house; and emulate, not men who confute these trifles, but those who have everyday life, glory, and many other good things" (Gorg., xli. 486 b).

This passage is curiously completed by the one that follows. The tone here is pre-eminently Christian, even as compared with some so-called Christian writings, almost *plus royaliste que le roi.*

"I for my part am persuaded . . . and consider how I may manifest as wholesome a soul as possible to the judge. Wherefore, disregarding the honours of the majority, and looking to the truth, I shall endeavour in real earnest to live and die as virtuously as I can. And I exhort all other men, to the utmost of my power, and you too in turn I urge, to this life and this contest, which I affirm surpasses all contests here; and I upbraid you because you will not be able to assist yourself when your sentence comes, and the judgment of which I have already told you. . . . But when the judge shall lay hold of you and bring you before his tribunal, you will there gape and become dizzy, no less than I should here, and perhaps some one will strike you ignominiously on the cheek, and treat you with all manner of contumely " (Gorg., lxxxii. 526 d).

At the spiritual altitude a man can arrive only by taking and holding to a very broad view of life : " What is there that can be great in a little time? for all the period from infancy to old age is but little in respect of the whole. . . . Do you think an immortal being ought to be much concerned about such a period, and not about the whole of time? . . . Have you not realized that your soul is immortal, and never perishes ? " (Rep., x. 608 b).

Jesus said openly, " My kingdom is not of this world," and was in distinct opposition to the worldly spirit, which had nothing in him. Plato is more tolerant, perhaps, as being on a plane nearer the human level, and not so near the angelic ; but he ends in discovering that the way of the world, even in politics, is not a way in which he could walk, without too serious a deflection from his ideal :—

" At first I was full of ardour towards engaging in affairs of the commonwealth, but when I looked into these and saw that they swayed about in every way from side to side, I ended in becoming giddy, yet not so as to withdraw from considering how at any time something better might come to pass in respect of these very matters, and above all, as regards the whole form of government, but to be ever awaiting opportunities of action. At last I perceived that all existing states are badly governed. . . . I was therefore compelled to say, in praise of true philosophy, that through it we are enabled to discern all that is righteous in regard to matters of state and of individuals ; and hence that the human race will never cease from ills until the race of those who are right and true wisdom-seekers shall come into political power, or until persons who have power in states shall by some divine fate seek wisdom in very truth" (Ep., vii. 325 e).

When Plato turns his mind to political or social topics, he as it were drafts a bill for the regulation of human affairs, and a bill that never became law. Nevertheless his work remains, "providing," as Professor Jowett phrases it, "the instruments of thought for future generations."

There is a hypothesis in the passage that follows that still remains as it was in Plato's day,—mooted now and again by philosophic minds :—

"'Tell me this, Glaucon; for in your house I see both sporting dogs and a number of fine birds—have you, I beg, ever applied yourself to their pairing, and bringing forth young?'

"'To what end?' said he.

"'First of all, among these, though all are fine, are not some of them both actually and potentially the best?'

"'They are.'

"'Do you breed, then, from all alike; or are you studious to do so, as far as possible, from the best breed?'

"'From the best.'

"'But how; from the youngest, or the oldest, or those fully in their prime?'

"'From those in their prime.'

"'And if they are not thus bred, you consider that the breed both of birds and dogs greatly degenerates?'

"'I do,' replied he.

"'And as to horses,' said I, 'and other animals, do you think their case otherwise?'

"'It would be paradoxical to suppose so.'

"'Bless me, my dear fellow,' said I, 'how urgently we require to have tiptop governors, that is to say, if the same applies to the human race!'" (Rep., v. 459 a).

A shrewd American, one of some experience in conscientious efforts in this direction, has suggested that perhaps it was for this bold stroke of criticism that Socrates was condemned to death. However that may be, and though we have devoted more attention to the scientific breeding of animals than ever ancient Greece could have done, society has not yet progressed so far as to produce the prize baby, or the all-round man. Indeed, some of the human tabernacles which we offer the unborn are so poor and rickety that it is a marvel tenants are ever found for them. A very large proportion do indeed surrender their lease at a very early date.

Nor, amid more than ample political clamour and profession, have we yet assimilated the truth that the State is based upon the individual, and that ill-bred, ill-fed, ill-trained children provide a continual supply of costly tenants of hospitals, almshouses, poor-houses, and prisons, and constitute a permanent weakness to our race.

How happy are young animals other than human! In a single English town of middle size * it was found that the chemists sold, every week, £70 worth of "Godfrey's cordial," "quietness," "child's preserver," "syrup of poppies," and laudanum.

Plato did not foresee this development of his theory, that instead of fostering the production of fine children, future lawgivers might in their wisdom license the slow poisoning of puling and unsatisfactory specimens of humanity.

The one quality that distinguishes the sane thinker or seer from the overheated enthusiast, is his patience: he accepts the necessity of growth. There is a very beautiful parabolic metaphor in the following passage, which will show us that Plato was not a merely fanciful dreamer, the sport of momentary impulse, or the votary of a sentimental asceticism urging a luxurious withdrawal from life:—

"We ought to endeavour to fly hence thither [from mortal nature to divine] as quickly as possible. But this flight con-

* Preston.

sists in resembling God to the utmost of our power; and this resemblance consists in becoming righteous and holy with wisdom. . . . God is never in any respect unjust, but the most righteous that can be, and there is not anything more like unto him than the man amongst us who is as righteous as possible" (Theætetus, 177 a, c).

We may be reminded of the words, "This is life eternal, to know thee the only true God," "Be ye perfect, as your heavenly Father is perfect."

The peculiar symbolic form of the thought, "The flight from mortal nature to divine consists in resembling God to our utmost," may remind us of an exquisite way of defining judgment, as applied to men who shut their eyes in sensual sleep; "this is the judgment [*i.e.* the judgment consists in the fact], that the light has come into the world."

In a wider sense than can be fully shown by a comparison of isolated passages, is the spirit of Plato at one with the original spirit of Christianity. With both, human life, while of primary importance to those tabernacling therein, is not life itself, or life of eternal quality, but a secondary, derivative, or removed phase of existence, proceeding from the first, and drawing therefrom, or lacking, its normal rule and governance.

But, to judge of Plato by isolated passages is not so great an injustice as it might be in the case of some philosophers: "Platonism is so organic throughout, that it may be developed from every genuine germ of it." There is spirit in Plato's work, not intellect only; and spirit has a glow discernible in the smallest fragment.

"Plato did not propose by his philosophy a mere theoretic perception of abstract truth, but to penetrate and elevate life was its highest aim and endeavour. And so he illustrates the saying of Pascal, that in Divine things one must love in order to know." In this there is a sympathy between his influence and the more personal and vivid appeal of Jesus, a sympathy that will be difficult to perceive only in proportion as "the old habit of thinking immediately, or even exclusively, of something doctrinal, when the Christian element or Christianity is spoken of," still adheres to us. "If any one chooses to put the will of God into practice, he will know concerning the doctrine."

It is manifest that we cannot be taught the whole secret of fate and freewill, of our place and condition here, and the reasons why we are in a material world. All truths, therefore, which may be attempted to be conveyed to us must be partial truths. Suggestive facts unnoticed by us busy sleepers, a great and inspired teacher is now and again enabled to convey; and from these and their solid sanctions in the lessons of life, we are left to deduce such conclusions as best fit the bigness of our appreciative faculty. We can receive no more than we can grasp from either Platonism or Christianity, and a blow from the resistless hand upon our factitious and temporary life is perhaps sometimes the necessary preliminary to the opening of our ears and hearts to the whisper of any gospel; even one that tells of a happy kingdom which waits only to be won.

END OF VOL. I.

A LIST OF

KEGAN PAUL, TRENCH, TRÜBNER, & CO.'S

PUBLICATIONS.

SIZES OF BOOKS.

A book is folio (fol.); quarto (4to.); octavo (8vo.); twelve mo (12mo.); sixteen mo (16mo.); eighteen mo (18mo.); thirty-two mo (32mo.), &c., according to the number of leaves or foldings of a printed sheet, whether the sheet be foolscap, crown, demy, medium, royal, super-royal, or imperial, and irrespective of the thickness of the volume. The following are *approximate* outside measurements in inches of the more common sizes.

	height	breadth		height	breadth
32mo. = royal 32mo.	$5\frac{1}{4}$ ×	$3\frac{3}{4}$	P-8vo. = post 8vo.	8 ×	$5\frac{1}{4}$
16mo. = demy 16mo.	$5\frac{1}{2}$ ×	$4\frac{1}{2}$	LP-8vo. = large post 8vo.	$8\frac{1}{2}$ ×	6
18mo. = royal 18mo.	6 ×	$4\frac{1}{4}$	8vo. = demy 8vo.	9 ×	6
fcp. = fcp. 8vo.	$6\frac{3}{4}$ ×	$4\frac{1}{2}$	M-8vo. = medium 8vo.	$9\frac{1}{2}$ ×	6
cr. = demy 12mo.	$7\frac{1}{4}$ ×	$4\frac{1}{2}$	SR-8vo. = super-royal 8vo.	10 ×	$6\frac{1}{2}$
cr. = small crown 8vo.	$7\frac{1}{4}$ ×	5	IMP-8vo. = imperial 8vo.	12 ×	$8\frac{1}{2}$
cr. = crown 8vo.	$7\frac{1}{2}$ ×	$5\frac{1}{2}$			
cr. = large crown 8vo.	$8\frac{1}{4}$ ×	$5\frac{1}{2}$			

Printed and folded in the reverse way—the breadth being greater than the height—the size is described as "oblong" 8vo., "oblong" 4to. &c.

Paternoster House,
Charing Cross Road,
August 21, 1893.

A LIST OF
KEGAN PAUL, TRENCH, TRÜBNER, & CO.'S PUBLICATIONS.

NOTE.—*Books are arranged in alphabetical order under the names or pseudonyms of author, translator, or editor. Biographies 'by the author of' are placed under the name of the subject. Anonymous works and 'selections' will be found under the first word of the title. The letters I.S.S. denote that the work forms a volume of the International Scientific Series.*

A. K. H. B., **From a Quiet Place**: some Discourses. Cr. 8vo. 5s.

ABEL, CARL, **Linguistic Essays.** Post 8vo. 9s. (*Trübner's Oriental Series.*)
    Slavic and Latin: Lectures on Comparative Lexicography. Post 8vo. 5s.

ABERCROMBY, Hon. RALPH, **Weather**: a popular Exposition of the Nature of Weather Changes from day to day. With 96 Figures. Second Edition. Cr. 8vo. 5s. (*I.S.S.*)

ABRAHAMS, L. B., **Manual of Scripture History for Jewish Schools and Families.** With Map. Eleventh Edition. Cr. 8vo. 1s. 6d.

ACLAND, Sir HENRY, Bart., **Science in Secondary Schools.** Cr. 8vo. 1s. 6d.

ACLAND, Hon. Mrs. W., **Love in a Life.** 2 vols. Cr. 8vo. 21s.

ADAMS, ESTELLE, **Sea Song and River Rhyme, from Chaucer to Tennyson.** With 12 Etchings. Large cr. 8vo. 10s. 6d.

ADAMS, Mrs. LEITH, **The Peyton Romance.** 3 vols. £1. 11s. 6d.

ADAMS, W. H. DAVENPORT, **The White King**; or, Charles the First, and Men and Women, Life and Manners, &c., in the first half of the 17th Century. 2 vols. 8vo. 21s.

ÆSCHYLUS. **The Seven Plays in English Verse.** Translated by Prof. LEWIS CAMPBELL. Cr. 8vo. 7s. 6d.

AHLWARDT, W., **The Diváns of the Six Ancient Arabic Poets**—Ennábiga, 'Antara, Tharafa, Zuhair, 'Alquama, and Imruulquais. With a complete list of the various readings of the text. 8vo. 12s.

AHN, F., **Grammar of the Dutch Language.** Fifth Edition, revised and enlarged. 12mo. 3s. 6d.
    Grammar of the German Language. New Edition. Cr. 8vo. 3s. 6d.
    Method of Learning German. 12mo. 3s. Key, 8d.
    Manual of German Conversation; or, Vade Mecum for English Travellers. Second Edition. 12mo. 1s. 6d.
    Method of Learning French. First and Second Courses. 12mo. 3s.; separately, 1s. 6d. each.
    Method of Learning French. Third Course. 12mo. 1s. 6d.
    Method of Learning Italian. 12mo. 3s. 6d.
    Latin Grammar for Beginners. Thirteenth Edition. Cr. 8vo. 3s.

AINSWORTH, W. F., **Personal Narrative of the Euphrates Expedition.** With Map. 2 vols. Demy 8vo. 30s.

AIZLEWOOD, J. W., Echo and Narcissus. Cr. 8vo. 2s. 6d.

Albanaise Grammaire, à l'usage de ceux qui désirent apprendre cette langue sans l'aide d'un maître. Par P. W. Cr. 8vo. 7s. 6d.

ALBÉRÛNÎ'S India: an Account of the Religion, Philosophy, Literature, Geography, Chronology, Astronomy, Customs, Laws, and Astrology of India, about A.D. 1030. Arabic text, edited by Prof. E. SACHAU. 4to. £3. 3s.

ALEXANDER, Major-Gen. G. G., Confucius, the Great Teacher. Cr. 8vo. 6s.

ALEXANDER, S., Moral Order and Progress: an Analysis of Ethical Conceptions. Second Edition. Post 8vo. 14s. (*Philosophical Library*.)

ALEXANDER, WILLIAM, D.D., Bishop of Derry, St. Augustine's Holiday, and other Poems. Cr. 8vo. 6s.

  The Great Question, and other Sermons. Cr. 8vo. 6s.

ALEXANDROW, A., Complete English-Russian and Russian-English Dictionary. 2 vols. 8vo. £2.

ALLEN, C. F. ROMILLY, Book of Chinese Poetry. Being the collection of Ballads, Sagas, Hymns, and other Pieces known as the Shih Ching, metrically translated. 8vo. 16s.

ALLEN, GRANT, The Colour-Sense: its Origin and Development. An Essay in Comparative Psychology. Second Edition. Post 8vo. 10s. 6d. (*Philosophical Library*.)

ALLEN, MARY L., Luncheon Dishes; comprising Menus in French and English, as well as Suggestions for Arrangement and Decoration of Table. Fcp. 8vo. cloth, 1s. 6d.; paper covers, 1s.

  Five-o'clock Tea. Containing Receipts for Cakes, Savoury Sandwiches, &c. Eleventh Thousand. Fcp. 8vo. 1s. 6d.; paper covers, 1s.

ALLIBONE, S. A., Dictionary of English Literature and British and American Authors, from the Earliest Accounts to the Latter Half of the 19th Century. 3 vols. Roy. 8vo. £5. 8s. SUPPLEMENT, 2 vols. roy. 8vo. (1891), £3. 3s.

ALTHAUS, JULIUS, The Spas of Europe. 8vo. 7s. 6d.

AMOS, Professor Sheldon, History and Principles of the Civil Law of Rome: an Aid to the Study of Scientific and Comparative Jurisprudence. 8vo. 16s.

  Science of Law. Seventh Edition. Cr. 8vo. 5s. (*I.S.S.*)

  Science of Politics. Third Edition. Cr. 8vo. 5s. (*I.S.S.*)

ANDERSON, DAVID, 'Scenes' in the Commons. Cr. 8vo. 5s.

ANDERSON, J., English Intercourse with Siam in the Seventeenth Century. Post 8vo. 15s. (*Trübner's Oriental Series*.)

ANDERSON, WILLIAM, Practical Mercantile Correspondence: a Collection of Modern Letters of Business, with Notes. Thirtieth Edition, revised. Cr. 8vo. 3s. 6d.

Antiquarian Magazine and Bibliographer, The. Edited by EDWARD WALFORD and G. W. REDWAY. Complete in 12 vols. 8vo. £3 net.

APEL, H., Prose Specimens for Translation into German. With copious Vocabularies and Explanations. Cr. 8vo. 4s. 6d.

APPLETON, J. H., and SAYCE, A. H., Dr. Appleton: his Life and Literary Relics. Post 8vo. 10s. 6d. (*Philosophical Library*.)

ARAGO, ÉTIENNE, Les Aristocraties: a Comedy in Verse. Second Edition. 12mo. 4s.

ARBUTHNOT, Sir A. J., Major-Gen. Sir Thomas Munro: a Memoir. Cr. 8vo. 3s. 6d.

ARCHER, WILLIAM, William Charles Macready. Cr. 8vo. 2s. 6d. (*Eminent Actors.*)

ARDEN, A. H., Progressive Grammar of Common Tamil. 5s.

ARISTOTLE, The Nicomachean Ethics. Translated by F. H. PETERS. Third Edition. Cr. 8vo. 6s.

ARNOLD, Sir EDWIN, Grammar of the Turkish Language. With Dialogues and Vocabulary. Pott 8vo. 2s. 6d.

    Death and Afterwards. Reprinted from the *Fortnightly Review* of August 1885, with a Supplement. Eleventh Edition. Cr. 8vo. cloth, 1s. 6d.; paper covers, 1s.

    In My Lady's Praise: Poems Old and New, written to the honour of Fanny, Lady Arnold. Fourth Edition. Imperial 16mo. parchment, 3s. 6d.

    India Revisited. With 32 Full-page Illustrations. Second Edition. Cr. 8vo. 6s.

    Indian Idylls. From the Sanskrit of the Mahâbhârata. Second Edition. Cr. 8vo. 6s.

    Indian Poetry. Containing 'The Indian Song of Songs' from the Sanskrit, two books from 'The Iliad of India,' and other Oriental Poems. Sixth Edition. 6s. (*Trübner's Oriental Series.*)

    Lotus and Jewel. Containing 'In an Indian Temple,' 'A Casket of Gems,' 'A Queen's Revenge,' with other Poems. Third Edition. Cr. 8vo. 6s.

    Pearls of the Faith, or Islam's Rosary. Being the Ninety-Nine Beautiful Names of Allah. Sixth Edition. Cr. 8vo. 6s.

    Poems, National and Non-Oriental, with some new Pieces. Second Edition. Cr. 8vo. 6s.

    The Light of Asia, or The Great Renunciation. Being the Life and Teaching of Gautama. Presentation Edition. With Illustrations and Portrait. Sm. 4to. 21s. Library Edition, cr. 8vo. 6s. Elzevir Edition, 6s. Cheap Edition (*Lotos Series*), cloth or half-parchment, 3s. 6d.

    The Secret of Death: being a Version of the Katha Upanishad, from the Sanskrit. Fifth Edition. Cr. 8vo. 6s.

    The Song Celestial, or Bhagavad-Gîtâ, from the Sanskrit. Fifth Edition. Cr. 8vo. 5s.

    With Sa'di in the Garden, or The Book of Love: being the 'Ishk,' or third chapter of the 'Bostân' of the Persian poet Sa'di, embodied in a Dialogue. Fourth Edition. Cr. 8vo. 6s.

    Poetical Works. Uniform Edition, comprising—The Light of Asia, Lotus and Jewel, Indian Poetry, Pearls of the Faith, Indian Idylls, The Secret of Death, The Song Celestial, With Sa'di in the Garden. 8 vols. Cr. 8vo. 48s.

ARNOLD, THOMAS, and SCANNELL, T. B., Catholic Dictionary. An account of the Doctrine, Discipline, Rites, Ceremonies, &c., of the Catholic Church. Fourth Edition, revised and enlarged. 8vo. 21s.

ASTON, W. G., Grammar of the Japanese Spoken Language. Fourth Edition. Cr. 8vo. 12s.

    Grammar of the Japanese Written Language. Second Edition. 8vo. 28s.

AUBERTIN, J. J., A Flight to Mexico. With 7 Full-page Illustrations and a Railway Map. Cr. 8vo. 7s. 6d.

    Six Months in Cape Colony and Natal. With Illustrations and Map. Cr. 8vo. 6s.

    A Fight with Distances. With Illustrations and Maps. Cr. 8vo. 7s. 6d.

    Wanderings and Wonderings. With Portrait, Map, and 7 Illustrations. Cr. 8vo. 8s. 6d.

AUGIER, ÉMILE, Diane: a Drama in Verse. Third Edition. 12mo. 2s. 6d.

AVELING, F. W., The Classic Birthday Book. 8vo. cloth, 8s. 6d.; paste grain, 15s.; tree calf, 21s.

AXON, W. E. A., The Mechanic's Friend. A Collection of Receipts and Practical Suggestions relating to Aquaria, Bronzing, Cements, Drawing, Dyes, Electricity, Gilding, Glass-working, &c. Numerous Woodcuts. Second Edition. Cr. 8vo. 3s. 6d.

AZARIAS, Brother, Aristotle and the Christian Church: an Essay. Sm. cr. 8vo. 3s. 6d.

BADER, CHARLES, Natural and Morbid Changes of the Human Eye, and their Treatment. 8vo. 16s. Atlas of Plates, in portfolio. Medium 8vo. 21s. Text and Atlas together, £1. 12s.

BADHAM, F. P., Formation of the Gospels. Second Edition, revised and enlarged. Cr. 8vo. 5s.

BAGEHOT, WALTER, The English Constitution. Seventh Edition. Cr. 8vo. 7s. 6d.
    Lombard Street. A Description of the Money Market. Tenth Edition. With Notes, bringing the work up to the present time, by E. JOHNSTONE. Cr. 8vo. 7s. 6d.
    Essays on Parliamentary Reform. Cr. 8vo. 5s.
    On the Depreciation of Silver, and Topics connected with it. 8vo. 5s.
    Physics and Politics; or, Thoughts on the Application of the Principles of 'Natural Selection' and 'Inheritance' to Political Society. Ninth Edition. Cr. 8vo. 5s. (I.S.S.)

BAGENAL, PHILIP H., American Irish and their Influence on Irish Politics. Cr. 8vo. 5s.

BAGOT, ALAN, Accidents in Mines: their Causes and Prevention. Cr. 8vo. 6s.
    Principles of Colliery Ventilation. Second Edition, greatly enlarged. Cr. 8vo. 5s.
    Principles of Civil Engineering as applied to Agriculture and Estate Management. Cr. 8vo. 7s. 6d.

BAIN, ALEX., Education as a Science. Seventh Edition. Cr. 8vo. 5s. (I.S.S.)
    Mind and Body. The Theories of their Relation. With 4 Illustrations. Eighth Edition. Cr. 8vo. 5s. (I.S.S.)

BAKER, Major EDEN, R.A., Preliminary Tactics. An Introduction to the Study of War. For the use of Junior Officers. Cr. 8vo. 6s.

BAKER, IRA, Treatise on Masonry Construction. Royal 8vo. 21s.

BAKER, Sir SHERSTON, Bart., Laws relating to Quarantine. Cr. 8vo. 12s. 6d.
    Halleck's International Law. Third Edition, thoroughly revised by Sir SHERSTON BAKER, Bart. 2 vols. Demy 8vo. 38s.

BALDWIN, Capt. J. H., Large and Small Game of Bengal and the North-Western Provinces of India. With 20 Illustrations. Sm. 4to. 10s. 6d.

BALFOUR, F. H., Leaves from my Chinese Scrap-Book. Post 8vo. 7s. 6d.

BALKWILL, F. H., The Testimony of the Teeth to Man's Place in Nature. With Illustrations. Cr. 8vo. 6s.

BALL, JOHN, Notes of a Naturalist in South America. With Map. Cr. 8vo. 8s. 6d.

BALL, Sir ROBERT, The Cause of an Ice Age. Cr. 8vo. 2s. 6d. (Modern Science Series.)

BALL, V., Diamonds, Coal, and Gold of India: their Mode of Occurrence and Distribution. Fcp. 8vo. 5s.

BALLANTYNE, J. R., Elements of Hindi and Braj Bhakha Grammar. Compiled for the East India College at Haileybury. Second Edition. Cr. 8vo. 5s.

BALLANTYNE, J. R., First Lessons in Sanskrit Grammar. Fifth Edition. 8vo. 3s. 6d.
— **Sankhya Aphorisms of Kapila.** With Illustrative Extracts from the Commentaries. Third Edition. Post 8vo. 16s. (*Trübner's Oriental Series.*)
BALLIN, ADA S. and **F. L., Hebrew Grammar.** With Exercises selected from the Bible. Cr. 8vo. 7s. 6d.
BANCROFT, H. H., Popular History of the Mexican People. 8vo. 15s.
BANKS, Mrs. G. LINNÆUS, God's Providence House. Cr. 8vo. 6s.
BARING-GOULD, S., Germany, Present and Past. New and Cheaper Edition. Large cr. 8vo. 7s. 6d.
BARLOW, J. W., The Ultimatum of Pessimism. An Ethical Study. 8vo. 6s.
BARNES, WILLIAM, Poems of Rural Life in the Dorset Dialect. New Edition. Cr. 8vo. 6s.
BARRIÈRE, THEODORE, and CAPENDU, ERNEST, Les Faux Bonshommes. A Comedy. 12mo. 4s.
BARTH, A., Religions of India. Translated by the Rev. J. Wood. Third Edition. Post 8vo. 16s. (*Trübner's Oriental Series.*)
BARTLETT, J. R., Dictionary of Americanisms: a Glossary of Words and Phrases colloquially used in the United States. Fourth Edition. 8vo. 21s.
BASU, K. P., Students' Mathematical Companion. Containing Problems in Arithmetic, Algebra, Geometry, and Mensuration, for Students of the Indian Universities. Cr. 8vo. 6s.
BASTIAN, H. CHARLTON, The Brain as an Organ of Mind. With 184 Illustrations. Fourth Edition. Cr. 8vo. 5s. (*I.S.S.*)
BAUGHAN, ROSA, The Influence of the Stars: a Treatise on Astrology, Chiromancy, and Physiognomy. Second Edition. 8vo. 5s.
BAUR, FERDINAND, Philological Introduction to Greek and Latin for Students. Translated and adapted from the German by C. Kegan Paul and E. D. Stone. Third Edition. Cr. 8vo. 6s.
BAYNES, Canon H. R., Home Songs for Quiet Hours. Fourth and Cheaper Edition. Fcp. 8vo. 2s. 6d.
BEAL, S., Catena of Buddhist Scriptures. From the Chinese. 8vo. 15s.
— **Romantic Legend of Sakya Buddha.** From the Chinese-Sanskrit. Cr. 8vo. 12s.
— **Life of Hiuen-Tsiang.** By the Shamans Hwui Li and Yen-Tsung. With an Account of the Works of I-Tsing. Post 8vo. 10s. (*Trübner's Oriental Series.*)
— **Si-Yu-Ki:** Buddhist Records of the Western World. Translated from the Chinese of Hiuen-Tsiang (A.D. 629). With Map. 2 vols. post 8vo. 24s. (*Trübner's Oriental Series.*)
— **Texts from the Buddhist Canon, commonly known as Dhammapada.** Translated from the Chinese. Post 8vo. 7s. 6d. (*Trübner's Oriental Series.*)
BEAMES, JOHN, Outlines of Indian Philology. With a Map showing the Distribution of Indian languages. Enlarged Edition. Cr. 8vo. 5s.
— **Comparative Grammar of the Modern Aryan Languages of India:** Hindi, Panjabi, Sindhi, Gujarati, Marathi, Oriya, and Bengali. 3 vols. 8vo. 16s. each.
BEARD, CHARLES, Martin Luther and the Reformation in Germany. 8vo. 16s.
BELL, A. M., Elocutionary Manual. Fifth Edition Revised. 12mo. 7s. 6d.
BELLASIS, EDWARD, Cardinal Newman as a Musician. Sewed, 1s. 6d.
BELLOWS, JOHN, French and English Dictionary for the Pocket. Containing the French-English and English-French Divisions on the same page; Conjugating all the Verbs; Distinguishing the Genders by Different Types; giving Numerous Aids to Pronunciation, &c. Fifty-third Thousand of the Second Edition. 32mo. morocco tuck, 12s. 6d.; roan, 10s. 6d.
— **Tous les Verbes.** Conjugations of all the Verbs in French and English. Second Edition. With Tables of Weights, Measures, &c. 32mo. 6d.

BENEDEN, P. J. van, Animal Parasites and Messmates. With 83 Illustrations. Fourth Edition. Cr. 8vo. 5s. (*I.S.S.*)

BENEDIX, RODERICK, Der Vetter. Comedy in Three Acts. 12mo. 2s. 6d.

BENFEY, THEODOR, Grammar of the Sanskrit Language. For the Use of Early Students. Second Edition. Roy. 8vo. 10s. 6d.

BENSON, A. C., William Laud, sometime Archbishop of Canterbury. With Portrait. Cr. 8vo. 6s.

BENSON, MARY ELEANOR, At Sundry Times and in Divers Manners. With Portrait and Memoir. 2 vols. cr. 8vo. 10s. 6d.

BENTHAM, JEREMY, Theory of Legislation. Translated from the French of Etienne Dumont by R. HILDRETH. Seventh Edition. Post 8vo. 7s. 6d.

'BERNARD,' From World to Cloister; or, My Novitiate. Cr. 8vo. 5s.

BERNSTEIN, Prof., The Five Senses of Man. With 91 Illustrations. Fifth Edition. Cr. 8vo. 5s. (*I.S.S.*)

BERTIN, GEORGE, Abridged Grammar of the Languages of the Cuneiform Inscriptions. Cr. 8vo. 5s.

BEVAN, THEODORE F., Toil, Travel, and Discovery in British New Guinea. With 5 Maps. Large cr. 8vo. 7s. 6d.

BHIKSHU, SUBHADRA, Buddhist Catechism. 12mo. 2s.

BIDDULPH, C. E., Four Months in Persia. 8vo. 3s. 6d.

BILLER, EMMA, Ulli: the Story of a Neglected Girl. Translated from the German by A. B. DAISY ROST. Cr. 8vo. 6s.

Bible Folk Lore: a Study in Comparative Mythology. Cr. 8vo. 10s. 6d.

BINET, A., and FERE, C., Animal Magnetism. Second Edition. Cr. 8vo. 5s. (*I.S.S.*)

BIRD, ROBERT, Jesus, the Carpenter of Nazareth. Seventh Edition, revised. Cr. 8vo. 5s. Also in Two Parts, price 2s. 6d. each.

BISHOP, M. C., The Prison Life of Marie Antoinette and her Children, the Dauphin and the Duchesse D'Angoulême. New and Revised Edition. With Portrait. Cr. 8vo. 6s.

BLADES, W., Biography and Typography of William Caxton, England's First Printer. 8vo. hand-made paper, imitation old bevelled binding, £1. 1s.; Cheap Edition, cr. 8vo. 5s.

Account of the German Morality Play, entitled, 'Depositio Cornuti Typographici.' As performed in the 17th or 18th Centuries. With facsimile illustrations. Sm. 4to. 7s. 6d.

BLAKE, WILLIAM, Selections from the Writings of. Edited, with Introduction, by LAURENCE HOUSMAN. With Frontispiece. Elzevir 8vo. Parchment, 6s.; vellum, 7s. 6d. (*Parchment Library*.)

BLASERNA, Prof. P., Theory of Sound in its Relation to Music. With numerous Illustrations. Fourth Edition. Cr. 8vo. 5s. (*I.S.S.*)

BLEEK, W. H. I., Reynard the Fox in South Africa, or, Hottentot Fables and Tales. Post 8vo. 3s. 6d.

BLOGG, H. B., Life of Francis Duncan. With Introduction by the BISHOP OF CHESTER. Cr. 8vo. 3s. 6d.

BLOOMFIELD, The Lady, Reminiscences of Court and Diplomatic Life. New and Cheaper Edition, with Frontispiece. Cr. 8vo. 6s.

BLUMHARDT, J. F., Charitabali, The; or, Instructive Biography. By ISVARA-CHANDRA VIDYASAGARA. With Vocabulary of all the Words occurring in the Text. 12mo. 5s. Vocabulary only, 2s. 6d.

BLUNT, WILFRID SCAWEN, The Wind and the Whirlwind. 8vo. 1s. 6d.

The Love Sonnets of Proteus. Fifth Edition. Elzevir 8vo. 5s.

In Vinculis. With Portrait. Elzevir 8vo. 5s.

A New Pilgrimage, and other Poems. Elzevir 8vo. 5s.

Esther, Love Lyrics, and Natalia's Resurrection. 7s. 6d.

BLYTH, E. KELL, Life of William Ellis, founder of the Birkbeck Schools. Second Edition. 8vo. 10s. 6d.

BODEMANN, TH. and KARL, Bruno: a Treatise on the Assaying of Lead, Copper, Silver, Gold, and Mercury. Translated by W. A. GOODYEAR. Illustrated with Plates. Cr. 8vo. 6s. 6d.

BOGER, Mrs. E., Myths, Scenes, and Worthies of Somerset. Cr. 8vo. 10s. 6d.

BOJESEN, MARIA, Guide to the Danish Language. 12mo. 5s.

BOSANQUET, BERNARD, Introduction to Hegel's Philosophy of Fine Art. Cr. 8vo. 5s.

BOWDEN, Fr. CHARLES HENRY, Life of B. John Juvenal Ancina. 8vo. 9s.

BOWEN, H. C., Studies in English. For the use of Modern Schools. Tenth thousand. Sm. cr. 8vo. 1s. 6d.

 English Grammar for Beginners. Fcp. 8vo. 1s.

 Simple English Poems. English Literature for Junior Classes, 3s. Parts I. II. and III. 6d. each. Part IV. 1s.

BOYD, P., Nágánanda; or, the Joy of the Snake World. From the Sanskrit of Sri-Harsha-Deva. Cr. 8vo. 4s. 6d.

BRACKENBURY, Major-General, Field Works: their Technical Construction and Tactical Application. 2 vols. Sm. cr. 8vo. 12s. *(Military Handbooks.)*

BRADLEY. F. H., The Principles of Logic. 8vo. 16s.

BRADSHAW'S Guide. Dictionary of Mineral Waters, Climatic Health Resorts, Sea Baths, and Hydropathic Establishments. With a Map. 2s. 6d.

Brave Men's Footsteps: a Book of Example and Anecdote for Young People. By the editor of 'Men who have Risen.' Illustrations by C. DOYLE. Ninth Edition. Cr. 8vo. 2s. 6d.

BRENTANO, LUJO, History and Development of Gilds, and the Origin of Trade Unions. 8vo. 3s. 6d.

BRETSCHNEIDER, E., Mediæval Researches from Eastern Asiatic Sources: Fragments towards the Knowledge of the Geography and History of Central and Western Asia, from the 13th to the 17th century, with 2 Maps. 2 vols. Post 8vo. 21s. *(Trübner's Oriental Series.)*

BRETTE, P. H., THOMAS, F., French Examination Papers set at the University of London. Part I. Matriculation, and the General Examination for Women. Cr. 8vo. 3s. 6d. Key, 5s. Part II. First B.A. Examinations for Honours and D. Litt. Examinations. Cr. 8vo. 7s.

BRIDGETT, T. E., Blunders and Forgeries: Historical Essays. Cr. 8vo. 6s.

 History of the Holy Eucharist in Great Britain. 2 vols. 8vo. 18s.

BROOKE, Rev. STOPFORD A., The Fight of Faith: Sermons preached on various occasions. Sixth Edition, cr. 8vo. 5s.

 The Spirit of the Christian Life. Fourth Edition. Cr. 8vo. 5s.

 Theology in the English Poets: Cowper, Coleridge, Wordsworth, and Burns. Sixth Edition. Post 8vo. 5s.

 Christ in Modern Life. Eighteenth Edition. Cr. 8vo. 5s.

 Sermons. Two Series. Thirteenth Edition. Cr. 8vo. 5s. each.

 Life and Letters of F. W. Robertson. With Portrait. 2 vols. Cr. 8vo. 7s. 6d. Library Edition, 8vo. with portrait, 12s. Popular Edition, cr. 8vo. 6s.

BROWN, C. P., Sanskrit Prosody and Numerical Symbols Explained. 8vo. 3s. 6d.

BROWN, HORATIO F., Venetian Studies. Cr. 8vo. 7s. 6d.

BROWN, Rev. J. BALDWIN, The Higher Life: its Reality, Experience, and Destiny. Seventh Edition. Cr. 8vo. 5s.

 Doctrine of Annihilation in the Light of the Gospel of Love. Fourth Edition. Cr. 8vo. 2s. 6d.

 The Christian Policy of Life: a Book for Young Men of Business. Third Edition. Cr. 8vo. 3s. 6d.

BROWN, J. C., People of Finland in Archaic Times. Cr. 8vo. 5s.
BROWN, J. P., The Dervishes; or, Oriental Spiritualism. With 24 Illustrations. Cr. 8vo. 14s.
BROWNE, EDGAR A., How to Use the Ophthalmoscope. Third Edition. Cr. 8vo. 3s. 6d.
BROWNING, OSCAR, Introduction to the History of Educational Theories. Second Edition. 3s. 6d. (*Education Library.*)
BRUGMANN, KARL, Comparative Grammar of the Indo-Germanic Languages. 3 vols. 8vo. Vol. I. Introduction and Phonology, 18s. Vol. II. Morphology (Stem-Formation and Inflexion), Part 1, 16s. Vol. III. 12s. 6d.
BRUN, L. LE, Materials for Translating English into French. Seventh Edition. Post 8vo. 4s. 6d.
BRYANT, SOPHIE, Celtic Ireland. With 3 Maps. Cr. 8vo. 5s.
BRYANT, W. CULLEN, Poems. Cheap Edition. Sm. 8vo. 3s. 6d.
BRYCE, J., Handbook of Home Rule: being Articles on the Irish Question. Second Edition. Cr. 8vo. 1s. 6d.; paper covers, 1s.
— Two Centuries of Irish History. 8vo. 16s.
BUDGE, E. A., History of Esarhaddon (Son of Sennacherib), King of Assyria, B.C. 681–668. Translated from the Cuneiform Inscriptions in the British Museum. Post 8vo. 10s. 6d. (*Trübner's Oriental Series.*)
— Archaic Classics: Assyrian Texts, being Extracts from the Annals of Shalmaneser II., Sennacherib, and Assur-Bani-Pal, with Philological Notes. Sm. 4to. 7s. 6d.
BUNGE, Prof. G., Text-Book of Physiological and Pathological Chemistry, for Physicians and Students. Translated from the German by L. C. WOOLDRIDGE. 8vo. 16s.
BUNSEN, ERNEST DE, Islam; or, True Christianity. Crown 8vo. 5s.
BURGESS, JAMES, The Buddhist Cave-Temples and their Inscriptions, containing Views, Plans, Sections, and Elevation of Façades of Cave-temples; Drawings of Architectural and Mythological Sculptures; Facsimiles of Inscriptions, &c.; with Descriptive and Explanatory Text, and Translations of Inscriptions. With 86 Plates and Woodcuts. Royal 4to. half-bound, £3. 3s. [*Archæological Survey of Western India.*]
— Elura Cave-Temples and the Brahmanical and Jaina Caves in Western India. With 66 Plates and Woodcuts. Royal 4to. half-bound, £3. 3s. [*Archæological Survey of Western India.*]
— Reports of the Amaravati and Jaggayyapeta Buddhist Stupas, containing numerous Collotype and other Illustrations of Buddhist Sculpture and Architecture, &c., in South-eastern India; Facsimiles of Inscriptions, &c., with Descriptive and Explanatory Text; together with Transcriptions, Translations, and Elucidations of the Dhauli and Jaugada Inscriptions of Asoka. With numerous Plates and Woodcuts. Royal 4to. half-bound, £4. 4s. [*Archæological Survey of Southern India.*]
BURNELL, A. C., Elements of South Indian Palæography, from the 4th to the 17th century: an Introduction to the Study of South Indian Inscriptions and MSS. Enlarged Edition. With Map and 35 Plates. 4to. £2. 12s. 6d.
— The Ordinances of Manu. Translated from the Sanskrit, with Introduction by the late A. C. BURNELL. Completed and Edited by E. W. HOPKINS. Post 8vo. 12s. (*Trübner's Oriental Series.*)
BURNEY, Capt., R.N., The Young Seaman's Manual and Rigger's Guide. Tenth Edition, revised and corrected. With 200 Illustrations and 16 Sheets of Signals. Cr. 8vo. 7s. 6d.
BURNS, ROBERT, Selected Poems of. With an Introduction by ANDREW LANG. Elzevir 8vo. vellum, 7s. 6d.; parchment or cloth, 6s. (*Parchment Library.*)
BUTLER, F., Spanish Teacher and Colloquial Phrase-Book. 18mo. half-roan, 2s. 6d.
BUXTON, Major, Elements of Military Administration. First part: Permanent System of Administration. Small cr. 8vo. 7s. 6d. (*Military Handbooks.*)

BYRNE, Dean JAMES, General Principles of the Structure of Language. 2 vols. Second and Revised Edition. 8vo. 36s.

Origin of Greek, Latin, and Gothic Roots. Second and Revised Edition. 8vo. 18s.

CABLE, G. W., Strange True Stories of Louisiana. 8vo. 7s. 6d.

CAIRD, MONA, The Wing of Azrael. Cr. 8vo. 6s.

CALDERON'S Dramas. Translated by DENIS FLORENCE MACCARTHY. Post 8vo. 10s.

CAMERINI, E., L'Eco Italiano: a Guide to Italian Conversation, with Vocabulary. 12mo. 4s. 6d.

CAMERON, Miss, Soups and Stews and Choice Ragoûts. Cr. 8vo. cloth, 1s. 6d.; paper covers, 1s.

CAMOENS' Lusiads. Portuguese Text, with Translation, by J. J. AUBERTIN. Second Edition. 2 vols. Cr. 8vo. 12s.

CAMPBELL, Prof. LEWIS, Sophocles. The Seven Plays in English Verse. Cr. 8vo. 7s. 6d.

Æschylus. The Seven Plays in English Verse. Cr. 8vo. 7s. 6d.

Candid Examination of Theism. By PHYSICUS. Second Edition, post 8vo. 7s. 6d. (*Philosophical Library.*)

CANDOLLE, ALPHONSE DE, Origin of Cultivated Plants. Second Edition. Cr. 8vo. 5s. (*I.S.S.*)

CARLYLE, THOMAS, Sartor Resartus. Elzevir 8vo. vellum, 7s. 6d.; parchment or cloth, 6s. (*Parchment Library.*)

CARPENTER, R. L., Personal and Social Christianity: Sermons and Addresses by the late RUSSELL LANT CARPENTER. With a Short Memoir by FRANCES E. COOKE. Edited by J. ESTLIN CARPENTER. Cr. 8vo. 6s.

CARPENTER, W. B., Principles of Mental Physiology, with their Applications to the Training and Discipline of the Mind, and the Study of its Morbid Conditions. Illustrated. Sixth Edition. 8vo. 12s.

Nature and Man. With a Memorial Sketch by J. ESTLIN CARPENTER. Portrait. Large cr. 8vo. 8s. 6d.

CARREÑO, Metodo para aprender a Leer, escribir y hablar el Inglés segun el sistema de Ollendorff. 8vo. 4s. 6d. Key, 3s.

CARRINGTON, H., Of the Imitation of Christ. By THOMAS À KEMPIS. A Metrical Version. Cr. 8vo. 5s.

CASSAL, CHARLES, Glossary of Idioms, Gallicisms, and other Difficulties contained in the Senior Course of the 'Modern French Reader.' Cr. 8vo. 2s. 6d.

CASSAL, CH., and **KARCHER, THEODORE.** Modern French Reader. Junior Course. Nineteenth Edition. Cr. 8vo. 2s. 6d. Senior Course. Seventh Edition. Cr. 8vo. 4s. Senior Course and Glossary in 1 vol. Cr. 8vo. 6s.

Little French Reader: extracted from the 'Modern French Reader.' Third Edition. Cr. 8vo. 2s.

CATLIN, GEORGE, O-Kee-Pa: a Religious Ceremony; and other Customs of the Mandans. With 13 coloured Illustrations. Small 4to. 14s.

The Lifted and Subsided Rocks of America, with their Influence on the Oceanic, Atmospheric, and Land Currents, and the Distribution of Races. With 2 Maps. Cr. 8vo. 6s. 6d.

Shut your Mouth and Save your Life. With 29 Illustrations. Ninth Edition. Cr. 8vo. 2s. 6d.

CHAMBERLAIN, Prof. B. H., Classical Poetry of the Japanese. Post 8vo. 7s. 6d. (*Trübner's Oriental Series.*)

Simplified Japanese Grammar. Cr. 8vo. 5s.

Romanised Japanese Reader. Consisting of Japanese Anecdotes and Maxims, with English Translations and Notes. 12mo. 6s.

Handbook of Colloquial Japanese. 8vo. 12s. 6d.

Things Japanese. Second, Revised Edition. Cr. 8vo. 8s. 6d.

CHAMBERS, J. D., Theological and Philosophical Works of Hermes Trismegistus, Christian Neoplatonist. Translated from the Greek. 8vo. 7s. 6d.

CHAUCER, G., Canterbury Tales. Edited by A. W. POLLARD. 2 vols. Elzevir 8vo. vellum, 15s.; parchment or cloth, 12s. (*Parchment Library*.)

CHEYNE, Canon T. K., The Prophecies of Isaiah. With Notes and Dissertations. 2 vols. Fifth Edition, Revised. 8vo. 25s.

   Job and Solomon; or, The Wisdom of the Old Testament. 8vo. 12s. 6d.

   The Book of Psalms; or, the Praises of Israel. With Commentary. 8vo. 16s.

   The Book of Psalms. Elzevir 8vo. vellum, 7s. 6d.; parchment or cloth, 6s. (*Parchment Library*.)

   The Origin and Religious Contents of the Psalter. The Bampton Lectures, 1889. 8vo. 16s.

CHICHELE, Mary, Doing and Undoing. Cr. 8vo. 4s. 6d.

CHILDERS, R. C., Pali-English Dictionary, with Sanskrit Equivalents. Imp. 8vo. £3. 3s.

CHRISTIAN, JOHN, Behar Proverbs, Classified and arranged according to subject matter, with Notes. Post 8vo. 10s. 6d. (*Trübner's Oriental Series*.)

Civil War (American), Campaigns of the. 12 vols., and Supplement. With Maps and Plans. 12mo. 5s. each vol. Navy in the Civil War. 3 vols. 5s. each.

CLAIRAUT, Elements of Geometry. Translated by Dr. KAINES. With 145 Figures. Cr. 8vo. 4s. 6d.

CLAPPERTON, JANE HUME, Scientific Meliorism and the Evolution of Happiness. Large cr. 8vo. 8s. 6d.

CLARKE, HENRY W., History of Tithes from Abraham to Queen Victoria. Cr. 8vo. 5s.

CLARKE, JAMES FREEMAN, Ten Great Religions: an Essay in Comparative Theology. 2 vols. 8vo. 10s. 6d. each.

CLERY, Gen. C. FRANCIS, Minor Tactics. With 26 Maps and Plans. Eleventh Edition, revised. Cr. 8vo. 9s.

CLIFF, MARIA, Poems on True Incidents, and other Poems. Cr. 8vo. 3s. 6d.

CLIFFORD, W. KINGDON, Common Sense of the Exact Sciences. Second Edition. With 100 Figures. Cr. 8vo. 5s. (*I.S.S.*)

CLODD, EDWARD, Childhood of the World: a Simple Account of Man in early times. Ninth Edition. Cr. 8vo. 3s. Special Edition for Schools, 1s.

   Childhood of Religions. Including a simple account of the birth and growth of Myths and Legends. Ninth Edition. Cr. 8vo. 5s. Special Edition for Schools, 1s. 6d.

   Jesus of Nazareth. With a brief Sketch of Jewish History to the time of His birth. Second Edition. Revised throughout and partly re-written. Sm. cr. 8vo. 6s. Special Edition for Schools, in 2 parts, 1s. 6d. each.

COGHLAN, J. COLE, D.D., The Modern Pharisee and other Sermons. Edited by the Very Rev. H. H. DICKINSON, D.D. New and Cheaper Edition. Cr. 8vo. 7s. 6d.

COLERIDGE. Memoir and Letters of Sara Coleridge. Edited by her Daughter. Cheap Edition. With Portrait. Cr. 8vo. 7s. 6d.

COLLETTE, C. H., Life, Times, and Writings of Thomas Cranmer, D.D., the First Reforming Archbishop of Canterbury. 8vo. 7s. 6d.

   Pope Joan. An Historical Study, from the Greek of Rhoïdis. 12mo. 2s. 6d.

COLLINS, MABEL, Through the Gates of Gold: a Fragment of Thought. Sm. 8vo. 4s. 6d.

   Light on the Path. Fcp. 8vo. 1s. 6d.

COMPTON, A. G., First Lessons in Metal-Working. Cr. 8vo. 6s. 6d.
COMPTON, C. G., Scot Free: a Novel. Cr. 8vo. 6s.
COMTE, AUGUSTE, Catechism of Positive Religion, from the French, by R. Congreve. Third Edition, revised and corrected. Cr. 8vo. 2s. 6d.
 Eight Circulars of Auguste Comte. Fcp. 8vo. 1s. 6d.
 Appeal to Conservatives. Cr. 8vo. 2s. 6d.
 Positive Philosophy of Auguste Comte, translated and condensed by Harriet Martineau. 2 vols. New and Cheaper Edition. Large post 8vo. 15s.
 Subjective Synthesis; or, Universal System of the Conceptions adapted to the Normal State of Humanity. Vol. I., containing the System of Positive Logic. 8vo. paper covers, 2s. 6d.
CONTE, JOSEPH LE, Sight: an Exposition of the Principles of Monocular and Binocular Vision. Second Edition. With 132 Illustrations. Cr. 8vo. 5s. (I.S.S.)
CONTOPOULOS, N., Lexicon of Modern Greek-English and English-Modern Greek. 2 vols. 8vo. 27s.
 Modern-Greek and English Dialogues and Correspondence. Fcp. 8vo. 2s. 6d.
CONWAY, M. D., Emerson at Home and Abroad. With Portrait. Post 8vo, 10s. 6d. (*Philosophical Library*.)
CONWAY, R. S., Verner's Law in Italy: an Essay in the History of the Indo-European sibilants. 8vo. 5s.
COOK, KENINGALE, The Fathers of Jesus. A Study of the Lineage of the Christian Doctrine and Traditions. 2 vols. 8vo. 28s.
COOK, LOUISA S., Geometrical Psychology; or, The Science of Representation. An Abstract of the Theories and Diagrams of B. W. Betts. 16 Plates. 8vo. 7s. 6d.
COOKE, M. C., British Edible Fungi: how to distinguish and how to cook them. With Coloured Figures of upwards of Forty Species. Cr. 8vo. 7s. 6d.
 Fungi: their Nature, Influences, Uses, &c. Edited by Rev. M. J. Berkeley. With numerous Illustrations. Fourth Edition. Cr. 8vo. 5s. (I.S.S.)
 Introduction to Fresh-Water Algæ. With an Enumeration of all the British Species. With 13 Plates. Cr. 8vo. 5s. (I.S.S.)
COOKE, Prof. J. P., New Chemistry. With 31 Illustrations. Ninth Edition. Cr. 8vo. 5s. (I.S.S.)
 Laboratory Practice. A Series of Experiments on the Fundamental Principles of Chemistry. Cr. 8vo. 5s.
CORDERY, J. G., Homer's Iliad. Greek Text, with Translation. 2 vols. 8vo. 14s. Translation only, cr. 8vo. 5s.
CORY, W., Guide to Modern English History. Part I. 1815-1830. 8vo. 9s. Part II. 1830-1835, 8vo. 15s.
COTTA, BERNHARD von, Geology and History. A Popular Exposition of all that is known of the Earth and its Inhabitants in Prehistoric Times. 12mo. 2s.
COTTON, LOUISE, Palmistry and its Practical Uses. With 12 Plates. Second Edition. Cr. 8vo. 2s. 6d.
COWELL, E. B., Short Introduction to the Ordinary Prakrit of the Sanskrit Dramas. Cr. 8vo. 3s. 6d.
 Prakrita-Prakasa; or, The Prakrit Grammar of Vararuchi, with the Commentary (Manorama) of Bhamaha. 8vo. 14s.
COWELL, E. B., and GOUGH, A. E., The Sarva-Darsana-Samgraha; or, Review of the Different Systems of Hindu Philosophy. Post 8vo. 10s. 6d. (*Trübner's Oriental Series*.)
COWIE, Bishop, Our Last Year in New Zealand, 1887. Cr. 8vo. 7s. 6d.
COX, SAMUEL, D.D., Commentary on the Book of Job. With a Translation. Second Edition. 8vo. 15s.
 Salvator Mundi; or, Is Christ the Saviour of all Men? Fourteenth Edition. Cr. 8vo. 2s. 6d.
 The Larger Hope: A Sequel to 'Salvator Mundi.' Second Edition. 16mo. 1s.

COX, SAMUEL, D.D., The Genesis of Evil, and other Sermons, mainly Expository. Fourth Edition. Cr. 8vo. 6s.
    Balaam : an Exposition and a Study. Cr. 8vo. 5s.
    Miracles : an Argument and a Challenge. Cr. 8vo. 2s. 6d.

COX, Sir G. W., Bart., Mythology of the Aryan Nations. New Edition. 8vo. 16s.
    Tales of Ancient Greece. New Edition. Sm. cr. 8vo. 6s.
    Tales of the Gods and Heroes. Sm. cr. 8vo. 3s. 6d
    Manual of Mythology in the Form of Question and Answer. New Edition. Fcap. 8vo. 3s.
    Introduction to the Science of Comparative Mythology and Folk-lore. Second Edition. Cr. 8vo. 7s. 6d.

COX, Sir G. W., Bart., and JONES, E. H., Popular Romances of the Middle Ages. Third Edition. Cr. 8vo. 6s.

CRAVEN, Mrs., A Year's Meditations. Cr. 8vo. 6s.

CRAVEN, T., English-Hindustani and Hindustani-English Dictionary. New Edition. 18mo. 4s. 6d.

CRAWFURD, OSWALD, Portugal, Old and New. With Illustrations and Maps. New and Cheaper Edition. Cr. 8vo. 6s.

CRUISE, F. R., Notes of a Visit to the Scenes in which the Life of Thomas à Kempis was spent. With numerous Illustrations. 8vo. 12s.

CUNNINGHAM, Major-Gen. ALEX., Ancient Geography of India. I. The Buddhist Period, including the Campaigns of Alexander and the Travels of Hwen-Thsang. With 13 Maps. 8vo. £1. 8s.

CURTEIS, Canon, Bishop Selwyn of New Zealand and of Lichfield : a Sketch of his Life and Work, with further gleanings from his Letters, Sermons, and Speeches. Large cr. 8vo. 7s. 6d.

CUST, R. N., Linguistic and Oriental Essays. Post 8vo. First Series, 10s. 6d. ; Second Series, with 6 Maps, 21s. ; Third Series, with Portrait, 21s. (*Trübner's Oriental Series.*)

DANA, E. S., Text-Book of Mineralogy. With Treatise on Crystallography and Physical Mineralogy. Third Edition, with 800 Woodcuts and Plate. 8vo. 15s.

DANA, J. D., Text-Book of Geology, for Schools. Illustrated. Cr. 8vo. 10s.
    Manual of Geology. Illustrated by a Chart of the World, and 1,000 Figures. 8vo. 21s.
    The Geological Story Briefly Told. Illustrated. 12mo. 7s. 6d.

DANA, J. D., and BRUSH, G. J., System of Mineralogy. Sixth Edition, entirely rewritten and enlarged. Roy. 8vo. £3. 3s.
    Manual of Mineralogy and Petrography. Fourth Edition. Numerous Woodcuts. Cr. 8vo. 8s. 6d.

DANTE'S Treatise 'De Vulgari Eloquentiâ.' Translated, with Notes, by A. G. F. HOWELL. 3s. 6d.
    The Banquet (Il Convito). Translated by KATHARINE HILLARD. Cr. 8vo. 7s. 6d.

DARMESTETER, ARSENE, Life of Words as the Symbols of Ideas. Cr. 8vo. 4s. 6d.

D'ASSIER, ADOLPHE, Posthumous Humanity : a Study of Phantoms. From the French by H. S. OLCOTT. With Appendix. Cr. 8vo. 7s. 6d.

DAVIDS, T. W. RHYS, Buddhist Birth-Stories ; or, Jataka Tales. The oldest Collection of Folk-lore extant. Being the Jātakatthavannanā. Translated from the Pali Text of V. FAUSBOLL. Post 8vo. 18s. (*Trübner's Oriental Series.*)
    The Numismata Orientalia. Part VI. The Ancient Coins and Measures of Ceylon. With 1 Plate. Royal 4to. Paper wrapper, 10s.

DAVIDSON, SAMUEL, D.D., Canon of the Bible : its Formation, History, and Fluctuations. Third Edition. Sm. Cr. 8vo. 5s.
    Doctrine of Last Things. Sm. Cr. 8vo. 3s. 6d.

DAVIDSON, T., Compendium of the Philosophical System of Antonio Rosmini-Serbati. Second Edition, 8vo. 10s. 6d.

DAVIES, G. CHRISTOPHER, Rambles and Adventures of Our School Field Club. With 4 Illustrations. New and Cheaper Edition. Cr. 8vo. 3s. 6d.

DAVIES, J., Sānkhya Kārikā of Iswara Krishna: an Exposition of the System of Kapila. Post 8vo. 6s. (*Trübner's Oriental Series.*)

The Bhagavad Gîtâ; or, the Sacred Lay. Translated, with Notes, from the Sanskrit. Third Edition. Post 8vo. 6s. (*Trübner's Oriental Series.*)

DAVITT, MICHAEL, Speech before the Special Commission. Cr. 8vo. 5s.

DAWSON, GEORGE, Prayers. First Series, Edited by his WIFE. Eleventh Edition. Sm. 8vo. 3s. 6d.

Prayers. Second Series. Edited by GEORGE ST. CLAIR. Second Edition. Sm. 8vo. 3s. 6d.

Sermons on Disputed Points and Special Occasions. Edited by his WIFE. Fifth Edition. Sm. 8vo. 3s. 6d.

Sermons on Daily Life and Duty. Edited by his WIFE. Fifth Edition. Sm. 8vo. 3s. 6d.

The Authentic Gospel. Sermons. Edited by GEORGE ST. CLAIR. Fourth Edition. Sm. 8vo. 3s. 6d.

Every-Day Counsels. Edited by GEORGE ST. CLAIR. Cr. 8vo. 6s.

Biographical Lectures. Edited by GEORGE ST. CLAIR. Third Edition. Large cr. 8vo. 7s. 6d.

Shakespeare; and other Lectures. Edited by GEORGE ST. CLAIR. Large Cr. 8vo. 7s. 6d.

DAWSON, Sir J. W., Geological History of Plants. With 80 Illustrations. Cr. 8vo. 5s. (*I.S.S.*)

DEAN, TERESA H., How to be Beautiful: Nature Unmasked. A Book for every Woman. Fcp. 8vo. 2s. 6d.

DELBRUCK, B., Introduction to the Study of Language: the History and Methods of Comparative Philology of the Indo-European Languages. 8vo. 5s.

DENNIS, J., Collection of English Sonnets. Sm. Cr. 8vo. 2s. 6d.

DENNYS, N. B., Folk-Lore of China, and its Affinities with that of the Aryan and Semitic Races. 8vo. 10s. 6d.

DENVIR, JOHN, The Irish in Britain, from the Earliest Times to the Fall and Death of Parnell. Cr. 8vo. 6s.

DEWEY, JOHN, Psychology. Large Cr. 8vo. 5s. 6d.

DEWEY, J. H., The Way, the Truth, and the Life: a Handbook of Christian Theosophy, Healing and Psychic Culture. 10s. 6d.

DIDON, Father, Jesus Christ. Cheaper Edition. 2 vols. 8vo. 12s.

DILLON, W., Life of John Mitchel. With Portrait. 2 vols. 8vo. 21s.

DOBSON, AUSTIN, Old World Idylls, and other Verses. With Frontispiece. Eleventh Edition. Elzevir 8vo. 6s.

At the Sign of the Lyre. With Frontispiece. Eighth Edition. Elzevir 8vo. 6s.

The Ballad of Beau Brocade; and other Poems of the Eighteenth Century. With Fifty Illustrations by Hugh Thomson. Cr. 8vo. 5s.

DOMVILE, Lady M., Life of Alphonse de Lamartine. Large Cr. 8vo. 7s. 6d.

D'ORSEY, A. J. D., Grammar of Portuguese and English. Adapted to Ollendorff's System. Fourth Edition. 12mo. 7s.

Colloquial Portuguese; or, the Words and Phrases of Every-day Life. Fourth Edition. Cr. 8vo. 3s. 6d.

Doubter's Doubt about Science and Religion, A. Cr. 8vo. 3s. 6d.

DOUGLAS, Prof. R. K., Chinese Language and Literature. Cr. 8vo. 5s.

The Life of Jenghiz Khan. Translated from the Chinese. Cr. 8vo. 5s.

DOWDEN, EDWARD, Shakspere: a Critical Study of His Mind and Art. Tenth Edition. Large post 8vo. 12s.
   Shakspere's Sonnets. With Introduction and Notes. Large post 8vo. 7s. 6d.
   Shakspere's Sonnets. Edited, with Frontispiece after the Death Mask. Elzevir 8vo. vellum, 7s. 6d.; parchment or cloth, 6s. (*Parchment Library.*)
   Studies in Literature. 1789-1877. Fifth Edition. Large post 8vo. 6s.
   Transcripts and Studies. Large post 8vo. 12s.
   Life of Percy Bysshe Shelley. With Portraits. 2 vols. 8vo. 36s.

DOWNING, C., Fruits and Fruit Trees of America: or, the Culture and Management of Fruit Trees generally. Illustrated. 8vo. 25s.

DOWSON, JOHN, Grammar of the Urdū or Hindūstānī Language. Second Edition. Cr. 8vo. 10s. 6d.
   Hindūstānī Exercise Book. Passages and Extracts for Translation into Hindūstānī. Cr. 8vo. 2s. 6d.
   Classical Dictionary of Hindu Mythology and History, Geography and Literature. Post 8vo. 16s. (*Trübner's Oriental Series.*)

DRAPER, J. W., The Conflict between Religion and Science. 21st Edition. Cr. 8vo. 5s. (*I.S.S.*)

DRAYSON, Major-General, Untrodden Ground in Astronomy and Geology. With Numerous Figures. 8vo. 14s.

DRUMMOND. Maria Drummond: a Sketch. Pott 8vo. 2s.

DUFF, E. GORDON, Early Printed Books. With Frontispiece and Ten Plates. Post 8vo. 6s. net. (*Books about Books.*)

DUFFY, Sir C. GAVAN, Thomas Davis: the Memoirs of an Irish Patriot, 1840-46. 8vo. 12s.

DUKA, THEODORE, Life and Works of Alexander Csoma de Körös between 1819 and 1842. With a Short Notice of all his Works and Essays, from Original Documents. Post 8vo. 9s. (*Trübner's Oriental Series.*)

DUNN, H. P., Infant Health: the Physiology and Hygiene of Early Life. Sm. Cr. 8vo. 3s. 6d.

DURUY, VICTOR, History of Greece. With Introduction by Prof. J. P. MAHAFFY. 8 vols. Super royal 8vo. £8. 8s.

DUSAR, P. FRIEDRICH, Grammar of the German Language. With Exercises. 2nd Edition. Cr. 8vo. 4s. 6d.
   Grammatical Course of the German Language. 3rd Edition. Cr. 8vo. 3s. 6d.

DUTT, ROMESH CHUNDER, History of Civilisation in Ancient India, based on Sanskrit literature. Cr. 8vo. Vol. I. Vedic and Epic Ages, 8s. Vol. II. Rationalistic Age, 8s. Vol. III. Buddhist and Pauranik Ages, 8s.

DUTT, TORU, Ancient Ballads and Legends of Hindustan. With an Introductory Memoir by EDMUND GOSSE. 18mo. cloth extra, gilt top, 5s.

EASTWICK, E. B., The Gulistan; or, Rose Garden of Shekh Mushliu-'d-Din Sadi of Shiraz. Translated from the Atish Kadah. 2nd Edition. Post 8vo. 10s. 6d. (*Trübner's Oriental Series.*)

EDGREN, H., Compendious Sanskrit Grammar. With a Brief Sketch of Scenic Prakrit. Cr. 8vo. 10s. 6d.

EDKINS, J., D.D., Religion in China. Containing a Brief Account of the Three Religions of the Chinese. 3rd Edition. Post 8vo. 7s. 6d. (*Philosophical Library* and *Trübner's Oriental Series.*)
   Chinese Buddhism: Sketches Historical and Critical. Post 8vo. 18s. (*Trübner's Oriental Series.*)

EDMONDS, HERBERT, Well-spent Lives: a Series of Modern Biographies. New and Cheaper Edition. Cr. 8vo. 3s. 6d.

EGER, GUSTAV, Technological Dictionary in the English and German Languages. 2 vols. roy. 8vo. £1. 7s.

Eighteenth Century Essays. Edited by AUSTIN DOBSON. With Frontispiece. Elzevir 8vo. vellum, 7s. 6d.; parchment or cloth, 6s. (*Parchment Library.*) Cheap Edition, fcap. 8vo. 1s. 6d.

EITEL, E. J., Buddhism: its Historical, Theoretical, and Popular Aspects. Third Edition, revised, 8vo. 5s.

Handbook for the Student of Chinese Buddhism. Second Edition. Cr. 8vo. 18s.

Electricity in Daily Life; a Popular Account of its Application to Every-day Uses. With 125 Illustrations. Sq. 8vo. 9s.

ELLIOTT, EBENEZER, Poems. Edited by his Son, the Rev. EDWIN ELLIOTT, of St. John's, Antigua. 2 vols. crown 8vo. 18s.

ELLIOTT, F. R., Handbook for Fruit Growers. Illustrated. Sq. 16mo. 5s.

Handbook of Practical Landscape Gardening. Illustrated. 8vo. 7s. 6d.

ELLIOT, Sir H. M., History, Folk-lore, and Distribution of the Races of the North-Western Provinces of India. Edited by J. BEAMES. With 3 Coloured Maps. 2 vols. 8vo. £1. 16s.

History of India, as told by its own Historians: the Muhammadan Period. From the Posthumous Papers of the late Sir H. M. ELLIOT. Revised and continued by Professor JOHN DOWSON. 8 vols. 8vo. £8. 8s.

ELLIOT, Sir W., Coins of Southern India. With Map and Plates. Roy. 4to. 25s. (*Numismata Orientalia.*)

ELLIS, W. ASHTON, Wagner Sketches: 1849. A Vindication. Cr. 8vo. cloth, 2s. 6d.; paper, 2s.

Richard Wagner's Prose Works. Translated by W. A. ELLIS. Vol. I. The Art Work of the Future. 8vo. 12s. 6d.

ELTON, CHARLES and MARY, The Great Book Collectors. With 10 Illustrations. Post 8vo. 6s. net. (*Books about Books.*)

Encyclopædia Americana. 4 vols. 4to. £8. 8s.

English Comic Dramatists. Edited by OSWALD CRAWFURD. Elzevir 8vo. vellum, 7s. 6d.; parchment or cloth, 6s. (*Parchment Library.*)

English Lyrics. Elzevir 8vo. vellum, 7s. 6d.; parchment or cloth, 6s. (*Parchment Library.*)

English Odes. Edited by E. GOSSE. With Frontispiece. Elzevir 8vo. vellum, 7s. 6d.; parchment or cloth, 6s. (*Parchment Library.*)

English Sacred Lyrics. Elzevir 8vo. vellum, 7s. 6d.; parchment or cloth, 6s. (*Parchment Library.*)

English Poets (Living). With Frontispiece by WALTER CRANE. Second Edition. Large cr. 8vo. Printed on hand-made paper, vellum, 15s.; cloth, 12s.

English Verse. CHAUCER TO BURNS. TRANSLATIONS. LYRICS OF THE NINETEENTH CENTURY. DRAMATIC SCENES AND CHARACTERS. BALLADS AND ROMANCES. Edited by W. J. LINTON and R. H. STODDARD. 5 vols. cr. 8vo. 5s. each.

EYTON, ROBERT, The Apostles' Creed: Sermons. Cr. 8vo. 3s. 6d.

The True Life, and Other Sermons. Cr. 8vo. 7s. 6d.

The Lord's Prayer: Sermons. Cr. 8vo. 3s. 6d.

A Rash Investment: Sermon on Salvation Army Scheme of Social Reform. Fcp. 8vo. 1s.

The Search for God, and other Sermons. Cr. 8vo. 3s. 6d.

FABER, E., The Mind of Mencius; or, Political Economy founded upon Moral Philosophy. A systematic digest of the doctrines of the Chinese philosopher, Mencius. Original text Classified and Translated. Post 8vo. 10s. 6d. (*Trübner's Oriental Series.*)

FAUSBÖLL, V., The Jataka, together with its Commentary: being Tales of the Anterior Birth of Gotama Buddha. 5 vols. 8vo. 28s. each.

FERGUSSON, T., Chinese Researches: Chinese Chronology and Cycles. Cr. 8vo. 10s. 6d.

FEUERBACH, L., Essence of Christianity. From the German, by MARIAN EVANS. Second Edition. Post 8vo. 7s. 6d. (*Philosophical Library.*)

FICHTE, J. GOTTLIEB, New Exposition of the Science of Knowledge. Translated by A. E. KROEGER. 8vo. 6s.

    Science of Knowledge. From the German, by A. E. KROEGER. With an Introduction by Prof. W. T. HARRIS. Post 8vo. 10s. 6d. (*Philosophical Library.*)

    Science of Rights. From the German by A. E. KROEGER. With an Introduction by Prof. W. T. HARRIS. Post 8vo. 12s. 6d. (*Philosophical Library.*)

    Popular Works: The Nature of the Scholar; The Vocation of the Scholar; The Vocation of Man; The Doctrine of Religion; Characteristics of the Present Age; Outlines of the Doctrine of Knowledge. With a Memoir by W. SMITH. Post 8vo. 2 vols. 21s. (*Philosophical Library.*)

FINN, ALEXANDER, Persian for Travellers. Oblong 32mo. 5s.

FITZARTHUR, T., The Worth of Human Testimony. Fcp. 8vo. 2s.

FITZGERALD, R. D., Australian Orchids. Part I., 7 Plates; Part II., 10 Plates; Part III., 10 Plates; Part IV., 10 Plates; Part V., 10 Plates; Part VI., 10 Plates. Each Part, coloured, 21s.; plain, 10s. 6d. Part VII., 10 Plates. Vol. II., Part I., 10 Plates. Each, coloured, 25s.

FITZPATRICK, W. J., Life of the Very Rev. T. N. Burke. With Portrait. 2 vols. 8vo. 30s.

FLETCHER, J. S., Andrewlina. Cr. 8vo. cloth, 1s. 6d.; paper covers, 1s.

    The Winding Way. Cr. 8vo. 6s.

FLINN, D. EDGAR, Ireland: its Health Resorts and Watering Places. With Frontispiece and Maps. 8vo. 5s.

FLOWER, W. H., The Horse: a Study in Natural History. Cr. 8vo. 2s. 6d. (*Modern Science Series.*)

FORNANDER, A., Account of the Polynesian Race: its Origin and Migrations, and the Ancient History of the Hawaiian People. Post 8vo. Vol. I., 7s. 6d. Vol. II., 10s. 6d. Vol. III., 9s. (*Philosophical Library.*)

FORNEY, MATTHIAS N., Catechism of the Locomotive. Second Edition, revised and enlarged. Fcp. 4to. 18s.

FRASER, Sir WILLIAM, Bart., Disraeli and His Day. Second Edition. Post 8vo. 9s.

FRAZAR, DOUGLAS, Practical Boat Sailing: a Treatise on Management of Small Boats and Yachts. Sm. cr. 4s. 6d.

FREEBOROUGH, E., and RANKEN, C. E., Chess Openings, Ancient and Modern. Revised and Corrected up to the Present Time from the best Authorities. Large post 8vo. 7s. 6d.

FREEBOROUGH, E., Chess Endings. A Companion to 'Chess Openings, Ancient and Modern.' Edited and Arranged. Large post 8vo. 7s. 6d.

FREEMAN, E. A., Lectures to American Audiences. I. The English People in its Three Homes. II. Practical Bearings of General European History. Post 8vo. 8s. 6d.

French Jansenists. By the Author of 'Spanish Mystics' and 'Many Voices.' Cr. 8vo. 6s.

French Lyrics. Edited by GEORGE SAINTSBURY. With Frontispiece. Elzevir 8vo. vellum, 7s. 6d.; parchment or cloth, 6s. (*Parchment Library.*)

FREWEN, MORETON, The Economic Crisis. Cr. 8vo. 4s. 6d.

FRIEDLÄNDER, M., Text-Book of Jewish Religion. Third Edition, revised. Cr. 8vo. 1s. 6d.

The Jewish Religion. Cr. 8vo. 5s.

FRIEDRICH, P., Progressive German Reader. With copious Notes. Cr. 8vo. 4s. 6d.

FRITH, I., Life of Giordano Bruno, the Nolan. Revised by Prof. MORIZ CARRIERE. With Portrait. Post 8vo. 14s. (*Philosophical Library.*)

FRŒMBLING, F. OTTO, Graduated German Reader: a Selection from the most popular writers. With a Vocabulary. Twelfth Edition. 12mo. 3s. 6d.

Graduated Exercises for Translation into German: Extracts from the best English Authors, with Idiomatic Notes. Cr. 8vo. 4s. 6d.; without Notes, 4s.

GALL, Capt. H. R., Tactical Questions and Answers on the Infantry Drill Book 1892. Third Edition. Cr. 8vo. 1s. 6d.

GARDINER, LINDA, His Heritage. With Frontispiece. Cr. 8vo. 6s.

GARDNER, PERCY, The Numismata Orientalia. Part V. The Parthian Coinage. With 8 Plates. Royal 4to. Paper wrapper, 18s.

GARLANDA, FEDERICO, The Fortunes of Words. Cr. 8vo. 5s.

The Philosophy of Words: a popular introduction to the Science of Language. Cr 8vo. 5s.

GASTER, M., Greeko-Slavonic Literature, and its Relation to the Folk-lore of Europe during the Middle Ages. Large Post 8vo. 7s. 6d.

GAY, JOHN, Fables. Edited by AUSTIN DOBSON. With Portrait. Elzevir 8vo. vellum, 7s. 6d.; parchment or cloth, 6s. (*Parchment Library.*)

GEIGER, LAZARUS, Contributions to the History of the Development of the Human Race. From the German by D. ASHER. Post 8vo. 6s. (*Philosophical Library.*)

GELDART, E. M., Guide to Modern Greek. Post 8vo. 7s. 6d. Key, 2s. 6d.

Simplified Grammar of Modern Greek. Cr 8vo. 2s. 6d.

GEORGE, HENRY, Progress and Poverty: an Inquiry into the Causes of Industrial Depressions, and of Increase of Want with Increase of Wealth; the Remedy. Fifth Edition. Post 8vo. 7s. 6d. Cabinet Edition, cr. 8vo. 2s. 6d. Cheap Edition, limp cloth, 1s. 6d.; paper covers, 1s.

Protection or Free Trade: an Examination of the Tariff Question, with especial regard to the interests of labour. Second Edition. Cr. 8vo. 5s. Cheap Edition, limp cloth, 1s. 6d.; paper covers, 1s.

Social Problems. Fourth Thousand. Cr. 8vo. 5s. Cheap Edition, limp cloth, 1s. 6d.; paper covers, 1s.

A Perplexed Philosopher: being an Examination of Mr. HERBERT SPENCER'S various utterances on the Land Question, &c. Cr. 8vo. 5s.

GERARD, E. and D., A Sensitive Plant: a Novel. With Frontispiece. Cr. 8vo. 6s.

GIBB, E. J. W., The History of the Forty Vezirs; or, The Story of the Forty Morns and Eves. Translated from the Turkish. Cr. 8vo. 10s. 6d.

GILBERT. Autobiography, and other Memorials of Mrs. Gilbert. Edited by JOSIAH GILBERT. Fifth Edition. Cr. 8vo. 7s. 6d.

GLANVILL, JOSEPH, Scepsis Scientifica. Edited, with Introductory Essay, by JOHN OWEN. Elzevir 8vo. 6s.

GLAZEBROOK, R. T., Laws and Properties of Matter. Cr. 8vo. 2s. 6d. (*Modern Science.*)

GLOVER, F., Exempla Latina: a First Construing Book, with Notes, Lexicon, and an Introduction to Analysis of Sentences. Second Edition. Fcp. 8vo. 2s.

GOETHE'S Faust. Translated from the German by JOHN ANSTER. With an Introduction by BURDETT MASON. With illustrations (18 in black and white, 10 in colour) by FRANK M. GREGORY. Grand folio, £3. 3s.

GOLDSMITH, Oliver, Vicar of Wakefield. Edited by AUSTIN DOBSON. Elzevir 8vo. vellum, 7s. 6d.; parchment or cloth, 6s. (*Parchment Library.*)

GOMME, G. L., Ethnology in Folklore. Cr. 8vo. 2s. 6d. (*Modern Science.*)

GOOCH, Diaries of Sir Daniel Gooch, Bart. With an Introductory Notice by Sir THEODORE MARTIN, K.C.B. With 2 Portraits and an Illustration. Cr. 8vo. 6s.

GOODENOUGH. Memoir of Commodore J. G. Goodenough. Edited by his Widow. With Portrait. Third Edition. Cr. 8vo. 5s.

GORDON, Major-General C. G., Journals at Khartoum. Printed from the original MS. With Introduction and Notes by A. EGMONT HAKE. Portrait, 2 Maps, and 30 Illustrations. 8vo. 21s. Cheap Edition, 6s.

    Last Journal: a Facsimile of the last Journal received in England from General Gordon, reproduced by Photo-lithography. Imp. 4to. £3. 3s.

GORDON, Sir H. W., Events in the Life of General Gordon, from the Day of his Birth to the Day of his Death. With Maps and Illustrations. Second Edition. 8vo. 7s. 6d.

Gospel according to Matthew, Mark, and Luke (The). Elzevir 8vo. vellum, 7s. 6d.; parchment or cloth, 6s. (*Parchment Library.*)

GOSSE, EDMUND, Seventeenth Century Studies: a Contribution to the History of English Poetry. 8vo. 10s. 6d.

    New Poems. Cr. 8vo. 7s. 6d.

    Firdausi in Exile, and other Poems. Second Edition. Elzevir 8vo. gilt top, 6s.

    On Viol and Flute: Lyrical Poems. With Frontispiece by L. ALMA TADEMA, and Tailpiece by HAMO THORNYCROFT. Elzevir 8vo. 6s.

    Life of Philip Henry Gosse. By his Son. 8vo. 15s.

GOSSIP, G. H. D., The Chess-Player's Text-Book: an Elementary Treatise on the Game of Chess. Numerous Diagrams. 16mo. 2s.

GOUGH, A. E., Philosophy of the Upanishads. Post 8vo. 9s. (*Trübner's Oriental Series.*)

GOUGH, EDWARD, The Bible True from the Beginning: a Commentary on all those portions of Scripture that are most questioned and assailed. Vols. I. to V. 8vo. 16s. each.

GOWER, Lord RONALD, Bric-à-Brac. Being some Photoprints illustrating Art Objects at Gower Lodge, Windsor. With Letterpress descriptions. Super roy. 8vo. 15s.; extra binding, 21s.

    Last Days of Marie Antoinette: an Historical Sketch. With Portrait and Facsimiles. Fcap. 4to. 10s. 6d.

    Notes of a Tour from Brindisi to Yokohama, 1883-1884. Fcp. 8vo. 2s. 6d.

    Rupert of the Rhine: a Biographical Sketch of the Life of Prince Rupert. With 3 Portraits. Cr. 8vo. buckram, 6s.

    Stafford House Letters. With 2 Portraits. 8vo. 10s. 6d.

GRAHAM, JEAN CARLYLE, Songs, Measures, Metrical Lines. Cr. 8vo. 5s.

GRAHAM, WILLIAM, The Creed of Science: Religious, Moral, and Social. Second Edition, revised. Cr. 8vo. 6s.

    The Social Problem, in its Economic, Moral and Political Aspects. 8vo. 14s.

    Socialism New and Old. Second Edition. Cr. 8vo. 5s. (*I.S.S.*)

GRAY, J., Ancient Proverbs and Maxims from Burmese Sources; or, The Niti Literature of Burma. Post 8vo. 6s. (*Trübner's Oriental Series.*)

GRAY, MAXWELL, Silence of Dean Maitland. Eighth Edition. With Frontispiece. Cr. 8vo. 6s.
    The Reproach of Annesley. Fifth Edition. With Frontispiece. Cr. 8vo. 6s.
    In the Heart of the Storm. With Frontispiece by GORDON BROWNE. Cr. 8vo. 6s.
    Westminster Chimes, and other Poems. Sm. 8vo. 5s.
GREEN, F. W. EDRIDGE, Colour Blindness and Colour Perception. With 3 Coloured Plates. Cr. 8vo. 5s. (I.S.S.)
GREG, R. P., Comparative Philology of the Old and New Worlds in Relation to Archaic Speech. With copious Vocabularies. Super royal 8vo. £1. 11s. 6d.
GREG, W. R., Literary and Social Judgments. Fourth Edition. 2 vols. Cr. 8vo. 15s.
    The Creed of Christendom. Eighth Edition. 2 vols. post 8vo. 15s. (Philosophical Library).
    Enigmas of Life. Seventeenth Edition. Post 8vo. 10s. 6d. (Philosophical Library).
    Enigmas of Life. With a Prefatory Memoir. Edited by his WIFE. Nineteenth Edition. Cr. 8vo. 6s.
    Political Problems for our Age and Country. 8vo. 10s. 6d.
    Miscellaneous Essays. Two Series. Cr. 8vo. 7s. 6d. each.
GREY, ROWLAND, In Sunny Switzerland: a Tale of Six Weeks. Second Edition. Sm. 8vo. 5s.
    Lindenblumen, and other Stories. Sm. 8vo. 5s.
    By Virtue of His Office. Cr. 8vo. 6s.
    Jacob's Letter, and other Stories. Cr. 8vo. 5s.
GRIFFIN, Sir Lepel, The Rajas of the Punjab: History of the Principal States in the Punjab, and their Political Relations with the British Government. Royal 8vo. 21s.
GRIFFIS, W. E., The Mikado's Empire. Book I. History of Japan from B.C. 660 to A.D. 1872. Book II. Personal Experiences, Observations, and Studies in Japan, 1870-1874. Second Edition, illustrated. 8vo. 20s.
    Japanese Fairy World: Stories from the Wonder-Lore of Japan. With 12 Plates. Square 16mo. 3s. 6d.
GRIFFITH, R. T. H., Birth of the War-God: a Poem from the Sanskrit of KÁLIDÁSÁ. Second Edition. Post 8vo. 5s. (Trübner's Oriental Series).
    Yúsef and Zulaikha: a Poem by JAMI. Translated from the Persian into English verse. Post 8vo. 8s. 6d. (Trübner's Oriental Series.)
GRIMLEY, H. N., The Prayer of Humanity: Sermons on the Lord's Prayer. Cr. 8vo. 3s. 6d.
    Tremadoc Sermons, chiefly on the Spiritual Body, the Unseen World, and the Divine Humanity. Fourth Edition. Cr. 8vo. 6s.
    The Temple of Humanity, and other Sermons. Cr. 8vo. 6s.
GRIMSHAW, R., Engine Runner's Catechism. A Sequel to the Author's 'Steam Engine Catechism.' Illustrated. 18mo. 8s. 6d.
GUBERNATIS, ANGELO DE, Zoological Mythology; or, The Legends of Animals. 2 vols. 8vo. £1. 8s.
GUICCIARDINI, FRANCESCO, Counsels and Reflections. Translated by N. H. Thomson. Cr. 8vo. 6s.
GURNEY, ALFRED, The Vision of the Eucharist, and other Poems. Cr. 8vo. 5s.
    A Christmas Faggot. Sm. 8vo. 5s.
    Voices from the Holy Sepulchre, and other Poems. Cr. 8vo. 5s.
    Wagner's Parsifal: a Study. Second Edition. Fcp. 8vo. 1s. 6d.
    Our Catholic Inheritance in the Larger Hope. Cr. 8vo. 1s. 6d.
    The Story of a Friendship. Cr. 8vo. 5s.
HADDON, CAROLINE, The Larger Life: Studies in Hinton's Ethics. Cr. 8vo. 5s.

HAECKEL, Prof. ERNST, The History of Creation. New Edition. Translation revised by Professor E. Ray Lankester, with 20 plates and numerous figures. Fourth Edition. 2 vols. Large post 8vo. 32s.
    The History of the Evolution of Man. With numerous Illustrations. 2 vols. Post 8vo. 32s.
    A Visit to Ceylon. Post 8vo. 7s. 6d.
    Freedom in Science and Teaching. With a Prefatory Note by Prof. T. H. Huxley. Cr. 8vo. 5s.

HAGGARD, H. RIDER, Cetywayo and His White Neighbours; or, Remarks on Recent Events in Zululand, Natal, and the Transvaal. Fourth Edition. Cr. 8vo. 6s.

HAGGARD, W. H., and LE STRANGE, G., The Vazir of Lankuran: a Persian Play. With a Grammatical Introduction, Translation, Notes, and Vocabulary. Cr. 8vo. 10s. 6d.

HAHN, T., Tsuni-Goam, the Supreme Being of the Khoi-Khoi. Post 8vo. 7s. 6d. (*Trübner's Oriental Series.*)

HALL, H. E., Leadership, not Lordship. Cr. 8vo. 2s.

HALLECK'S International Law; or, Rules Regulating the Intercourse of States in Peace and War. Third Edition, thoroughly revised by Sir Sherston Baker, Bart. 2 vols. 8vo. 38s.

HALLOCK, CHARLES, The Sportsman's Gazetteer and General Guide to the Game Animals, Birds, and Fishes of North America. Maps and Portrait. Cr. 8vo. 15s.

HAMILTON. Memoirs of Arthur Hamilton, B.A., of Trinity College, Cambridge. Cr. 8vo. 6s.

HARDY, W. J., Book Plates. With Frontispiece and 36 Illustrations of Book Plates. Post 8vo. 6s. net. (*Books about Books.*)

HARRISON, CLIFFORD, In Hours of Leisure. Second Edition. Cr. 8vo. 5s.

HARRISON, Col. R., Officer's Memorandum Book for Peace and War. Fourth Edition, revised. Oblong 32mo. red basil, with pencil, 3s. 6d.

HARRISON, J. A., and BASKERVILL, W., Handy Dictionary of Anglo-Saxon Poetry. Sq. 8vo. 12s.

HART, J. W. T., Autobiography of Judas Iscariot. A Character Study. Cr. 8vo. 3s. 6d.

HARTMANN, EDUARD von, Philosophy of the Unconscious. Translated by W. C. Coupland. 3 vols. Post 8vo. 31s. 6d. (*Philosophical Library.*)

HARTMANN, FRANZ, Magic, White and Black; or, The Science of Finite and Infinite Life. Fourth Edition, revised. Cr. 8vo. 6s.
    The Life of Paracelsus, and the Substance of his Teachings. Post 8vo. 10s. 6d.
    Life and Doctrines of Jacob Boehme: an Introduction to the Study of his Works. Post 8vo. 10s. 6d.

HARTMANN, R., Anthropoid Apes. With 63 Illustrations. Second Edition. Cr. 8vo. 5s. (*I.S.S.*)

HARVEY, W. F., Simplified Grammar of the Spanish Language. Cr. 8vo. 3s. 6d.

HAUG, M., Essays on the Sacred Language, Writings, and Religion of the Parsis. Third Edition. Edited and Enlarged by E. W. West. Post 8vo. 16s. (*Trübner's Oriental Series.*)

HAWEIS, H. R., Current Coin. Materialism—The Devil—Crime—Drunkenness—Pauperism—Emotion—Recreation—The Sabbath. Sixth Edition. Cr. 8vo. 5s.
    Arrows in the Air. Fifth Edition. Cr. 8vo. 5s.
    Speech in Season. Sixth Edition. Cr. 8vo. 5s.
    Thoughts for the Times. Fourteenth Edition. Cr. 8vo. 5s.
    Unsectarian Family Prayers. Fourth Edition. Fcp. 8vo. 1s. 6d.

HAWTHORNE, NATHANIEL, Works. Complete in 12 vols. Large post 8vo. 7s. 6d. each. (Scarlet Letter. New Illustrated Edition. Post 8vo. 10s. 6d.)

HEAD, BARCLAY V., The Numismata Orientalia. Part III. The Coinage of Lydia and Persia, from the Earliest Times to the Fall of the Dynasty of the Achæmenidæ. With 3 Plates. Royal 4to. Paper wrapper, 10s. 6d.

HEALES, Major ALFRED, The Architecture of the Churches of Denmark, 8vo. 14s.

HEATH, FRANCIS GEORGE, Autumnal Leaves. With 12 Coloured Plates. Third and Cheaper Edition. 8vo. 6s.

    Sylvan Winter. With 70 Illustrations. 14s.

HEATH, RICHARD, Edgar Quinet: His Early Life and Writings. With Portraits, Illustrations, and an Autograph Letter. Post 8vo. 12s. 6d. (*Philosophical Library.*)

HEGEL. Lectures on the History of Philosophy. Translated by E. S. HALDANE. 3 vols. Vol. I. 12s.

The Introduction to Hegel's Philosophy of Fine Art, translated by BERNARD BOSANQUET. Cr. 8vo. 5s.

HEIDENHAIN, RUDOLPH, Hypnotism, or Animal Magnetism. With Preface by G. J. ROMANES. Second Edition. Sm. 8vo. 2s. 6d.

HEILPRIN, Prof. A., Bermuda Islands. 8vo. 18s.

    Geographical and Geological Distribution of Animals. With Frontispiece. Cr. 8vo. 5s. (*I.S.S.*)

HEINE, H., Religion and Philosophy in Germany. Translated by J. SNODGRASS. Post 8vo. 6s. (*Philosophical Library.*)

HENDRIKS, DOM LAWRENCE, The London Charterhouse; its Monks and its Martyrs. Illustrated. 8vo. 15s.

HENSLOW, Prof. G., Origin of Floral Structures through Insect and other Agencies. With 88 Illustrations. Cr. 8vo. 5s.

HEPBURN, J. C., Japanese and English Dictionary. Second Edition. Imp. 8vo. half-roan, 18s.

    Japanese-English and English-Japanese Dictionary. Third Edition. Royal 8vo. half-morocco, cloth sides, 30s. Pocket Edition, square 16mo. 14s.

HERMES TRISMEGISTUS, Works. Translated by J. D. CHAMBERS. Post 8vo. 7s. 6d.

    The Virgin of the World. Translated and Edited by the Authors of 'The Perfect Way.' Illustrations. 4to. imitation parchment, 10s. 6d.

HERSHON, P. J., Talmudic Miscellany; or, One Thousand and One Extracts from the Talmud, the Midrashim, and the Kabbalah. Post 8vo. 14s. (*Trübner's Oriental Series.*)

HILLEBRAND, KARL, France and the French in the Second Half of the 19th Century. From the third German Edition. Post 8vo. 10s. 6d.

HINTON. Life and Letters of James Hinton. With an Introduction by Sir W. W. GULL, and Portrait engraved on steel by C. H. JEENS. Sixth Edition. Cr. 8vo. 8s. 6d.

    Philosophy and Religion. Selections from the Manuscripts of the late James Hinton. Edited by CAROLINE HADDON. Second Edition. Cr. 8vo. 5s.

    The Law-Breaker and **The Coming of the Law.** Edited by MARGARET HINTON. Cr. 8vo. 6s.

    The Mystery of Pain. New Edition. Fcp. 8vo. 1s.

HIRSCHFELD, H., Arabic Chrestomathy in Hebrew Characters. With a Glossary. 8vo. 7s. 6d.

HODGSON, B. H., Essays on the Languages, Literature, and Religion of Nepal and Tibet. Roy. 8vo. 14s.

    Essays relating to Indian Subjects. 2 vols. Post 8vo. 28s. (*Trübner's Oriental Series.*)

HODGSON, J. E., Academy Lectures. Cr. 8vo. 7s. 6d.

HOLBOROW, A., Evolution and Scripture; with an Inquiry into the nature of the Scriptures and Inspiration. Cr. 8vo. 4s. 6d.

HOLMES-FORBES, A. W., The Science of Beauty: an Analytical Inquiry into the Laws of Æsthetics. Second Edition. Post 8vo. 3s. 6d.

HOLMES, OLIVER WENDELL, John Lothrop Motley: a Memoir. Cr. 8vo. 6s.
    Life of Ralph Waldo Emerson. With Portrait. English Copyright Edition. Cr. 8vo. 6s.

HOLTHAM, E. G., Eight Years in Japan, 1873-1881. With 3 Maps. Large Cr. 8vo. 9s.

HOMER'S Iliad. Greek Text, with Translation by J. G. CORDERY. 2 vols. 8vo. 14s. Translation only, cr. 8vo. 5s.

HOOPER, MARY, Little Dinners: How to Serve them with Elegance and Economy. Twenty-second Edition. Cr. 8vo. 2s. 6d.
    Cookery for Invalids, Persons of Delicate Digestion, and Children. Fifth Edition. Cr. 8vo. 2s. 6d.
    Every-day Meals: being Economical and Wholesome Recipes for Breakfast, Luncheon, and Supper. Seventh Edition. Cr. 8vo. 2s. 6d.

HOPKINS, ELLICE, Work amongst Working Men. Sixth Edition. Cr. 8vo. 3s. 6d.

HORATIUS FLACCUS, Q., Opera. Edited by F. A. CORNISH. With Frontispiece. Elzevir 8vo. vellum, 7s. 6d.; parchment or cloth, 6s. (*Parchment Library*.)

HORNADAY, W. T., Two Years in a Jungle. With Illustrations. 8vo. 21s.
    Taxidermy and Zoological Collecting; with Chapters on Collecting and Preserving Insects, by W. J. HOLLAND, D.D. With 24 Plates and 85 Illustrations. 8vo. 10s. 6d.

HOSPITALIER, E., The Modern Applications of Electricity. Translated and Enlarged by JULIUS MAIER. Second Edition, revised, with many Additions and Numerous Illustrations. 2 vols. 8vo. 25s.

HOWARD, H. C., Christabel (concluded), with other Poems. Cr. 8vo. 2s. 6d.

HOWE, HENRY MARION, The Metallurgy of Steel. Vol. I. Second Edition, revised and enlarged. Royal 4to. £2. 12s. 6d.

HULME, F. EDWARD, Mathematical Drawing Instruments, and How to Use Them. With Illustrations. Fifth Edition, imperial 16mo, 3s. 6d.

HUMBOLDT, Baron W. von, The Sphere and Duties of Government. From the German by J. COULTHARD. Post 8vo, 5s.

HUNTER, HAY, and WHYTE, WALTER. My Ducats and My Daughter. With Frontispiece. Cr. 8vo. 6s.

HUSMANN, G., American Grape Growing and Wine Making. Illustrated. 12mo. 7s. 6d.

HUTCHINSON, A. B., The Mind of Mencius; or, Political Economy founded upon Moral Philosophy. A Systematic Digest of the Doctrines of the Chinese Philosopher Mencius. Translated from the German of FABER, with Additional Notes. Post 8vo. 10s. 6d. (*Trübner's Oriental Series*.)

HUTCHINSON, Colonel, and MACGREGOR, Major, Military Sketching and Reconnaissance. Fifth Edition, with 16 Plates. Sm. cr. 8vo. 4s. (*Military Handbooks*.)

HUXLEY, Prof. T. H., The Crayfish: an Introduction to the Study of Zoology. With 82 Illustrations. Fifth Edition. Cr. 8vo. 5s. (*I.S.S.*)

IHNE, W., Latin Grammar for Beginners. Ahn's System. 12mo. 3s.

IM THURN, EVERARD F., Among the Indians of Guiana: Sketches, Chiefly Anthropologic, from the Interior of British Guiana. With 53 Illustrations and a Map. 8vo. 18s.

INGELOW, JEAN, Off the Skelligs: a Novel. With Frontispiece. Cr. 8vo. 6s.

INMAN, JAMES, Nautical Tables. Designed for the use of British Seamen. New Edition, revised and enlarged. 8vo. 16s.

IVANOFF'S Russian Grammar. Sixteenth Edition. Translated, Enlarged, and Arranged for use of Students by Major W. E. GOWAN. 8vo. 6s.

JACOB, G. A., Manual of Hindu Pantheism: the Vedântasâra. Third Edition, post 8vo. 6s. (*Trübner's Oriental Series.*)

JAPP, ALEXANDER H., Days with Industrials: Adventures and Experiences among Curious Industries. With Illustrations. Cr. 8vo. 6s.

JÄSCHKE, H. A., Tibetan Grammar. Prepared by Dr. H. WENZELL. Second Edition. Cr. 8vo. 5s.

JEAFFRESON, HERBERT H., Magnificat: a Course of Sermons. With Frontispiece. Cr. 8vo. 2s. 6d.

JENKINS, E., A Modern Paladin: Contemporary Manners. Cr. 8vo. 5s.

JENKINS, E., and RAYMOND, J., Architect's Legal Handbook. Fourth Edition, revised. Cr. 8vo. 6s.

JENKINS, JABEZ, Vest-Pocket Lexicon. An English Dictionary of all except Familiar Words, including the principal Scientific and Technical Terms. 64mo. roan, 1s. 6d.; cloth, 1s.

JENKINS, Canon R. C., Heraldry, English and Foreign. With a Dictionary of Heraldic Terms and 156 Illustrations. Sm. 8vo. 3s. 6d.

JENNINGS, HARGRAVE, The Indian Religions; or, Results of the Mysterious Buddhism. 8vo. 10s. 6d.

JESSOP, C. MOORE, Past and Future; or, Fable and Fact. Cr. 8vo. 5s.

JEVONS, W. STANLEY, Money and the Mechanism of Exchange. Ninth Edition. Cr. 8vo. 5s. (*I.S.S.*)

JOEL, L., Consul's Manual, and Shipowner's and Shipmaster's Practical Guide in their Transactions Abroad. 8vo. 12s.

Johns Hopkins University Studies in History and Politics. Edited by HERBERT B. ADAMS. Nine Annual Series, and nine Extra Volumes. 8vo. £10. 10s. Also sold separately.

JOHNSON, J. B., Theory and Practice of Surveying. Designed for use of Students in Engineering. Illustrated. Second Edition. 8vo. 15s.

JOHNSON, S. W., How Crops Feed: a Treatise on the Atmosphere and the Soil as related to Nutrition of Plants. Illustrated. Cr. 8vo. 10s.

    How Crops Grow: a Treatise on the Chemical Composition, Structure, and Life of the Plant. Illustrated. Cr. 8vo. 10s.

JOHNSON, SAMUEL, Oriental Religions and their Relation to Universal Religion—Persia. 8vo. 18s.

    Oriental Religions and their Relation to Universal Religion—India. 2 vols. 21s. (*Philosophical Library.*)

JOHNSTON, H. H., The Kilima-njaro Expedition: a Record of Scientific Exploration in Eastern Equatorial Africa. With 6 Maps and 80 Illustrations. 8vo. 21s.

    History of a Slave. With 47 Illustrations. Square 8vo. 6s.

JOLLY, JULIUS, Naradiya Dharma-Sastra: or, The Institutes of Narada. Translated from the Sanskrit. Cr. 8vo. 10s. 6d.

    Manava-Dharma-Castra: the Code of Manu. Original Sanskrit Text. With Critical Notes. Post 8vo. 10s. 6d. (*Trübner's Oriental Series.*)

JOLY, N., Man before Metals. With 148 Illustrations. Fourth Edition. Cr. 8vo. 5s. (*I.S.S.*)

JONCOURT, Madame MARIE DE, **Wholesome Cookery.** Fifth Edition. Cr. 8vo. cloth, 1s. 6d.; paper covers, 1s.

JUDD, Prof. J. W., **Volcanoes**: what they are and what they teach. With 96 Illustrations on Wood. Fourth Edition. Cr. 8vo. 5s. (I.S.S.)

Kalender of Shepherdes. Facsimile Reprint. With Introduction and Glossary by Dr. H. OSKAR SOMMER. £2. 2s. net.

KARCHER, THÉODORE, **Questionnaire Français**: Questions on French Grammar, Idiomatic Difficulties, and Military Expressions. Fourth Edition. Cr. 8vo. 4s. 6d.; interleaved with writing paper, 5s. 6d.

KARMARSCH, KARL, **Technological Dictionary.** Fourth Edition, revised. Imp. 8vo. 3 vols.
- Vol. 1.—German-English-French, 12s.
- Vol. 2.—English-German-French, 12s.
- Vol. 3.—French-German-English, 15s.

KAUFMANN, M., **Socialism**: its Nature, its Dangers, and its Remedies considered. Cr. 8vo. 7s. 6d.

Utopias; or, Schemes of Social Improvement, from Sir Thomas More to Karl Marx. Cr. 8vo. 5s.

Christian Socialism. Cr. 8vo. 4s. 6d.

KAY, JOSEPH, **Free Trade in Land.** Edited by his WIDOW. With Preface by Right Hon. JOHN BRIGHT. Seventh Edition. Cr. 8vo. 5s. Cheap Edition. Cloth, 1s. 6d.; paper covers, 1s.

KEATS, JOHN, **Poetical Works.** Edited by W. T. ARNOLD. Large Cr. 8vo. choicely printed on hand-made paper, with etched portrait, vellum, 15s.; parchment or cloth, 12s. Cheap edition, crown 8vo, cloth, 3s. 6d.

KEBLE, J., **Christian Year.** With Portrait. Elzevir 8vo. vellum, 7s. 6d.; parchment or cloth, 6s. (*Parchment Library*.)

KELKE, W. H. H., **An Epitome of English Grammar.** For the Use of Students. Adapted to London Matriculation Course. Cr. 8vo. 4s. 6d.

KELLOGG, G. H., **Grammar of the Hindi Language.** Second Edition, revised and enlarged. 8vo. 18s.

KEMPIS, THOMAS À, **The Imitation of Christ.** Revised Translation. Elzevir 8vo. (*Parchment Library*), vellum, 7s. 6d.; parchment or cloth, 6s. Red line Edition, fcp. 8vo. 2s. 6d. Cabinet Edition, sm. 8vo. 1s. 6d.; cloth limp, 1s. Miniature Edition, 32mo. with red lines, 1s. 6d.; without red lines, 1s.

A Metrical Version. By H. CARRINGTON. Cr. 8vo. 5s.

De Imitatione Christi. Latin Text, Rhythmically Arranged, with Translation on Opposite Pages. Cr. 8vo. 7s. 6d.

KETTLEWELL, S., **Thomas à Kempis and the Brothers of Common Life.** With Portrait. Cr. 8vo. 7s. 6d.

KHAYYÁM, OMAR, **The Quatrains of.** Persian Text, with an English Verse Translation. Post 8vo. 10s. 6d. Translation only, 5s. (*Trübner's Oriental Series*.)

KIDD, JOSEPH, **Laws of Therapeutics.** Second Edition. Cr. 8vo. 6s.

KINAHAN, G. H., **Valleys and their Relation to Fissures, Fractures, and Faults.** Cr. 8vo. 7s. 6d.

KING, Mrs. HAMILTON, **The Disciples.** Eleventh Edition. Elzevir 8vo. 6s. Fourteenth Edition. Sm. 8vo. 5s.

A Book of Dreams. Third Edition. Cr. 8vo. 3s. 6d.

Sermon in the Hospital (from 'The Disciples'). Fifth Edition. Fcp. 8vo. 1s. Cheap Edition, 3d.

Ballads of the North, and other Poems. Cr. 8vo. 5s.

KINGSFORD, ANNA, The Perfect Way in Diet: a Treatise advocating a Return to the Natural and Ancient Food of our Race. Sixth Edition. Sm. 8vo. 2s.
— Spiritual Hermeneutics of Astrology and Holy Writ. Illustrated. 4to. parchment, 10s. 6d.

KINGSFORD, ANNA, and MAITLAND, EDWARD, The Virgin of the World of Hermes Mercurius Trismegistus, rendered into English. 4to. imit. parchment, 10s. 6d.

KINGSFORD, W., History of Canada. 5 vols. 8vo. 15s. each.

KISTNA, OTTO, Buddha and His Doctrines: a Bibliographical Essay. 4to. 2s. 6d.

KITTON, FRED. G., John Leech, Artist and Humourist: a Biographical Sketch. 18mo. 1s.

KNOWLES, J. HINTON, Folk-Tales of Kashmir. Post 8vo. 16s. (*Trübner's Oriental Series.*)

KNOX, A. A., The New Playground; or, Wanderings in Algeria. New and Cheaper Edition. Large cr. 8vo. 6s.

KOLBE, F. W., A Language-Study based on Bantu: an Inquiry into the Laws of Root-formation. 8vo. 6s.

KRAMER, J., Pocket Dictionary of the Dutch Language. Fifth Edition. 16mo. 4s.

KRAPF, L., Dictionary of the Suahili Language. 8vo. 30s.

KRAUS, J., Carlsbad: its Thermal Springs and Baths, and how to use them. Fourth Edition, revised and enlarged. Cr. 8vo. 6s. 6d.

KUNZ, G. F., Gems and Precious Stones of North America. Illustrated with 8 Coloured Plates and numerous Engravings. Super-royal 8vo. £2. 12s. 6d.

LAGRANGE, F., Physiology of Bodily Exercise. Second Edition. Cr. 8vo. 5s. (*I.S.S.*)

LANDON, JOSEPH, School Management; including a General View of the Work of Education, Organisation, and Discipline. Seventh Edition. Cr. 8vo. 6s. (*Education Library.*)

LANE, E. W., Selections from the Koran. New Edition, with Introduction by STANLEY LANE-POOLE. Post 8vo. 9s. (*Trübner's Oriental Series.*)

LANG, ANDREW, In the Wrong Paradise, and other Stories. Cr. 8vo. 6s.
— Ballades in Blue China. Elzevir 8vo. 5s.
— Rhymes à la Mode. With Frontispiece. Fourth Edition. Elzevir 8vo. 5s.
— Lost Leaders. Cr. 8vo. 5s. Second Edition.

LANGE, Prof. F. A., History of Materialism, and Criticism of its present importance. Authorised Translation by ERNEST C. THOMAS. Fourth Edition. 3 vols. Post 8vo. 10s. 6d. each. (*Philosophical Library.*)

LANGE, F. K. W., Germania: a German Reading-book. Part I. Anthology of Prose and Poetry, with vocabulary. Part II. Essays on German History and Institutions. 8vo. 2 vols. 5s. 6d.; separately, 3s. 6d. each.

LANGSTROTH on the Hive and Honey Bee. Revised and Enlarged Edition. With numerous Illustrations. 8vo. 9s.

LARMOYER, M. de, Practical French Grammar. Cr. 8vo. New Edition, in one vol. 3s. 6d. Two Parts, 2s. 6d. each.

LARSEN, A., Dano-Norwegian Dictionary. Cr. 8vo. 10s. 6d.

LAURIE, S. S., Rise and Early Constitution of Universities. With a Survey of Mediæval Education. Cr. 8vo. 6s.

LEE, G., Manual of Politics. Sm. cr. 8vo. 2s. 6d.

LEE, MATTHEW HENRY, Diaries and Letters of Philip Henry, M.A., o Broad Oak, Flintshire. Cr. 8vo. 7s. 6d.

LEFEVRE, Right Hon. G. SHAW, Peel and O'Connell. 8vo. 10s. 6d.

    Incidents of Coercion: a Journal of Visits to Ireland. Third Edition. Cr. 8vo. limp cloth, 1s. 6d.; paper covers, 1s.

    Irish Members and English Gaolers. Cr. 8vo. limp cloth, 1s 6d.; paper covers, 1s.

    Combination and Coercion in Ireland: Sequel to 'Incidents of Coercion.' Cr. 8vo. cloth, 1s. 6d.; paper covers, 1s.

LEFFMANN, HENRY, and **BEAM, W., Examination of Water for Sanitary and Technical Purposes.** Second Edition, revised and enlarged. With Illustrations. Cr. 8vo. 5s.

Legend of Maandoo, The: a Poem. With Fifteen Collotype Plates. Second Edition. 8vo. 10s. 6d.

LEGGE, J., Chinese Classics. Translated into English. Popular Edition. Cr. 8vo.
    Vol. I. Life and Teachings of Confucius. 6th edition, 10s. 6d.
    Vol. II. Works of Mencius, 12s.
    Vol. III. She-King, or Book of Poetry, 12s.

LELAND, C. G., Breitmann Ballads. The only Authorised Edition. Including Nineteen Original Ballads, illustrating his Travels in Europe. Cr. 8vo. 6s. Cheap Edition, 3s. 6d. (*Lotos Series.*)

    Gaudeamus: Humorous Poems from the German of JOSEPH VICTOR SCHEFFEL and others. 16mo. 3s. 6d.

    English Gipsies and their Language. Second Edition. Cr. 8vo. 7s. 6d.

    Fu-Sang; or, The Discovery of America by Chinese Buddhist Priests in the 5th Century. Cr. 8vo. 7s. 6d.

    Pidgin-English Sing-Song; or, Songs and Stories in the China-English Dialect. Third Edition. Cr. 8vo. 5s.

    The Gipsies. Cr. 8vo. 10s. 6d.

LEOPARDI, GIACOMO, Essays and Dialogues. Translated by CHARLES EDWARDES, with Biographical Sketch. Post 8vo. 7s. 6d. (*Philosophical Library.*)

LESLEY, J. P., Man's Origin and Destiny. Sketches from the Platform of the Physical Sciences. Second Edition. Cr. 8vo. 7s. 6d.

LESSING, GOTTHOLD E., Education of the Human Race. From the German by F. W. Robertson. Fcp. 8vo. 2s. 6d.

LEVI, Prof. LEONE, International Law, with Materials for a Code of International Law. Cr. 8vo. 5s. (*I.S.S.*)

LEWES, GEORGE HENRY, Problems of Life and Mind. 8vo.
    Series I. Foundations of a Creed. 2 vols. 28s.
    Series III. The Study of Psychology. 2 vols. 22s. 6d.

    The Physical Basis of Mind. With Illustrations. New Edition, with Prefatory Note by Prof. J. SULLY. Large post 8vo. 10s. 6d.

Life's Greatest Possibility: an Essay on Spiritual Realism. Fcp. 8vo. 2s. 6d.

Light on the Path. For the Personal Use of those who are Ignorant of the Eastern Wisdom. Written down by M. C. Fcp. 8vo. 1s. 6d.

LILLIE, ARTHUR, Popular Life of Buddha. Containing an Answer to the Hibbert Lectures of 1881. With Illustrations. Cr. 8vo. 6s.

    Buddhism in Christendom; or, Jesus the Essene. With Illustrations. 8vo. 15s.

LILLY, W. S., Characteristics from the Writings of Cardinal Newman. Selections from his various Works. Ninth Edition. With Portrait. Cr. 8vo. 6s.

LINTON, W. J., Rare Poems of the 16th and 17th Centuries. Cr. 8vo. 5s.

LINTON, W. J., and STODDARD, R. H., English Verse. Chaucer to Burns—Translations—Lyrics of the Nineteenth Century—Dramatic Scenes and Characters—Ballads and Romances. 5 vols. Cr. 8vo. 5s. each.

LIOY, DIODATO, The Philosophy of Right, with special reference to the Principles and Development of Law Translated from the Italian by W. Hastie, B.D. 2 vols. Post 8vo. 21s. (*Philosophical Library.*)

LOCHER, CARL, Explanation of Organ Stops. With Hints for Effective Combinations. 8vo. 5s.

LOCKER, F., London Lyrics. Twelfth Edition. With Portrait. Elzevir 8vo. 5s.

LOCKYER, J. NORMAN, Studies in Spectrum Analysis. With 6 Photographic Illustrations of Spectra, and numerous Engravings on Wood. Fourth Edition. Cr. 8vo. 6s. 6d. (*I.S.S.*)

LOMMEL, Dr. EUGENE, Nature of Light. With a General Account of Physical Optics. With 188 Illustrations and a Table of Spectra in Chromo-lithography. Fifth Edition. Cr. 8vo. 5s. (*I.S.S.*)

LONG, J., Eastern Proverbs and Emblems, illustrating Old Truths. Post 8vo. 6s. (*Trübner's Oriental Series.*)

LONGFELLOW. Life of H. Wadsworth Longfellow. By His Brother. With Portraits and Illustrations. 3 vols. 8vo. 42s.

LONSDALE, MARGARET, Sister Dora: a Biography. With Portrait. Thirtieth Edition. Small 8vo. 2s. 6d.

LOVAT, Lady, Seeds and Sheaves: Thoughts for Incurables. Cr. 8vo. 5s.

LOWDER. Charles Lowder: a Biography. By the Author of 'St. Teresa.' Twelfth Edition. With Portrait. Cr. 8vo. 3s. 6d.

LOWE, R. W., Thomas Betterton. Cr. 8vo. 2s. 6d. (*Eminent Actors.*)

LOWELL, JAMES RUSSELL, Biglow Papers. Edited by Thomas Hughes, Q C. Fcp. 8vo. 2s. 6d.

LUBBOCK, Sir JOHN, Ants, Bees, and Wasps: a Record of Observations on the Habits of the Social Hymenoptera. With 5 Chromo-lithographic Plates. Tenth Edition. Cr. 8vo. 5s. (*I.S.S.*)

    On the Senses, Instincts, and Intelligence of Animals. With Special Reference to Insects. With 118 Illustrations. Third Edition. Cr. 8vo. 5s. (*I.S.S.*)

    A Contribution to our Knowledge of Seedlings. With nearly 700 figures in text. 2 vols. 8vo. 36s. net.

LÜCKES, EVA C. E., Lectures on General Nursing, Delivered to the Probationers of the London Hospital Training School for Nurses. Fourth Edition. Cr. 8vo. 2s. 6d.

LUKIN, J., Amateur Mechanics' Workshop: Plain and Concise Directions for the Manipulation of Wood and Metals. Sixth Edition. Numerous Woodcuts. 8vo. 6s.

    The Lathe and its Uses: or, Instruction in the Art of Turning Wood and Metal. Seventh Edition. Illustrated. 8vo. 10s. 6d.

    Amongst Machines: a Description of Various Mechanical Appliances Used in the Manufacture of Wood, Metal, &c. A Book for Boys. Third Edition With 64 Engravings. Cr. 8vo. 3s. 6d

    The Boy Engineers: What They Did, and How They Did It. A Book for Boys. With 30 Engravings. Third Edition. Imp. 16mo. 3s. 6d.

    The Young Mechanic: a Book for Boys Containing Directions for the Use of all Kinds of Tools, and for the Construction of Steam-engines and Mechanical Models, including the Art of Turning in Wood and Metal. Seventh Edition. With 70 Engravings. Cr. 8vo. 3s. 6d.

LUYS, J., The Brain and its Functions. With Illustrations. Third Edition. Cr. 8vo. 5s. (*I.S.S.*)

LYALL, Sir ALFRED, Verses written in India. Second Edition. Elzevir 8vo. gilt top, 5s.

LYTTON, Earl of, Life, Letters, and Literary Remains of Edward Bulwer, Lord Lytton. With Portraits, Illustrations, and Facsimiles. 8vo, 2 vols. 32s.

    Lucile. Illustrated. 16mo. 4s. 6d.

MACAULAY'S Essays on Men and Books: Lord Clive, Milton, Earl of Chatham, Lord Byron. Edited by ALEX. H. JAPP. Pott 8vo. 3s. 6d. (*Lotos Series*.)

MacCARTHY, DENIS FLORENCE, Calderon's Dramas. Translated by. Post 8vo. 10s.

MACDONALD, GEORGE, Malcolm. With Portrait of the Author engraved on Steel. Cr. 8vo. 6s. New and cheaper Edition, 3s. 6d.

    Castle Warlock. With Frontispiece. Cr. 8vo. 6s. New and cheaper Edition, 3s. 6d.

    There and Back. With Frontispiece. 6s.

    Donal Grant. With Frontispiece. Cr. 8vo. 6s. New and cheaper Edition, 3s. 6d.

    Home Again. With Frontispiece. Cr. 8vo. 6s.

    The Marquis of Lossie. With Frontispiece. Cr. 8vo. 6s. New and cheaper Edition, 3s. 6d.

    St. George and St. Michael. With Frontispiece. Cr. 8vo. 6s. New and cheaper Edition, 3s. 6d.

    What's Mine's Mine. With Frontispiece. Cr. 8vo. 6s. New and cheaper Edition, 3s. 6d.

    Annals of a Quiet Neighbourhood. With Frontispiece. Cr. 8vo. 6s. New and cheaper Edition. 3s. 6d.

    The Seaboard Parish: a Sequel to 'Annals of a Quiet Neighbourhood.' With Frontispiece. Cr. 8vo. 6s. New and cheaper Edition. 3s. 6d.

    Wilfrid Cumbermede: an Autobiographical Story. With Frontispiece. Cr. 8vo. 6s. New and cheaper Edition, 3s. 6d.

    Thomas Wingfold, Curate. With Frontispiece. Cr. 8vo. 6s. New and cheaper Edition, 3s. 6d.

    Paul Faber, Surgeon. With Frontispiece. Cr. 8vo. 6s. New and Cheaper Edition, 3s. 6d.

    The Elect Lady. With Frontispiece. Cr. 8vo. 6s.

    Flight of the Shadow. With Frontispiece. Cr. 8vo. 6s.

McGRATH, TERENCE, Pictures from Ireland. New Edition. Cr. 8vo. 2s.

MACHIAVELLI, NICCOLO, Discourses on the First Decade of Titus Livius. From the Italian by N. HILL THOMPSON. Large cr. 8vo. 12s.

MACKAY, DONALD J., Bishop Forbes: a Memoir. With Portrait and Map. Cr. 8vo. 7s. 6d.

MACKAY, ERIC, A Lover's Litanies, and other Poems. With Portrait of Author. 3s. 6d. (*Lotos Series*.)

MAC KENNA, S. J., Plucky Fellows: a Book for Boys. With 6 Illustrations. Fifth Edition. Cr. 8vo. 3s. 6d.

MACKONOCHIE. Alexander Heriot Mackonochie: a Memoir. By E. A. T. Edited, with Preface, by E. F. RUSSELL. With Portrait and Views. Large cr. 8vo. 7s. 6d. Cheap Edition, cr. 8vo. 3s. 6d.

MACMASTER, J., The Divine Purpose of Capital Punishment. Cr. 8vo. 6s.

MACNEILL, J. G. SWIFT, How the Union was Carried. Cr. 8vo. cloth, 1s. 6d.; paper covers, 1s.

MADAN, FALCONER, Books in Manuscript. With 8 Plates. Post 8vo. 6s. net. (*Books about Books*.)

MADDEN, F. W., Coins of the Jews; being a History of the Jewish Coinage and Money in the Old and New Testaments. With 279 Woodcuts and a Plate of Alphabets. Roy. 4to. £2. 2s.

    The Numismata Orientalia. Vol. II. Coins of the Jews. Being a History of the Jewish Coinage and Money in the Old and New Testaments. With 279 Woodcuts and Plate. Royal 4to. £2.

MAGNUS, Lady, About the Jews since Bible times. Sm. Cr. 8vo. 6s.

MAGNUS, Sir PHILIP, Industrial Education. Cr. 8vo. 6s. (*Education Library*.)

MAGUIRE, W. R., Domestic Sanitary Drainage and Plumbing. 8vo. 12s.

MAHAFFY, Prof., Old Greek Education. Second Edition. Cr. 8vo. 3s. 6d. (*Education Library.*)

MAIMONIDES, Guide of the Perplexed. Translated and annotated by M. Friedländer. 3 vols. post 8vo. 31s. 6d. (*Philosophical Library.*)

MAISEY, Gen. F. C., Sanchi and its Remains. With Introductory Note by Maj.-Gen. Sir Alex. Cunningham, K.C.I.E. With 40 Plates. Royal 4to. £2. 10s.

MALET, LUCAS, Little Peter: a Christmas Morality for Children of any Age. With numerous Illustrations. Fourth Thousand. Imp. 16mo. 5s.

    Colonel Enderby's Wife. With Frontispiece. Cr. 8vo. 6s.

    A Counsel of Perfection. With Frontispiece. Cr. 8vo. 6s.

MALLET, Right Hon. Sir LOUIS, Free Exchange. Papers on Political and Economical Subjects, including Chapters on the Law of Value and Unearned Increment. Edited by Bernard Mallet. 8vo. 12s.

MANNING. Towards Evening: Selections from the Writings of Cardinal Manning. Fifth Edition. With Facsimile. 16mo. 2s.

Many Voices. Extracts from Religious Writers of Christendom from the 1st to the 16th Century. With Biographical Sketches. Cr. 8vo. 6s.

MARCHANT, W. T., In Praise of Ale: Songs, Ballads, Epigrams, and Anecdotes. Cr. 8vo. 10s. 6d.

MAREY, Prof. E. J., Animal Mechanism: a Treatise on Terrestrial and Aerial Locomotion. With 117 Illustrations. Third Edition. Cr. 8vo. 5s. (*I.S.S.*)

MARKHAM, Capt. ALBERT HASTINGS, R.N., The Great Frozen Sea: a Personal Narrative of the Voyage of the *Alert* during the Arctic Expedition of 1875-6. With Illustrations and Maps. Sixth and Cheaper Edition. Cr. 8vo. 6s.

MARSDEN, J. PENNINGTON, The Personal History of Jim Duncan: a Chronicle of Small Beer. 3 vols. 31s. 6d.

MARSDEN, WILLIAM, Numismata Orientalia Illustrata. 57 Plates of Oriental Coins, from the Collection of the late William Marsden, F.R.S., engraved from drawings made under his directions. 4to. 31s. 6d.

MARTIN, G. A., The Family Horse: its Stabling, Care, and Feeding. Cr. 8vo. 3s. 6d.

MARTINEAU, GERTRUDE, Outline Lessons on Morals. Sm. cr. 8vo. 3s. 6d.

MARTINEAU, HARRIET, The Positive Philosophy of Auguste Comte. Translated and condensed. New and cheaper Edition. 2 vols. Large post 8vo.

MARTINEAU, JAMES, Essays, Philosophical and Theological. 2 vols. cr. 8vo. £1. 4s.

MASON, CHARLOTTE M., Home Education: a Course of Lectures to Ladies. Cr. 8vo. 3s. 6d.

MASON, Capt. F. H., Life and Public Service of James A. Garfield, President U.S.A. With a Preface by Bret Harte. Portrait. Cr. 8vo. 2s. 6d.

MATHER, G., and BLAGG, C. J., Bishop Rawle: a Memoir. Large cr. 8vo. 7s. 6d.

MATHERS, S. L. M., The Key of Solomon the King. Translated from ancient MSS. in the British Museum. With Plates. Cr. 4to. 25s.

    The Kabbalah Unveiled. Containing the Three Books of the Zohar, translated from the Chaldee and Hebrew Text. Post 8vo. 10s. 6d.

    The Tarot: its Occult Signification, use in Fortune-telling, and method of Play. With pack of 78 Tarot Cards, 5s.; without the Cards, 1s. 6d.

MATUCE, H. OGRAM, A Wanderer. Cr. 8vo. 5s.

MAUDSLEY, H., Body and Will: an Essay concerning Will, in its Metaphysical, Physiological, and Pathological Aspects. 8vo. 12s.

    Natural Causes and Supernatural Seemings. Second Edition. Cr. 8vo. 6s.

    Responsibility in Mental Disease. Fourth Edition. Cr. 8vo. 5s. (I.S.S.)

MAXWELL, W. E., Manual of the Malay Language. Second Edition. Cr. 8vo. 7s. 6d.

MEAD, C. M., D.D., Supernatural Revelation: an Essay concerning the basis of the Christian Faith. Royal 8vo. 14s.

MEAKIN, J. E. BUDGETT, Introduction to the Arabic of Morocco. English-Arabic Vocabulary, Grammar, Notes, &c. Fcp. 8vo. 6s.

Meditations on Death and Eternity. Translated from the German by FREDERICA ROWAN. Published by Her Majesty's gracious permission. Cr. 8vo. 6s.

Meditations on Life and its Religious Duties. Translated from the German by FREDERICA ROWAN. Published by Her Majesty's gracious permission. Cr. 8vo. 6s.

MENDELSSOHN'S Letters to Ignaz and Charlotte Moscheles. Translated by FELIX MOSCHELES. Numerous Illustrations and Facsimiles. 8vo. 12s.

MERRILL, G. P., Stones for Building and Decoration. Royal 8vo. 21s.

MEYER, G. HERMANN von, Organs of Speech and their Application in the Formation of Articulate Sounds. With 47 Illustrations. Cr. 8vo. 5s. (I.S.S.)

MEYNELL, WILFRID, John Henry Newman, the Founder of Modern Anglicanism, and a Cardinal of the Roman Church. Cr. 8vo. 2s. 6d.

MILL, JOHN STUART, Auguste Comte and Positivism. Fourth Edition. Post 8vo. 3s. 6d. (Philosophical Library.)

MILLER, EDWARD, The History and Doctrines of Irvingism; or, The So-called Catholic and Apostolic Church. 2 vols. Large post 8vo. 15s.

MILLER, ELLEN E., Alone Through Syria. With Introduction by Prof. A. H. SAYCE. With 8 Illustrations. Second Edition. Cr. 8vo. 5s.

MILLHOUSE, JOHN, Italian Dictionary. 2 vols. 8vo. 12s.

    Manual of Italian Conversation. 18mo. 2s.

MILLS, HERBERT, Poverty and the State; or, Work for the Unemployed. Cr. 8vo. 6s.; cheap edition, limp cloth, 1s. 6d.; paper covers, 1s.

MILNE, J., Earthquakes and other Earth Movements. With 38 Figures. Third and Revised Edition. Cr. 8vo. 5s. (I.S.S.)

MILTON, JOHN, Prose Writings. Edited by E. MYERS. Elzevir 8vo. vellum, 7s. 6d.; parchment or cloth, 6s. (Parchment Library.)

    Poetical Works. 2 vols. elzevir 8vo. vellum, 15s.; parchment or cloth, 12s. (Parchment Library.)

    Sonnets. Edited by MARK PATTISON. With Portrait. Elzevir 8vo. vellum, 7s. 6d.; parchment or cloth, 6s. (Parchment Library.)

MITCHELL, LUCY M., History of Ancient Sculpture. With Numerous Illustrations. Super-royal 8vo. 42s.

MIVART, ST. GEORGE, On Truth. 8vo. 16s.

    Origin of Human Reason. 8vo. 10s. 6d.

MOLTKE, Count Von, Notes of Travel. Cr. 8vo. 2s. 6d.

MONCEL, Count DU, The Telephone, the Microphone, and the Phonograph. With 74 Illustrations. 3rd Edition. Sm. 8vo. 5s.

MONIER-WILLIAMS, Sir M., Modern India and the Indians: a Series of Impressions, Notes, and Essays. Fifth Edition. Post 8vo. 14s. (*Trübner's Oriental Series.*)

MOORE, AUBREY L., Essays, Scientific and Philosophical. With Memoir of the Author. Cr. 8vo. 6s.

    Lectures and Papers on the History of the Reformation in England and on the Continent. 8vo. 10s.

    Science and the Faith: Essays on Apologetic Subjects. Third Edition. Cr. 8vo. 6s.

MOORE, T. W., Treatise and Handbook of Orange Culture in Florida, Louisiana, and California. Fourth Edition Enlarged. 18mo. 5s.

MORFILL, W. R., Simplified Grammar of the Polish Language. Cr. 8vo. 3s. 6d.

    Simplified Serbian Grammar. Crown 8vo. 4s. 6d.

MORFIT, CAMPBELL, Manufacture of Soaps. With Illustrations. 8vo. £2. 12s. 6d.

    Pure Fertilizers, and the Chemical Conversion of Rock Guanos, &c., into various Valuable Products. With 28 Plates. 8vo. £4. 4s.

MORISON, J. COTTER, The Service of Man: an Essay towards the Religion of the Future. Cr. 8vo. 5s.

MORRIS. Diary and Letters of Gouverneur Morris, Minister of the U.S. to France. With Portraits. 2 vols. 8vo. 30s.

MORRIS, HENRY, Simplified Grammar of the Telugu Language. With Map of India showing Telugu Country. Cr. 8vo. 10s. 6d.

MORRIS, LEWIS, Poetical Works. New and Cheaper Edition. 5 vols. fcap. 8vo. 5s. each.

    Songs of Two Worlds. Fourteenth Edition. Fcap. 8vo. 5s.

    Gwen, and the Ode of Life. Ninth Edition. Fcap. 8vo. 5s.

    Songs Unsung, and Gycia. Fifth Edition. Fcap. 8vo. 5s.

    Songs of Britain. Fourth Edition. Fcap. 8vo. 5s.

    A Vision of Saints. Fourth Edition. Fcap. 8vo. 6s.

    Poetical Works. Eighth Thousand. In 1 vol. cr. 8vo. 6s. Cloth extra, gilt edges, 7s. 6d.

    The Epic of Hades. Thirty-fifth Thousand. Fcap. 8vo. 5s.

    The Epic of Hades. With 16 Autotype Illustrations, after the Drawings of the late GEORGE R. CHAPMAN. 4to. cloth extra, gilt edges, 21s.

    The Epic of Hades. Presentation Edition. 4to. cloth extra, gilt edges, 10s. 6d. Elzevir Edition, 6s.

    Ode on the Marriage of H.R.H. the Duke of York and H.S.H. Princess Victoria Mary of Teck, July 6, 1893. Royal 4to. hand-made paper, 1s. 6d. net.

    Birthday Book. Edited by S. S. COPEMAN. With Frontispiece. 32mo. cloth extra, gilt edges, 2s.; cloth limp, 1s. 6d.

MORSE, E. S., First Book of Zoology. With numerous Illustrations. New Edition. Cr. 8vo. 2s. 6d.

MORSELLI, Prof. H., Suicide: an Essay on Comparative Moral Statistics. Second Edition, with Diagrams. Cr. 8vo. 5s. (*I.S.S.*)

MOSENTHAL, J. De, and **HARTING, JAMES E., Ostriches and Ostrich Farming.** Second Edition. With 8 full-page Illustrations and 20 woodcuts, royal 8vo. 10s. 6d.

MUIR, JOHN, Original Sanskrit Texts, on the Origin and History of the People of India. 5 vols. 8vo.

    Mythical and Legendary Accounts of the Origin of Caste. Third Edition. £1. 1s. Also issued as a volume of *Trübner's Oriental Series,* at the same price.

    The Trans-Himalayan Origin of the Hindus. Second Edition. £1. 1s.

MUIR, JOHN, The Vedas. Second Edition. 16s.
    Comparison of the Vedic with the Principal Indian Deities. Second Edition. £1. 1s.
    Cosmogony, Mythology, &c., of the Indians in the Vedic Age. Third Edition. £1. 1s.
    Metrical Translations from Sanskrit Writers. Post 8vo. 14s. (*Trübner's Oriental Series*.)

MULHALL, M. G. & E. T., Handbook of the River Plate, comprising the Argentine Republic, Uruguay, and Paraguay. With Railway Map. Sixth Edition. Cr. 8vo. 6s.

MULHOLLAND, ROSA, Marcella Grace: an Irish Novel. Cr. 8vo. 6s.
    A Fair Emigrant. With Frontispiece. Cr. 8vo. 6s.

MÜLLER, E., Simplified Grammar of the Pali Language. Cr. 8vo. 7s. 6d.

MÜLLER, F. MAX, Outline Dictionary, for the Use of Missionaries, Explorers, and Students of Language. 12mo. morocco, 7s. 6d.
    Sacred Hymns of the Brahmins, as preserved in the oldest Collection of Religious Poetry, the Rig-Veda-Sanhita. Vol. I. Hymns to the Maruts, or the Storm-Gods. 8vo. 12s. 6d.
    Hymns of the Rig-Veda, in the Sanhita and Pada Texts. 2 vols. Second Edition. 8vo. £1. 1s.

Munchausen's Travels and Surprising Adventures. Illustrated by ALFRED CROWQUILL. 3s. 6d. (*Lotos Series*.)

My Lawyer; or, the People's Legal Adviser. A Concise Abridgement of and Popular Guide to the Laws of England. By a BARRISTER-AT-LAW. Second Edition. Cr. 8vo. 6s. 6d.

NARADIYA DHARMA-SASTRA; or, The Institutes of Narada. Translated by Dr. JULIUS JOLLY. Cr. 8vo. 10s. 6d.

NEWHOUSE, S., Trapper's Guide; a Manual of Instructions for Capturing all Kinds of Fur-bearing Animals, and Curing their Skins, &c. Eighth, Revised Edition. 8vo. 5s.

NEWMAN. Characteristics from the Writings of Cardinal Newman. Selections from his various Works, arranged by W. S. LILLY. Ninth Edition. With Portrait. Cr. 8vo. 6s.
    *** Portrait of the late Cardinal Newman, mounted for framing, 2s. 6d.

NEWMAN, F. W., Miscellanies. 8vo. Vol. I., Chiefly Addresses, Academical and Historical, 7s. 6d.
    A Handbook of Modern Arabic. Post 8vo. 6s.

NICOLS, ARTHUR, Chapters from the Physical History of the Earth: an Introduction to Geology and Palæontology. With numerous Illustrations. Cr. 8vo. 5s.

NILSSON, L. G., WIDMARK, P. F., and COLLIN, A. Z., Swedish Dictionary. New Edition. 8vo. 16s.

NOEL, Hon. RODEN, A Modern Faust, and other Poems. Sm. cr. 8vo. 5s.
    Essays on Poetry and Poets. 8vo. 12s.

NOIRIT, JULES, French Course in Ten Lessons. Cr. 8vo. 1s. 6d.
    French Grammatical Questions, for the use of Gentlemen preparing for the Army, Civil Service, Oxford Examinations, &c. Cr. 8vo. 1s.; interleaved, 1s. 6d.

NOPS, M., Class Lessons on Euclid. Cr. 8vo. 2s. 6d.

NORTHALL, G. F., English Folk Rhymes. A Collection of Traditional Verses relating to Places and Persons, Customs, Superstitions, &c. Cr. 8vo. 10s. 6d.

Notes on Cavalry Tactics, Organisation, &c. By a CAVALRY OFFICER. With Diagrams. 8vo. 12s.

NUGENT'S French Pocket Dictionary. 24mo. 3s.

Numismata Orientalia (The), Royal 4to. in Paper Wrapper. Part I. Ancient Indian Weights, by E. THOMAS, with a Plate and Map, 9s. 6d. Part II. Coins of the Urtuki Turkumáns, by S. LANE POOLE, with 6 Plates, 9s. Part III. Coinage of Lydia and Persia, by BARCLAY V. HEAD, with 3 Plates, 10s. 6d. Part IV. Coins of the Tuluni Dynasty, by E. T. ROGERS, with 1 Plate, 5s. Part V. Parthian Coinage, by PERCY GARDNER, with 8 Plates, 18s. Part VI. Ancient Coins and Measures of Ceylon, by T. W. RHYS DAVIDS, with 1 Plate, 10s.

Vol. I. containing Six Parts, as specified above, half-bound, £3. 13s. 6d.

Vol. II. **Coins of the Jews:** being a History of the Jewish Coinage in the Old and New Testaments. By F. W. MADDEN. With 279 Woodcuts and Plate. Royal 4to. £2.

Vol. III. Part I. **The Coins of Arakan, of Pegu, and of Burma.** By Lieut.-General Sir ARTHUR PHAYRE. Also contains the Indian Balhara, and the Arabian Intercourse with India in the Ninth and following Centuries. By EDWARD THOMAS. With 5 Illustrations. Royal 4to. 8s. 6d.

Vol. III. Part II. **The Coins of Southern India.** By Sir W. ELLIOT. With Map and Plates. Royal 4to. 25s.

OATES, FRANK, Matabele Land and the Victoria Falls: a Naturalist's Wanderings in the Interior of South Africa. Edited by C. G. OATES. With numerous Illustrations and 4 Maps. Second Edition. 8vo. 21s.

O'BRIEN, R. BARRY, Irish Wrongs and English Remedies, with other Essays. Cr. 8vo. 5s.

Home Ruler's Manual. Cr. 8vo. cloth, 1s. 6d.; paper covers, 1s.

Life and Letters of Thomas Drummond, Under-Secretary in Ireland, 1835-40. 8vo. 14s.

O'CLERY, The, The Making of Italy, 1856-70. With Sketch Maps. 8vo. 16s.

O'CONNELL, Mrs. MORGAN J., The Last Colonel of the Irish Brigade, Count O'Connell, and Old Irish Life at Home and Abroad, 1745-1833. 2 vols. 8vo. 25s.

O'CONNOR, EVANGELINE, Index to Shakspere's Works. Cr. 8vo. 5s.

O'HAGAN, JOHN, Joan of Arc: an Historical Essay. Cr. 8vo. 3s. 6d.

OLCOTT, Colonel, Posthumous Humanity: a Study of Phantoms, from the French of Adolphe D'Assier. With Appendix and Notes. Cr. 8vo. 7s. 6d.

Theosophy, Religion, and Occult Science, with Glossary of Eastern words. Cr. 8vo. 7s. 6d.

OLLENDORFF. Metodo para aprender a Leer, escribir y hablar el Inglés, segun el sistema de Ollendorff. 8vo. 7s. 6d. Key, 4s.

Metodo para aprender a Leer, escribir y hablar el Frances, segun el sistema de Ollendorff. Cr. 8vo. 6s. Key, 3s. 6d.

OMAN, F. G., Swedish Dictionary. Cr. 8vo. 8s.

O'MEARA, KATHLEEN, Henri Perreyve and his Counsels to the Sick. Sm. cr. 8vo. 5s.

One-and-a-Half in Norway. By EITHER and BOTH. Sm. cr. 8vo. 3s. 6d.

OTTÉ E. C., Dano-Norwegian Grammar: a Manual for Students of Danish, based on the Ollendorffian System. Third Edition. Cr. 8vo. 7s. 6d. Key, 3s.

Simplified Grammar of the Danish Language. Cr. 8vo. 2s. 6d.

Simplified Grammar of the Swedish Language. Cr. 8vo. 2s. 6d.

OWEN, ROBERT DALE, Footfalls on the Boundary of another World. With Narrative Illustrations. Post 8vo. 7s. 6d.

Debatable Land between this World and the Next. With Illustrative Narrations. Second Edition. Cr. 8vo. 7s. 6d.

Threading My Way: Twenty-seven Years of Autobiography. Cr. 8vo. 7s. 6d.

PACKARD, A. S., The Labrador Coast. A Journal of two Summer Cruises to that Region. With Maps and Illustrations. 8vo. 18s.

PALGRAVE, W. GIFFORD, Hermann Agha: an Eastern Narrative. Third Edition. Cr. 8vo. 6s.

PALMER, E. H., English-Persian Dictionary. With Simplified Grammar of the Persian Language. Royal 16mo. 10s. 6d.

Persian-English Dictionary. Second Edition. Royal 16mo. 10s. 6d.

Simplified Grammar of Hindustani, Persian, and Arabic. Second Edition. Cr. 8vo. 5s.

Papers relating to Indo-China. Reprinted from Dalrymple's 'Oriental Repertory,' 'Asiatic Researches,' and the 'Journal' of the Asiatic Society of Bengal. Post 8vo. 2 vols. 21s.

MISCELLANEOUS ESSAYS ON SUBJECTS CONNECTED WITH THE MALAY PENINSULA AND THE INDIAN ARCHIPELAGO. From the Journals of the Royal Asiatic, Royal Geographical Societies, &c. Edited by R. ROST. With 5 Plates and a Map. Second Series, 2 vols. 25s. (*Trübner's Oriental Series.*)

PARAVICINI, FRANCES de, Early History of Balliol College. 8vo. 12s.

PARKER, G. W., Concise Grammar of the Malagasy Language. Cr. 8vo. 5s.

PARKER, THEODORE, Discourse on Matters pertaining to Religion. People's Edition. Cr. 8vo. cloth, 2s.; paper covers, 1s. 6d.

Collected Works of Theodore Parker, Minister of the Twenty-eighth Congregational Society at Boston, U.S. 14 vols. Cr. 8vo. 6s. each.

PARRY, EDWARD ABBOTT, Charles Macklin. Cr. 8vo. 2s. 6d. (*Eminent Actors.*)

PARRY, E. GAMBIER, Biography of Reynell Taylor, C.B., C.S.I. With Portrait and Map. 8vo. 14s.

PARSLOE, JOSEPH, Our Railways: Sketches, Historical and Descriptive. With Information as to Fares and Rates, &c. Cr. 8vo. 6s.

PASCAL, BLAISE, Thoughts. Translated by C. KEGAN PAUL. Large cr. 8vo. Parchment, 12s.; vellum, 15s. Cheap edition. Cr. 8vo. 6s.

PATON, A. A., History of the Egyptian Revolution, from the Period of the Mamelukes to the Death of Mohammed Ali. Second Edition. 2 vols. 8vo. 7s. 6d.

PAUL, ALEXANDER, Short Parliaments. History of National Demand for Frequent General Elections. Sm. cr. 8vo. 3s. 6d.

PAUL, C. KEGAN, Faith and Unfaith, and other Essays. Cr. 8vo. 7s. 6d.

Biographical Sketches. Second Edition. Cr. 8vo. 7s. 6d.

Confessio Viatoris. Fcp. 8vo. 2s.

Thoughts of Blaise Pascal. Translated. Large cr. 8vo. Parchment, 12s.; vellum, 15s. Cheap Edition, cr. 8vo. 6s.

Paul of Tarsus. By the Author of 'Rabbi Jeshua.' Cr. 8vo. 4s. 6d.

PAULI, REINHOLD, Simon de Montfort, Earl of Leicester, the Creator of the House of Commons. Cr. 8vo. 6s.

PEMBERTON, T. EDGAR, Charles Dickens and the Stage: a Record of his Connection with the Drama. Cr. 8vo. 6s.

PERRY, ARTHUR LATHAM, Principles of Political Economy. Large post 8vo. 9s.

PESCHEL, OSCAR, The Races of Man and their Geographical Distribution. Second Edition. Large cr. 8vo. 9s.

PETTIGREW, J. B., **Animal Locomotion**; or, Walking, Swimming, and Flying. With 130 Illustrations. Third Edition. Cr. 8vo. 5s. (*I.S.S.*)

PHAYRE, Lieut.-Gen. Sir A., **History of Burma.** Including Burma Proper, Pegu, Taungu, Tenasserim, and Arakan, from the Earliest Time to the end of the First War with British India. Post 8vo. 14s. (*Trübner's Oriental Series.*)

PHAYRE, Lieut.-Gen. Sir A., and THOMAS, E., **Coins of Arakan, of Pegu, and of Burma.** With 5 Illustrations. Royal 4to. 8s. 6d. (*Numismata Orientalia.*)

PHILLIPS, Col. A. N., **Hindustani Idioms.** With Vocabulary and Explanatory Notes. Cr. 8vo. 5s.

PHILLIPS, W., **Manual of British Discomycetes.** With Descriptions of all the Species of Fungi hitherto found in Britain included in the Family, and Illustrations of the Genera. Cr. 8vo. 5s. (*I.S.S.*)

'PHYSICUS,' **Candid Examination of Theism.** Third Edition. Post 8vo. 7s. 6d. (*Philosophical Library.*)

PICARD, A., **Pocket Dictionary of the Dutch Language.** Fifth Edition. 16mo. 10s.

PICKFORD, JOHN, **Maha-vira-Charita**; or, the Adventures of the Great Hero Rama. From the Sanskrit of BHAVABHÚTI. Cr. 8vo. 5s.

PIESSE, C. H., **Chemistry in the Brewing Room**: a Course of Lessons to Practical Brewers. Fcp. 8vo. 5s.

PILCHER, J. E., **First Aid in Illness and Injury.** With 174 Illustrations. Cr. 8vo. 6s.

PLOWRIGHT, C. B., **British Uredineæ and Ustilagineæ.** With Illustrations. 8vo. 10s. 6d.

PLUMPTRE, C. J., **Lectures on Elocution**, delivered at King's College. Fourth Edition. Post 8vo. 15s.

POE, EDGAR ALLAN, **Poems.** Edited by ANDREW LANG. With Frontispiece. Elzevir 8vo. vellum, 7s. 6d.; parchment or cloth, 6s. (*Parchment Library.*)

    The Raven. With Commentary by JOHN H. INGRAM. Cr. 8vo. parchment, 6s.

POLE, W., **Philosophy of Music.** Lectures delivered at the Royal Institution. Third Edition. Post 8vo. 7s. 6d. (*Philosophical Library.*)

POLLEN, JOHN, **Rhymes from the Russian.** Translations from the best Russian Poets. Cr. 8vo. 3s. 6d.

PONSARD, F., **Charlotte Corday:** a Tragedy. Edited by Professor C. CASSAL. Fourth Edition. 12mo. 2s. 6d.

    L'Honneur et l'Argent: a Comedy. Edited by Professor C. CASSAL. Fourth Edition. 12mo. 3s. 6d.

PONTOPIDDAN, HENRIK, **The Apothecary's Daughters.** Translated from the Danish by GORDIUS NIELSEN. Cr. 8vo. 3s. 6d.

POOLE, STANLEY LANE, **The Numismata Orientalia.** Part II. Coins of the Urtuki Turkumáns. With 6 Plates. Royal 4to. Paper wrapper, 9s.

POOLE, W. F., **Index to Periodical Literature.** Revised Edition. Royal 8vo. £3. 13s. 6d. net. FIRST SUPPLEMENT, 1882 to 1887. Royal 8vo. £2 net. SECOND SUPPLEMENT, 1887 to 1892. Royal 8vo. £2 net.

POSNETT, H. M., **Comparative Literature.** Crown 8vo. 5s. (*I.S.S.*)

POULTON, E. B., **Colours of Animals**: their Meaning and Use, especially considered in the case of Insects. With Coloured Frontispiece and 66 Illustrations in Text. Cr. 8vo. 5s. (*I.S.S.*)

Practical Guides, to see all that ought to be seen in the shortest period and at the least expense. 113th Thousand, Illustrated. Sm. 8vo. paper covers. France, Belgium, Holland, and the Rhine, 1s. Italian Lakes, 1s. Wintering Places of the South, 2s. Switzerland, Savoy, and North Italy, 2s. 6d. General Continental Guide, 5s. Geneva, 1s. Paris, 1s. Bernese Oberland, 1s. Italy, 4s.

PRATT, GEORGE, Grammar and Dictionary of the Samoan Language. Second Edition. Cr. 8vo. 18s.

PRATT, Lieut.-Colonel S. C., Field Artillery: its Equipment, Organisation, and Tactics. Fourth Edition. Sm. cr. 8vo. 6s. (*Military Handbooks.*)

    Military Law: its Procedure and Practice. Seventh revised Edition. Sm. cr. 8vo. 4s. 6d. (*Military Handbooks.*)

PREL, CARL DU, Philosophy of Mysticism. Translated from the German by C. C. Massey. 2 vols. 8vo. cloth, 25s.

PRICE, Prof. BONAMY, Chapters on Practical Political Economy. New Edition. Cr. 8vo. 5s.

PRIG, The Prigment: 'The Life of a Prig,' 'Prig's Bede,' 'How to Make a Saint,' 'Black is White.' Second Edition. In 1 vol. Cr. 8vo. 5s.

    A Romance of the Recusants. Cr. 8vo. 5s.

    Dulce Domum. Fcap. 8vo. 5s.

    Black is White; or, Continuity Continued. Second Edition. Fcp. 8vo. 3s. 6d.

    Prig's Bede: the Venerable Bede Expurgated, Expounded, and Exposed. Second Edition. Fcp. 8vo. 3s. 6d.

    Riches or Ruin. Fcp. 8vo. 3s. 6d.

    Egosophy. Fcp. 8vo. 3s. 6d.

PRIOR, MATTHEW, Selected Poems. Edited by Austin Dobson. Elzevir 8vo. vellum, 7s. 6d.; parchment or cloth, 6s. (*Parchment Library.*)

PROTHERO, G. W., Henry Bradshaw: a Memoir, with Portrait and Facsimile. 8vo. 16s.

Psalms of the West. Second Edition. Sm. 8vo. 1s. 6d.

Pulpit Commentary, The (Old Testament Series). Edited by the Very Rev. Dean H. D. M. Spence, D.D., and the Rev. J. S. Exell. Super royal 8vo.

    Genesis, by the Rev. T. Whitelaw, D.D.; Homilies by the Very Rev. J. F. Montgomery, D.D., Rev. Prof. R. A. Redford, Rev. F. Hastings, Rev. W. Roberts; Introduction to the Study of the Old Testament, by Ven. Archdeacon Farrar, D.D.; Introductions to the Pentateuch, by the Right Rev. H. Cotterill, D.D., and Rev. T. Whitelaw, D.D. Ninth Edition. 15s.

    Exodus, by the Rev. Canon Rawlinson; Homilies by the Rev. J. Orr, D.D., Rev. D. Young, Rev. C. A. Goodhart, Rev. J. Urquhart, and the Rev. H. T. Robjohns. Fifth Edition. 2 vols. 9s. each.

    Leviticus, by the Rev. Prebendary Meyrick; Introductions by the Rev. R. Collins, Rev. Professor A. Cave; Homilies by the Rev. Prof. Redford, Rev. J. A. Macdonald, Rev. W. Clarkson, Rev. S. R. Aldridge, and Rev. McCheyne Edgar. Fifth Edition. 15s.

    Numbers, by the Rev. R. Winterbotham; Homilies by the Rev. Prof. W. Binnie, D.D., Rev. E. S. Prout, Rev. D. Young, Rev. J. Waite; Introduction by the Rev. Thomas Whitelaw, D.D. Fifth Edition. 15s.

    Deuteronomy, by the Rev. W. L. Alexander, D.D.; Homilies by the Rev. C. Clemance, D.D., Rev. J. Orr, D.D., Rev. R. M. Edgar, Rev. J. D. Davies. Fourth Edition. 15s.

    Joshua, by the Rev. J. J. Lias; Homilies by the Rev. S. R. Aldridge, Rev. R. Glover, Rev. E. de Pressensé, D.D., Rev. J. Waite, Rev. W. F. Adeney; Introduction by the Rev. A. Plummer, D.D. Sixth Edition. 12s. 6d.

    Judges and Ruth, by the Bishop of Bath and Wells, and Rev. J. Morison, D.D.; Homilies by the Rev. A. F. Muir, Rev. W. F. Adeney, Rev. W. M. Statham, and Rev. Prof. J. Thomson. Fifth Edition. 10s. 6d.

    1 and 2 Samuel, by the Very Rev. R. Payne Smith, D.D.; Homilies by the Rev. Donald Fraser, D.D., Rev. Prof. Chapman, Rev. B. Dale, and Rev. G. Wood. Seventh Edition. 2 vols. 15s. each.

Pulpit Commentary, The (Old Testament Series)—

1 Kings, by the Rev. JOSEPH HAMMOND; Homilies by the Rev. E. DE PRESSENSÉ, D.D., Rev. J. WAITE, Rev. A. ROWLAND, Rev. J. A. MACDONALD, and Rev. J. URQUHART. Fifth Edition. 15s.

2 Kings, by the Rev. Canon RAWLINSON; Homilies by the Rev. J. ORR, D.D., Rev. D. THOMAS, D.D., and Rev. C. H. IRWIN. Second Edition. 15s.

1 Chronicles, by the Rev. Prof. P. C. BARKER; Homilies by the Rev. Prof. J. R. THOMSON, Rev. R. TUCK, Rev. W. CLARKSON, Rev. F. WHITFIELD, and Rev. RICHARD GLOVER. Second Edition. 15s.

2 Chronicles, by the Rev. PHILIP C. BARKER; Homilies by the Rev. W. CLARKSON and Rev. T. WHITELAW, D.D. Second Edition. 15s.

Ezra, Nehemiah, and Esther, by the Rev. Canon G. RAWLINSON. Homilies by the Rev. Prof. J. R. THOMSON, Rev. Prof. R. A. REDFORD, Rev. W. S. LEWIS, Rev. J. A. MACDONALD, Rev. A. MACKENNAL, Rev. W. CLARKSON, Rev. F. HASTINGS, Rev. W. DINWIDDIE, Rev. Prof. ROWLANDS, Rev. G. WOOD, Rev. Prof. P. C. BARKER, and the Rev. J. S. EXELL. Seventh Edition. 12s. 6d.

Job, by the Rev. Canon G. RAWLINSON. Homilies by the Rev. T. WHITELAW, D.D., the Rev. Prof. E. JOHNSON, the Rev. Prof. W. F. ADENEY, and the Rev. R. GREEN. 21s.

Proverbs, by the Rev. W. J. DEANE and the Rev. S. T. TAYLOR-TASWELL. Homilies by the Rev. Prof. W. F. ADENEY, the Rev. Prof. E. JOHNSON, and the Rev. W. CLARKSON. Second Edition. 15s.

Ecclesiastes and Song of Solomon, by the Rev. W. J. DEANE and Rev. Prof. R. A. REDFORD. Homilies by the Rev. T. WHITELAW, D.D., Rev. B. C. CAFFIN, Rev. Prof. J. R. THOMSON, Rev. S. CONWAY, Rev. D. DAVIES, Rev. W. CLARKSON, and Rev. J. WILLCOCK. 21s.

Isaiah, by the Rev. Canon G. RAWLINSON; Homilies by the Rev. Prof. E. JOHNSON, Rev. W. CLARKSON, Rev. W. M. STATHAM, and Rev. R. TUCK. Third Edition. 2 vols. 15s. each.

Jeremiah and Lamentations, by the Rev. Canon T. K. CHEYNE, D.D.; Homilies by the Rev. Prof. J. R. THOMSON, Rev. W. F. ADENEY, Rev. A. F. MUIR, Rev. S. CONWAY, Rev. D. YOUNG, Rev. J. WAITE. 2 vols. Fourth Edition. 15s. each.

Ezekiel, by the Very Rev. E. H. PLUMPTRE, D.D. Homilies by the Rev. Prof. W. F. ADENEY, the Rev. Prof. J. R. THOMSON, the Rev. J. D. DAVIES, the Rev. W. JONES, and the Rev. W. CLARKSON. Introduction by the Rev. T. WHITELAW, D.D. 2 vols. 12s. 6d. each.

Hosea and Joel, by the Rev. Prof. J. J. GIVEN, D.D.; Homilies by the Rev. Prof. J. R. THOMSON, Rev. A. ROWLAND, Rev. C. JERDAN, Rev. J. ORR, D.D., and Rev. D. THOMAS, D.D. Second Edition. 15s.

Amos, Obadiah, Jonah, and Micah, by the Rev. W. J. DEANE; Homilies by the Rev. J. EDGAR HENRY, Rev. Prof. J. R. THOMSON, Rev. S. D. HILLMAN, Rev. A. ROWLAND, Rev. D. THOMAS, Rev. A. C. THISELTON, Rev. E. S. PROUT, Rev. G. T. COSTER, Rev. W. G. BLAIKIE. 15s.

Pulpit Commentary, The (New Testament Series). Edited by the Very Rev. H. D. M. SPENCE, D.D., and Rev. JOSEPH S. EXELL.

St. Matthew, by the Rev. A. L. WILLIAMS. Homilies by the Rev. B. C. CAFFIN, Rev. Prof. W. F. ADENEY, Rev. P. C. BARKER, Rev. M. DODS, D.D., Rev. J. A. MACDONALD, and Rev. R. TUCK.

St. Mark, by the Very Rev. Dean E. BICKERSTETH, D.D.; Homilies by the Rev. Prof. J. R. THOMSON, Rev. Prof. J. J. GIVEN, D.D., Rev. Prof. E. JOHNSON, Rev. A. ROWLAND, Rev. A. F. MUIR, and Rev. R. GREEN. Sixth Edition. 2 vols. 10s. 6d. each.

St. Luke, by the Very Rev. Dean H. D. M. SPENCE; Homilies by the Rev. J. MARSHALL LANG, D.D., Rev. W. CLARKSON, and Rev. R. M. EDGAR. Second Edition. 2 vols. 10s. 6d. each.

St. John, by the Rev. Prof. H. R. REYNOLDS, D.D.; Homilies by the Rev. Prof. T. CROSKERY, D.D., Rev. Prof. J. R. THOMSON, Rev. D. YOUNG, Rev. B. THOMAS, and Rev. G. BROWN. Third Edition. 2 vols. 15s. each.

Pulpit Commentary, The (New Testament Series)—

    The Acts of the Apostles, by the Right Rev. Bishop of BATH and WELLS; Homilies by the Rev. Prof. P. C. BARKER, Rev. Prof. E. JOHNSON, Rev. Prof. R. A. REDFORD, Rev. R. TUCK, Rev. W. CLARKSON. Fifth Edition. 2 vols. 10s. 6d. each.

    Romans, by the Rev. J. BARMBY; Homilies by Rev. Prof. J. R. THOMSON, Rev. C. H. IRWIN, Rev. T. F. LOCKYER, Rev. S. R. ALDRIDGE, and Rev. R. M. EDGAR. 15s.

    Corinthians and Galatians, by the Ven. Archdeacon FARRAR, D.D., and Rev. Prebendary E. HUXTABLE; Homilies by the Rev. Ex-Chancellor LIPSCOMB, Rev. DAVID THOMAS, D.D., Rev. DONALD FRASER, D.D., Rev. R. TUCK, Rev. E. HURNDALL, Rev. Prof. J. R. THOMSON, Rev. R. FINLAYSON, Rev. W. F. ADENEY, Rev. R. M. EDGAR, and Rev. T. CROSKERY, D.D. 2 vols. Vol I., containing I. Corinthians, Fifth Edition, 15s. Vol. II., containing Corinthians and Galatians, Second Edition, 21s.

    Ephesians, Philippians, and Colossians, by the Rev. Prof. W. G. BLAIKIE, D.D., Rev. B. C. CAFFIN, and Rev. G. G. FINDLAY; Homilies by the Rev. D. THOMAS, D.D., Rev. R. M. EDGAR, Rev. R. FINLAYSON, Rev. W. F. ADENEY, Rev. Prof. T. CROSKERY, D.D., Rev. E. S. PROUT, Rev. Canon VERNON HUTTON, and Rev. U. R. THOMAS, D.D. Third Edition. 21s.

    Thessalonians, Timothy, Titus, and Philemon, by the Right Rev. Bishop of BATH and WELLS, Rev. Dr. GLOAG, and Rev. Dr. EALES; Homilies by the Rev. B. C. CAFFIN, Rev. R. FINLAYSON, Rev. Prof. T. CROSKERY, D.D., Rev. W. F. ADENEY, Rev. W. M. STATHAM, and Rev. D. THOMAS, D.D. Second Edition. 15s.

    Hebrews and James, by the Rev. J. BARMBY, and Rev. Prebendary E. C. S. GIBSON; Homilies by the Rev. C. JERDAN and Rev. Prebendary E. C. S. GIBSON, Rev. W. JONES, Rev. C. NEW, Rev. D. YOUNG, Rev. J. S. BRIGHT, and Rev. T. F. LOCKYER. Third Edition. 15s.

    Peter, John, and Jude, by the Rev. B. C. CAFFIN, Rev. A. PLUMMER, D.D., and Rev. Prof. S. D. F. SALMOND, D.D.; Homilies by the Rev. A. MACLAREN, D.D., Rev. C. CLEMANCE, D.D., Rev. Prof. J. R. THOMSON, Rev. C. NEW, Rev. U. R. THOMAS, Rev. R. FINLAYSON, Rev. W. JONES, Rev. Prof. T. CROSKERY, D.D., and Rev. J. S. BRIGHT, D.D. Second Edition. 15s.

    Revelation. Introduction by the Rev. T RANDELL, principal of Bede College, Durham. Exposition by the Rev. A. PLUMMER, D.D., assisted by Rev. T. RANDELL and A. T. BOTT. Homilies by the Rev. C. CLEMANCE, D.D., Rev. S. CONWAY, Rev. R. GREEN, and Rev. D. THOMAS, D.D. Second Edition. 15s.

PUSEY. Sermons for the Church's Seasons from Advent to Trinity. Selected from the published Sermons of the late EDWARD BOUVERIE PUSEY, D.D. Cr. 8vo. 5s.

PYE, W., Surgical Handicraft: a Manual of Surgical Manipulations, &c. With 235 Illustrations. Third Edition, Revised and Edited by T. H. R. CROWLE. Cr. 8vo. 10s. 6d.

    Elementary Bandaging and Surgical Dressing, for the use of Dressers and Nurses. Twelfth Thousand. 18mo. 2s.

Public Schools (Our): Eton, Harrow, Winchester, Rugby, Westminster, Marlborough, and The Charterhouse. Cr. 8vo. 6s.

QUATREFAGES, Prof. A. de, The Human Species. Fifth Edition. Cr. 8vo. 5s. (I.S.S.)

QUINCEY, DE, Confessions of an English Opium Eater. Edited by RICHARD GARNETT. Elzevir 8vo. vellum, 7s. 6d.; parchment or cloth, 6s. (*Parchment Library.*)

RALSTON, W. R. S., Tibetan Tales, derived from Indian Sources. Done into English from the German of F. ANTON VON SCHIEFNER. Post 8vo. 14s. (*Trübner's Oriental Series.*)

Rare Poems of the 16th and 17th Centuries. Edited by W. J. LINTON. Cr. 8vo. 5s.

RASK, ERASMUS, Grammar of the Anglo-Saxon Tongue. From the Danish, by B. THORPE. Third Edition. Post 8vo, 5s. 6d.

READE, WINWOOD, The Martyrdom of Man. Fourteenth Edition. Cr. 8vo. 7s. 6d.

REANEY, Mrs. G. S., Waking and Working; or, From Girlhood to Womanhood. New and Cheaper Edition, with Frontispiece. Cr. 8vo. 3s. 6d.

    Blessing and Blessed: a Sketch of Girl Life. New and Cheaper Edition. Cr. 8vo. 3s. 6d.

    Rose Gurney's Discovery: a Story for Girls, dedicated to their Mothers. Cr. 8vo. 3s. 6d.

    English Girls: their Place and Power. With Preface by the Rev. R. W. DALE. Fifth Edition. Fcp. 8vo. 2s. 6d.

    Just Anyone, and other Stories. With 3 Illustrations. 16mo. 1s. 6d.

    Sunbeam Willie, and other Stories. With 3 Illustrations. 16mo. 1s. 6d.

    Sunshine Jenny, and other Stories. With 3 Illustrations. 16mo. 1s. 6d.

REDHOUSE, J. W., Simplified Grammar of the Ottoman-Turkish Language. Cr. 8vo. 10s. 6d.

    Turkish Vade-Mecum of Ottoman Colloquial Language. English-Turkish and Turkish-English, the whole in English Characters, the Pronunciation being fully indicated. Third Edition. 32mo. 6s.

    The Mesnevi (usually known as the Mesneviyi Sherif, or Holy Mesnevi) of Mevlānā (Our Lord) Jelālu'd-Din Muhammed Er-Rūmi. Illustrated by a selection of Characteristic Anecdotes. Post 8vo. £1. 1s. (*Trübner's Oriental Series.*)

    History, System, and Varieties of Turkish Poetry. Illustrated by Selections in the original English Paraphrase. 8vo. 2s. 6d.

    Tentative Chronological Synopsis of the History of Arabia and its Neighbours, from B.C. 500,000 (?) to A.D. 679. 8vo. 2s.

REES, J. D., H.R.H. The Duke of Clarence and Avondale in Southern India. With a Narrative of Elephant Catching in Mysore, by G. P. SANDERSON. With Map, Portraits, and Illustrations. Medium 8vo. 31s. 6d.

    Lord Connemara's Tours in India, 1886-1890. 8vo. 15s.

RENAN, ERNEST, Age and Antiquity of the Book of Nabathæan Agriculture. Cr. 8vo. 3s. 6d.

    Life of Jesus. Cr. 8vo. 1s. 6d.; paper covers, 1s.

    The Apostles. Cr. 8vo. 1s. 6d.; paper covers, 1s.

RENDELL, J. M., Handbook of the Island of Madeira. With Plan and Map. Second Edition. Fcp. 8vo. 1s. 6d.

REYNOLDS, J. W., The Supernatural in Nature: a Verification by Free Use of Science. Third Edition, Revised and Enlarged. 8vo. 14s.

    Mystery of the Universe our Common Faith. 8vo. 14s.

    Mystery of Miracles. Third Edition, Enlarged. Cr. 8vo. 6s.

    The World to Come: Immortality a Physical Fact. Cr. 8vo. 6s.

REYNOLDS, Sir JOSHUA, Discourses. Edited by E. GOSSE. Elzevir 8vo. vellum, 7s. 6d.; parchment or cloth, 6s. (*Parchment Library.*)

RHOIDIS, EMMANUEL, Pope Joan: an Historical Study. From the Greek by C. H. COLLETTE. 12mo. 2s. 6d.

RHYS, JOHN, Lectures on Welsh Philology. Second Edition. Cr. 8vo. 15s.

RIBOT, Prof. Th., **Diseases of Memory:** an Essay in the Positive Psychology. Third Edition. Cr. 8vo. 5s. (*I.S.S.*)
 Heredity: a Psychological Study of its Phenomena, Laws, Causes, and Consequences. Second Edition. Large cr. 8vo. 9s.
 English Psychology. Cr. 8vo. 7s. 6d.
RICHARD, Ap, **Marriage and Divorce.** Including the Religious, Practical, and Political Aspects of the Question. Cr. 8vo. 5s.
RICHARDSON, AUSTIN, '**What are the Catholic Claims?**' With Introduction by Rev. LUKE RIVINGTON. Cr. 8vo. 3s. 6d.
RICHARDSON, M. T., **Practical Blacksmithing.** With 400 Illustrations. 4 vols. Cr. 8vo. 5s. each.
 Practical Horse-shoer. With 170 Illustrations. Cr 8vo. 5s.
RICHTER, Prof. VICTOR von, **Text-book of Inorganic Chemistry.** Authorised Translation. By EDGAR F. SMITH. Third American Edition, from the Fifth German Edition. Cr. 8vo. 8s. 6d.
 Chemistry of the Carbon Compounds; or, Organic Chemistry. Authorised Translation. By EDGAR F. SMITH. Second American Edition, from the Sixth German Edition. Cr. 8vo. 20s.
RIOLA, HENRY, **How to learn Russian**: a Manual for Students. Based upon the Ollendorffian System. Fourth Edition. Cr. 8vo. 12s. Key, 5s.
 Russian Reader. With Vocabulary. Cr. 8vo. 10s. 6d.
RIVINGTON, LUKE, **Authority**; or, A Plain Reason for Joining the Church of Rome. Sixth Edition. Cr. 8vo. 3s. 6d.
 Dependence; or, The Insecurity of the Anglican Position. Cr. 8vo. 5s.
 The English Martyrs. Sewed, 6d.
 The Church Visible. Sewed, 6d.
 The Appeal to History: a Letter to the Bishop of Lincoln. Sewed, 6d.
ROBERTS, H., **Grammar of the Khassi Language.** Cr. 8vo. 10s. 6d.
ROBERTSON, F. W., **Life and Letters.** Edited by STOPFORD BROOKE.
  I. Library Edition. With Portrait. 8vo. 12s.
  II. Two vols. With Portrait. Cr. 8vo. 7s. 6d.
  III. Popular Edition. Cr. 8vo. 6s.
 Sermons. 5 vols. Sm. 8vo. 3s. 6d. each.
 Notes on Genesis. New and Cheaper Edition. Sm. 8vo. 3s. 6d.
 St. Paul's Epistles to the Corinthians: Expository Lectures. New Edition. Sm. 8vo. 5s.
 Lectures and Addresses. With other Literary Remains. New Edition. Sm. 8vo. 5s.
 Analysis of Tennyson's 'In Memoriam.' Dedicated by Permission to the Poet-Laureate. Fcp. 8vo. 2s.
 Education of the Human Race. Translated from the German of GOTTHOLD EPHRAIM LESSING. Fcp. 8vo. 2s. 6d.
 ** Portrait of the late Rev. F. W. Robertson, mounted for framing, 2s. 6d.
ROBINSON, A. MARY F., **The Fortunate Lovers.** Twenty-seven Novels of the Queen of Navarre. Frontispiece by G. P. JACOMB HOOD. Large cr. 8vo. 10s. 6d.
 The Crowned Hippolytus. Sm. cr. 8vo. 5s.
ROBINSON, E. FORBES, **The Early History of Coffee Houses in England.** With Illustrations. Cr. 8vo. 6s.
ROCHE, A., **French Grammar.** Adopted by the Imperial Council of Public Instruction. Cr. 8vo. 3s.
 Prose and Poetry, from English Authors. For Reading, Composition, and Translation. Second Edition. Fcp. 8vo. 2s. 6d.
ROCKHILL, W. W., **Life of the Buddha and the Early History of his Order.** Derived from Tibetan Works in the Bkah-Hgyur and the Bstan-Hgyur. Post 8vo. 9s. (*Trübner's Oriental Series.*)
 UDANAVARGA: a Collection of Verses from the Buddhist Canon. Compiled by DHARMATRĀTA and Translated from the Tibetan. Post 8vo. 9s. (*Trübner's Oriental Series.*)

Kegan Paul, Trench, Trübner, & Co.'s Publications. 43

RODD, E. H., Birds of Cornwall and the Scilly Islands. Edited by J. E. HARTING. With Portrait and Map. 8vo. 14s.

ROGERS, E. T., The Numismata Orientalia. Part IV. The Coins of the Tulun Dynasty. With 1 Plate. Royal 4to. Paper wrapper, 5s.

ROGERS, WILLIAM, Reminiscences. Compiled by R. H. HADDEN. With Portrait. Cr. 8vo. 6s.; Cheap Edition, 2s. 6d.

ROMANES, G. J., Mental Evolution in Animals. With Posthumous Essay on Instinct by CHARLES DARWIN. 8vo. 12s.

 Mental Evolution in Man: Origin of the Human Faculty. 8vo. 14s.
 Animal Intelligence. Fourth Edition. Cr. 8vo. 5s. (*I.S.S.*)
 Jelly-Fish, Star-Fish, and Sea-Urchins: being a Research on Primitive Nervous Systems. With Illustrations. Second Edition. Cr. 8vo. 5s. (*I.S.S.*)

ROOD, OGDEN N., Colour: a Text-book of Modern Chromatics. With Applications to Art and Industry. With 130 Original Illustrations. Third Edition. Cr. 8vo. 5s. (*I.S.S.*)

ROOT, A. I., The A B C of Bee Culture. A Cyclopædia of everything pertaining to the care of the Honey Bee. Illustrated. Royal 8vo. 7s. 6d.

ROOSEVELT, BLANCHE, Victorien Sardon: a Personal Study. Fcp. 8vo. 3s. 6d.

ROOSEVELT, THEODORE, Hunting Trips of a Ranchman. With 26 Illustrations. Royal 8vo. 18s.

ROSENTHAL, Prof. J., General Physiology of Muscles and Nerves. Third Edition. With 75 Illustrations. Cr. 8vo. 5s. (*I.S.S.*)

ROSING, S., Danish Dictionary. Cr. 8vo. 8s. 6d.

ROSS, JANET, Italian Sketches. With 14 full-page Illustrations. Cr. 8vo. 7s. 6d.

ROSS, PERCY, A Professor of Alchemy. Cr. 8vo. 3s. 6d.

ROSS, Lieut.-Col. W. A., Alphabetical Manual of Blowpipe Analysis. Cr. 8vo. 5s.

 Pyrology, or Fire Chemistry. Sm. 4to. 36s.

ROUTLEDGE, Canon C. F., History of St. Martin's Church, Canterbury. Cr. 8vo. 5s.

ROUTLEDGE, JAMES, English Rule and Native Opinion in India. 8vo. 10s. 6d.

ROWLEY, A. C., The Christ in the Two Testaments. With an Introduction by the BISHOP OF LINCOLN. Cr. 8vo. 2s.

RULE, MARTIN, Life and Times of St. Anselm, Archbishop of Canterbury and Primate of the Britains. 2 vols. 8vo. 32s.

ST. CLAIR, GEORGE, Buried Cities and Bible Countries. Second Edition. Large cr. 8vo. 7s. 6d.

SAINTSBURY G., Specimens of English Prose Style from Malory to Macaulay. Selected and Annotated. With Introductory Essay. Large cr. 8vo. Printed on hand-made paper. Vellum, 15s.; parchment antique or cloth, 12s.

SALAMAN, J. S., Trade Marks: their Registration and Protection. Cr. 8vo. 5s.

SALMONÉ, H. A., Arabic-English Dictionary, comprising about 120,000 Arabic Words, with English Index of about 50,000 Words. 2 vols. post 8vo. 36s.

SAMUELSON, JAMES, Bulgaria, Past and Present: Historical, Political, and Descriptive. With Map and numerous Illustrations. 8vo. 10s. 6d.

SANDWITH, F. M., Egypt as a Winter Resort. Cr. 8vo. 3s. 6d.

SANTIAGOE, DANIEL, Curry Cook's Assistant. Fcp. 8vo. 1s. 6d.; paper covers, 1s.

SAYCE, A. H., Introduction to the Science of Language. New and Cheaper Edition. 2 vols. cr. 8vo. 9s.

— The Principles of Comparative Philology. Fourth Edition, revised and enlarged. Cr. 8vo. 10s. 6d.

SCANNELL, THOMAS B., and WILHELM, JOSEPH, D.D., Manual of Catholic Theology, based on SCHEEBEN'S 'Dogmatik.' Vol. I. 15s.

SCHAW, Col. H., Defence and Attack of Positions and Localities. Fifth Edition. Cr. 8vo. 3s. 6d.

SCHLAGINTWEIT, EMIL, Buddhism in Tibet. Illustrated by Literary Documents and Objects of Religious Worship. With 20 Plates. 2 vols. roy. 8vo. and folio, £2. 2s.

SCHLEICHER, AUGUST, Comparative Grammar of the Indo-European, Sanskrit, Greek, and Latin Languages. From the Third German Edition by H. BENDALL. 8vo. 13s. 6d.

SCHLEIERMACHER, F., On Religion: Speeches to its Cultured Despisers. Translated, with Introduction, by J. OMAN. 8vo. 7s. 6d.

SCHMIDT, Prof. O., Doctrine of Descent and Darwinism. With 26 Illustrations. Seventh Edition. Cr. 8vo. 5s. (I.S.S.)

— Mammalia in their Relation to Primeval Times. With 51 Woodcuts. Cr. 8vo. 5s. (I.S.S.)

SCHOOLING, J. HOLT, Handwriting and Expression: a Study of Written Gesture, with 150 Facsimile Reproductions of the Handwritings of Men and Women of various Nationalities. Translated. 8vo. 6s.

SCHOPENHAUER, A., The World as Will and Idea. From the German by R. B. HALDANE and J. KEMP. Third Edition. 3 vols. post 8vo. £2. 12s. (*Philosophical Library.*)

SCHÜTZENBERGER, Prof., Fermentation. With 28 Illustrations. Fourth Edition. Cr. 8vo. 5s. (I.S.S.)

SCHWENDLER, LOUIS, Instructions for Testing Telegraph Lines. 2 vols. 8vo. 21s.

SCOONES, W. B., Four Centuries of English Letters: a Selection of 350 Letters by 150 Writers, from the period of the Paston Letters to the Present Time. Third Edition. Large cr. 8vo. 6s.

SCOTT, JAMES GEORGE, Burma as it Was, as it Is, and as it Will Be. Cheap Edition. Cr. 8vo. 2s. 6d.

SCOTT, ROBERT H., Elementary Meteorology. Fifth Edition. With numerous Illustrations. Cr. 8vo. 5s. (I.S.S.)

SEDDING, JOHN D., Gardencraft, Old and New. With Memorial Notice by the Rev. E. F. RUSSELL. 16 Illustrations. Second Edition. 8vo. 12s.

— Art and Handicraft. Six Essays. 8vo. 7s. 6d.

SELBY, H. M., Shakespeare Classical Dictionary; or, Mythological Allusions in the Plays of Shakespeare explained. Fcap. 8vo. 1s.

SEMPER, KARL, Natural Conditions of Existence as they affect Animal Life. With 2 Maps and 106 Woodcuts. Fourth Edition. Cr. 8vo. 5s. (I.S.S.)

SERJEANT, W. C. ELDON, The Astrologer's Guide (Anima Astrologiæ). 8vo. 7s. 6d.

SEVERNE, FLORENCE, The Pillar House. With Frontispiece. Cr. 8vo. 6s.

SEYMOUR, W. DIGBY, Home Rule and State Supremacy. Cr. 8vo. 3s. 6d.

SHAKSPERE. WORKS. Avon Edition. In One Volume. With Glossarial Index. Super roy. 8vo. 7s. 6d.

    Works. Avon Edition. 12 vols. Elzevir 8vo. (*Parchment Library*), vellum, 7s. 6d. per vol.; parchment or cloth, 6s. per vol.; Cheap Edition, 1s. 6d. per vol.

    *** The Cheap Edition may also be had complete, 12 vols. in cloth box, 21s., or bound in 6 vols. 15s.

    Works. New Variorum Edition. Edited by HORACE HOWARD FURNESS. Roy. 8vo. Vol. I. Romeo and Juliet, 18s. Vol. II. Macbeth, 18s. Vols. III. and IV. Hamlet, 2 vols. 36s. Vol. V. King Lear, 18s. Vol. VI. Othello, 18s. Vol. VII. Merchant of Venice, 18s. Vol. VIII. As You Like It, 18s.

    Concordance to Shakspere's Poems. By Mrs. FURNESS. Roy. 8vo. 18s.

    Sonnets. Edited by EDWARD DOWDEN. With Frontispiece. Elzevir 8vo. (*Parchment Library*), vellum, 7s. 6d.; parchment or cloth, 6s.

SHAW, FLORA L., Castle Blair: a Story of Youthful Days. Cr. 8vo. 3s. 6d.

SHAW, Lieut.-Col. WILKINSON, Elements of Modern Tactics practically applied to English Formations. Seventh Edition. With 31 Plates and Maps. Small cr. 8vo. 9s. (*Military Handbooks*.)

SHELLEY. Life of P. B. Shelley. By EDWARD DOWDEN, LL.D. With Portraits. 2 vols. 8vo. 36s.

    Poems. Edited, with Preface, by RICHARD GARNETT. Frontispiece. Elzevir 8vo. vellum, 7s. 6d.; parchment or cloth, 6s. (*Parchment Library*.)

    Select Letters. Edited by RICHARD GARNETT. Elzevir 8vo. vellum, 7s. 6d.; parchment or cloth, 6s. (*Parchment Library*.)

SHORE. Journal of Emily Shore. With Portrait and Facsimile. Cr. 8vo. 6s.

SIBREE, JAMES, The Great African Island, Madagascar: its Physical Geography, &c. With Maps and Illustrations. 8vo. 10s. 6d.

SIDGWICK, A., Fallacies: a View of Logic from the Practical Side. Second Edition. Cr. 8vo. 5s. (*I.S.S.*)

SIDNEY, Sir PHILIP, Knt., The Countess of Pembroke's Arcadia. Edited by H. OSKAR SOMMER. The original 4to. Edition (1590) in Photographic Facsimile, with Bibliographical Introduction. £2. 2s.

SIMCOX, EDITH, Episodes in the Lives of Men, Women, and Lovers. Cr. 8vo. 7s. 6d.

    Natural Law: an Essay in Ethics. Second Edition. Post 8vo. 10s. 6d. (*Philosophical Library*.)

SIME, JAMES, Lessing: his Life and Writings. Second Edition, with Portraits. 2 vols. Post 8vo. 21s. (*Philosophical Library*.)

SIMONNÉ, Metodo para aprender a Leer Escribir y hablar el Frances, segun el verdadero sistema de Ollendorff. Cr. 8vo. 6s. Key, 3s. 6d.

SIMPSON, M. C. M., Letters and Recollections of Julius and Mary Mohl. With Portraits and 2 Illustrations. 8vo. 15s.

SINGER, I., Simplified Grammar of the Hungarian Language. Cr. 8vo. 4s. 6d.

SINNETT, A. P., The Occult World. Sixth Edition. Cr. 8vo. 3s. 6d.

    Incidents in the Life of Madame Blavatsky. With Portrait. 8vo. 10s. 6d.

    The Rationale of Mesmerism. Cr. 8vo. 3s. 6d.

Sister Augustine. Superior of the Sisters of Charity at the St. Johannis Hospital at Bonn. Translated by HANS THARAU. Cheap Edition. Large cr. 8vo. 4s. 6d.

SKINNER. James Skinner: a Memoir. By the Author of 'Charles Lowder.' With Preface by the Rev. Canon CARTER, and Portrait. Large cr. 8vo. 7s. 6d. Cheap Edition, cr. 8vo. 3s. 6d.

SMITH, A. H., Chinese Characteristics. 8vo. 7s. 6d.

SMITH, E., Foods. With numerous Illustrations. Ninth Edition. Cr. 8vo. 5s. (*I.S.S.*)

SMITH, EDGAR F., Electro-Chemical Analysis. With 25 Illustrations. Square 16mo. 5s.

SMITH, H. PERCY, Glossary of Terms and Phrases. Cheap Edition. Medium 8vo. 3s. 6d.

SMITH, HAMILTON, Hydraulics: the Flow of Water through Orifices, over Weirs, and through open Conduits and Pipes. With 17 plates. Royal 4to. 30s.

SMITH, HUNTINGTON, A Century of American Literature: Benjamin Franklin to James Russell Lowell. Cr. 8vo. 6s.

SMITH, JAMES C., The Distribution of the Produce. Cr. 8vo. 2s. 6d.

SMITH, L. A., The Music of the Waters: Sailors' Chanties and Working Songs of the Sea. Words and Music. 8vo. 12s.

SMITH, M., and HORNEMAN, H., Norwegian Grammar. With a Glossary for Tourists. Post 8vo. 2s.

SMYTH, R. BROUGH, The Aborigines of Victoria. Compiled for the Government. With Maps, Plates, and Woodcuts. 2 vols. royal 8vo. £3. 3s.

SOPHOCLES. The Seven Plays in English Verse. Translated by Prof. LEWIS CAMPBELL. Cr. 8vo. 7s. 6d.

Spanish Mystics. By the Editor of 'Many Voices.' Cr. 8vo. 5s.

Specimens of English Prose Style from Malory to Macaulay. Selected and Annotated. With an Introductory Essay by GEORGE SAINTSBURY. Large cr. 8vo, printed on hand-made paper, vellum, 15s.; parchment antique or cloth, 12s.

SPENCER, HERBERT, Study of Sociology. Fifteenth Edition. Cr. 8vo. 5s. (*I.S.S.*)

SPINOZA. Life, Correspondence, and Ethics of Spinoza. By R. WILLIS. 8vo. 21s.

SPRAGUE, CHARLES E., Handbook of Volapuk, the International Language. Second Edition. Cr. 8vo. 5s.

STALLO, J. B., Concepts and Theories of Modern Physics. Third Edition. Cr. 8vo. 5s. (*I.S.S.*)

STANHOPE, The British Army and our Defensive Position in 1892. Preface by Rt. Hon. E. STANHOPE. Cr. 8vo. 1s.

STARCKE, C. N., The Primitive Family in its Origin and Development. Cr. 8vo. 5s. (*I.S.S.*)

STEBBING, T. R. R., The Naturalist of Cumbrae: a True Story, being the Life of David Robertson. Cr. 8vo. 6s.

    A History of Crustacea. Recent Malacostraca. With numerous Illustrations. Cr. 8vo. 5s. (*I.S.S.*)

STEELE, TH., An Eastern Love-Story: Kusa Játakaya. Cr. 8vo. 6s.

STEVENSON, W. FLEMING, Hymns for the Church and Home. 32mo. 1s.

STEWART, BALFOUR, Conservation of Energy. With 14 Illustrations. Seventh Edition. Cr. 8vo. 5s. (*I.S.S.*)

STONE, J. M., Faithful unto Death: an Account of the Sufferings of the English Franciscans during the 16th and 17th centuries. With Preface by Rev. J. MORRIS, S.J. 8vo. 7s. 6d.

STORR, F., and TURNER, H., Canterbury Chimes; or, Chaucer Tales Re-told to Children. With 6 Illustrations from the Ellesmere Manuscript. Third Edition. Fcap. 8vo. 3s. 6d.

STRACHEY, Sir JOHN, India. With Map. 8vo. 15s.

STRAHAN, S. A. K., Marriage and Disease. A Study of Heredity and the more important Family Degenerations. Cr. 8vo. 6s.

Stray Papers on Education, and Scenes from School Life. By B. H. Second Edition. Sm. cr. 8vo. 3s. 6d.

STRECKER, ADOLPH, Text-book of Organic Chemistry. Edited by Prof. WISLICENUS. Translated and Edited, with Extensive Additions, by W. R. HODGKINSON and A. J. GREENAWAY. Second and Cheaper Edition. 8vo. 12s. 6d.

STREET, J. C., The Hidden Way across the Threshold; or, The Mystery which hath been Hidden for Ages and from Generations. With Plates. Large 8vo. 15s.

STRETTON, HESBA, David Lloyd's Last Will. With 4 Illustrations. New Edition. Royal 16mo, 2s. 6d.

Through a Needle's Eye; a Story. With Frontispiece. Cr. 8vo. 6s.

SULLY, JAMES, Pessimism: a History and a Criticism. Second Edition. 8vo. 10s. 6d.

Illusions: a Psychological Study. Third Edition. Cr. 8vo. 5s. (I.S.S.)

SWINBURNE, ALGERNON CHARLES, A Word for the Navy. (Only 250 copies printed.) Imperial 16mo. paper covers, 5s.

SWINBURNE. Bibliography of A. C. Swinburne, 1857-87. Cr. 8vo. vellum gilt, 6s.

SYMONDS, JOHN ADDINGTON, Vagabunduli Libellus. Cr. 8vo. 6s.

SWIFT, JON., Letters and Journals. Edited by STANLEY LANE-POOLE. Elzevir 8vo. vellum, 7s. 6d.; parchment or cloth, 6s. (*Parchment Library.*)

Prose Writings. Edited by STANLEY LANE-POOLE. With Portrait. Elzevir 8vo. vellum, 7s. 6d.; parchment or cloth, 6s. (*Parchment Library.*)

TARRING, C. J., Elementary Turkish Grammar. Cr. 8vo. 6s.

'TASMA,' A Sydney Sovereign, and other Tales. Crown 8vo. cloth, 6s.

In her Earliest Youth. Cheap Edition. Cr. 8vo. 6s.

TAYLOR, Col. MEADOWS, Seeta: a Novel. With Frontispiece. Cr. 8vo. 6s.

Tippoo Sultaun: a Tale of the Mysore War. With Frontispiece. Cr. 8vo. 6s.

Ralph Darnell. With Frontispiece. Cr. 8vo. 6s.

A Noble Queen. With Frontispiece. Cr. 8vo. 6s.

The Confessions of a Thug. With Frontispiece. Cr. 8vo. 6s.

Tara: a Mahratta Tale. With Frontispiece. Crown 8vo. 6s.

TAYLOR, Canon ISAAC, The Alphabet: an Account of the Origin and Development of Letters. With numerous Tables and Facsimiles. 2 vols. 8vo. 36s.

Leaves from an Egyptian Note-Book. Cr. 8vo. 5s.

TAYLOR, R. WHATELEY COOKE, The Modern Factory System. 8vo. 14s.

TAYLOR, Sir H., Works. 5 vols. Cr. 8vo. 30s.

Philip Van Artevelde. Fcap. 8vo. 3s. 6d.

The Virgin Widow, &c. Fcap. 8vo. 3s. 6d.

The Statesman. Fcap. 8vo. 3s. 6d.

Technological Dictionary of the Terms employed in the Arts and Sciences (Architecture, Engineering, Mechanics, Shipbuilding and Navigation, Metallurgy, Mathematics, &c.), with Preface by KARL KAMARSCH. Fourth Revised Edition. 3 vols. Imperial 8vo.

Vol. I. German-English-French. 12s.
Vol. II. English-German-French. 12s.
Vol. III. French-German-English. 15s.

THACKERAY, S. W., The Land and the Community. Crown 8vo. 3s. 6d.

THACKERAY, W. M., **Essay on the Genius of George Cruickshank.** Reprinted verbatim from the *Westminster Review*. With 40 Illustrations. Royal 8vo. 7s. 6d.

   Sultan Stork, and other Stories and Sketches, 1829–44, now first collected; to which is added the Bibliography of Thackeray. Large 8vo. 10s. 6d.

THOM, J. HAMILTON, **Laws of Life after the Mind of Christ.** Two Series. Fourth Edition. Cr. 8vo. 7s. 6d. each.

THOMAS, E., **The Numismata Orientalia.** Part I. Ancient Indian Weights. With Plates and Map of the India of MANU. Royal 4to. paper wrapper, 9s. 6d.

THOMPSON, E. MAUNDE, **Handbook of Greek and Latin Palæography.** With numerous facsimiles. Cr. 8vo. 5s. (*I.S.S.*)

THOMPSON, Sir H., **Diet in Relation to Age and Activity.** Fcp. 8vo. 1s. 6d.; paper covers, 1s.

   Modern Cremation. Second Edition, revised and enlarged. Cr. 8vo. 2s.; paper covers, 1s.

Through North Wales with a Knapsack. By FOUR SCHOOLMISTRESSES. With a Sketch Map. Sm. 8vo. 2s. 6d.

THURSTON, Prof. R. H., **History of the Growth of the Steam Engine.** With numerous Illustrations. Fourth Edition. Cr. 8vo. 5s. (*I.S.S.*)

   Manual of the Steam Engine. For Engineers and Technical Schools. Parts I. and II. Royal 8vo. 31s. 6d. each Part.

TIELE, Prof. C. P., **Outlines of the History of Religion to the Spread of the Universal Religions.** From the Dutch by J. ESTLIN CARPENTER. Fifth Edition. Post 8vo. 7s. 6d. (*Philosophical Library, and Trübner's Oriental Series.*)

   History of the Egyptian and Mesopotamian Religions. Translated by J. BALLINGAL. Post 8vo. 7s. 6d. (*Trübner's Oriental Series.*)

TIRARD, H. M. and **N.**, **Sketches from a Nile Steamer**, for the use of Travellers in Egypt. With Map and numerous Illustrations. Cr. 8vo. 6s.

TISDALL, W. ST. CLAIR, **Simplified Grammar and Reading Book of the Panjabi Language.** Cr. 8vo. 7s. 6d.

   Simplified Grammar of the Gujarati Language. Cr. 8vo. 10s. 6d.

TOLSTOI, Count LEO, **Christ's Christianity.** Translated from the Russian. Large cr. 8vo. 7s. 6d.

TORCEANU, R., **Simplified Grammar of the Roumanian Language.** Cr. 8vo. 5s.

TORREND, J., **Comparative Grammar of the South African Bantu Languages**, comprising those of Zanzibar, Mozambique, the Zambezi, Kafirland, Benguela, Angola, The Congo, The Ogowe, The Cameroons, the Lake Region, &c. Super-royal 8vo. 25s.

TRANT, WILLIAM, **Trade Unions**: their Origin, Objects, and Efficacy. Sm. 8vo. 1s. 6d.; paper covers, 1s.

TRENCH. **Letters and Memorials of Archbishop Trench.** By the Author of 'Charles Lowder.' With 2 Portraits. 2 vols. 8vo. 21s.

TRENCH, Archbishop, **English Past and Present.** Fourteenth Edition, revised and improved. Fcp. 8vo. 5s.

   On the Study of Words. Twenty-third Edition, revised. Fcp. 8vo. 5s.

   Notes on the Parables of Our Lord. Fifteenth Edition. 8vo. 12s. Cheap Edition, 61st thousand, 7s. 6d.

   Notes on the Miracles of Our Lord. Twelfth Edition. 8vo. 12s.; Cheap Edition, Fourteenth Edition, 7s. 6d.

TRENCH, Archbishop, **Household Book of English Poetry.** Fifth Edition, revised. Extra fcp. 8vo. 5s.

Essay on the Life and Genius of Calderon. With Translations from his 'Life's a Dream' and 'Great Theatre of the World.' Second Edition, revised and improved. Extra fcp. 8vo. 5s. 6d.

Gustavus Adolphus in Germany, and other Lectures on the Thirty Years' War. Fourth Edition, enlarged. Fcp. 8vo. 4s.

Plutarch: His Life, His Lives, and His Morals. Second Edition, enlarged. Fcp. 8vo. 3s. 6d.

Remains of the late Mrs. Richard Trench. Being Selections from her Journals, Letters, and other Papers. Edited by her Son, Archbishop TRENCH. New and Cheaper Edition. With Portraits. 8vo. 6s.

Lectures on Mediæval Church History. Being the substance of Lectures delivered at Queen's College, London. 2nd edition, 8vo. 12s.

Poems. Eleventh Edition. Fcp. 8vo. 7s. 6d. Library Edition. 2 vols. sm. 8vo. 10s.

Proverbs and their Lessons. Eighth Edition, enlarged. Fcp. 8vo. 4s.

Sacred Latin Poetry, chiefly Lyrical. Third Edition, corrected and improved. Fcp. 8vo. 7s.

Select Glossary of English Words used formerly in Senses different from their present. Seventh Edition, revised and enlarged. Fcp. 8vo. 5s.

Brief Thoughts and Meditations on some Passages in Holy Scripture. Third Edition. Cr. 8vo. 3s. 6d.

Commentary on the Epistles to the Seven Churches in Asia. Fifth Edition, revised. 8vo. 8s. 6d.

On the Authorised Version of the New Testament. Second Edition. 8vo. 7s.

Sermons New and Old. Cr. 8vo. 6s.

Westminster and other Sermons. Cr. 8vo. 6s.

The Sermon on the Mount: an Exposition drawn from the Writings of St. Augustine. Fourth Edition, enlarged. 8vo. 10s. 6d.

Shipwrecks of Faith: three Sermons preached before the University of Cambridge. Fcap. 8vo. 2s. 6d.

Studies in the Gospels. Fifth Edition, revised. 8vo. 10s. 6d.

Synonyms of the New Testament. Eleventh Edition, enlarged. 8vo. 12s.

TRENCH, Major-General, **Cavalry in Modern War.** Sm. cr. 8vo. 6s. (*Military Handbooks.*)

TRIMEN, ROLAND, **South African Butterflies:** a Monograph of the Extra-tropical Species. With 12 Coloured Plates. 3 vols. 8vo. £2. 12s. 6d.

TROUESSART, E. L., **Microbes, Ferments, and Moulds.** With 107 Illustrations. Second Edition. Cr. 8vo. 5s. (*I.S.S.*)

TROWBRIDGE, J. M., **The Cider Maker's Handbook:** a Complete Guide for Making and Keeping Pure Cider. Illustrated. Cr. 8vo. 5s.

TRÜBNER'S **Bibliographical Guide to American Literature.** From 1817 to 1857. 8vo. half-bound, 18s.

Catalogue of Dictionaries and Grammars of the Principal Languages and Dialects of the World. Second Edition. 8vo. 5s.

TRUMBULL, H. CLAY, **The Blood-Covenant:** a Primitive Rite and its Bearings on Scripture. Post 8vo. 7s. 6d.

TURNER, C. E., **Count Tolstoï, as Novelist and Thinker.** Lectures delivered at the Royal Institution. Cr. 8vo. 3s. 6d.

Modern Novelists of Russia. Lectures delivered at the Taylor Institution, Oxford. Cr. 8vo. 3s. 6d.

Tyll Owlglass' **Marvellous and Rare Conceits.** Translated by KENNETH MACKENZIE. Illustrated by ALFRED CROWQUILL. 3s. 6d. (*Lotos Series.*)

TYNAN, KATHARINE, Louise de la Vallière, and other Poems. Sm. 8vo. 3s. 6d.
    Shamrocks. Sm. cr. 8vo. 5s.
    Ballads and Lyrics. Sm. cr. 8vo. 5s.
    A Nun: her Friends and her Order. Being a Sketch of the Life of Mother Mary Xaveria Fallon. Second Edition. Cr. 8vo. 5s.

TYNDALL, J., Forms of Water: in Clouds and Rivers, Ice and Glaciers. With 25 Illustrations. Tenth Edition. Cr. 8vo. 5s. (I.S.S.)

TYRRELL, WALTER, Nervous Exhaustion: its Causes, Outcomes, and Treatment. Cr. 8vo. 3s.

UMLAUFT, Prof. F., The Alps. Translated by LOUISA BROUGH. With 110 Illustrations. 8vo. 25s.

Under King Constantine. Cr. 8vo. 6s.

VAN EYS, W., Outlines of Basque Grammar. Cr. 8vo. 3s. 6d.

VAN LAUN, H., Grammar of the French Language. Cr. 8vo. Accidence and Syntax, 4s.; Exercises, 3s. 6d.

VELASQUEZ, M. de la CADENA, Dictionary of the Spanish and English Languages. For the use of Young Learners and Travellers. Cr. 8vo. 6s.
    Pronouncing Dictionary of the Spanish and English Languages. Royal 8vo. £1. 4s.
    New Spanish Reader. Passages from the most approved Authors, with Vocabulary. Post 8vo. 6s.
    Introduction to Spanish Conversation. 12mo. 2s. 6d.

VELASQUEZ and SIMONNE, New Method of Learning the Spanish Language. Adapted to Ollendorff's system. Revised and corrected by Señor VIVAR. Post 8vo. 6s.; Key, 4s.

VIEYRA'S Pocket Dictionary of the Portuguese and English Languages. 2 vols. Post 8vo. 10s.

VIGNOLI, TITO, Myth and Science: an Essay. Third Edition. With Supplementary Note. Cr. 8vo. 5s. (I.S.S.)

VINCENT, FRANK, Around and About South America. Twenty Months of Quest and Query. With Maps, Plans, and 54 Illustrations. Medium 8vo. 21s.

VIRGIL. The Georgics of Virgil. Translated into English Verse by J. RHOADES. Sm. cr. 8vo. Second Edition. 2s. 6d.

VOGEL, HERMANN, Chemistry of Light and Photography. With 100 Illustrations. Fifth Edition. Cr. 8vo. 5s. (I.S.S.)

VOLCKXSOM, E. W. von, Catechism of Elementary Modern Chemistry. Sm. cr. 8vo. 3s.

WAGNER. Richard Wagner's Prose Works. Translated by W. ASHTON ELLIS. Vol. I. The Art Work of the Future &c. 8vo. 12s. 6d.

WAITE, A. E., Lives of Alchemystical Philosophers. 8vo. 10s. 6d.
    Magical Writings of Thomas Vaughan. Sm. 4to. 10s. 6d.
    Real History of the Rosicrucians. With Illustrations. Cr. 8vo. 7s. 6d.
    Mysteries of Magic: a Digest of the Writings of Eliphas Lévi. With Illustrations. 8vo. 10s. 6d.
    The Occult Sciences. Cr. 8vo. 6s.

WAKE, C. S., Serpent-Worship, and other Essays. With a chapter on Totemism. 8vo. 10s. 6d.
    Development of Marriage and Kinship. 8vo. 18s.

WALLACE, ALFRED RUSSELL, Miracles and Modern Spiritualism. Second Edition. Cr. 8vo. 5s.

WALLACE, WILFRID, Life of St. Edmund of Canterbury from Original Sources. With Five Illustrations and Map. 8vo. 15s.

WALPOLE, C. G., Short History of Ireland. With 5 Maps and Appendices. Third Edition. Cr. 8vo. 6s.

WALSHE, W. H., Dramatic Singing Physiologically Estimated. Cr. 8vo. 3s. 6d.

WANKLYN, J. A., Milk Analysis: a Practical Treatise on the Examination of Milk and its Derivatives, Cream, Butter, and Cheese. Second Edition. Cr. 8vo. 5s.

—— **Tea, Coffee, and Cocoa:** a Practical Treatise on the Analysis of Tea, Coffee, Cocoa, Chocolate, and Maté (Paraguay tea). Cr. 8vo. 5s.

WANKLYN, J. A., and COOPER, W. J., Bread Analysis: a Practical Treatise on the Examination of Flour and Bread. Cr. 8vo. 5s.

—— **Air Analysis:** a Practical Treatise. With Appendix on Illuminating Gas. Cr. 8vo. 5s.

WANKLYN, J. A., and CHAPMAN, E. T., Water Analysis: a Treatise on the Examination of Potable Water. Eighth Edition. Entirely re-written. Cr. 8vo. 5s.

WARD, BERNARD, History of St. Edmund's College, Old Hall (Ware). With Illustrations. 8vo. 10s. 6d.

WARD, H. MARSHALL. The Oak: a Popular Introduction to Forest Botany. Cr. 8vo. 2s. 6d. (*Modern Science Series.*)

WARD, W. G., Essays on the Philosophy of Theism. Edited, with an Introduction, by WILFRID WARD. 2 vols. 8vo. 21s.

WARNER, Prof. F., Physical Expression: its Modes and Principles. With 50 Illustrations. Second Edition. Cr. 8vo. 5s. (*I.S.S.*)

WARTER, J. W., An old Shropshire Oak. 4 vols. 8vo. 56s.

WATERHOUSE, Col. J., Preparation of Drawings for Photographic Reproduction. With Plates. Cr. 8vo. 5s.

WATSON, JOHN FORBES, Index to the Native and Scientific Names of Indian and other Eastern Economic Plants and Products. Imp. 8vo. £1. 11s. 6d.

WATSON, R. G., Spanish and Portuguese South America during the Colonial Period. 2 vols. Post 8vo. 21s.

WEAVER, F. W., Wells Wills. Arranged in Parishes, and Annotated. 8vo. 10s. 6d.

WEBER, A., History of Indian Literature. From the German by J. MANN and T. ZACHARIAE. Third Edition. Post 8vo. 10s. 6d. (*Trübner's Oriental Series.*)

WEDDING'S Basic Bessemer Process. Translated from the German by W. B. PHILLIPS and ERNST PROCHASKA. Roy. 8vo. 18s.

WEDGWOOD, H., Dictionary of English Etymology. Fourth Edition. Revised and Enlarged. 8vo. £1. 1s.

—— **Contested Etymology in the Dictionary of the Rev. W. W. Skeat.** Cr. 8vo. 5s.

WEDGWOOD, JULIA, The Moral Ideal; an Historic Study. Second Edition. 8vo. 9s.

WEISBACH, JULIUS, Theoretical Mechanics: a Manual of the Mechanics of Engineering. Designed as a Text-book for Technical Schools and for the Use of Engineers. From the German by E. B. COXE. With 902 Woodcuts. Second Edition. 8vo. 31s. 6d.

WELLER, E., Improved French Dictionary. Roy. 8vo. 7s. 6d.

WESTROPP, HODDER M., Primitive Symbolism as Illustrated in Phallic Worship; or, The Reproductive Principle. With Introduction by Major-Gen. FORLONG. 8vo. 7s. 6d.

WHEELDON, J. P., Angling Resorts near London: the Thames and the Lea. Cr. 8vo. paper covers, 1s. 6d.

WHEELER, J. TALBOYS, History of India from the Earliest Ages. 8vo. (Vol. I. *out of print*.) Vol. II., 21s. Vol. III., 18s. Vol. IV., Part I., 14s. Vol. IV., Part II., 12s.

    *** Vol. III. is also published as an independent work under the title of 'History of India: Hindu, Buddhist, and Brahmanical.'

    Early Records of British India: a History of the English Settlements in India, as told in the Government Records and other Contemporary Documents. Roy. 8vo. 15s.

WHERRY, E. M., Comprehensive Commentary to the Quran. With SALE'S Preliminary Discourse, Translation and Additional Notes. Post 8vo. (Vol. I. *out of print*.) Vols. II. and III. 12s. 6d. each. Vol. IV. 10s. 6d. (*Trübner's Oriental Series*.)

WHIBLEY, CHAS., In Cap and Gown: Three Centuries of Cambridge Wit. Second Edition. Cr. 8vo. 7s. 6d.

WHINFIELD, E. H., The Quatrains of Omar Khayyám. The Persian Text, with an English Verse Translation. Post 8vo. 10s. 6d.; Translation only, 5s. (*Trübner's Oriental Series*.)

    Masnavi I Ma'navi: the Spiritual Couplets of Maulána Jalálu-'d-Din Muhammad I Rúmí. Translated and Abridged. Post 8vo. 7s. 6d. (*Trübner's Oriental Series*.)

WHITAKER, FLORENCE, Christy's Inheritance: a London Story. Illustrated. Roy. 16mo, 1s. 6d.

WHITNEY, Prof. W. D., Life and Growth of Language. Sixth Edition. Cr. 8vo. 5s. (*I.S.S.*)

    Essentials of English Grammar. Second Edition. Cr. 8vo. 3s. 6d.

    Language and the Study of Language. Fourth Edition. Cr. 8vo. 10s. 6d.

    Language and its Study. With especial Reference to the Indo-European Family of Languages. Edited by R. MORRIS. Second Edition. Cr. 8vo. 5s.

    Sanskrit Grammar. Including both the Classical Language and the older Dialects of Veda and Brahmana. Second Edition. 8vo. 12s.

WHITWORTH, G. C., Anglo-Indian Dictionary: a Glossary of Indian Terms used in English, and of such English or other non-Indian Terms as have obtained Special Meanings in India. 8vo. cloth, 12s.

WICKSON, E. J., California Fruits, and How to Grow Them. 8vo. 18s.

WIECHMANN, FERDINAND G., Sugar Analysis. For Refineries, Sugar-Houses, Experimental Stations, &c. 8vo. 10s. 6d.

WILBERFORCE. Life of Bishop Wilberforce of Oxford and Winchester. By HIS SON. Cr. 8vo. 6s.

WILDE, HENRY, Origin of Elementary Substances. 4to. 4s.

WILDRIDGE, T. TYNDAL, The Dance of Death, in Painting and in Print. With Woodcuts. Sm. 4to. 3s. 6d.

WILLARD, X. A., Practical Dairy Husbandry. Complete Treatise on Dairy Farms and Farming. Illustrated. 8vo. 15s.

    Practical Butter Book. Complete Treatise on Butter Making, &c. 12mo. 5s.

WILLIAMS, S. WELLS, Syllabic Dictionary of the Chinese Language: arranged according to the Wu-Fang Yuen Yin, with the Pronunciation of the Characters as heard in Pekin, Canton, Amoy, and Shanghai. Third Edition. 4to. £3. 15s.

WILLIS, R., Life, Correspondence, and Ethics of Benedict de Spinoza. 8vo. 21s.

WILSON, H. H., Rig-Veda-Sanhita: a Collection of Ancient Hindu Hymns. From the Sanskrit. Edited by E. B. COWELL and W. F. WEBSTER. 6 vols. 8vo. (Vols. I. V. VI. 21s. each; Vol. IV. 14s.; Vols. II. and III. in sets only.)

    The Megha-Duta (Cloud Messenger). Translated from the Sanskrit of KALIDASA. New Edition. 4to. 10s. 6d.

    Essays and Lectures, chiefly on the Religion of the Hindus. Collected and Edited by Dr. REINHOLD ROST. 2 vols. 21s.

    Essays, Analytical, Critical, and Philological, on Subjects connected with Sanskrit Literature. Collected and Edited by Dr. REINHOLD ROST. 3 vols. 36s.

    Vishnu Puráná: a System of Hindu Mythology and Tradition. From the Original Sanskrit. Illustrated by Notes derived chiefly from other Puránás. Edited by FITZEDWARD HALL. 6 vols. (including Index), £3. 4s. 6d.

    Select Specimens of the Theatre of the Hindus. From the Original Sanskrit. Third Edition. 2 vols. 21s.

WILSON, Mrs. R. F., The Christian Brothers: their Origin and Work. With Sketch of Life of their Founder. Cr. 8vo. 6s.

Within Sound of the Sea. With Frontispiece. Cr. 8vo. 6s.

WOLTMANN, ALFRED, and **WOERMANN, KARL,** History of Painting. With numerous Illustrations. Med. 8vo. Vol. I. Painting in Antiquity and the Middle Ages, 28s. Vol. II. The Painting of the Renascence, 42s. The two volumes may be had bound in cloth with bevelled boards and gilt leaves, price 30s. and 45s. respectively.

Woman's Crusade, A. By a DAME OF THE PRIMROSE LEAGUE. 3 vols. 31s. 6d.

WOOD, M. W., Dictionary of Volapük: Volapük-English and English-Volapük. Cr. 8vo. 10s. 6d.

WOODBURY, CHAS. J., Talks with Ralph Waldo Emerson. Cr. 8vo. 5s.

WOOLDRIDGE, L. C., On the Chemistry of the Blood, and other Scientific Papers. Arranged by VICTOR HORSLEY and ERNEST STARLING. With Introduction by VICTOR HORSLEY. With Illustrations. 8vo. 16s.

WORDSWORTH Birthday Book. Edited by ADELAIDE and VIOLET WORDSWORTH. 32mo. 2s.; cloth limp, 1s. 6d.

WORDSWORTH, Selections from. By WILLIAM KNIGHT and other Members of the Wordsworth Society. Printed on hand-made paper. Large cr. 8vo. With Portrait. Vellum, 15s.; parchment, 12s. Cheap Edition, cr. 8vo. 4s. 6d.

WORSAAE, CHAMBERLAIN J. J. A., The Pre-history of the North. Based on contemporary Memorials. Translated by H. F. MORLAND SIMPSON. Cr. 8vo. 6s.

WORTHAM, B. HALE, Satakas of Bhartrihari. Translated from the Sanskrit. Post 8vo. 5s. (*Trübner's Oriental Series.*)

WORTHY, CHARLES, Practical Heraldry: an Epitome of English Armoury. With 124 Illustrations. Cr. 8vo. 7s. 6d.

WRIGHT, G. FREDERICK, The Ice Age in North America, and its Bearing upon the Antiquity of Man. With Maps and Illustrations. 8vo. 21s.

    Man and the Glacial Period. With 111 Illustrations and Map. Cr. 8vo. 5s. (*I.S.S.*)

WRIGHT, THOMAS, The Celt, the Roman, and the Saxon: a History of the Early Inhabitants of Britain down to the Conversion of the Anglo-Saxons to Christianity. Fifth Edition, corrected and enlarged. With nearly 300 Engravings. Cr. 8vo. 9s.

WRIGHT, W., The Book of Kalilah and Dimnah. Translated from Arabic into Syriac, with Preface and Glossary in English. 8vo. 21s.

WURTZ, Prof., The Atomic Theory. Translated by E. CLEMINSHAW. Fifth Edition. Cr. 8vo. 5s. (I.S.S.)

WYLDE, W. The Inspection of Meat: a Guide and Instruction Book to Officers supervising Contract Meat, and to all Sanitary Inspectors. With 32 Coloured Plates. 8vo. 10s. 6d.

YOUNG, Prof. C. A., The Sun. With Illustrations. Third Edition. Cr. 8vo. 5s. (I.S.S.)

YOUMANS, ELIZA A., First Book of Botany. Designed to Cultivate the Observing Powers of Children. With 300 Engravings. New and Cheaper Edition. Cr. 8vo. 2s. 6d.

SHAKSPERE'S WORKS.

THE AVON EDITION,

Printed on thin opaque paper, and forming 12 handy volumes, cloth, 18s., or bound in 6 volumes, 15s.

The set of 12 volumes may also be had in a cloth box (*see Illustration*), price 21s., or bound in roan, persian, crushed persian levant, calf, or morocco, and enclosed in an attractive leather box, at prices from 31s. 6d. upwards.

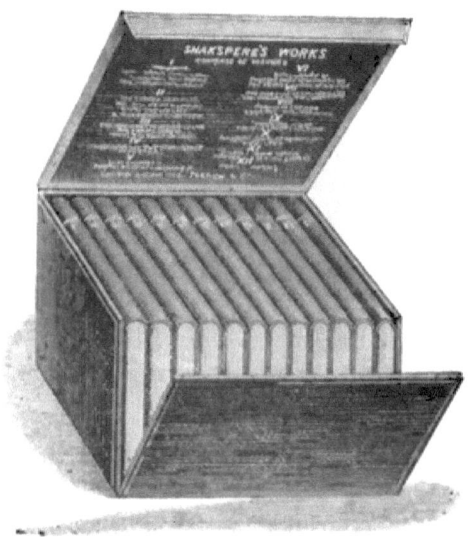

THE PARCHMENT LIBRARY EDITION,

In 12 volumes elzevir 8vo., choicely printed on hand-made paper, and bound in parchment or cloth, price £3. 12s., or in vellum, price £4. 10s.

The set of 12 volumes may also be had in a strong cloth box, price £3. 17s., or with an oak hanging shelf (*see Illustration*), £3. 18s.

LONDON: KEGAN PAUL, TRENCH, TRÜBNER, & CO., LTD.

THE AMERICAN PATENT
REVOLVING BOOKCASE.

The Revolving Bookcase will be found a great convenience by those who wish to have from 80 to 200 volumes accessible while seated at a table or by the fireside. This bookcase occupies no more space than an ordinary whatnot, and can be wheeled from one part of a room to another. It is particularly suitable for Private Libraries, for Studies, and for the Consulting Chambers of Barristers, Physicians, &c.

Size No. 1, 36 inches high.

PRICE FROM 4 GUINEAS.

These Bookcases are made in various sizes, 24 inches square, 36 to 59 inches high, with eight, twelve, or sixteen shelves, in ash, walnut, mahogany, oak, and ebonised, and neatly finished so as to form handsome pieces of furniture. A special form of Revolving Bookcase has been designed to hold the set of 'Encyclopædia Britannica.'

Specimens of the different sizes and woods can be seen in use at

PATERNOSTER HOUSE,
CHARING CROSS ROAD, LONDON.
KEGAN PAUL, TRENCH, TRÜBNER, & CO., Ltd.,

SOLE AUTHORISED AGENTS.

Illustrated Price List on receipt of one Stamp.